Enterprise Java™ Programming with IBM® WebSphere®

Enterprise Java™ Programming with IBM® WebSphere®

Kyle Brown

Dr. Gary Craig

Greg Hester

Jaime Niswonger

David Pitt

Russell Stinehour

Addison-Wesley

Boston • San Francisco • New York • Toronto • Montreal
London • Munich • Paris • Madrid
Capetown • Sydney • Tokyo • Singapore • Mexico City

The publisher offers discounts on this book when ordered in quantity for special sales. For more information, please contact:

> Pearson Education Corporate Sales Division
> One Lake Street
> Upper Saddle River, NJ 07458
> (800) 382-3419
> corpsales@pearsontechgroup.com

Visit AW on the Web: www.awl.com/cseng/

Library of Congress Cataloging-in-Publication Data

Enterprise Java™ programming with IBM® WebSphere®/Kyle Brown...[et al.].
    p. cm.
    Includes bibliographical references and index.
    ISBN 0-201-61617-3
       1. Java (Computer program language) I. Brown, Kyle.
  QA76.73.J38 E548 2001
  005.2'762—dc21

                            2001018851

ISBN 0-201-61617-3
Text printed on recycled paper
12345678910—MA—0504030201
First printing, May 2001

This book is dedicated to . . .

Bob Feather for first piquing my interest in these silly machines.
We're glad to have you back.—K.B.

My wife Judy, and my kids, Andrew, Megan, and Taylor, for surviving
this odyssey with me.—G.C.

My wife and kids, without whose love, encouragement, and shared
vision, this would not have been possible.—G.H.

My wife, who truly is my "Angel."—J.N.

My wife Sheila, for her patience and support—D.P.

The many CrossLogic consultants who contributed time and input to
this endeavor: thank you!—R.S.

Contents

Figures, Tables, and Listings

Foreword

I don't often find books like this one terribly interesting. Books on a specific technology, such as WebSphere and VisualAge, are often handy if you're using that technology—but they don't contain any great insights. I look to these books to tell me exactly which animal I need to sacrifice with which incense in order to get a job done. And this book does tell you that for these tools.

What makes this book stand out is that it doesn't stop at that. As the old adage says, a fool with a tool is still a fool. If you're developing enterprise applications with a technology like J2EE, it's easy to be a fool. There are lots of ways you can mess things up, and all the wizards and cute graphical interfaces in the world can't save you!

So this book also tells you how to reduce your foolishness by passing on design advice. The authors have been building these kinds of applications since before Java was invented. Kyle Brown, in particular, has more than once steered me around a nasty distributed rock. So here, you don't just find chapters on how to build a servlet, and what the transaction attributes are for Enterprise JavaBeans—they actually give you some advice on how to design these things. Rather than just give a simple solution, suitable for a hands-on tutorial, they talk about the trade-offs you'll need to make in putting an Enterprise Java application together. As a result, you may find some of this book hard work, but by putting the effort in to understand it you'll avoid many of the pitfalls that regularly send these kinds of projects to the great cubicle farm in the sky.

In particular, the authors put a strong emphasis on layering—centering their design around a five-layer architecture. While carefully separated layers are an odd complexity for simple examples, they are a key life vest for serious enterprise applications. Time and time again, I've seen teams begin by reluctantly following layers, shrinking from the fact that simple logic gets separated into several different classes. Then slowly, they appreciate that the layers allow changes to be made more easily, that layers make a system easier to test and easier to root out bugs. If there is any advice in this book that I must echo, it is to follow the layering architecture, even if it seems awkward to you. Your future self will thank you for it.

So if you're a Websphere developer, buy this book for its tutorial on Websphere, but treasure it for its design advice. If you don't develop in Websphere, get this book for its design advice anyway. At the moment, the Java world has lots of books on technology, but precious few on on how to use it well. Thank goodness this book is one of the exceptions!

—Martin Fowler
Chief Scientist, ThoughtWorks

Preface

How We Got Here

In the mid 1990s, a book on server-side Java would have been an oxymoron. It's funny how quickly things change. When Java first burst onto the programming language scene, Java on the client was all the rage. Oracle was pushing Network Computers (NCs) as the replacement for the PC, Netscape was running full-speed to beat Microsoft in the browser wars, and no one was talking much about putting programs on servers anymore.

How things change. Oracle is out of the NC business and is instead selling server "appliances." Netscape was purchased by AOL and is now giving away its browser source code, and Marc Andressen has unequivocally stated, "Java on the client is dead."

What happened? Why did Java on the client "die"? And if Java is dead on the client, where is it still "alive"? Understanding the answers to these questions requires examining some object-oriented (OO) development history, the history of the Web, and a little bit of Java history. In the process, we will reach an understanding of the most exciting new technologies for Java: the Java 2 Enterprise Edition (J2EE) technologies. In this way, we can discover how the J2EE programming model has incorporated the best elements from some older programming models together with some radically new ideas. In particular, we will focus on understanding how IBM's WebSphere Standard Edition and Advanced Edition make "Java on the server" a reality. You have to have a context in order to understand how to use the new J2EE technologies, and in this book, the context will be the WebSphere Application Server and the VisualAge for Java, Enterprise Edition development environment.

All of us writing this book share a similar background. We all came to Java after programming for several years in another OO programming language. In some cases, our first language was Smalltalk; in others, it was

C++. In this respect, we're probably like a lot of you. For a good part of the last ten years, we have been involved in developing client/server applications using these languages. Although the details of the systems that we have worked on have differed, they all shared some common features. What we hope to do in this book is to introduce the new parts of J2EE, WebSphere, and VisualAge for Java by referring back to the things you already know and at the same time show you some best practices that we've learned in building client/server and enterprise systems both before the age of Java and in the new J2EE universe.

What We Want to Accomplish

We set forward to achieve several goals in the writing of this book:

- Introduce developers to key J2EE technologies, such as Java servlets, JavaServer Pages, and Enterprise JavaBeans
- Teach developers how to apply these J2EE technologies within the correct architectural framework
- Demonstrate how WebSphere Application Server, Advanced Edition, implements the J2EE standard and what advantages it gives to developers as a J2EE application server
- Demonstrate the advantages VisualAge for Java, Enterprise Edition, conveys as a platform for developing J2EE programs for deployment on WebSphere Application Server, Advanced Edition

Of these four goals, perhaps the most important one is to teach developers how to apply J2EE technologies within the correct architectural context. It has been our experience that teaching someone a new technology without also teaching how that technology should be applied is a terrible mistake. A lot of our time as consultants is spent in getting customers out of problems that have been created either by trying to make a technology do something it was not intended to do or by viewing one particular technology as a "hammer" and all problems as "nails."

Although we can convey some of this architectural context by teaching you the dos and don'ts of the technologies, most of you are like us: You learn best by doing. In order to help you really gain a "feel" for the J2EE technologies we will cover, you will want to walk with us through the example system that we are building and find out for yourselves how the pieces fit together. It is only by seeing the entire system end to end and by working through the example on your own that you will really start to understand how the different APIs interrelate and how WebSphere and VisualAge for Java implement the abstract specifications.

So, we want to welcome you on an adventure. It's been a long, hard road for us in mastering these technologies, tools, and techniques; we hope that we can make the way easier for those of you who are following us. It will still take a lot of preparation and effort for you to really learn how and why to apply these technologies and how best to take advantage of the features of WebSphere and VisualAge for Java, but we feel that the effort is worthwhile. J2EE is a terrific architecture for building scalable, manageable server-side systems, and IBM has developed a wonderful set of tools that make those technologies "real." We hope that by the time you reach the end of this book, you will understand and agree with us why we think so highly of these tools. We also hope that this book will enable you to start designing and building these kinds of large-scale, "enterprise" systems that J2EE, WebSphere, and VisualAge for Java make possible. Thanks for coming along with us on this journey, and good luck in reaching your destination.

Acknowledgments and Thanks

Building a book like this is a team effort. We would like to acknowledge all those team members who contributed to this book but whose names are not mentioned on the cover: Keys Botzum, Geoff Hambrick, Peter Jakab, Rachel Reinitz, Scott Rich, and Skyler Thomas. Without the important contributions from these people this book would not have been possible. We would also like to thank those who have participated as reviewers of this project and provided remarkably insightful feedback and help: Dan Kehn, Dan Kehn, Dale Nilsson, Andre Tost, and again Keys Botzum and Scott Rich. You have our gratitude and our thanks.

May, 2001
Raleigh, N.C.
Asheville, N.C.
Kansas City, Mo.

CHAPTER 1

Internet Business Environment

Today's unprecedented Internet business-to-business (B2B) and business-to-consumer (B2C) opportunities have captured the minds of executives of companies large and small alike. The dot-com gold rush that has swept the business world has come about not only because of the dollar and market share opportunities but also because people can envision using technology to fundamentally improve the way they do business. The new technologies can be used to

- *Enhance communications* through a distributed, connectionless network, providing access to information and data from anywhere. Mobile computing solutions will expand communications even more by providing wireless solutions that use the same technologies and network.
- *Leverage existing technologies,* making legacy resources more productive and useful to an increased number of users. Client/server solutions of the early 1990s called for the reduction of legacy systems, making distributed computing expensive and inflexible. Client/server solutions of the new millennium fully use legacy systems and take advantage of distributed resources.
- *Improve the visibility of information and data* by opening up new and existing sources of information to a larger population of customers, vendors, employees, and others. Static information can be quickly and easily updated, and dynamic solutions can be delivered with minimal effort and programming resources.
- *Fulfill the promises of distributed computing* with flexible, easy-to-implement programming languages, tools, components, and interfaces. Many of the client/server design templates of the early 1990s never

1

produced viable solutions in the marketplace. The Web-based client/server design templates of the new millennium have been used to deliver flexible, high-performance, and standard solutions that can be easily changed to reflect new requirements and design needs.

- *Streamline and reengineer business processes* to do business in ways never imagined before. Self-service applications have moved information closer to the end user and have reduced administrative personnel. Electronic-commerce (e-commerce) transaction-based applications have increased marketplace competition and have changed the way that many companies present and sell goods and services. Internet technologies have lowered the barrier of entry for many start-up ventures and entrepreneurs, allowing them to compete with larger companies. The Web has equalized the playing field for many businesses, making many small businesses to appear larger and many larger companies to move like smaller businesses.

In this chapter, we look at the projected amount of business over the Web and suggest some possible business requirements facing players in this emerging technology-driven marketplace. We also discuss potential pressures facing Internet business and legal issues that will require additional attention when doing business over the Web. We look at information technology (IT) management issues and what is required for bringing Web solutions to the enterprise. We conclude this chapter with what is needed overall to respond to competition, business pressures, and new requirements.

Web Revenue Projections

E-commerce is projected to grow rapidly. The Multimedia Marketing Group Inc. (MMG Inc.) quotes a *Time Magazine*/Gartner Group study, a Simba Information report, and e-Marketer projections as $195 billion in 2001, $202 billion in 2002, and $294 billion in 2002, respectively.[1] MMG Inc. estimates B2B and B2C revenue as approximately $5,168.70 per second, or $163 billion in 2000. An IDC study projects that e-commerce will grow 39 percent annually through 2003.

Although no one can predict Web revenue with any certainty, it is clear that the numbers will be large and that the opportunity will be unprecedented for innovative companies that can deliver solutions quickly. Compa-

---

1. *http://www.mmg.com/clock*

nies that respond to customer requirements and that find new ways to serve customers, vendors, and employees will benefit greatly.

Financial analysts have divided e-commerce solutions into five categories:

- *Web publishing:* static Web pages with no dynamic content or user-to-application interaction
- *Collaboration:* dynamic client-side solutions with calculations, graphing, or transforming data for viewing
- *Supply chain management:* server-side dynamic solutions to help manage vendor relationships
- *Customer self-service:* server-side dynamic solutions to help manage customer relationships
- *Full back-end integration:* server-side dynamic solutions that integrate back-end legacy systems

Taking into account revenue generation, cost reduction, productivity enhancements, cycle time reduction, and quality improvements, analysts project return on investment (ROI) for static Web publishing solutions to produce 21 percent, whereas solutions with back-end integration can deliver up to 68 percent.[2]

Marketplace Competition

The Internet ushered in a wave of entrepreneurial expansion that fueled much of the economic growth in the late 1990s. On the Internet, small companies can appear to be much larger than they are. Large companies can use the Web to cut costs and to move quickly, like a small company in the marketplace. The result is that the e-commerce marketplace has increased the number of players competing for demand. The e-commerce supply is more visible to customers. E-commerce has created a worldwide shopping mall complete with price comparison engines, wholesale efficiency, and retail convenience. Figure 1.1 illustrates what happens when the visible supply of goods and services increases. Increased competition increases supply and demand fulfillment, resulting in lower prices, which require that e-commerce participants be more efficient in order to compete.

E-commerce has supplied innovations to reengineer business processes. A wave of self-service applications has appeared, accompanied by the

---

2. Jenny Szawlewicz, IBM WebSphere Education Program Manager.

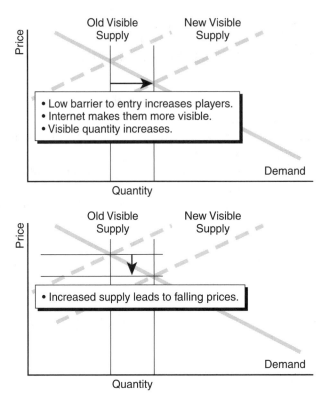

Figure 1.1   Internet Induced Increased Competition and Falling Prices

formation of a new marketing channel, which resulted in initial profit margins that further encouraged additional competition in e-commerce. Increased competition, shopping comparison engines, and information overload resulted in customers becoming very price sensitive and overloaded with options.

Falling prices led to falling gross margins. Many e-commerce participants focused on market share rather than on immediate profits, resulting in increased pressures on prices and margins. Eventually, those companies that learn how to best serve their customers will rise above their competitors. Increased bandwidth and economies of scale will improve the Web experience and increase the number of Web users and shoppers. Eventually, the market will weed out those players that cannot meet their customers' requirements. Innovators and efficient providers will survive to find higher gross margins and will dominate market share. Early application providers will learn how to grow with their customers and will have a better chance of surviving the eventual weed-out process. (See Figure 1.2.)

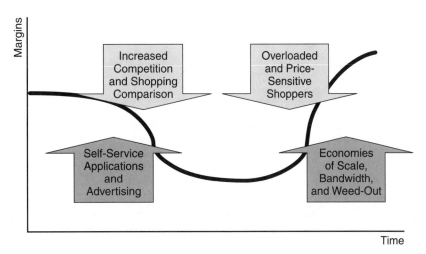

Figure 1.2 E-Commerce Business Pressures

IT Management Issues

Managing Web-based projects will require an iterative development process (Figure 1.3) that

- *Focuses on feasibility issues early in the development cycle.* The project can be delivered in iterations, with feasibility items prioritized early in the overall development effort.
- *Builds on early success.* Breaking the project up into smaller "chunks" allows the development team to deliver iterations early in the development cycle instead of waiting for the "big-bang" delivery of the project as in the more traditional waterfall development process.
- *Ensures early participation and commitment by end users.* At the same time, the process facilitates early discovery of requirements.
- *Uses a standard, repeatable process.* The process uses Unified Modeling Language (UML) development process deliverables.
- *Reduces risk to the overall project.* Increasing concrete-deliverables risk can be reduced with each subsequent iteration deliverable.

Forrester Research's Marry Modahl has defined the new role and focus of the "whole-view IT" organization.[3] The Web is transforming IT deliverables into strategic weapons that can build customer satisfaction and loyalty,

---

3. Marry Modahl, *Now or Never: How Companies Must Change Today to Win the Battle for Internet Consumers* (New York: Harperbusiness, 1999).

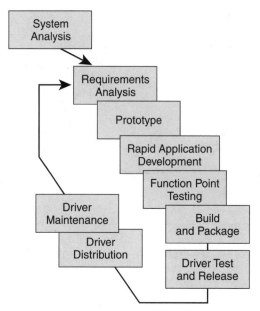

Figure 1.3   Iterative Development Process

create experimental brands, and redefine enterprise missions. This new focus will require additional investment and speed to market for new applications, as indicated in Table 1.1.

What Is Needed

Increased competition, lower projected e-commerce profit margins, increased legal issues, and new IT management requirements call for

- *Solution value:* reliance on a layered architecture that leverages reuse and dynamic, scalable solutions that can be easily changed.
- *Speed to market:* a focus on the business domain and not the application infrastructure to help meet the ever-growing backlog of strategic applications. By using a repeatable standard development process that reuses legacy information and systems, a development team can begin to bring solutions to the marketplace sooner.
- *Secure solutions:* assets protection—legally and technically—so that an IT organization can not only produce flexible solutions but also give the enterprise a strategic advantage in the marketplace.

Table 1.1 Whole-View IT Management

Issues	Classical IT management	Whole-view IT management
Technology reach	Mission critical	Mission redefining
Focus of Systems	Internal productivity	Customer sales and service
Key goals	Reduce costs and keep systems running	Create experimental brands and build customer satisfaction and loyalty
Time to develop new capabilities	12 to 24 months	2 to 6 months
Percent of sales spent on technology and technology people	Less than 5%	5% to 25%
Status in company	Lower level; tactical	Higher level; strategic

Summary and Preview

You've now seen why the Web is so important for IT organizations to master. In the next chapter, we look at traditional client/server computing and see where it all started, and then we look at Web-based client/server computing and see what distributed computing has evolved into. Specifically, we look at Java 2 Enterprise Edition (J2EE) to see how Java and the Web have met customers' unfulfilled expectations of client/server solutions.

CHAPTER 2

Web-Based Client/Server Solutions

By the mid 1990s, client/server computing had lost its shine with many IT managers and professionals. Traditional client/server solutions missed the mark for several reasons.

- *Client/server solutions moved only the view closer to the end users.* Traditional client/server applications were expected to move the solution closer to the end user. However, client machines with large applications were difficult to distribute, scale, and maintain. The "thick client" was an attempt to place function and data with the end user. Legacy back-end systems could not be easily moved or replaced. Transactions could not be processed on the front end or middle tier, so transaction processing remained on the back-end system. Connecting to the back end became more of a challenge than enhancing the legacy system itself.

- *Performance impeded the usability of applications.* Multimedia graphical user interface (GUI) objects fueled expectations about enhanced end user productivity. Many of the solutions did not have the required communications bandwidth or transaction-processing throughput to satisfy end users. Many solutions were soon shelved because of performance shortcomings. Performance issues negated end user productivity gains from enhanced user interface objects. Other solutions were designed by copying the legacy system functionality without reengineering the business process. This approach placed a GUI front end on the same application. Traditional client/server solutions did not provide the necessary productivity gains to justify new system expenditures.

- *Application backlog grew with new technologies.* Traditional client/server development processes were to increase development productivity and to reduce IT application backlog. IT professionals had difficulties deciding where to place data and function. New solution types, new development tools, and a growing number of vendors that promised great results made project start-up arduous at best. Many development teams had false starts, as their first attempts did not scale to the enterprise. Hurdles caused by feasibility issues slowed application development efforts. Development teams required training and retooling to get started. Promises of productivity gains were spent in the attempts to reengineer business processes and in building new architectures.

- *Business processes were molded to fit technology shortfalls.* Attempts to reengineer business processes were fraught with technology feasibility issues. Instead of reengineering the business, many development teams tried to duplicate the legacy system with a "green screen"–style GUI tied to the same back end. Requirements for data and function placement were not well understood. In many cases, the decision of where to place data did not take into consideration the lack of network bandwidth to support old-process data volumes being transferred to the client. Debates over "fat versus thin" client solutions demonstrated a lack of skills in dealing with end user needs and process efficiencies. Many developers and vendors were more concerned with "one-size-fits-all" architectures and design.

- *Overall computing costs rose.* All the solution shortcomings, client/server project false starts, poor solution performance, and lack of scalable solutions increased the costs of computing. Many IT groups were faced with supporting duplicate departmental solutions and continuing to maintain the legacy systems that they were supposed to be replacing. Retraining the development teams and infusing new tools and technologies into the enterprise also contributed to rising costs of computing. Object technologies were supposed to reduce development costs through object inheritance and code reuse. Although object-oriented (OO) programming did bring a valid new technology to IT organizations, the IT staff required extensive training, and the promise of code reuse would take years to be fulfilled through the creation and growth of reuse libraries and frameworks.

The real focus of client/server solutions was to deliver more for less, moving solutions closer to the end users, and to use more intuitive user interfaces to reduce end user learning. In many cases, these expectations were met with frustration. Web-based client/server technologies have overcome many of the frustrations and have changed the way we think of distributed computing.

Web-Based Client/Server Design Templates

In many ways, Web-based client/server solutions offer as many options as traditional client/server solutions do. The Web-based design templates look very much like the client/server design templates. (See Figure 2.1.) The real difference is in the introduction of Java. Java is a robust object technology and a scalable networking language that supports more robust distributed solutions. These Web-based templates have the following characteristics:

- *Remote presentation,* or scripting, which uses a server-side scripting, or programming, language to produce the view logic, or user interface.
- *Distributed logic,* which places the view on the client and splits the business logic across the client and the server machines. Data management logic remains on the server.
- *Remote data management,* which accesses server data from the client machine.
- *Distributed data management,* which manages data on both the client and the server machines.

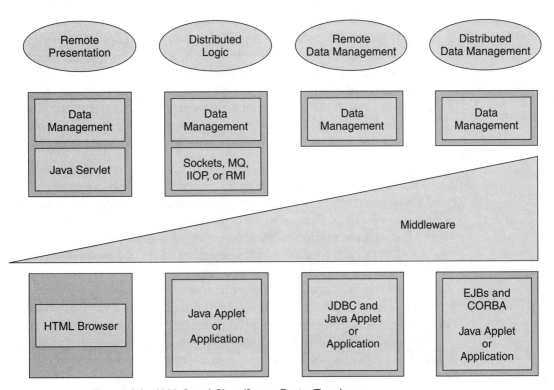

Figure 2.1   Web-Based Client/Server Design Templates

Remote Presentation

One of the simplest Web-based client/server solutions is remote presentation, which places the presentation logic as "paint" on the client machine but keeps the remaining application logic on the server. The end user invokes the server application from the client from a Web browser through the Hyper-Text Transfer Protocol (HTTP). The server also contains view controller logic written in C, C++, or Perl language as a common gateway interface (CGI) solution or in Java servlets. In traditional client/server computing, this was a primitive type of solution. In Web-based client/server computing, this is an advanced distributed solution. The Web-based remote-presentation solution has the following primary benefits.

- The business logic, servlet, and data management parts of the application usually sit on the server, protected behind the enterprise firewall.
- No additional client application code is needed to make the solution work.
- The client investment in hardware, software and application development, and distribution requirements is minimal.
- The legacy application is protected behind the firewall and usually requires little to no additional programming.
- The server-side controller provides dynamic content to the client.
- Software distribution to the client is not an issue, as the user interface is streamed to the client browser as Hypertext Markup Language (HTML) text over HTTP.
- Client configuration is a minimal concern, as all the client machine needs is a standard Web browser. (*Note:* testing against proper behavior across various browsers and browser versions requires notable effort.)

Challenges with this solution include potential browser inconsistencies and exception-handling complexities. Traditional remote-presentation solutions were viewed as "low tech" or as a client/server stopgap at best. Web-based remote-presentation solutions are viewed as high-end client/server solutions. Servlets respond to user interface messages and send interface information to the client. Pulling, or streaming, user interface information from the server supports dynamic content on a Web browser as controlled by the CGI or servlet program. This is sometimes called the *thin client solution* and is discussed in more detail later in this chapter.

A servlet is a standard server-side Java program that extends the functionality of a Web server. A Web server is a server-side program that manages and executes a server application. When it gets a request for a servlet from a Web browser, the Web server loads the servlet, if needed, into the server machine's memory and executes the servlet. When it completes its task, the servlet sends any generated output back to the Web browser.

Servlets can interface to existing JavaBeans or Enterprise JavaBeans (EJB), which then access a database or a transactional system to perform the real work as business objects. Servlets act as the controller layer for applications that run on the Web. Servlets serve as the glue between HTML and the business objects. Servlets can add functionality to the Web application by providing session management, user authentication, and user authorization. The servlet life cycle defines the process used to load the servlet into memory, execute the servlet, and unload the servlet from memory. A Web browser requests a servlet through a URL, which can be either on the URL line of the Web browser or a link from an HTML form being updated.

Servlets offer advantages over CGI in the areas of portability, performance, and security. Sun Microsystems describes Java as a "write once run anywhere" language. This makes servlets platform independent where there is a compatible Web server. Servlet architecture is open and can easily tie into legacy databases, transaction management systems, and other servers (Figure 2.2).

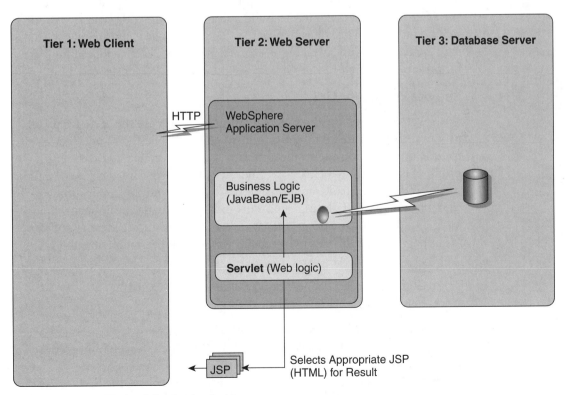

Figure 2.2 Servlet Architecture

Servlets offer better performance than CGI. After the Web server loads a servlet into memory, the servlet stays there and listens for requests. When a request arrives, a new Java thread is created, and the servlet code is executed in that thread. Java threads are lightweight, and their creation is more efficient than standard CGI, which creates a new operating system process for each request. Because a servlet remains resident in memory, connections to databases can remain open. Servlets also provide a session object that can be used to maintain session information across multiple accesses by the same user. Use of the session object can reduce access to the same information over and over again.

Servlets offer better security than standard CGI. A servlet runs within the Web server context. Servlets can use authentication and authorization features of the Web server.

Distributed Logic

Distributed–logic solutions split the application across the client and the server. Although distributed–logic applications provide a flexible solution, the IT development team has to build and to maintain code built on two different platforms. The solution provides flexibility that meets many of the mission-critical application requirements. Two types of distributed-logic solutions are presented here: remote procedure call (RPC) and messaging.

Remote Procedure Call

With Web-based client/server, RPC communications are the easiest type of program-to-program communications to develop. The RPC looks like a subroutine or a function call to the applications programmer. The call-return protocol is typically synchronous, and the calling program is blocked until the procedure returns. Communication is hidden from the application, except when network failures occur. This solution provides a simple programming paradigm for the programmer with a complex administrative solution in support of the runtime environment. RPCs have been implemented via

- Remote method invocation (RMI)
- Common object request broker architecture (CORBA)
- Enterprise JavaBeans (EJBs)

The RMI mechanism allows Java object instances to send messages over the network to remote objects (Figure 2.3). RMI includes a naming registry, which tracks instances, associates them to an object name, and allows a client object to locate a remote object. Remote objects use the RMI activation service to activate a server object when a client object requests it. RMI also uses a remote reference manager to support the runtime transport of ob-

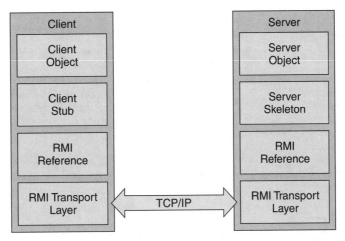

Figure 2.3 RMI Runtime

jects. Objects communicate with objects on a remote machine through proxies, or references. RMI can communicate over the Internet Inter-ORB Protocol (IIOP), which allows RMI clients to work with CORBA objects, which may or may not be implemented in Java.

The application development process includes the following steps.

1. The application developer creates a type that directly or indirectly extends the java.rmi.Remote Interface. This interface defines the remote methods that can be invoked by the client object.

2. The application developer then defines a server class that implements the newly defined subtype that extends the java.rmi.Remote Interface.

3. The RMI compiler (rmic) is then used to take the subtype of the remote interface as input and to generate client stub and server skeleton classes and object instances. The stubs and the skeletons are used to work with the RMI reference layer. (See Figure 2.4.)

Another solution that uses RPC for communications between the client and server objects is the common object resource broker architecture (CORBA). At its core, CORBA shares many of the features found in Java RMI. A description of a remote object is used to generate client stub and server skeleton interfaces. A client object uses the client stub to invoke methods of a remote server object. The method request is transmitted through the underlying CORBA communications infrastructure to the server skeleton. The server skeleton invokes the method on the remote object. Method return values and exceptions are transmitted back to the client through the CORBA infrastructure.

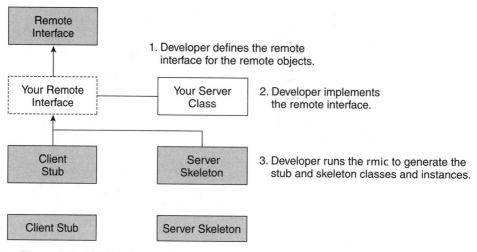

Figure 2.4   RMI Development Process

CORBA contains general nondomain-specific distributed object frameworks. These services include events, naming, transactions, concurrency, relationships, property, trader, collections, and start-up. CORBA components include the following:

- *Object services,* such as initialize and destroy, which standardize the lifecycle management of objects
- *Object request broker (ORB),* the heart of the standard, which accepts requests, coordinates communications, and makes them transparent to the applications programmer
- *Common facilities*—printing, document management, database, and electronic mail facilities—that provide a set of generic application functions that sit closer to the user
- *Domain interfaces,* which represent services that support application domains and may combine some common facilities and object services
- *Application objects,* which perform component-based application tasks for a user
- *Interface repository,* which provides dynamic client access to interface definitions to construct a request, dynamic type checking of request signatures, traversal of inheritance graphs, and ORB-to-ORB interoperability

Application development for CORBA is similar to the process used to create a Java RMI solution. (See Figure 2.5.)

1. The remote object is specified by using an interface definition language (IDL) to specify the remote object name, state, and behavior.

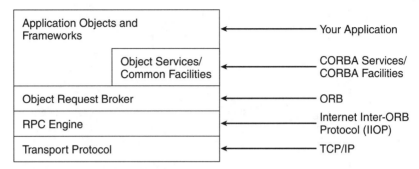

Figure 2.5   CORBA Application Architecture

2. The remote object description is compiled into Java by using an IDL-to-Java compiler. The compiler generates a Java interface, a Java client stub, and a Java server skeleton.

Another RPC-based solution can be found in the EJB framework. EJB frameworks separate high-level business logic from low-level infrastructure services. The EJB model contains an RMI object that runs in an EJB container on an EJB server. The EJB container and server provide such services as transaction management, security, name services, distribution services, resource pooling, life-cycle management, and object persistence.

A user or a client of an EJB has the same view of an EJB object, regardless of the implementation of the EJB and its container. This ensures that a client application is portable across all container implementations. An EJB container is where EJBs reside. Multiple EJB classes can be contained in a single EJB container. The developer provides a home interface that allows the client to create, to look up, and to remove EJB objects. An EJB server may host one or multiple EJB containers. The EJB container is transparent to the client. There is no client API to manipulate the container, and there is no way for a client to tell in which container an EJB is found. A client locates an EJB interface by using the J2EE naming service, Java Naming and Directory Interface (JNDI). The location of an EJB container is transparent to the client. In order to fully describe an EJB object to an EJB container, an application developer must implement three types:

- *Home interface,* used to specify how to find or to create an EJB
- *Remote interface,* used to specify business logic
- *Enterprise Bean implementation,* used to implement the home and remote interfaces (Figure 2.6)

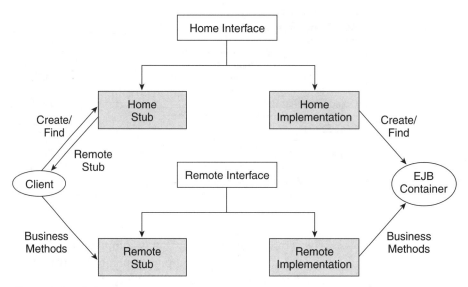

Figure 2.6   EJB Implementation

EJBs are of two types:

- *Session Beans:* used to manage a session
- *Entity Beans:* used to persist an object

EJBs offer the best of RMI and CORBA and will most likely become the standard for distributing objects. Using EJBs offers application developers several benefits.

- The EJB architecture is open and interoperable with nonJava applications.
- EJBs are portable and can be developed once and deployed on multiple platforms without source code modification or recompilation.
- EJBs are easy and flexible to use. Application developers can write to either a high-level abstract API or a set of low-level APIs that deal with state management, multithreading, transaction processing, and resource pooling.
- Many independent software vendors (ISVs) have developed EJB tools offering application developers a wide range of tools to select from to develop and to deploy application components.
- EJBs are compatible with CORBA.

Java Message Service

The Java message service (JMS) is a J2EE API for working with networked messaging services, such as the IBM MQ Series. JMS is used for writing message-oriented middleware solutions. JMS sits on top of vendor-specific messaging middleware and provides an abstract interface for messaging. JMS can be thought of as a distributed event notification system.

JMS 1.0 supports two models:

- *Point to point,* which revolves around message queues. The client creates a message and addresses it to a recipient. The message is queued for delivery. The recipient queues messages for handling. The point-to-point model is analogous to e-mail.
- *Publish/subscribe,* which uses hierarchical content topic trees. The client publishes messages to specific nodes of the topic tree. Other clients can retrieve messages from specific nodes on the trees they subscribe to. The publish/subscribe model is analogous to Internet newsgroups.

JMS is ideal for use with the J2EE Java Transaction API (JTA). JMS supports transactions, asynchronous processing, and multithreaded processes. JMS hides communications programming from the application and brings consistency to message-oriented middleware. Message-oriented middleware quite often works in concert with other types of Web-based client/server solutions.

Remote Data Management

Remote data management solutions provide a consistent method of accessing from a client remote databases on different servers. The Java Database Connectivity (JDBC) API provides a common interface to vendor-specific relational database implementations. Net JDBC drivers come with support to access databases over the network. The JDBC API provides support to

- Send structured query language (SQL) query and update statements to a database server
- Retrieve and scroll through query results returned by the server
- Get metadata about the database and its tables from the database server
- Treat database query results as JavaBeans, which helps map physical data to domain business objects at a very low level
- Manage database connection pools and obtain pool information
- Store Java objects in relational databases
- Batch updates

Applications can either use an intermediate DriverManager to access a JDBC driver or access a JDBC driver directly (Figure 2.7). Most of the major relational database systems come with a DriverManager with which to access relational data.

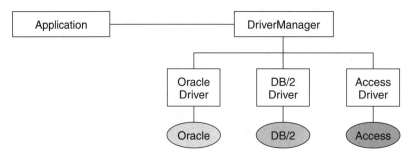

Figure 2.7 JDBC Drivers

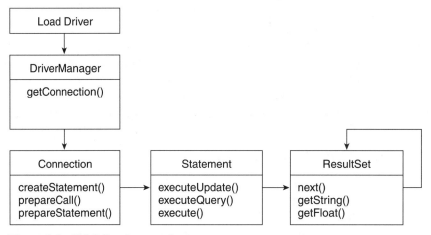

Figure 2.8 JDBC Development Steps

The steps required to access and to manipulate data are as follows (Figure 2.8).

1. Initialize and allocate drivers and connections.
2. Create, prepare, and process statements for execution.
3. Process and navigate result sets.
4. Manage housekeeping and cleanup.

Although JDBC has been improved in Java 2, it still has not abstracted SQL at a high enough level to simplify database access for the applications programmer who wants to work with objects rather than with physical data. We discuss mapping database data into business objects in Chapter 3.

Distributed Data Management

Distributed data management provides data management on both the client and the server platforms. This Web-based solution is made possible by database system replication of server database updates to and from remote client users. IBM DB/2, Lotus Notes, Oracle, and other database products support replication as a way to maintain database updates concurrently across platforms. This solution is proprietary. Replication is an administrative process used to synchronize the client and server databases. Either the end user or the database administrator corrects a conflict caused from concurrent update of the same data. Because it is not a connectivity solution, except when in replication mode, this type of solution is not covered in any detail in this book.

J2EE and Server-Side Solutions

The focus of this book is on server-side Web-based solutions and the following Java 2 Enterprise Edition (J2EE) APIs and frameworks that have become the standard for Web-based programming in Java.

- RMI (remote method interface)
- CORBA (common object request broker architecture)
- Servlets (Java server-side applications)
- EJB (Enterprise JavaBeans)
- JNDI (Java Naming and Directory Interface)
- JMS (Java message service)
- JDBC (Java Database Connectivity)
- JTA (Java Transaction Architecture)

Although we've described the APIs and how they are used in application templates, we haven't yet talked about how the APIs are implemented. To do so, we need to introduce a little more terminology before we can proceed. The J2EE technologies that we have seen allow a programmer to write Java programs that use these APIs, but there must be a platform and a framework that the APIs run in. In the industry today, the common name for this kind of platform is called an *application server*. The two competing programming models that application servers may implement today are the J2EE programming model and Microsoft's DNA (Distributed Network Architecture) model. In this book, we will be concerned only with J2EE and will not address DNA. The IBM WebSphere Application Server, Advanced Edition, implements most of the J2EE APIs. Other J2EE application servers are BEA's WebLogic and products from Oracle and Inprise.

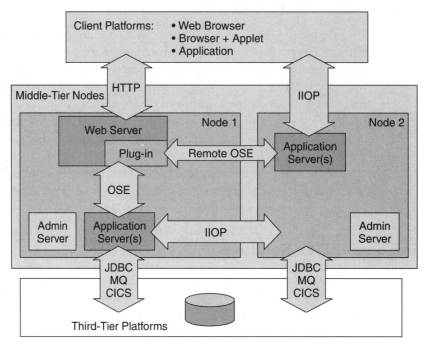

Figure 2.9   IBM WebSphere Architecture

We will be using the IBM WebSphere Application Server and IBM Visual-Age for Java products to create, deploy, and manage dynamic solutions that access legacy transactions and data. The IBM WebSphere Application Server, Advanced Edition, V3.x architecture model (Figure 2.9) contains a Web server plug-in that communicates with local application server servers via the Open Servlet Engine (OSE) protocol. IBM WebSphere can be configured with a number of application servers per node, or host. The application servers are all started and monitored by a local administration server process (admin server). Application servers can be configured to serve servlets/JSPs, EJBs, or both. The admin server also is home to the security service and the administration domain's name service. All configuration data is managed within a relational database instance: DB2, Oracle, or Sybase.

Summary and Preview

In this chapter, we reviewed the solutions for solving the inadequacies of client/server programming by using the World Wide Web. J2EE takes advantage of the Internet while still preserving the best parts of the client/server model and significantly expanding it into a scalable set of enterprise solutions. To conclude our look at Web architectures, we will review in Chapter 3 some software architectures suitable for use with J2EE. Then, in Chapter 4, we will describe the servlet interface in detail and begin to provide coding solutions.

CHAPTER 3

MVC and Layered Architectures

Chapter 2 described the technologies and the application templates used to build applications with J2EE technologies. But that discussion was only the tip of the proverbial iceberg. Remember that the three major technologies we focus on are servlets, JavaBeans and Enterprise JavaBeans (EJBs), and JavaServer Pages (JSPs). Together, these three object types form the core of a powerful architecture expressed in the MVC (Model-View-Controller) design pattern.

The control flow associated with this architecture starts with the browser's request being handled by a servlet that determines which program elements—JavaBeans, EJBs, or other objects—are required to carry out the specified request. The servlet then directs them to perform the business logic and to subsequently encapsulate the results of the execution. Finally, the servlet selects a presentation template—a JSP—for delivering the content back to the client. The JSP generates a specific response by accessing the resultant content available through the JavaBean(s) and/or EJB(s) (Figure 3.1).

This architecture provides a clean separation between the business logic implementation (Model) and the presentation (View). This separation makes it possible to independently develop, modify, and manage the implementation of the business logic and the form and style of the resulting presentation (HTML). Another layer of objects preserves the independence of the Model and the View and ties the two together. That Controller layer is made up of servlets that adapt the Model-layer objects to those needed by the View layer and mediate among various parts of the View layer by dealing with navigation and error-handling and reporting duties. The details of each of these pieces are discussed in later chapters. However, before we begin our overview of the J2EE, we need to examine the MVC notion more in depth and to discuss a few more architectural elements.

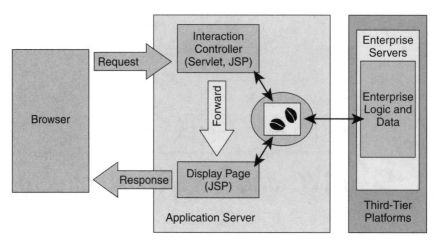

Figure 3.1   MVC Mapping to Servlets, Components, and JSPs

What's an MVC?

Computer scientists have an annoying tendency to overload terms, assigning multiple meanings to one word. A prime example of this, and an interesting study in how meanings change when conveyed from person to person, is the term *Controller*. Because we rely on an interpretation of MVC in our discussion, we need to see the alternative meaning to understand how the term is used in the Java community.

One of the central ideas of the Smalltalk-80 system was the Model-View-Controller (MVC) user interface paradigm, in which Controller had a well-defined, limited meaning. One of the best-known early public descriptions of MVC was that by [Krasner]: "Model-View-Controller (MVC) programming is the application of this three-way factoring whereby objects of different classes take over the operations related to the application domain (the Model), the display of the application's state (the View), and the user interaction with the Model and the View (the Controller)" (p. 26). In "classical" MVC, the Controller acted as a strategy for user interaction used by the View and the Model.

About the same time that this paper was published, in the late 1980s, Joelle Coutaz proposed another architecture. In this architecture, called *Presentation-Control-Abstraction* (PCA), the Presentation layer was responsible for the display of the application's state and interaction with the user—equivalent to both the View and the Controller in "classical" MVC. The Abstraction layer performed the same function as the Model layer in MVC. In between was a middle layer, termed, unfortunately, the *Control layer*, which acted as a mediator between parts of the Presentation layer and as a focal point for navigation.

Over the years, the division of roles in PCA has gained supporters, with presentations and reinterpretations in such books as [Jacobson 92] and [Buschmann]. However, over the same time, the PCA architecture has been increasingly referred to as the *MVC architecture*. We won't try to correct this reapplication of terminology but instead will go along with referring to a PCA-like architecture as MVC.

Layering

You've seen how the MVC design pattern can be used to structure applications built using J2EE technologies. Layering is a generalization of this concept. Application development is commonly accomplished in a vertical fashion, or at least the division and the estimation of work are determined by defining the application's primary user interfaces.

Underneath these interfaces, business rules, behavior, and data are obtained and manipulated, based on activity via the user interface. Architecture should provide a blueprint that will guide developers on when and how objects are defined during the development process. The importance of establishing this blueprint is realized in support of the iterative development process, whereby vertical slices of application functionality are delivered in iterations made up of planning, development, and assessment activities. The architecture must support both vertical and horizontal dimensions of an application. Horizontal development activities consist of applying logging, exception-handling, and start-up/shut-down mechanisms—behaviors that must be provided by all applications. Vertical activities involve implementing slices of application functionality from presentation to data source access. Having the infrastructure in place to allow development to occur in these two dimensions is the responsibility of the architecture.

Most experienced IT professionals agree that developing and adhering to an architecture are key to the success of large-scale software development, a notion validated by computer science pioneer Dijkstra in 1968. Since then, layered architectures have proved their viability in technological domains, such as hardware and networking. Today, corporate and retail computing are moving away from the desktop into a realm of distributed thin client computing.

Layering has proved itself in the operating system domain; however, the same benefits are available when applied to e-commerce or to thin client–oriented applications. Layered architectures have also proved themselves beyond the original centralized computing environments and have become essential in supporting the iterative development process by promoting reusability, scalability, and maintainability. In the following sections, we define and justify a layered architecture for J2EE.

Layered Architecture

Layering partitions the functionality of an application into separate layers that are stacked vertically. In layering, each layer interacts only with the layer directly underneath (Figure 3.2).

It is easy to see that changes can be effected on layer 3 with minimal side effects on layer 1. Moreover, layer 3 could be totally replaced, as long as it met layer 2's contract, without affecting layer 1. This property is known as *strict layering*.

Critics of strictly layered architectures argue that performance and sometimes extensibility are sacrificed, as more activity is required to propagate down through the layers. Extensibility can suffer if contracts defined between the layers are not robust enough to handle future requirements. However, being able to strategically distribute the application layers, use the domain layer across applications, and easily configure various data sources and user interfaces overcomes these criticisms. *Nonstrict layering* (Figure 3.3) allows a

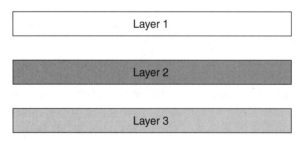

Figure 3.2   Layers

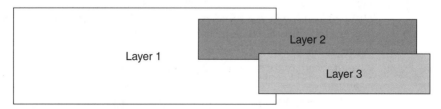

Figure 3.3   Nonstrict Layering

higher layer to access any layer defined below it and answers the critics' arguments against performance and extensibility; however, it nullifies the benefits of strict layering.

Common Layering Schemes

Traditional two-tier client/server-based applications can be partitioned into two layers: presentation and data access. A GUI application would simply query a data source, compute, and display the information to the user. Object technology encouraged the abstraction and reuse of not only presentation logic but also business processes and data. Therefore, decoupling application logic from application presentation was encouraged and has resulted in scalable three-tier distributed systems, allowing objects defined to model business data and processes to be used across application boundaries. With the explosion of the Internet and related technologies, requirements to scale, rapidly develop, deploy, and react to business changes have made the existence of layered application architecture imperative.

The most obvious layers of an application can be partitioned into presentation, domain, and data source sections (Figure 3.4). Arguably the most important layer is the domain, where business process and state are captured. Presentation-layer objects simply consume or exercise domain objects. Data source objects defined in the data source layer simply access specific data sources on behalf of domain objects requesting or saving state.

It is not enough to simply stipulate the layers in a graphic and expect developers to properly partition application elements into a layered architecture. Developers must implement functionality within each layer in a consistent fashion; moreover, message interaction between layers must be formalized.

Formalizing layer interaction should involve a decoupled design that includes the proper indirection in support of layer substitution. Additionally, behavior prescribed across all applications, namely, exception handling,

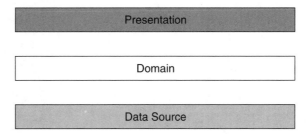

Figure 3.4 Client/Server Layers

logging, and start-up and shut-down operations, should be formalized and applied consistently.

Layered Architecture Defined

The primary motivation for layering is to create and to preserve an enterprise-reusable domain model that spans application boundaries. Of course, this can be accomplished with three layers, but introducing two additional layers between the presentation and data source layers further decouples the domain from application presentation and data source requirements (Figure 3.5).

Let's now take a closer look at the roles and responsibilities of the layers in this proposed five-layer architecture.

Presentation Layer

The presentation layer consists of objects defined to accept user input and to display application outputs. Presentation technologies that can be used with J2EE include

- HTML/JSP, with servlets acting as *Controllers*, as we see in the next section
- Applets, using Abstract Windowing Toolkit (AWT) or Swing
- Applications, using AWT or Swing

We will focus on the first option, the most common for supporting thin clients and the one that uses the most J2EE technologies, but we will at times bring up issues related to the other two.

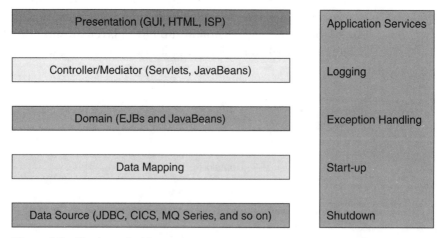

Figure 3.5   Five-Layer Architecture

Controller/Mediator Layer

Whatever the presentation technology happens to be, requests for domain state and behavior are done through a Controller object defined for the particular presentation requirements. This Controller object implements the Mediator design pattern from [Gamma]. An important design requisite involves making sure that domain-specific logic is not defined in presentation object methods but rather is obtained from a Mediator-referenced domain object. Application navigation topology also is defined within this layer.

Servlets control a client request for dynamic HTML content. Servlets produce HTML by either delegating to a JSP page or simply putting raw HTML tags onto the available PrintWriter. The JSP approach naturally separates the servlet from HTML presentation logic, as JSPs are physical documents, independent of the servlet. However, for producing raw HTML tags, the developer might be tempted to accomplish this with a method defined in a servlet. A better design involves creating a separate HTML-generating class, effectively isolating this functionality (Figure 3.6).

Servlets don't generate HTML but rather facilitate the production of dynamic HTML content by providing an entry point into a server-side JVM through a Web server. This entry point, known as a servlet, enables the developer to resolve session objects for individual users, access HTML form parameters, and respond with dynamically generated HTML. For a more detailed explanation of the Servlet API, refer to Chapter 4.

Application presentation objects interact with a domain model in generalized ways, regardless of the presentation technology. For instance, a GUI presents a list of choices, a collection of domain model objects; the same collection can be used to populate an HTML list. For that matter, the same collection could be used to provide a list of choices in a voice-response unit interface (Figure 3.7).

Mediators capture and decouple application-specific functionality from presentation technology by performing domain model requests for presentation or Controller objects that drive a specific application use case. Mediator classes are defined to satisfy a specific application user interface function or use case; therefore, they are less granular than controllers that usually exist at a component level. Mediators implement behavior that would usually end up in presentation classes as methods/scripts. Moreover, consistently applying mediator objects offers more than just loose coupling a domain model from

Figure 3.6 A Servlet as a Controller

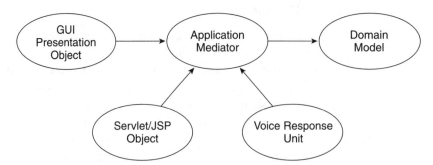

Figure 3.7   Mediators Used by Various Presentation Technologies

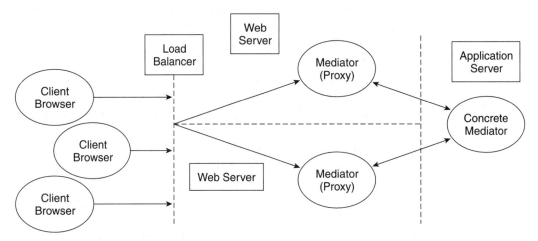

Figure 3.8   Distributed Mediator Topology

presentation technologies. Mediators provide a convenient and consistent way to transfer application state between user interfaces, eliminating the typical highly parameterized approach. Additionally, transaction behavior finds an appropriate location in mediator objects, as constraints of navigation and units of work are tied to application-specific functionality.

Mediators also play a role supporting scalability using distributed object technologies, such as EJBs or CORBA. In the case of mediators in a GUI application, making the mediator a distributed object makes for a thin client, and Web-based applications using servlets can keep sessions lightweight by referencing distributed mediator proxies (Figure 3.8).

The key to mediators' presentation independence is the enforcement of strict layering, meaning that mediators should not contain any references to presentation objects. However, mediators are free to reference domain object public state and behavior. Care must also be taken not to define domain logic in mediators. This pitfall can be avoided by asking yourself, "Can I still perform or obtain the requested domain operation by using only existing domain objects?" If the answer is, "No, I need a mediator object," the mediator is implementing behavior that belongs in the domain.

Mediators implement the same design intent as controllers. But instead of loosely coupling presentation objects, such as GUI components, mediators help decouple and capture the application presentation requirements of a domain model.

Mediator objects are application specific and possess intimate knowledge of the domain they are mediating on behalf of. So, typically they define methods that quickly delegate requests through to the domain. A common mediator operation involves producing a vector of objects that will be displayed in a drop-down selection list. A developer implementing a JSP page to display this list does not have to write domain-specific code to obtain this list but instead can simply obtain it from a mediator instance. Likewise, a selection will be made from this list and ultimately will result in a "selected" domain instance that an operation will be performed against. Again, instead of defining this application-specific behavior in presentation-specific code, such as a JSP page, the behavior can be captured in methods defined in a mediator class.

It is also worth mentioning that the mediator design is not specific to an HTML/servlet-based application. Mediators are coupled to the domain in an application-specific fashion; however, they do not reference a specific application technology, making them reusable by various presentation technologies. It is realistic to think that a single mediator type can "mediate" for both servlet and GUI-based applications (Figure 3.9).

In the context of servlet-based applications, mediators provide a convenient and consistent way to store user-specific application session objects. Several servlets are typically defined to support a single Web-based application function. Of course, the Servlet API provides a mechanism to associate domain object state with a user session; however, multiple domain objects could be involved in the function, and having to "get" and "put" multiple objects from the session requires extra bookkeeping. For a detailed discussion on how mediators can be used to help session management, see Chapter 8.

Domain Layer

The domain layer is possibly both the most difficult part of a layered system to understand and the most challenging to implement. To understand what a domain object is, we have to go back to the basic roots of object-oriented programming. When we learn Java programming or OO design, the first

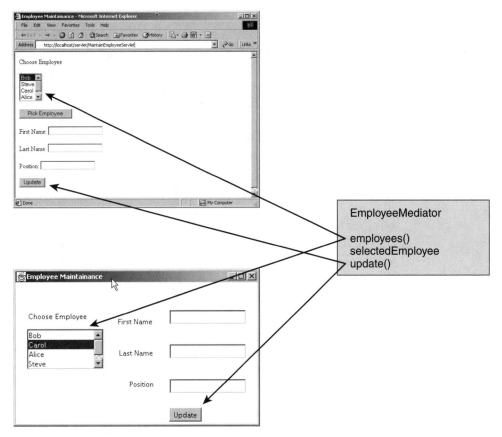

Figure 3.9   Mediator Servicing Various Presentation Types

examples seen are usually in terms of concrete objects. This might be an example of a control system as in Booch, in which the objects modeled, such as
temperature sensors and air conditioners, are physical, or through a simple
game in which objects, such as playing cards, are modeled.

Unfortunately, when starting to look at their own day-to-day problems,
many programmers instead see more abstract things, such as windows and
database tables, not the nice concrete things seen in the books and tutorials.
This is unfortunate, as modeling the aspects of a business in software can be
one of the most powerful tools that a programmer can bring to bear on solving the most difficult problems in software development. Capturing business
abstractions in objects can make a system much more powerful by making it
more flexible and can also create a critical distinction between the parts of a
system that represent the business problem being solved—its essence—and

the "accidents" of implementation resulting from choices in technology that might be transitory.

Domain objects are usually implemented as standard Java classes, which may or may not implement or follow the JavaBeans specification. If domain objects are implemented as JavaBeans, later users of these classes will have more options of how they can be manipulated in visual programming tools, such as VisualAge for Java. Correspondingly, there will be extra features required by the JavaBean specification that must be implemented for these options to be available.

As we have already discussed, J2EE provides another option for implementing domain objects. A programmer can choose to implement domain objects as EJBs, which offers some benefits in distribution, transaction capabilities, and persistence. Even when EJBs are used, a mix of standard Java classes and EJBs can be used, as we will examine in greater detail in the chapters on EJB architecture (Chapters 13 and 22).

Data Mapping Layer

One consequence of building a domain layer as we have described is that if we take a more abstract view of a domain object, it should not be concerned with purely implementation-specific details. For instance, one of the most common questions in enterprise programming is how to extract data from or update data in a database. Rather than making this behavior part of the domain object, a second set of objects is required to perform this function. Separating the behavior out in this way has a number of benefits, including making it possible to change implementation details, such as database vendor or database schema, without changing the domain implementation.

A design like this requires a separate layer, often called a *mapping,* or *persistence,* layer, that can move data from domain objects to back-end data sources and vice versa. Several commercial products, such as the VisualAge Persistence Builder, JavaBlend, and TOPLink, can add this behavior. However, for a programmer using J2EE, this behavior will commonly be used through the APIs provided by the EJB container. The EJB container in WebSphere provides a simple and consistent interface for data persistence for entity EJBs. However, we may still need to implement some mapping functions even in designs using EJBs when we need to move data between JavaBeans and EJBs. We cover this topic in depth in a later chapter.

From an architecture design perspective, how mapping operations are engaged from a JavaBean domain should be vendor neutral. Domain models should be implemented as JavaBeans that inherit from a common base class. Methods defined in this class allow an extended class to consistently issue persistent operations for retrieving, saving, and deleting of objects from underlying, "mapped" data sources. A discussion of the Mapper design and implementation details that appear in this book's case study are discussed in Appendix A.

Data Source Access Layer

Relational databases, such as DB2, Oracle, and Informix, are arguably the most common way IT organizations store and query enterprise data. Recognizing this profound market share, Sun delivered the JDBC (Java Database Connectivity) API, which allows the production and execution of vendor-neutral SQL.[1] Developers can use standard ANSI SQL against any JDBC-compliant driver. The specific API and types of available JDBC drivers are beyond the scope of this discussion; refer to the JDBC specification, available on Sun's Java Web site, for more information.

How does this fit into the J2EE architecture? Data source access exists within the EJB portion of the architecture. EJB containers perform mapping and specific persistent operations on behalf of entity objects. Containers accomplish this by using data source access frameworks and such APIs as JDBC. Other objects like servlets and JavaBeans may also use JDBC directly to access enterprise data as well.

Other Considerations

Application Services

Developers must apply application responsibilities to all application development efforts. Implementing these activities consistently using a design that is extensible will facilitate reuse and minimize side effects when requirements change. Moreover, standardizing these services across all applications can yield efficiencies in determining and communicating new development and maintenance activities.

Obvious application responsibilities include error handling, status tracing, application start-up and shutdown, accessing externalized properties, and applying interface preferences. A design must allow developers to consistently apply error handling across all applications and also support the ability to install and to change these behaviors on an application basis. For example, application status is sometimes reported to a console, but what happens if the application is server based and a console does not exist? The design should allow tracing to be routed to a flat file or maybe to the console. For a discussion of design and implementation issues for application service layers, see Appendix B.

---

1. The JDBC specification also applies to nonrelational data sources.

Test Scripts

The primary design intent of a layered architecture is decoupling a problem-space domain model from presentation and data source requirements. Reuse of the domain, at least across application boundaries, can be achieved if isolation is accomplished.

Creating test scripts that exercise domain model behavior helps to verify domain isolation and also to

- Verify domain functionality
- Support white box[2]–oriented regression testing
- Document usage intent through implementation examples
- Provide project plan milestones for domain implementation
- Provide a convenient place to apply performance timings

Test scripts should be created to exercise retrieval and output of individual top-level domain classes. Because all domain objects will inherit persistent operations, these types of test scripts can be created without physical data sources. An example test script that retrieves and outputs project objects and displays their state to the console is given in Listing 3.1.

Listing 3.1 An example of a test script.

```
import com.wsbook.casestudy.domain.*;
import java.util.*;
public class RetrieveAndDisplayEmployees {
/**
 * Retrieve and display Employees
 * @param args an array of command-line arguments
 */
public static void main(java.lang.String[] args) {
// Retrieve Employees
Vector employees = new Employee().retrieveAllObjects();
//  Enumerate over Employees
Enumeration elements = employees.elements();
    while (elements.hasMoreElements()) {
    Employee anEmployee = (Employee) elements.nextElement();
    // Display anEmployee...
    System.out.println(anEmployee);
    }
}
}
```

No hard-and-fast rules dictate what type of test scripts to create. Test scripts can also be created to exercise and verify, create, read, and update requirements or to implement operations to satisfy a use case that came out of the design process. A domain design that performs an interesting operation

---

2. Black-box testing, by contrast, exercises an application from an end user's perspective.

can also be captured in a use case. Each test script should be defined using a descriptive class name, regardless of length. For example, some of the test script class names defined for this book's case study on time sheets are

- CreateAndSaveTimeSheet
- DisplayTimeSheets
- DisplayPendingTimeSheets
- ApplyPendingTimeSheet

Creating test scripts is a simple notion and exercise that if incorporated in the development process can result in many benefits during and throughout an application's life cycle.

Summary and Preview

We've covered a lot of ground in this chapter. We've examined how the J2EE technologies introduced as the solution to the problems seen in Chapter 2 form a coherent MVC architecture and how the principles of application layering can be applied to make applications manageable, maintainable, and testable. In the next chapter, we begin to look more closely at the Servlet API: the first of the J2EE technologies that form the focus of this book.

CHAPTER 4

Introduction to Servlets

Now that we've examined some of the architectural issues surrounding the use of server-side programming and J2EE, we can proceed to an in-depth look at the first of the APIs that make up the programming model. In this chapter, we introduce the concept of a *servlet* and discuss what servlet programming entails. We discuss the following topics:

- HyperText Transfer Protocol (HTTP) basics
- Servlet concepts
- Servlet life cycle
- Example servlet
- Key classes
- Reasons for using servlets

The purpose of this chapter is to advance your knowledge of these fundamental concepts about the servlet API. In the next chapter we will examine how to take the examples and principles that we review in this chapter and execute them within the VisualAge for Java development environment.

HTTP Technology Primer

HyperText Transfer Protocol (HTTP) is the basis for the Web. HTTP is built on Transmission Control Protocol/Internet Protocol (TCP/IP) and is considered an application-level protocol for distributed, collaborative, hypermedia information systems. HTTP is a request/response–oriented protocol; an HTTP client makes a request, and then an HTTP server services that request and subsequently responds.

Background

The first available version of HTTP was HTTP/0.9, which was used in 1990 as a part of the World Wide Web global information initiative. This first HTTP version was a simple protocol for raw data transfer across the Internet.

HTTP/1.0, as defined by [RFC 1945], greatly improved the protocol by allowing requests and responses to exist as MIME-like messages. MIME (Multipurpose Internet Mail Extensions) provides definitions of various types of messages. For example, the MIME type text/html describes an HTML message, whereas the MIME type image/gif defines a message containing a GIF (graphics interchange format) bitmap. HTTP/1.0 also provided the ability for messages to contain metainformation about the data transferred and modifiers on the request/response semantics. HTTP/1.0 is the most common version of HTTP in use today, primarily because of the speed at which the Internet community adopts newer protocol versions. HTTP/1.1, as defined in [RFC 2616], is the most recent version, providing solutions to problems encountered with using hierarchical proxies, caching, persistent connections, and virtual hosts. Microsoft's Internet Explorer (IE) 4.x and above and Netscape Navigator 4.5 and above support HTTP/1.1.

When looking at HTTP from the perspective of application programming, the first thing to understand is that HTTP is connectionless and stateless. HTTP is based on a Web server—sometimes referred to as HTTPD, for HTTP daemon—receiving a request and then formulating a response back to a client. HTTP is connectionless because neither the client nor the server retains any state information about the application data. In HTTP/1.1, a connection can be maintained between the client and the server; however, this connection is mainly for batching response information for performance considerations. A request is sent; then, after the server-side task is completed, a response is given. It is up to the application programmer to maintain any state information necessary to the application.[1] In most cases, the client is a Web browser but could be an application, a Java applet, or another Web server. Although not as sophisticated as the newer connection-oriented protocols, such as Internet Inter-ORB Protocol (IIOP), this request/response protocol has proved very flexible in allowing a wide variety of vendors to create Web servers, Web browsers, and other HTTP-based systems.

Uniform Resource Identifiers

URIs have been called many different names: universal resource identifiers, universal resource locators, WWW addresses, and uniform resource locators

---

1. We will see later that the Servlet API provides ways of maintaining application state information, but this is not part of HTTP.

(URLs) and names (URNs). URLs and URNs are kinds of URIs. URL is specific to the HTTP scheme, but URN is not. URIs are simply formatted strings that identify—via name, location, or any other characteristic—a resource. URIs in HTTP can be represented in absolute form or relative to a known base, depending on the context of their use. The two forms differ in that absolute URIs always begin with a scheme name followed by a colon.

HTTP does not place any limits on the length of URIs. Therefore, HTTP servers should handle URIs of any length. However, programmers formulating URIs ought to be cautious about depending on URI lengths above 255 bytes, because some older client or proxy implementations might not properly support these lengths.

HTTP URL

Each Web resource—an HTML page, a JSP, a servlet, and so on—that can be requested from a Web server must have a unique name associated with it. That unique name is called a URL, or uniform resource locator. For discussion purposes, let's consider a URL as a way to uniquely identify a Web service that exists on a particular Web server. For example, to access the *index. html* page on the *www.abc.com* Web server, the absolute and explicit URL would be *http://www.abc.com/index.html*. The format of a URL is as follows:

```
protocol://hostname<:port>/identifiers
```

As you can see, the URL is made up of several components. Table 4.1 defines them and give examples.

URI versus URL

According to the specification [RFC 2396] all URLs are URIs. However, URIs allow Web services to be defined in a way that they are not bound to a specific server. This has important advantages.

- A URL explicitly locates a service to a specific Web server and port. If services and pages that can be hosted on various Web servers must be created, a way is needed to identify those pages without locating them. The URI provides the unique name for a service, hosted on any Web server.
- In addition to being able to relocate a service or a set of pages to another Web server, it is often desirable to replicate these services or pages to several servers to avoid the single-point-of-failure problem. If one of these servers terminates, other mechanisms, such as a network dispatcher, can safely send requests to another Web server, which has replicas of those services or pages. The existence of a nonlocated URI helps the developer avoid making code changes to the service or the page when deploying to different machines.

Table 4.1   Components of the HTTP URL

Component	Example	Explanation
Protocol, or access scheme	*http://*	The default protocol is always HTTP. However, other protocols, such as File Transfer Protocol (FTP) *(ftp://)*, Network News Transfer Protocol (NNTP) *(nntp://)*, and others can be specified.
Port	*80*	The port is optional and if omitted is set to the default port for the protocol specified in the URL. For example, port 80 is the default port for HTTP. FTP uses port 20 for connections and control.
Host	*www.abc.com*	The host name must be a valid TCP/IP address or domain naming service (DNS) host name. Other examples are *209.137.71.120*, *www.internic.net*, and *www.ncsu.edu*.
Identifiers	*Index.html*	This portion of the URL is loosely defined to allow the server program on the other side of HTTP to interpret in various ways. Usually, this identifier is the name of a file on the Web server. However, the identifier section of the URL may look something like */servlet/ MyServlet?parm1=8&parm2=10* In this case, the identifiers name a Java servlet and two parameters—parameter 1 and parameter 2—the servlet can use to perform its task.

> ### An Example of URLs and URIs
> A fully specified URL is always of the form
>
>   *http://www.mycompany.com/mydirectory/mypage.html*
>
> However, a URI may be fragmentary, as in
>
>   */mydirectory/mypage.html*
>
> This difference is important in specifying URIs that refer to HTML and to JSPs. By referring to only a partial address—a URI—you keep your HTML tags and JSP and servlet code from being tied to a single machine name.

Requests, Responses, and Headers

HTTP is a simple protocol based on a client sending a request to a Web server and then getting a response. When the client sends a request, it contains all the information that the Web server needs to process the request. Both the request and the response contain a *start-line;* zero or more *header fields,* or headers; an *empty line,* one with nothing preceding the carriage return/line feed (CR/LF) indicating the end of the header fields; and, possibly, a *message body.*

Headers

The headers section of a message contains a general-header section—headers that are applicable to both the request and the response and specific headers—an entity-header section, and either a request-header section or a response-header section, depending on the type of message.

- The general-header section contains such items as Cache-Control, Date, and Transfer-Encoding. The Transfer-Encoding header can impact the message length, as the encoding type may increase the size of the body of the message.
- The request-header section contains such headers as Host, Accept-Charset, and Referer. The Referer header specifies the URL of the page from which the request came whereas the Host header contains the name of the target host specified in the request, or the host processing the request.
- The response-header section contains such headers as Age, Location, and Server. The Server header specifies the name of the server that generated the response.
- The entity-headers section defines metainformation about the entity body or, if no body is present, the resource identified by the request. This section contains such headers as Allow, Content-Encoding, and Last-Modified.

Requests

The start line of a request message is the request itself. An HTTP request is characterized by a *method token,* followed by a request URI and a protocol version, ending with a CR/LF. The method token is one of GET, POST, OPTIONS, HEAD, PUT, DELETE, TRACE, CONNECT, or an extension method as defined by the implementation. When using HTTP methods to create a request, the application programmer should understand that the writers of HTTP consider some methods as safe and others as unsafe. This definition of a safe method was noted in the HTTP specification so that user agents can be written to make a user aware of the fact that a possibly unsafe action is being requested. It is thought that the safe methods will not generate side effects as a result of calling them. The protocol neither does nor can enforce this idea of safe methods, as implementers are free to create servers that handle these requests in any way that they see fit.

Two key HTTP request methods of importance to the programmer are GET and POST.

- GET happens when you type in a URL at a browser. Literally "Get a file and return its contents," this request in the context of a servlet means "Send some dynamic content to the user as HTML."
- POST happens, usually, when you type information into an HTML form and click the *Submit* button. The POST request is so named because it was originally intended to represent posting to an Internet newsgroup.

Table 4.2 summarizes all the HTTP methods.

Responses

After receiving and interpreting a response, the server must respond. The response message contains a start line, which is the status of the request. This

Table 4.2   HTTP Method Descriptions

Method	Description	Safe
GET	Obtains the contents associated with the request URI. GET can contain parameters, can be conditional, and can return only a portion of the contents if the Range header fields have been supplied. GET parameters must be contained in the request URI as a query string. To call the */register* service on the *abc.com* server with name and age parameters, *http://abc.com/ register?name=greg& age=34* could be used, where *?name=greg&age=34* is the query string. Note that the *?* starts the query string and that the parameters are shown as name/value pairs separated by *&*. This request URI would then be placed in a GET request as GET http://abc.com/register?name=greg&age=34 HTTP/1.1 Because parameters to the server must be added to the request URI as a query string, the GET request is, obviously, not designed to send large amounts of data. In fact, the size of the request URI equals that of the command line on the client operating system.	Yes
POST	Used to send data to the server so that it can annotate existing resources or update an existing resource based on the data sent. As with any request, a response is given. POST could be used for a bulletin board system, newsgroup, mailing list, or other group of articles. Unlike GET, POST is designed to send large amounts of data to the server. POST has potentially multiple connections to the server. The first is to send the request; subsequent ones may then be used to send the data to the server. Once the server has obtained the request and the headers, it can determine the length of the request body—the data—and read the data for an appropriate number of bytes.	No

Table 4.2 HTTP Method Descriptions *(continued)*

Method	Description	Safe
OPTIONS	Obtains the information about the communication options available on the request/response chain identified by the request URI. This method allows the client to determine the options and/or requirements associated with a resource, or the capabilities of a server, without implying a resource action or initiating resource retrieval. The following OPTIONS request obtains all communication options from the server: OPTIONS * HTTP/1.1	No
HEAD	Like a GET request except that the server must not return a message body in the response. The metainformation in the HTTP headers in response to a HEAD request should be identical to the information sent in response to a GET request. For example: HEAD http://abc.com/index.html HTTP/1.1	Yes
PUT	Used to send data to the server so that the data can be stored as a new resource on the server. If the resource already exists, PUT should view the request as one to update the existing resource. PUT and POST are almost identical, differing in the meaning of the request URI. The URI in a POST request identifies the resource that will handle the enclosed entity. That resource might be a data-accepting process, a gateway to another protocol, or a separate entity that accepts annotations. In contrast, the URI in a PUT request identifies the entity enclosed with the request; the user agent knows what URI is intended, and the server must not attempt to apply the request to another resource. If it wants the request to be applied to a different URI, the server must send a 301 "Moved Permanently" response; the user agent may then make its own decision about whether to redirect the request.	No
DELETE	Requests that the server delete the resource identified by the request URI. The server must provide the implementation of the delete, which may be to delete a record from a database or a resource from the Web server itself.	No
TRACE	Invokes a remote, application-layer loopback of request message. The final recipient is the origin server or the first proxy or gateway to receive a Max-Forwards value of 0 in the request. A TRACE request must not include an entity. If the TRACE is successful, the response should contain the entire request message in the entity body, with a Content-Type of message/http.	No
CONNECT	Reserved for use with a proxy that can dynamically switch to being a tunnel, such as Secure Sockets Layer tunneling.	No

status line contains the HTTP version followed by a numeric status code and its associated textual phrase, with elements separated by spaces. The status code is a three-digit integer result code of the attempt to understand and to satisfy the request. The textual phrase is for debugging purposes. The first digit in the three-digit code defines the class of the response. The last two digits do not have any categorization role but instead help to uniquely identify the response. Five values are possible for the first digit:

- 1xx: Informational—request received; continuing process
- 2xx: Success—action was successfully received, understood, and accepted
- 3xx: Redirection—further action needed to complete the request
- 4xx: Client error—request contains bad syntax or cannot be fulfilled
- 5xx: Server error—server failed to fulfill an apparently valid request

As with any HTTP message, after the start line (status line in the response case), the message headers are given, followed by the message body. The message body contains the data, which will be displayed in the Web browser.

Pulling It All Together

Many scenarios can be described when using HTTP. In an effort to pull together the ideas presented here about URIs and messages over HTTP, we need to take a look at the GET and POST requests and how the interaction between the client and the server occurs.

We show a roundtrip GET request in Figure 4.1. The request is for the URL of *http://webserver/index.html*. Note that when using a Web browser

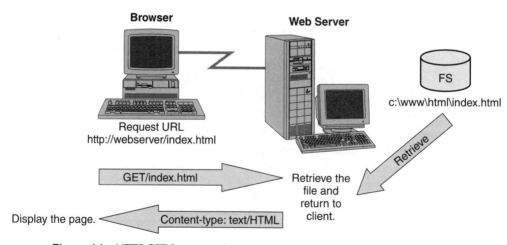

Figure 4.1   HTTP GET Request in Action

and HTML to make HTTP requests, a GET request could be made in several ways, as follows:

- By typing the URL into the URL line of the Web browser and pressing *Enter.*
- By clicking on a link that appears inside an HTML page. The link is coded using the <A HREF=url...> tag.
- By clicking a button on a form that appears inside an HTML page. The form would need to specify a method of GET, as in the tag <FORM method=GET action= url...>.

After receiving this request, the Web server maps it to a file located on the Web server file system—*C:\www\html\index.html*—and then responds with the contents of that file to the browser. The entire transaction involves one connection to the Web server and an almost immediate response.

Figure 4.2 shows a POST request roundtrip. This request is for the URL *http://webserver/servlet/Register.* When using a Web browser and HTML to make HTTP requests, the user must click a button on a form that appears inside an HTML page to make a POST request. The form would need to specify a method of POST, as in the tag <FORM method=POST action= url...>.

After receiving this request, the Web server maps it to the servlet's class file located on the Web server, or servlet engine, file system—*C:\WebSphere*

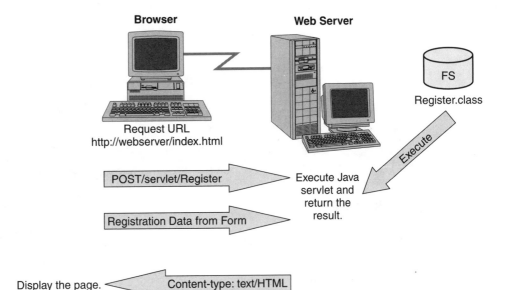

Figure 4.2 HTTP POST Request in Action

AppServer\servlets\Register.class—and then runs the servlet. Next, the Web server, or servlet engine, reads the posted data, using a second connection, and then performs the requested POST operation. Finally, the Web server, or servlet engine, responds with a message that is displayed in the browser. The entire transaction involves at least two connections to the Web server, with an almost immediate response.

Servlet Concepts

A servlet is a Java class, similar to an applet, that runs entirely within a Java Virtual Machine (JVM) associated with a Web server. Java is equally well suited for client use and server use.

Because Java is portable and mobile, server writers can freely change platforms for their server applications without having to rewrite or even to recompile their Java programs. In addition, Java as shipped with the Java Development Kit (JDK) comes with a complete set of communications classes for using TCP/IP sockets and URLs. IBM WebSphere Application Server and IBM VisualAge for Java include all these classes. Additionally, Java has built-in support for threads, a mechanism for allowing your Java program to do more than one task at once; serialization of objects, a persistence mechanism for objects; and the ability to call native C/C++ functions.

As a standard server-side Java program, a servlet extends the functionality of a Web server. The overall architecture of a servlet appears in Figure

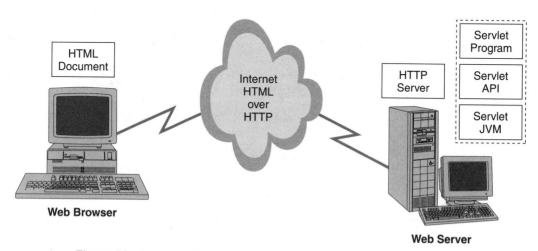

Figure 4.3   Servlet Architecture

4.3. When it receives a request for a servlet through a URL, a Web server loads the servlet, if necessary, into the JVM associated with the Web server—and executes the servlet. When it completes its task, the servlet sends any generated output—the response—back to the Web browser. You can write servlets for administrative purposes, such as managing Web server log files or sending e-mail alerts to administrators. However, what is more interesting and more pervasive is the use of servlets in information technology (IT) applications that run on the Web.

We have already seen how the Model-View-Controller (MVC) design pattern can help break a system down into layers. In this scenario, the servlets cooperate with a set of JavaBeans or Enterprise JavaBeans (EJBs) to perform the "real" work of an application. When following this principle, servlets act as a part of the controller layer for applications that run on the Web. Servlets become "glue" between ordinary HTML (View) and the JavaBeans or EJBs. Servlets can then add functionality to the overall Web application by providing session management, user authentication, and user authorization.

Support for Servlets

Sun Microsystems provides a reference implementation of the JavaServlet API and the JavaServer API called Tomcat, in conjunction with the Apache Software Foundation. You can download Tomcat from www.apache.org. At present, IBM WebSphere Application Server version 3.5 uses the servlet API version 2.1. As a result, all references in this book to the Servlet API are for the 2.1 version.

Because VisualAge for Java has an open design, you could use the Tomcat from within VisualAge for Java to develop and to test your servlets. However, the Professional and Enterprise editions of IBM VisualAge for Java IBM contain the WebSphere Test Environment (WTE), a servlet development and test environment based on IBM WebSphere. The WTE can be used in IBM VisualAge for Java instead of Tomcat to develop and to test servlets more effectively.

Servlet Engines

The various servlet engines available are implemented in a variety of ways. The three basics types of servlet engines are standalone, add-on, and embedded. Each has its advantages and disadvantages.

Standalone Servlet Engines

A standalone engine includes the normal HTTP server functions and also has built-in support for servlets. This is a desirable solution in that installation and configuration concerns are greatly minimized in the beginning, as the Web server and the servlet engine come integrated. However, as Sun releases new Servlet APIs, a potential problem becomes being able to use the latest Servlet API with the standalone solution. One might find them in a waiting pattern until the vendor of the standalone solution does the testing and reintegration of the Servlet API into the product.

Add-on Servlet Engines

Add-on servlet engines function as plug-ins to existing Web servers—adding servlet support to servers that were not originally designed with servlets in mind. This solution solves the problem mentioned in the standalone solution of allowing the user to keep up with the latest Servlet APIs apart from the Web server. However, the trade-off is that initial configuration may be difficult, as integration problems may have to be solved by the user rather than the vendor. IBM WebSphere Application Server falls into this category. IBM WebSphere provides a small plug-in that installs into the HTTP server. The HTTP server then forwards servlet requests to the standalone application server through a proprietary protocol over TCP/IP.

Embeddable Servlet Engines

An embeddable engine is generally a lightweight servlet deployment platform that can be embedded in another application. That application becomes the true server. An example of this kind of servlet engine can be found in Sun's JavaServer Engine, which can be embedded into other servlet engines that complement or add on to the basic functionality of the embedded servlet engine. The IBM WebSphere Test Environment under IBM VisualAge for Java is such a servlet engine.

Servlet Life Cycle

The servlet life cycle defines the process used to load the servlet into memory, execute the servlet, and then unload the servlet from memory. Figure 4.4 shows the servlet life cycle. A Web browser requests a servlet through a URL. The URL can be on the location line of the Web browser or can be a link embedded in the HTML document being viewed. A typical servlet URL appears as *http://localhost/servlet/HelloServlet*. In the simplest case, the word *servlet* in the URI path lets the Web server know that the request is for a servlet, not

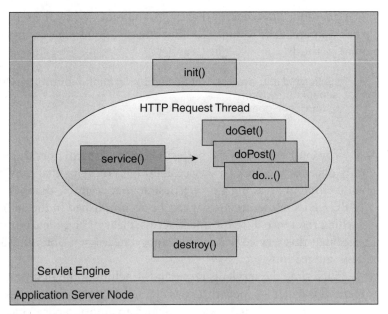

Figure 4.4 Servlet Life Cycle

an HTML page or a CGI program. In the preceding example, HelloServlet is the class name of the desired servlet.

To create a servlet, you must create a subclass of the GenericServlet class or one of its subclasses. Typically, you subclass the class javax.servlet.http. HttpServlet, which means that your servlet will be invoked through HTTP. You are not required to add any code to your servlet at this point. However, if you issue an HTTP request to your new servlet in this state, the servlet will respond with the default error saying that a GET or a POST request is not supported. Thus, from a compile-time perspective, there are no required methods. However, as you will see, you will want to code at the very least a doGet() or a doPost() method to make your servlet useful.

When your servlet is first requested, the Web server requests that the servlet engine load the requested servlet class and all the associated classes into memory on the servlet engine node. Control then passes to the init() method in the servlet. GenericServlet provides an empty init() method. If you wish to perform initialization tasks, such as connecting to a database, you need to provide an init() method in your subclass. The init() method receives only one call, immediately after your servlet is loaded into memory. It is a good idea to always call the superclass' init() method if you provide your own init() method. This ensures that any setup required by the servlet engine or other superclasses is done. To illustrate this point, let's examine the following init() method:

```
public void init(javax.servlet.ServletConfig config) throws ServletException
{super.init (config);
// Your code goes here . . .
}
```

The init() method is the perfect place to perform operations that are done only once for the life of a servlet. Examples of items that may be done in the init method are reading a properties file that contains database names and JDBC URLs. Other items that can be accomplished in the init() method are caching reference data for quick access, clearing log files, notifying other services that this service is available, and, if necessary, obtaining a pool of database connections.

Each time the servlet is requested—including the first time after the init() method is called—a new thread is created,[2] and that thread executes over the service() method. GenericServlet provides an empty service() method. You must override this method if you want to do any real work. Because the service() method is called in its own thread, the servlet engine is free to take additional requests for the same servlet or another servlet that it executes in another thread. The service() method is where the work of the servlet is accomplished. Because the service() method is always executed inside a new thread, you must be careful to ensure that everything done in the service() method is thread safe (reentrant).

Later, when the Web server deems it necessary, the destroy() method of the servlet is called, and then the servlet is unloaded from the server's memory. If you provide a destroy() method in your servlet, that method is called. Common tasks performed by the destroy() method are disconnecting all database connections and closing all files and other administrative items.

An Example Servlet

Now that we have explained what a servlet is and have discussed its life cycle, let's examine the code for a complete servlet. As we mentioned, a servlet is presented to the outside world by a single URL, exactly as a CGI script is represented to the Web browser. However, unlike a CGI script, information

---

2. In WebSphere, a new thread is usually not created, but instead an already created thread is assigned from a pool of existing threads.

about the request made of the servlet is not passed as environment variables that have to be manually parsed but instead is given to the servlet as a set of well-defined Java objects. To illustrate this point, let's examine the simplest possible servlet, "Hello World" (Listing 4.1).

Listing 4.1   "Hello World."

```
/**
 * This class is a simple sample servlet
 */
import java.io.*;
import javax.servlet.*;
import javax.servlet.http.*;
public class HelloServlet extends HttpServlet {
/**
 * This method handles an HTTP GET request and outputs
 * HTML to print "Hello IBM WebSphere World" to a browser.
 */
public void doGet (HttpServletRequest req, HttpServletResponse res)
throws ServletException, IOException{
    PrintWriter out = null;
    res.setContentType("text/html");
    out = res.getWriter ();
    out.println("<html>");
    out.println("<head><title>Sample</title></head>");
    out.println("<body>");
    out.println("Hello IBM WebSphere World!");
    out.println("</body>");
    out.println("</html>");
    }
}
```

To run this servlet, assuming that the host *localhost* is defined, that the Web server and application server are appropriately configured, and that the *HelloServlet.class* file is placed in the appropriate location, you would enter the URL *http://localhost/servlet/HelloServlet* on the URL line of a Web browser. The words "Hello IBM WebSphere World" would then be printed to your Web browser.

Our simple Servlet class extends the class javax.servlet.http.HttpServlet. Think about HttpServlet and its descendants as being servlets that speak HTTP as their native language. The key thing to understand about HTTP servlets is that they typically handle GET and POST requests. HttpServlet subclasses handle one or both of these methods by overriding either the method doGet() or doPost() methods, respectively. In our case, we're overriding doGet(), so the information sent back will be displayed on a client browser if the URL corresponding to our servlet is typed in by, for example, sending a GET request.

Which Servlet Methods Do I Override?

The HttpServlet class defines a special do[Request Type] method, or a *service handler,* for each of the HTTP request types discussed previously. These methods are simply defined as protected void methods; they are not declared abstract. The service() method defined in HttpServlet is written to automatically call the appropriate service handler, based on the type of request received. In your servlets, you will generally choose to override only a small subset of these methods–generally, either doGet() or doPost().

Sometimes, the same servlet will need to handle both GET and POST requests. If you want to do something different for each request type, you should override both doGet() and doPost(). On the other hand, if you need to implement the same logic for both request types, you should probably override service() instead.

Now, exactly how is the reply "Hello IBM WebSphere World" sent back to the browser? As you can see from the example, the route we use is an object that implements the interface HttpServletResponse. HttpServletResponse allows you to do several things:

- Set the MIME type, or content type, of the HTTP response header to any valid MIME type, such as image/jpeg or audio/wav. Most of the time, the response type will be text/html, which means that you are sending back HTML to be interpreted and displayed by the browser. The method setContentType(String) sets the content type.
- Obtain a PrintWriter for output with getWriter(). When you are sending HTML as your content type, you want to make it human readable. PrintWriter facilitates this, using the println() method to add CR/LF on the end of your text lines. Additionally, other "writers" allow for national language support and translation of Unicode characters to UCS transformation formats (UTFs). In all other respects, PrintWriter acts like an output stream. You can also obtain an output stream with getOutputStream().
- Set the HTTP header values with setHeader(String, String). This method is useful if you want to disable browser and server page caching for a response page.
- Redirect the browser to a different page with sendRedirect(String).

In our example, we're simply setting the content type of the response, opening a PrintWriter for output, and then sending several lines of HTML text back to the browser. This is what most servlets end up doing for output. They may obtain part of the information they display from an outside source—say, from a socket to another server, or a JDBC query. However, the mechanics of sending HTML to the client are the same, regardless of the source.

Those of you with keen attention to detail will have noticed that the doGet() method also takes a second parameter, HTTPServletRequest, which we did not use. Servlets that need to process input from the browser use this interface. The code in a doGet() or a doPost() method typically uses the HttpServletRequest methods getParameterNames(), getParameter(), and getParameterValues() to read in the HTTP parameters sent as part of a POST request or as part of a query string. The code can then make decisions on the basis of those parameters or record them to persistent storage. If we make a small modification to the "Hello World" servlet, we can send a message parameter to the servlet and have it display that message instead of the common "Hello IBM WebSphere World" message. Examine the new code (Listing 4.2) and note the lines in bold face.

Listing 4.2   Modified "Hello World."

```
/**
 * This class is a simple sample servlet, which takes a message parameter
 */
import java.io.*;
import javax.servlet.*;
import javax.servlet.http.*;

public class HelloServlet extends HttpServlet {
/**
 * This method handles an HTTP GET request and outputs
 * HTML to print "Hello IBM WebSphere World" to a browser.
 */
public void doGet (HttpServletRequest req, HttpServletResponse res)
      throws ServletException, IOException{
   PrintWriter out = null;
   res.setContentType("text/html");
   out = res.getWriter ();

   // Changed Code
   String theMessage = req.getParameter("mymessage");
   If (theMessage == null) {
      theMessage = "Hello IBM WebSphere World!";
   }
   out.println("<html>");
   out.println("<head><title>Sample</title></head>");
   out.println("<body>");
   out.println(theMessage);
   out.println("</body>");
   out.println("</html>");
      }
}
```

To run this servlet, you use the same URL as before but with an additional query string. An example URL of this type might be *http://localhost/ servlet/HelloServlet?mymessage=Hello+Parameter.* The words "Hello Parameter" would then be printed to your Web browser. Note that the + sign is used for spaces to ensure that the full message will survive the network send.

If you examine the code changes, you can see that the difference is the use of req.getParameter("mymessage") to obtain the data passed on the URL. The getParameter() method takes one argument, which must be a string and is the case-sensitive identifier of the parameter in the request. The name of this parameter key must match exactly the name used on the query string. Otherwise, the getParameter() method will return a null, and the method will set the variable theMessage to "Hello WebSphere World." The last thing done to the code was to change out.println() to use the newly created variable, theMessage.

Some Comments

Even the simplest examples, like the one we have shown here, are not truly representative of how servlets are used in practice. In particular, you should avoid hard-coding HTML into your servlets. Remember from our overview discussion of the J2EE APIs and the MVC design pattern that servlets act as mediators that will tie together domain logic and display logic in the form of JSPs. So, in general, you should avoid placing HTML in your servlet code; if you do place HTML in your servlets, changing the "look" of your Web sites becomes more difficult, as you must change your Java code even if all that changes is the HTML that is returned.

Key Classes and Interfaces

The Java Servlet API 2.1 contains a rich set of classes and methods that enables the servlet developer to code complex Web applications in a well-implemented manner. The API is contained in three packages: javax.servlet, javax.servlet. http, and javax.servlet.jsp. Each of these packages contains several interfaces and classes that define the API.[3] In this section, we will only begin to cover the javax.servlet and javax.servlet.http packages. As we look at the interfaces defined in these packages, you should understand that the servlet engine provider would supply implementations for these interfaces.

---

3. For more details on the Servlet API, refer to the Servlet API javadocs, available from the *Help* menu in VisualAge for Java or for download from *http://java.sun.com.*

Table 4.3   Classes and Interfaces in the javax.servlet Package

Classes	Interfaces
GenericServlet	RequestDispatcher
ServletException	Servlet
ServletInputStream	ServletConfig
ServletOutputStream	ServletContext
UnavailableException	ServletRequest
	ServletResponse
	SingleThreadModel

However, you will want to write code that uses the API only as it appears in an interface where supplied and not any vendor-specific class.

The javax.servlet *Package*

The javax.servlet package contains the basic API for servlets but is not tied to a particular scheme or protocol for how servlets may be used. We will briefly describe some of the key classes contained in this package. Table 4.3 lists the classes and interfaces in the javax.servlet package.

The Servlet Interface

The Servlet interface defines the basic API for all servlets and includes the init(), service(), and destroy() methods, as described earlier. All servlets implement this interface, either directly or by subclassing the GenericServlet class or the HttpServlet class.

The ServletContext Interface

A context is needed for each servlet so that communication with the servlet engine can be accomplished in a nonrequest-specific manner. This context includes finding path information, accessing other servlets running on the server, and writing to the server log file. Different virtual servers may return different servlet contexts.

If the server supports multiple or "virtual" hosts,[4] the ServletContext object must be at least as unique as the host, otherwise there exists the possibil-

---

4. A "virtual host" is a configuration enabling a single Web server machine to act like many machines. Many virtual hosts can reside on the same physical machine. Each virtual host name is defined in the DNS and must be configured in both the Web server and the application server.

ity that information might be shared between unrelated applications, causing application problems or security risks. Servlet engines can also create Servlet-Context objects that are unique to a group of servlets and tied to a specific part of the host's URL namespace. You can assign this grouping through the administrative functions of the application server. In this way you can combine a group of related servlets together with a single ServletContext so that they can share information in a logical application.

The ServletContext object is contained within the ServletConfig object, which the Web server gives the servlet when it is initialized. You can access the ServletConfig object by using the Servlet.getServletConfig() method.

The GenericServlet Class

The abstract class GenericServlet provides the basic behavior for the Servlet interface in a protocol-independent way. As a programmatic convenience, this class also implements the ServletConfig interface, which provides easy access to the ServletContext and initalization parameters. This class provides implementations for the init() and the destroy() methods, which provide basic servlet setup, such as managing the ServletConfig object. It is a best practice for all subclasses of GenericServlet that override the init() or the destroy() method to call the superclass version of the method. Additionally, GenericServlet contains a log() method that provides easy access to the built-in servlet logging functions through the ServletContext.

The ServletRequest Interface

The ServletRequest interface defines an object passed as the first parameter on a call to the service() method on a GenericServlet. This interface provides the servlet with information about the request for service that originated from a client. A ServletRequest object provides data, including parameter name and values, attributes, and an input stream. Interfaces that extend ServletRequest can provide additional protocol-specific data; for example, HttpServletRequest provides HTTP data. This interface and the interfaces that descend from it provide the servlet's only access to this data.

A servlet request is a MIME body request, and the response is a MIME body response. MIME bodies are either text or binary data. When the bodies are text, including character encoding, the programmer should use the getReader() method. When the bodies are binary data, use the getInputStream() method. Multipart MIME bodies are treated as binary data.

The ServletResponse Interface

The ServletResponse interface defines an object used in sending MIME-encoded data from the servlet to the client. The servlet engine creates a

ServletResponse object and passes it as an argument to the servlet's service method. To send binary data in a MIME body response, use the ServletOutputStream returned by the getOutputStream() method. Likewise, to send character data, use the PrintWriter object returned by the getWriter() method. If you need to mix binary and text data—for example, if you are creating a multipart response—use a ServletOutputStream to write the multipart headers, and then use the headers to build your own text bodies. If you do not specify a character set for the MIME body response with setContentType(java.lang.String), the servlet engine will select one and will modify the content accordingly. Call the setContentType() method before you call either the getWriter() method or the getOutputStream() method.

The RequestDispatcher Interface

The RequestDispatcher interface defines an object that receives requests from the client and sends them to any resource, such as a servlet, HTML file, or JSP file, on the server. The servlet engine creates the RequestDispatcher object, which is used as a wrapper around a server resource located at a particular path. This interface is intended to wrap servlets, but a servlet engine can create RequestDispatcher objects to wrap any type of resource.

A RequestDispatcher is obtained from the ServletContext by using the ServletContext.getRequestDispatcher("resource-name") method. Once a dispatcher is obtained, the servlet can then forward the request to the resource named in the getRequestDispatcher() method or include the output from the resource named in the getRequestDispatcher() method. Use the RequestDispatcher interface to forward a request to a JSP for output display.

The RequestDispatcher interface is new to the JSDK version 2.1 and provides a well-defined way for servlets to communicate with one another. A typical use of the RequestDispatcher is to forward control from one servlet to another. The following example shows how a servlet might use RequestDispatcher to forward control to a servlet named "NextServlet."

```
// Code fragment from a service(), doGet() or doPost() method in an HttpServlet
ServletContext context = getServletContext();
RequestDispatcher disp = context.getRequestDispatcher("/servlet/NextServlet");
disp.forward();
```

The javax.servlet.http Package

The javax.servlet.http package contains the API for servlets that will be used as HTTP servlets. We will briefly describe some of the key classes contained in this package. Table 4.4 lists the classes and interfaces in the javax.servlet.http package.

Table 4.4   Classes and Interfaces in the javax.servlet.http Package

Classes	Interfaces
Cookie	HttpServletRequest
HttpServlet	HttpServletResponse
HttpSessionBindingEvent	HttpSession
HttpUtils	HttpSessionBindingListener
NoBodyOutputStream	HttpSessionContext
NoBodyResponse	

The HttpServlet Class

GenericServlet provides the basic behavior of a servlet, but a mechanism for handling HTTP requests must also be provided. As such, HttpServlet, which is a subclass of GenericServlet, provides the additional behavior for HTTP requests through its Java methods for each of the HTTP request methods. Although all the HTTP methods are supported, GET and POST are the most prevalent. HttpServlet provides the doGet() and doPost() Java methods to handle the HTTP GET and POST methods.

When an HttpServlet is requested via a URL, the service() method reads the HTTP header and determines which HTTP method to call. That method is then invoked. A programmer needs to then simply provide overrides for the doGet() and/or doPost() methods to accomplish the tasks of the servlet. The service() method and the do...() methods accept two parameters, which are defined as instances of HttpServletRequest and HttpServletResponse. These specialized versions of the request and response objects contain HTTP-specific items, such as headers, cookies, and sessions.

The HttpServletRequest Interface

The HttpServletRequest interface extends the ServletRequest interface and defines a request object that coincides with an HTTP request. Some of the items available on an HttpServletRequest are the authentication type, through the getAuth() method; the list of cookies, through the getCookies() method; and the query string, through the getQueryString() method. The servlet engine implements this interface.

The HttpServletResponse Interface

The HttpServletResponse interface extends the ServletResponse interface and defines a response object that matches an HTTP response. This interface allows the servlet's service() method to access and set HTTP headers and to return data (e.g., HTML) to its client. The servlet engine provides a class that implements this interface.

The HttpSession Interface

The HttpSession interface defines an application-level connection between the Web browser and the Web server. By using sessions, a programmer can store session-specific data in the servlet engine for multiple requests to the same servlet or another servlet by the same user. The session persists for a specified time period, across more than one connection or page request from the user. A session usually corresponds to one user who may visit a site many times. The server can maintain a session either by using cookies or by rewriting URLs. HttpSession is discussed more fully later.

The HttpUtils Class

This concrete class provides a collection of methods useful to a programmer creating HttpServlet subclasses. One of the highly useful methods provides the ability to reconstruct the request URI for use by the server. This method, called getRequestURI(), is a static method. Nonstatic methods include parse-PostData(), for parsing the parameters of a POST; and parseQueryString(), for parsing a GET request's query string.

Rationale for Servlets

At this point, you might be thinking, "I have CGI and Perl; why should I use Java servlets?" The simple answer is that servlets offer a better CGI. In most Web applications that use servlets, the client code—HTML—accesses the servlets in the same way that it would access a Perl script through CGI. As such, using servlets does not in any way impact how HTML developers do their job.

Although CGI was the first server-side dynamic-solution standard developed, it has the following disadvantages.

- *CGI program life-cycle inefficiencies.* The Web server creates a new copy of the program each time it is requested. CGI does not take advantage of multithreading. CGI gets reinitialized each time a request is made. Connections to databases could get dropped and reconnected with each new request.
- *Lack of integration with reusable software component technologies.* Unlike Java servlet integration with JavaBeans and EJBs, CGI does not integrate efficiently with reusable, object-oriented software component technologies.

- *Lack of portability across platforms.* Unlike Java, most CGI programs are not portable. Compilers and runtime environments for the various CGI-supported languages differ, making portability difficult at best. CGI uses environment variables and strings, not objects, to maintain session information or to request data.

Servlets offer advantages over standard CGI mechanisms in the areas of portability, performance, and security. Because Java is "write once run anywhere," your server-side programs are platform independent. Additionally, servlets can take advantage of prepackaged component technologies through the use of JavaBeans and EJBs.

Servlets offer better performance than does standard CGI. Once the Web server loads a servlet into the server memory, the servlet stays there and listens for requests. When a request arrives, a new Java thread is automatically created, and the servlet code is executed in that thread. Java threads are lightweight, and their creation is far more efficient than standard CGI, which creates a new operating system process for each request. Because a servlet remains resident in memory, connections to databases can remain open. An intelligent servlet can create pools of database connections and manage those between concurrent users to further improve performance over standard CGI. IBM WebSphere provides a connection manager object to create and to manage pools of connections to JDBC databases. Servlets also provide a session object that you can use to maintain session information, across multiple accesses by the same user, to the servlets on a Web server. Use of the session object can reduce the need to retrieve the same information over and over again each time a user accesses a server-side application. Sessions can be set up to expire or to persist indefinitely.

Servlets offer better security than does standard CGI. Because a servlet runs within the Web server context and under the control of the Web server, you can use the authentication and authorization features of the Web server. Additionally, the JDK includes the java.security and java.security.acl packages, which offer Java interfaces for creating authentication and authorization functionality. IBM WebSphere provides an implementation of the Java interfaces in the java.security and java.security.acl packages. Additionally, IBM WebSphere provides security mechanisms that allow servlets, EJBs, and files to be secured, as well as administrative screens for maintaining the security.

Summary and Preview

In this chapter, we covered the basics of HTTP, servlet concepts, and the basics of servlet programming. Whenever you begin to code in a client/server environment, the complexity of the task increases. However, with the robust HTTP as an underlying mechanism for servlets and the highly usable Java Servlet API 2.1, a programmer of moderate skill can be very productive with servlets in a very short period of time. In the next chapter, we turn to a tool for creating and testing servlets.

CHAPTER 5

Using VisualAge for Java to Develop Servlets

The previous chapter discussed the basics of HTTP and how servlets are used. In this chapter, we focus on how to use the tools available to create and to test these servlets. The first tool we consider is IBM VisualAge for Java. In later chapters, we discuss the IBM WebSphere Application Server and the IBM WebSphere Studio.

VisualAge for Java is a general-purpose Java development and testing tool that can also be used to build and to test servlets. In this chapter, we show you how to create and to test servlets with VisualAge for Java, using the IBM Web-Sphere Test Environment (WTE). Specifically, we cover the following topics:

- Installing the IBM WTE
- Testing with the WTE, using the WTE Control Center and Servlet Runner
- Building a form-processing servlet

In this chapter, we will first present the code of an extended form processing servlet example and then demonstrate how to add this code to the VisualAge for Java environment. If you would rather simply read along with the example instead of typing the code in yourself, you may want to first skip ahead to Chapter 12 and follow the instructions for loading the case study into VisualAge for Java, then return to this chapter and examine the example.

IBM WebSphere Test Environment (WTE)

The IBM WTE is included in both the Professional and the Enterprise versions of VisualAge for Java. We will use the WTE to test our servlet examples and later for the book's case study. VisualAge and the WTE provide the following features:

- All the function found in the JSWDK
- An implementation for the JSPs versions 0.91 and 1.0 specifications
- A servlet engine that also has a plug-in facility for handling standard HTML pages and JSP files, thereby allowing for complete testing of servlets
- A JSP monitor for debugging JSP-generated servlets

The IBM WTE, a unit-testing version of the WebSphere 3.5 advanced runtime, allows you to test HTML; JSPs using either the JSP 0.91 or the 1.0 specifications; and servlets as you build them. You can also use the standard VisualAge Debugger to set breakpoints in servlets and JSP files, helping you with debugging. Additionally, a special JSP Execution Monitor is provided and is discussed in a later chapter.

VisualAge for Java has two central, unique technologies that make it especially useful for developing servlets and JSP files: the ability to simulate multiple Java Virtual Machine instances and a provision for incremental compilation and hot-linking code into running programs. One problem with the servlet life cycle is that, normally, you must stop and restart the Web server to update the servlet class or to reload the Java component code called by a JSP file. During development, you will change the servlet code or JSP source very frequently. Frequent restarts of a Web server or the Servlet Runner could get very tedious, especially if you have to debug a problem that occurs only after the servlet has been running for a while or at some part of a long loop. Fortunately, the WTE offers a much more productive way to develop servlets and JSP files for WebSphere. When you change a method in the servlet, VisualAge for Java incrementally compiles only the modified method in the class, not the entire class, and hot-links the modified method into the running program.

Incremental compilation is valuable, but equally valuable is the productivity boost that comes from not having to restart the program that you're debugging and not having to recreate the program execution state that caused the problem you are trying to debug. With VisualAge for Java, you can modify the running servlet, Bean, tag, or EJB code without stopping and restarting the WTE Application Server. In addition, you have all the features of the development environment at your disposal while the server is running. This allows you to both modify existing code and even develop new code while other code is running. Even more powerful is the fact that you do not need to start and stop the server even when you change Beans or other classes that comprise the business logic in components called from servlets or JSP—for example, EJBs running in a container in another simulated Java Virtual Machine (VM) instance.

Installing the WTE

The WTE is provided with VisualAge version 3.5 but must be installed and configured before it can be used. The first thing to do, of course, is to install VisualAge for Java, version 3.5. We strongly recommend that you use version 3.5 or higher to work the samples in this book. Also, you should understand the differences among the Entry, Professional, and Enterprise editions of VisualAge for Java.

- The Entry edition is a fully functional environment. However, you are limited to one project, 500 classes, no team support, and no enterprise support; the WTE is not included. The Entry edition is used for learning and adoption, not for project development.
- The Professional edition is fully functional and not as limited as the Entry edition but does not contain enterprise builder support or team development support. The Professional edition does contain the WTE, however.
- The Enterprise edition contains everything in the Professional edition, as well as enterprise support and team development support. The enterprise support includes a complete EJB development and testing environment, along with several other Enterprise Access Builders for such items as Customer Information Control System (CICS), a Transaction Processing (TP) monitor from IBM, and CORBA.

This book focuses on the Enterprise edition of VisualAge for Java; however, the Professional edition could be used for portions of this book dealing solely with servlets and Web applications.

After successfully installing VisualAge for Java and then starting it, you will notice that the *Workbench* views the Java code as a containment hierarchy of *projects* that contain *Java packages* that contain *Java classes and interfaces* that contain *Java methods and fields*. A project is a collection of Java packages needed for an application or part of an application. The concept of project is unique to VisualAge for Java. The highest container defined in the Java language specification is a package. As shown in Figure 5.1, the primary user interface is a notebook with tabs named *Projects, Packages, Resources, Classes, Interfaces, Managing,* and *All Problems*. This window is called the *Workbench* and is the primary window used in development.

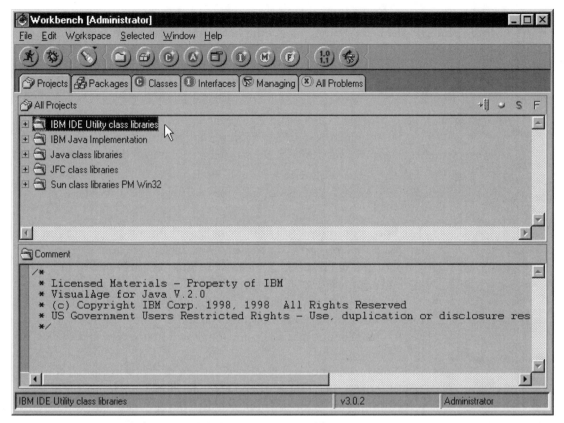

Figure 5.1   IBM VisualAge for Java: *Projects* Tab

With the exceptions of the *Managing* and *All Problems* tabs, the tabs are self-explanatory. The *Managing* tab allows a developer to view the Java code with respect to versions, owners, and developers. The *All Problems* tab shows all the classes and methods that have compilation errors.

With VisualAge installed, you now need to add the IBM WTE feature. To do this, select the *File->Quick Start* menu option. This will open a dialog, as shown in Figure 5.2.

Select *Features* and then *Add Feature* to obtain a list of features that can be added to the *Workbench*. When the list of features is shown, as in Figure 5.3, select the *IBM WTE 3.5* feature so that it will be added to your VisualAge workspace.

When you click the *OK* button, VisualAge starts the process of loading the WTE into VisualAge for Java. When this process is complete, you will see

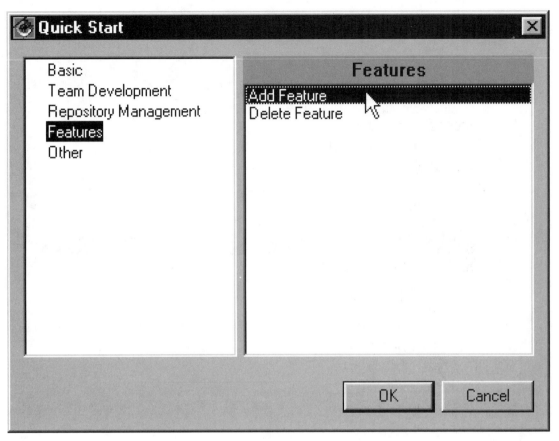

Figure 5.2 *Quick Start* Dialog: Choose *Features, Add Feature*

that several projects have been added to the VisualAge for Java *Workbench*; namely, the *IBM WTE* project has been added.

The WTE provides two ways to launch, or start, the Web server servlet engine from within VisualAge for Java. The first way is to use the WTE Control Center. Invoking the servlet engine directly through the class ServletEngine is the second. The Control Center approach is the default launching mechanism described in the VisualAge for Java documentation. In some cases, however, you might want to launch the ServletEngine class directly when you need greater control. This chapter covers using the Control Center, the approach used in all later chapters; the details of using the ServletEngine class directly are covered in the product documentation.

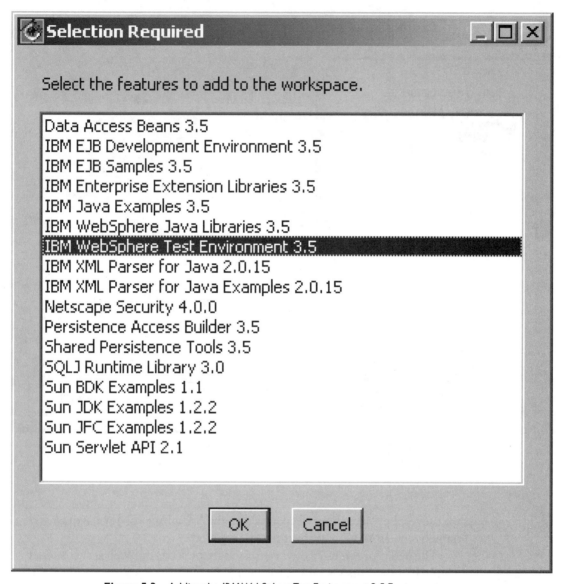

Figure 5.3   Adding the *IBM WebSphere Test Environment 3.5* Feature

Using the WTE Control Center

The main vehicle used inside VisualAge for Java to test our servlets is the
WTE Control Center, which you start, or launch, from a *Workbench* menu.
To launch from the menu, click on *Workspace->Tools->Launch WebSphere
Test Environment*. The *WebSphere Test Environment Control Center* will
then appear (Figure 5.4).

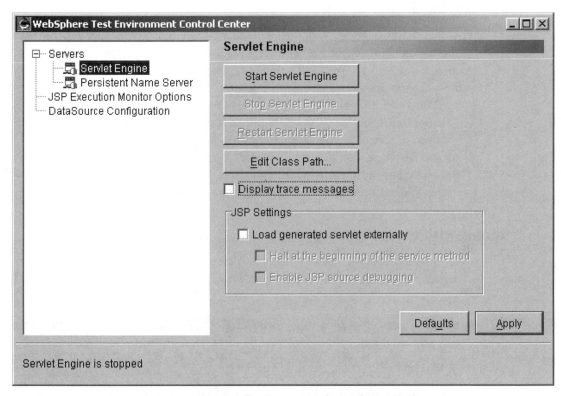

Figure 5.4   The *WebSphere Test Environment Control Center* Window

The *WTE Control Center* is made up of two major parts. The left-hand pane, which we will call the services pane, shows a tree view of the services available. The right-hand pane, which we will call the options pane, shows the configuration option for the selected service. The various services that can be configured in the *WTE Control Center* are

- Available *Servers.* These are application servers as would be deployed in WebSphere. By default, this tree contains the *Servlet Engine* and the *Persistent Name Server.* As you add new servers through the EJB Development Environment, which we cover in a later chapter, this list will expand to include them.
- *JSP Execution Monitor Options.* We cover how to use and configure the JSP Execution Monitor in a later chapter.
- *DataSource Configuration.* We cover how to use and configure JDBC 2.0 data sources in a later chapter.

Starting the Servlet Engine

At this point, we are interested only in the servlet engine. To start it, click the button marked *Start Servlet Engine* on the *WTE Control Center.* The console will open, if not already open, and a series of messages will be written to it. When the servlet engine is finished loading, the console will look as in Figure 5.5.

You know that the servlet engine has started successfully when you see the final message: "***Servlet Engine is started***." At this point, the WTE Web server servlet engine is listening on port 8080 and is waiting for requests. Also, the icon next to the words *Servlet Engine* in the services pane will change from red-and-white semicircles to four blue-and-white quarter-circles, indicating that the servlet engine is running.

Testing with the Servlet Engine

To ensure that the servlet engine is working, both the Web server and the servlet engine parts need to be tested. First, test the Web server part of

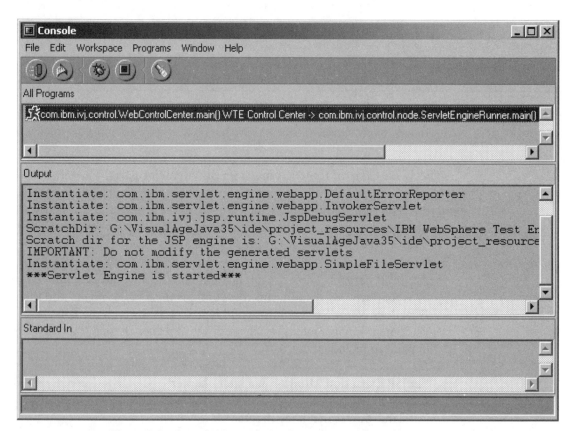

Figure 5.5　Console Messages after Starting the Servlet Engine

the servlet engine by opening a Web browser and entering the URL *http://localhost:8080/index.html*. The index.html page is provided by the WTE under the *project_resources* directory. If everything is working properly, you will get the response shown in Figure 5.6.

Next, test the servlet engine by opening a Web browser and typing in the URL *http://localhost:8080/servlet/HelloWorldServlet*. This servlet is provided with the WTE in the default package. If everything is functioning properly, you will get the response shown in Figure 5.7.

Stopping the Servlet Engine

Now that you have seen how to start the WTE servlet engine, you need to find out how to stop it. Stopping the servlet engine is a simple matter of clicking the *Stop Servlet Engine* button on the *WTE Control Center*. When you click this button, you will see the message "***Servlet Engine is stopped***" displayed to the console. The server icon for the *Servlet Engine* in the *WTE Control Center* will then change back to the stopped state of two red-and-white semicircles. Usually, you will not need to stop the servlet engine unless you are finished with development; one of the advantages of VisualAge and the WTE is that you can leave the servlet engine running while you make changes to your servlet code, and the new code will be automatically linked into the running process.

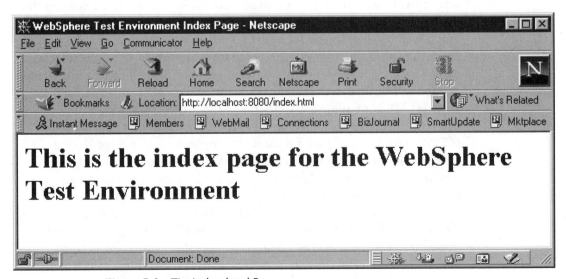

Figure 5.6 The index.html Page

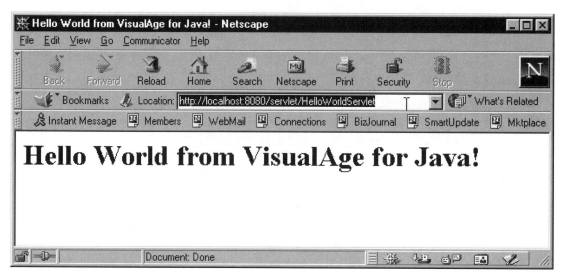

Figure 5.7 Response from "HelloWorldServlet"

Building an Example Servlet in VisualAge

Before continuing, we need to explore a servlet example that will demonstrate how to use the HTML <FORM> tag to send data to a servlet. This key concept will be used over and over again in servlet programming. Also, because the WTE is being used, we will also explain how to use the VisualAge interactive development environment (IDE). To best understand how a servlet works with data that is passed from an HTML form, we will develop the "CreateEmployeeServlet." First, we will call the servlet by typing its URL into a Web browser: *http://localhost:8080/servlet/com.wsbook.casestudy. servlet.CreateEmployeeServlet.* Note that we are simply using the full class name to name the servlet with a /servlet/ prefix. This will cause the doGet() method to be called in the servlet class. Inside the doGet() method, we will write HTML containing a <FORM> tag to the browser. This HTML form will demonstrate all the various types of HTML form tags that can be used in HTML version 4.0. Figure 5.8 shows the input form generated by "CreateEmployeeServlet." Note the two *Submit* buttons: *Submit1* and *Submit2*. We will discuss later how your servlet code can determine which button is clicked and thus do one of many operations.

Next, the user fills in the form. When the user clicks *Submit1* or *Submit2*, the same servlet will be called, using the POST HTTP method, which will cause the doPost() method in the servlet to be called. Inside the doPost() method, we will echo the data passed from the HTML form to the Web browser. Only selections made and buttons clicked are passed to the doPost()

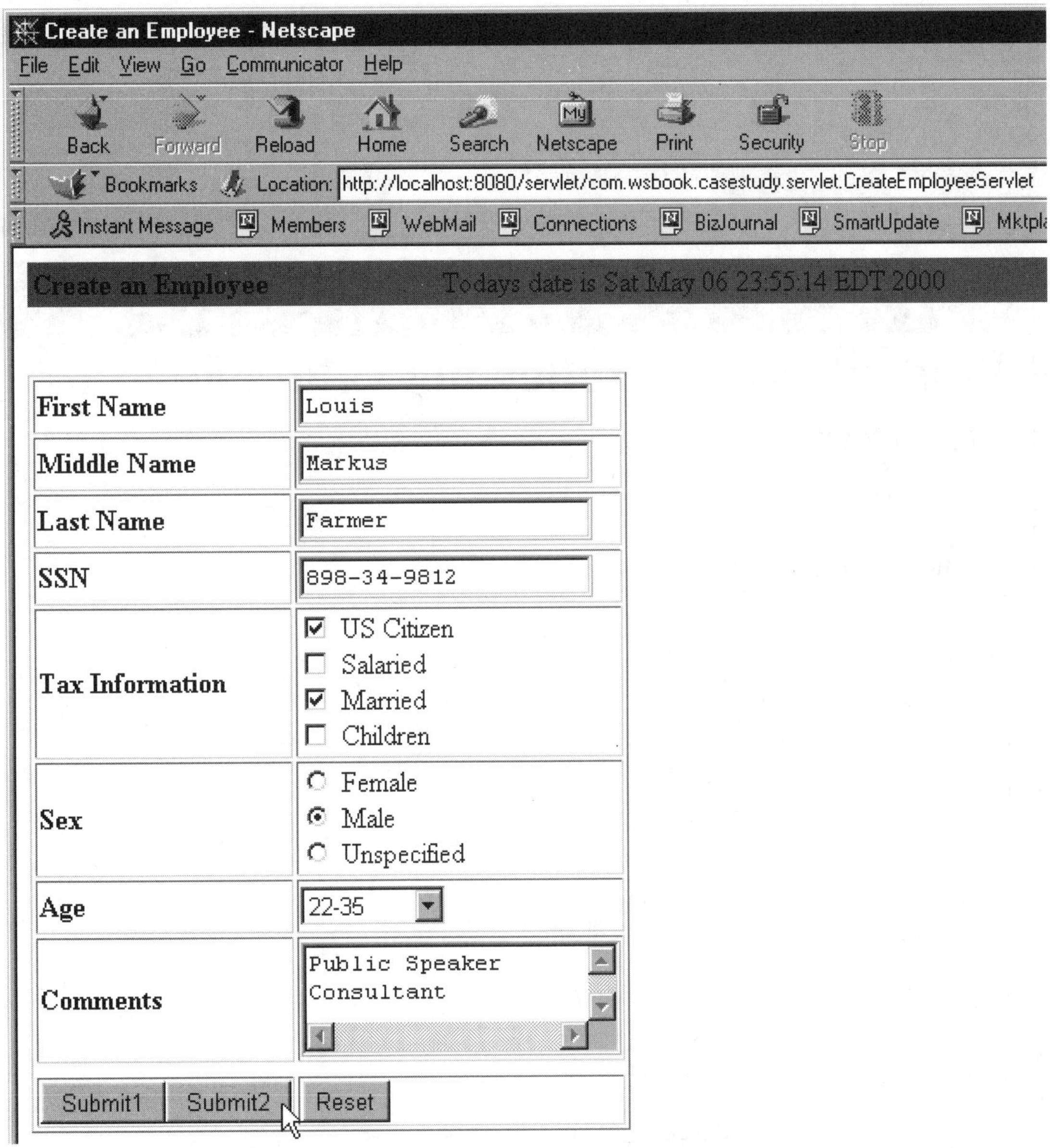

Figure 5.8 The Input Form Generated by "CreateEmployeeServlet"

method. This makes our job as servlet programmers easier. Figure 5.9 shows the output of clicking the *Submit2* button on the form.

Before examining the Java source for this sample, first note that our selections are displayed on the output page. For example, the *Children* check box was not selected, and so the taxinfo2 parameter was not passed to our

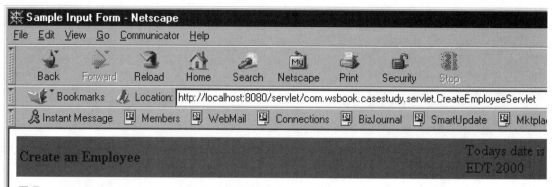

Figure 5.9   Output of Calling "CreateEmployeeServlet"

servlet. Also note that other selections, such as the sex and age parameters, contain the expected values. Finally, note that the action parameter contains the value Submit2. Therefore, we know that the *Submit2* button, not the *Submit1* button, was clicked. The class definition for CreateEmployeeServlet is given in Listing 5.1.

Listing 5.1 The CreateEmployeeServlet Class Definition.

```
package com.wsbook.casestudy.servlet;
import java.io.*;
import javax.servlet.*;
import javax.servlet.http.*;
public class CreateEmployeeServlet  extends javax.servlet.http.HttpServlet {
}
```

To make coding easier, three packages have been imported. The java.io package defines the streams and writers this servlet uses to communicate with the browser. The javax.servlet package defines the basic servlet classes and interfaces. The javax.servlet.http package defines the HTTP-specific classes and interfaces, such as HttpServlet. Also, CreateEmployeeServlet is a subclass of HttpServlet, which provides several methods, such as doGet() and doPost(), for handling HTTP requests. To enable our servlet to handle GET requests, we need to override the doGet() method. The doGet() method is called when one of the following happens.

- An HTML form, which uses the GET method, is used to call the servlet. An example tag follows:

```
<FORM action=servlet_url method=GET>
```

- The URL of the servlet is typed into the URL line of a Web browser.
- The URL of the servlet is placed in an HTML link. An example tag follows:

```
<A HREF=servlet_url>
```

The doGet() method is provided in Listing 5.2.

Listing 5.2 The doGet Method for the CreateEmployeeServlet Class.

```
/*
* This method will paint back an HTML form, which has an action
* set to call this same servlet using the POST method.
*/
public void doGet(HttpServletRequest req, HttpServletResponse res)
      throws IOException{
    res.setContentType("text/html");
    PrintWriter out = res.getWriter();
    // Write Header info
    out.println(
      "<HTML><HEAD>\n" +
      "<TITLE>Create an Employee</TITLE>\n" +
      "</HEAD>\n" +
      "<BODY>\n" +
      "<TABLE width=\"100%\" border=\"0\" bgcolor=\"#FFFFFF\" " +
```

```
        " cellspacing=\"0\" cellpadding=\"3\">\n" +
        "<TR>\n" +
        "<TD colspan=\"3\" bgcolor=\"#009900\">" +
        "<B>Create an Employee</B></TD>\n" +
        "<TD bgcolor=\"#009900\">" +
        "Todays date is " + new java.util.Date() + "</TD> \n" +
        "</TR>\n" +
        "</TABLE>\n"
);

// Write Form with embedded table for layout
out.println(
    "<FORM NAME=\"" + req.getRequestURI() + "\"" +
    " ACTION= \"" + req.getRequestURI() + "\" " +
    " METHOD=\"POST\">\n" +
    "<BR>\n" +
// Start Table for layout
    "<TABLE BORDER=1>\n" +
// First Name Text Field
    "<TR><TD>\n" +
    "<B>First Name</B>\n" +
    "</TD><TD>\n" +
    "<INPUT TYPE=\"text\" SIZE=20 MAXLENGTH=30" +
    " NAME=\"firstName\" VALUE=\"enterFirstName\">" +
    "</TD></TR>\n" +
// Middle Name Text Field
    "<TR><TD>\n" +
    "<B>Middle Name</B>\n" +
    "</TD><TD>\n" +
    "<INPUT TYPE=\"text\" SIZE=20 MAXLENGTH=30" +
    " NAME=\"MiddleName\" VALUE=\"enterMiddleName\">" +
    "</TD></TR>\n" +
// Last Name Text Field
    "<TR><TD>\n" +
    "<B>Last Name</B>\n" +
    "</TD><TD>\n" +
    "<INPUT TYPE=\"text\" SIZE=20 MAXLENGTH=30" +
    " NAME=\"LastName\" VALUE=\"enterLastName\">" +
    "</TD></TR>\n" +
// Social Security Number Text Field
    "<TR><TD>\n" +
    "<B>SSN</B>\n" +
    "</TD><TD>\n" +
    "<INPUT TYPE=\"text\" SIZE=20 MAXLENGTH=30" +
    " NAME=\"ssn\" VALUE=\"enterSSN\">" +
    "</TD></TR>\n" +
// Tax Information Check boxes
    "<TR><TD>\n" +
    "<B>Tax Information</B> \n" +
    "</TD><TD>\n" +
    "<INPUT type=\"checkbox\" name=\"taxinfo1\"" +
    " value=\"US Citizen\" CHECKED> US Citizen\n" +
    "<BR>\n" +
```

```
        "<INPUT type=\"checkbox\" name=\"taxinfo2\"" +
        " value=\"Salaried\"> Salaried\n" +
        "<BR>\n" +
        "<INPUT type=\"checkbox\" name=\"taxinfo3\"" +
        " value=\"Married\"> Married\n" +
        "<BR>\n" +
        "<INPUT type=\"checkbox\" name=\"taxinfo4\"" +
        " value=\"Children\"> Children\n" +
        "</TD></TR>\n" +

    // Sex radio buttons
        "<TR><TD>\n" +
        "<B>Sex</B> \n" +
        "</TD><TD>\n" +
        "<INPUT type=\"radio\" name=\"sex\" " +
        " VALUE=\"Female\"> Female\n" +
        "<BR>\n" +
        "<INPUT type=\"radio\" name=\"sex\" " +
        " VALUE=\"Male\"> Male\n" +
        "<BR>\n" +
        "<INPUT type=\"radio\" name=\"sex\" " +
        " VALUE=\"Unspecified\" CHECKED> Unspecified\n" +
        "</TD></TR>\n" +
    // Age Selection
        "<TR><TD>\n" +
        "<B>Age</B> \n" +
        "</TD><TD>\n" +
        "<SELECT id=\"AgeSelectBox\" name=\"age\">\n" +
            "\t<OPTION value=\"Under 18\" SELECTED>Under 18</OPTION>\n"+
            "\t<OPTION value=\"18-21\">18-21</OPTION> \n" +
            "\t<OPTION value=\"22-35\">22-35</OPTION> \n" +
            "\t<OPTION value=\"36-45\">36-45</OPTION> \n" +
            "\t<OPTION value=\"Over 55\">Over 55</OPTION> \n" +
        "</SELECT> \n" +
        "</TD></TR>\n" +

    // Comments Text Area Box
        "<TR><TD>\n" +
        "<B>Comments</B> \n" +
        "</TD><TD>\n" +
        "<TEXTAREA NAME =\"comments\" cols=\"20\"" +
        " rows=\"2\">Enter any comments </TEXTAREA>" +
        "</TD></TR>\n" +
// Blank Line
        "<TR><TD>\n" +
        "<!— Blank line —>\n" +
        "</TD></TR>\n" +
    // Submit and Reset Buttons
        "<TR><TD>\n" +
        "<INPUT TYPE=\"submit\"" +
        "NAME=\"action\" VALUE=\"Submit1\">" +
        "<INPUT TYPE=\"submit\"" +
        "NAME=\"action\" VALUE=\"Submit2\">" +
```

```
            "</TD><TD>\n" +
            "<INPUT TYPE=\"reset\"" +
            "NAME=\"reset\" VALUE=\"Reset\">" +
            "</TD></TR>\n"
        );
   // Write the ending tags.
        out.println(
            "</TABLE>\n" +
            "</FORM>\n" +
            "</BODY>\n" +
            "</HTML>\n"
        );
    return;
    }
```

In this sample, the doGet() method is very straightforward. The basic goal
is to create a response that contains an HTML <FORM> tag with several
<INPUT> tags that will be passed as parameters when one of the *Submit* but-
tons is clicked. Note that on the <FORM> tag, the method is set to POST, and
the action is set to the result of calling the getRequestURI() method on the
HttpRequest object. This will resolve to the URL */servlet/com.wsbook.*
casestudy.servlet.CreateEmployeeServlet. This URL does not contain a protocol, host, or port number. How does this work? The rule is that if you
provide a relative URL, such as has been done here, the browser will add the
protocol, host, and port number that generated the URL. In this case, that
would be *http://localhost:8080.*

Next, let's examine the doPost() method. In the doPost() method, we need
to loop through all the available parameters as presented by the HttpServletRequest object. Also, you should be aware of the fact that HTML and HTTP do
not treat the parameters as unique by name. An HTML form can have multiple parameters that in fact share the same parameter name. This can be useful in the case of buttons, check boxes, and radio buttons. However, in other
cases, this fact can be very confusing to the servlet programmer. Therefore,
we recommend that unique lowercase names be used for all nonbutton INPUT
fields in a form. Listing 5.3 shows the entire doPost() method.

Listing 5.3 The Complete CreateEmployeeServlet doPost() Method.

```
/*
 * The doPost method is called when an HTML Form which has been
 * coded to use a method=POST is used. This method will process
 * the form data and then echo the data in the response.
 */
public void doPost(HttpServletRequest req, HttpServletResponse res)
    throws IOException{
    res.setContentType("text/html");
    PrintWriter out = res.getWriter();
```

```
// Write the Header information and create a table of parms
   out.println(
      "<HEAD>\n" +
      "<TITLE>Sample Input Form</TITLE>\n" +
      "<BODY>\n" +
      "<TABLE width=\"100%\" border=\"0\" bgcolor=\"#FFFFFF\" " +
      "cellspacing=\"0\" cellpadding=\"3\">\n" +
      "<TR>\n" +
      "<TD colspan=\"3\" bgcolor=\"#009900\">" +
      "<B>Create an Employee</B></TD>\n" +
      "<TD bgcolor=\"#009900\">" +
      "Todays date is " + new java.util.Date() + "</TD> \n" +
      "</TR>\n" +
      "<TR>\n" +
      "<TD>\n" +
      "<FONT COLOR=\"blue\" SIZE=\"+2\">\n" +
      "<H1>You entered the following values on the form:</H1>\n" +
      "</FONT>\n" +
      "</TD>\n " +
      "</TR>\n" +
      "</TABLE>\n" +
      "<FORM NAME=\"" + req.getRequestURI() + "\"" +
      " ACTION= \"" + req.getRequestURI() + "\" " +
      " METHOD=\"POST\">\n" +
      "<TABLE Border=1>\n" +
      "<TR><TH>\n" +
      "Parameter Name \n" +
      "</TH><TH>\n" +
      "Parameter Value \n" +
      "</TH></TR>\n"
   );
// Process each form parameter found in the Request
   java.util.Enumeration enumeration = req.getParameterNames();
   for (int i = 0; enumeration.hasMoreElements(); i++) {
      // Use the form Parm name to obtain the parm values
      String formVarName = (String) enumeration.nextElement();
      String[] formVarValues = req.getParameterValues(formVarName);
   // For each form parm name, there could potentially be
   // multiple parm values.
      for (int j=0; j < formVarValues.length; j++) {
         String formVarValue = formVarValues[j];
         out.println(
            "<TR><TD>\n" +
            formVarName +
            "</TD><TD>\n" +
            formVarValue +
            "</TD></TR>\n"
            );
      }
   }
// Finish the table and write an ending message
   String color = null;
   if (req.getParameter("action").equals("Submit1")) {
```

```
        color = "blue";
    } else {
        color = "red";
    }
    out.println(
        // Submit and Reset Buttons
        "<TR><TD>\n" +
        "<INPUT TYPE=\"submit\"" +
        "NAME=\"action\" VALUE=\"Confirm\">" +
        "</TD><TD>\n" +
        "<INPUT TYPE=\"submit\"" +
        "NAME=\"action\" VALUE=\"Return\">" +
        "</TD></TR>\n" +
        "</TABLE>\n" +
        "</FORM>\n" +
        "<BR>\n" +
        "<FONT COLOR=\"" + color + "\" SIZE=\"+2\">" +
        " Parameter List Complete </FONT>\n" +
        "<BR>\n" +
        "</BODY> \n" +
        "</HTML>"
        );
    return;
    }
```

This doPost() is very simple but does in fact match many of the doPost()
methods that you may find yourself writing in the future, with the exception
that your servlets will not include hard-coded HTML but will instead use JSPs.
However, instead of echoing parameters back to the browser, parameters are
usually used as input data for a database operation or as switching parameters
to determine which portion of the servlet behavior to invoke. Note that the
statements near the end of the doPost() method do in fact demonstrate how
some of these decisions should be made. The color of the Parameter List Complete text is made blue when the *Submit1* button was clicked and red when the
Submit2 button was clicked. This is a small example of how the actions taken
by the user can then be interpreted in the servlet to do the appropriate action.

Note that the instructions for building a servlet with VisualAge for Java
that follow expect you to create a new VisualAge project and type the servlet
code directly from the examples given here into the IDE. If you do not want
to type in the code, you can jump ahead to Chapter 12 and follow the instructions there for loading the completed case study project into VisualAge
for Java. After that, you can come back here and read along with the examples in VisualAge for Java.

To add this code into VisualAge, you must create a new VisualAge for
Java project. After that, you must create a new package and, finally, add the
class and its methods. To create a new project, use the *Selected->Add->*
Project menu from the *Workbench* menu bar. A *SmartGuide* dialog (Figure
5.10) will be displayed so that the project can be named and configured.

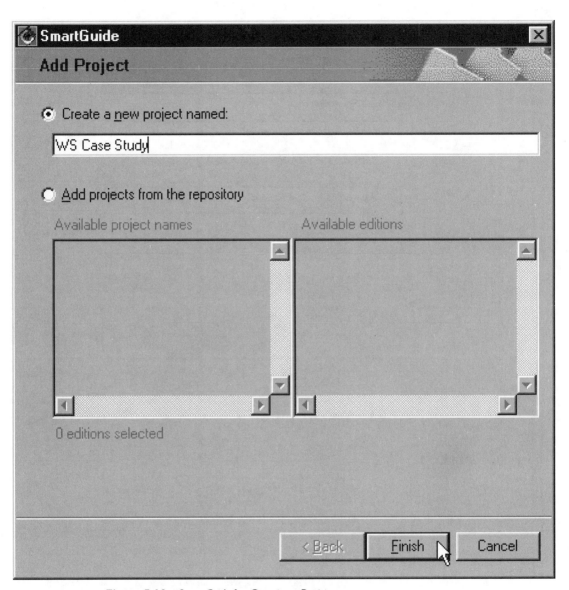

Figure 5.10 *SmartGuide* for Creating a Project

Name the project *WS Case Study*. Click the *Finish* button to close the dialog and to create the project. Next, use the *Selected->Add->Package* menu option from the *Workbench* to add a new package named com.wsbook. casestudy.servlet. Figure 5.11 shows this package being created.

Click the *Finish* button to close the *SmartGuide* and to create the package. Next, create the class by selecting the *Selected->Add->Class* menu from the

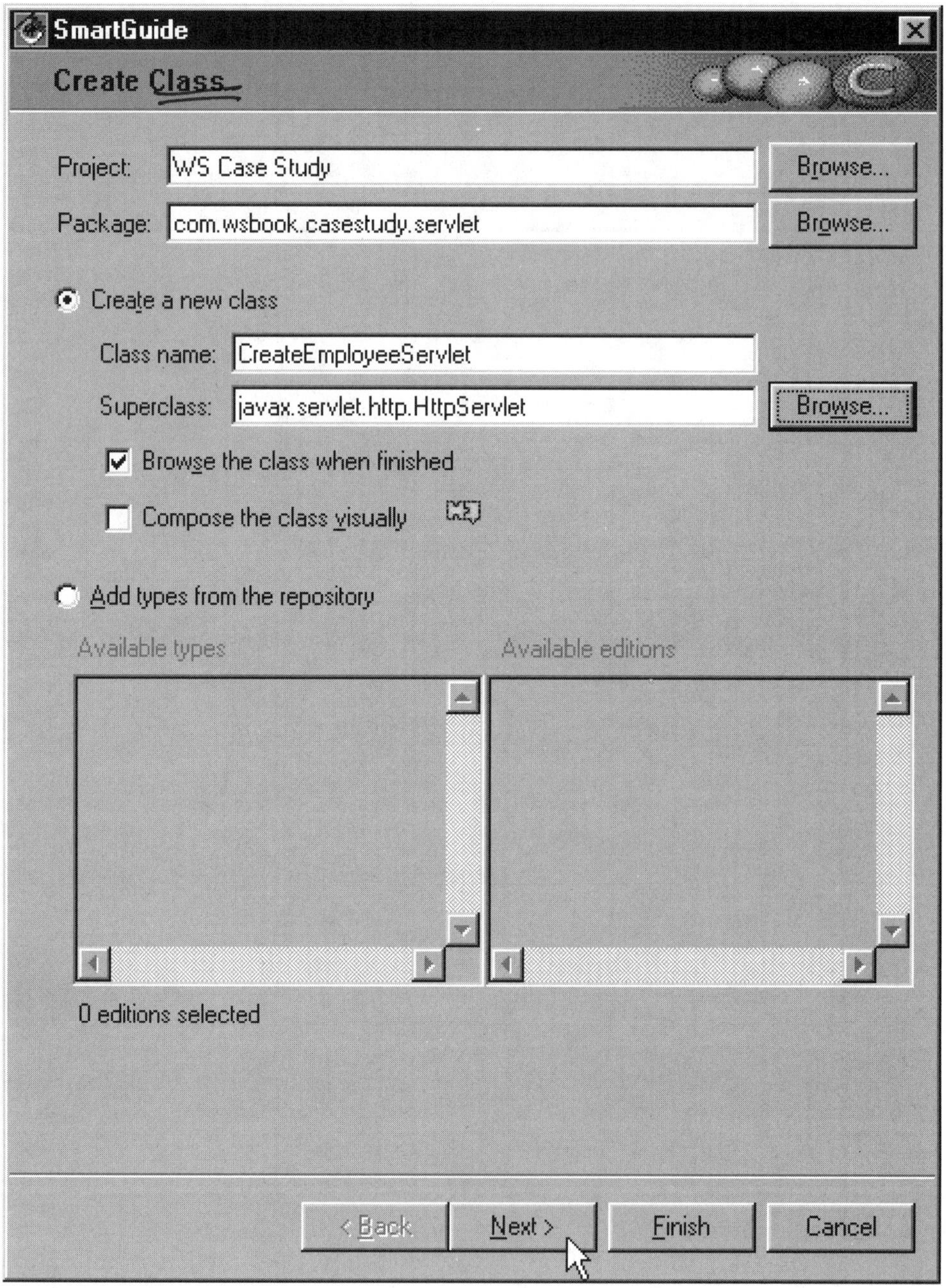

Figure 5.11   *SmartGuide* for Creating a Package

Wrong
Screen Shot

Workbench menu bar. This class will be named CreateEmployeeServlet and will extend the javax.servlet.http.HttpServlet abstract class. When the *SmartGuide* is displayed as in Figure 5.12, enter the class name and the superclass name.

Checking the box named *Browse the class when finished* opens a new window with this class definition in it when we are done with this *Smart-Guide*. Click the *Next* button to go to the next tab, where import statements, interface implementations, and other attributes for this class can be defined (Figure 5.13).

Most servlets will need to import at least three packages: java.io, javax.servlet, and javax.servlet.http. Click the *Add Package* button to add these package imports. Also, make sure that the *public* check box is checked and that no other check boxes are checked. Click the *Finish* button to create the class. The class will be created, and its definition will match that in Listing 5.1.

Next, the doGet() and the doPost() methods need to be created. We will walk through the creation of the doGet() method, examining the *SmartGuides* used. To create a method in VisualAge for Java, select the CreateEmployee Servlet class in the *Projects* tab of the *Workbench*. Next, select the *Selected >Add->Method* menu from the *Workbench* menu bar. When the *SmartGuide* appears (Figure 5.14), click the *Next* button without changing anything.

This first page of the *SmartGuide* allows you to code the method declaration by hand. As you become more familiar with VisualAge for Java, you may want to use this first page of the *SmartGuide* to create your methods. For now, let's discover how we can use the remaining pages to define the method declaration. Figure 5.15 shows the *Attributes* page of the *SmartGuide*.

On the second page of the *SmartGuide*, you can specify the method name, return type, and parameters. A convenient feature provided by Visual-Age for Java is the *Add* button for adding the parameters. When you click the *Add* button, a dialog appears that allows you to search for the type—class—and to then provide a name for the parameter. When you click the *Next* button, you will see the exceptions page (Figure 5.16).

The exceptions page allows you to specify exceptions that might be thrown by your method. Because we are coding a sample, not a real-world application, we will specify that both the ServletException and IOException might be thrown by our method. In a production application, this practice would be unacceptable. Your servlets should handle such exceptions so the user's Web browser does not display an error message from the Java VM. Click the *Finish* button to cause the method declaration to be generated. The body of the method is also generated; however, it consists only of {}. If you select the newly created doGet() method, you will see that it contains the proper declaration and the {} as a body. Here you need to add the code from Listing

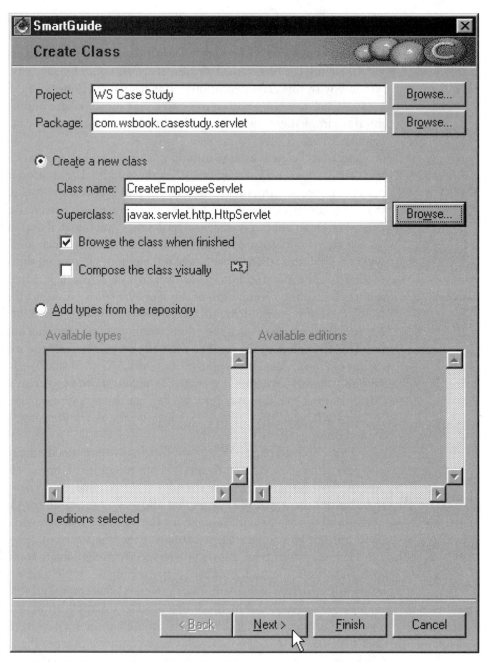

Figure 5.12   *SmartGuide* for Creating a Class

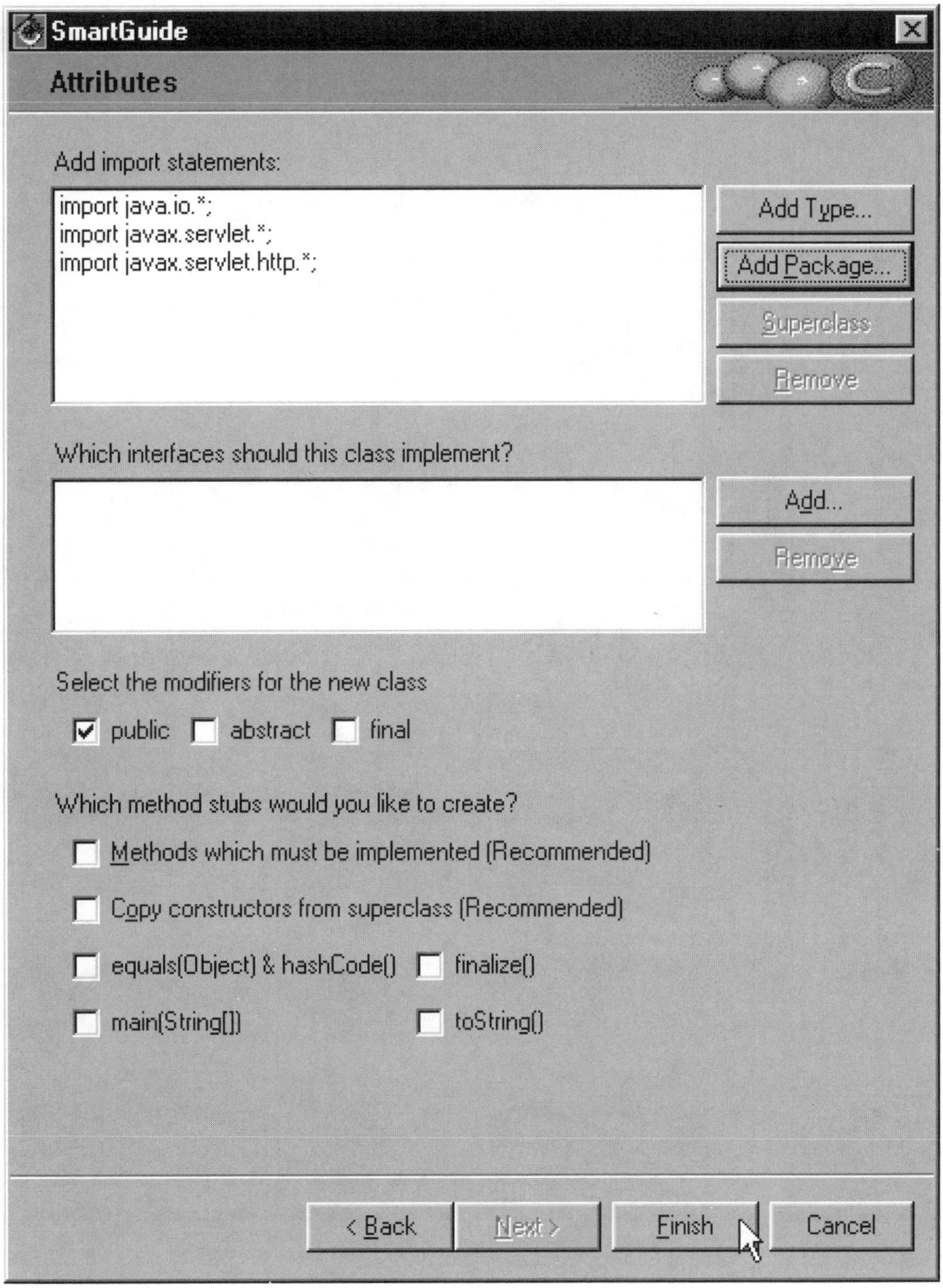

Figure 5.13 *SmartGuide* to Add Attributes to Class Definition

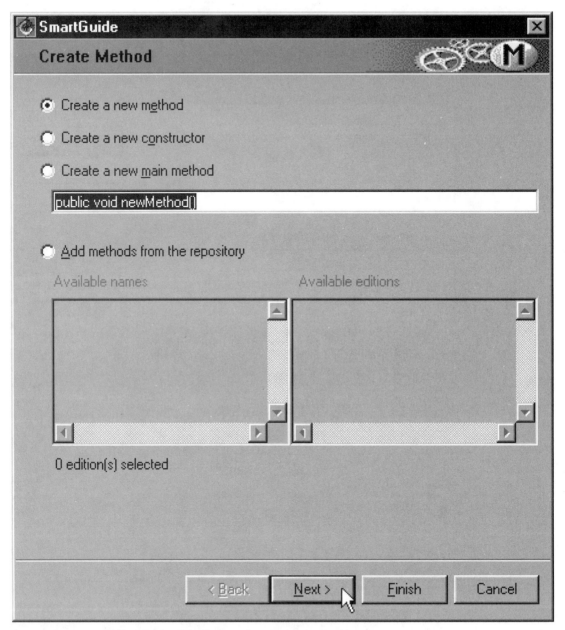

Figure 5.14　*SmartGuide* to Create a Method Declaration

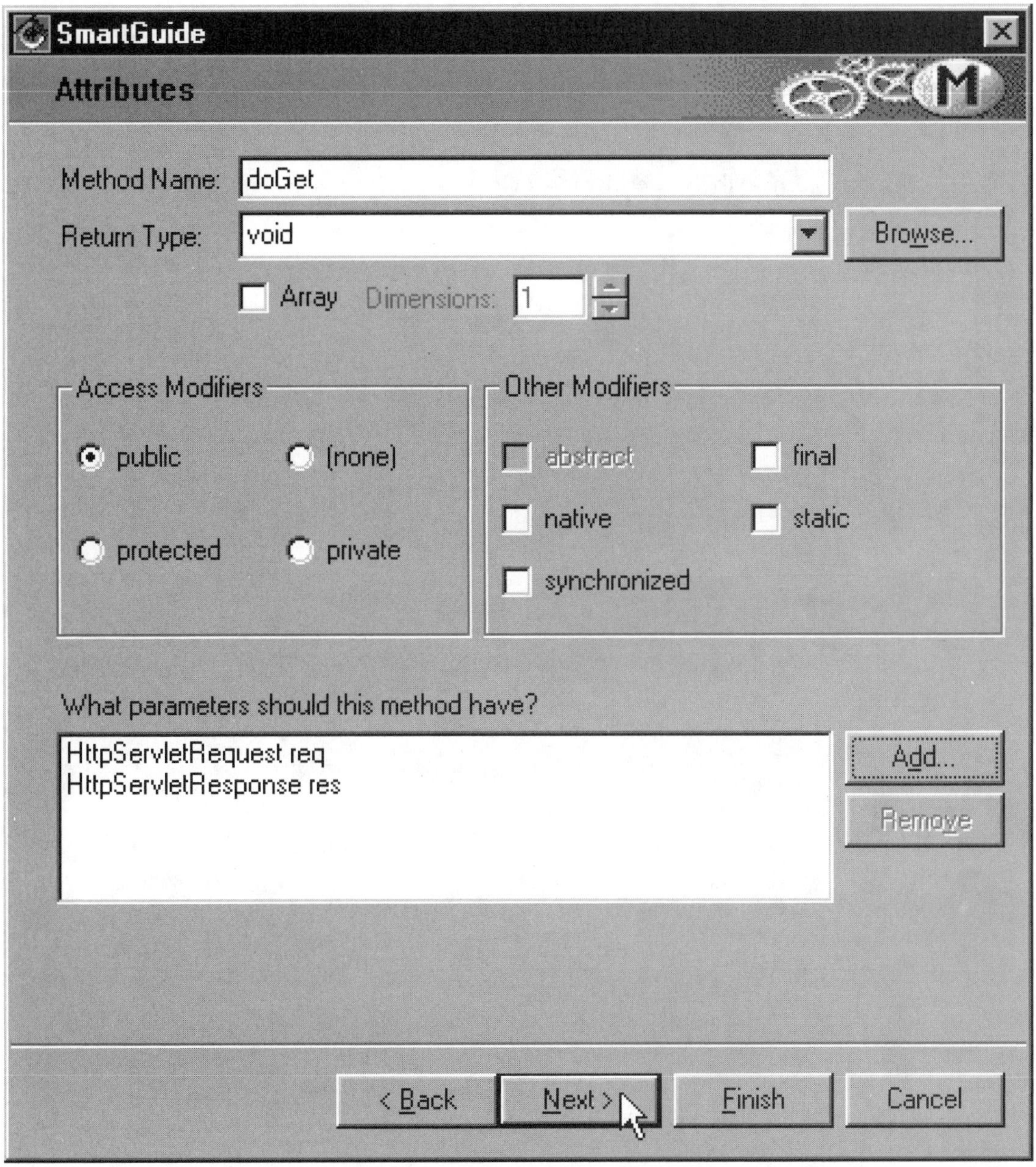

Figure 5.15 *SmartGuide* for Specifying the Attributes of a Method Declaration

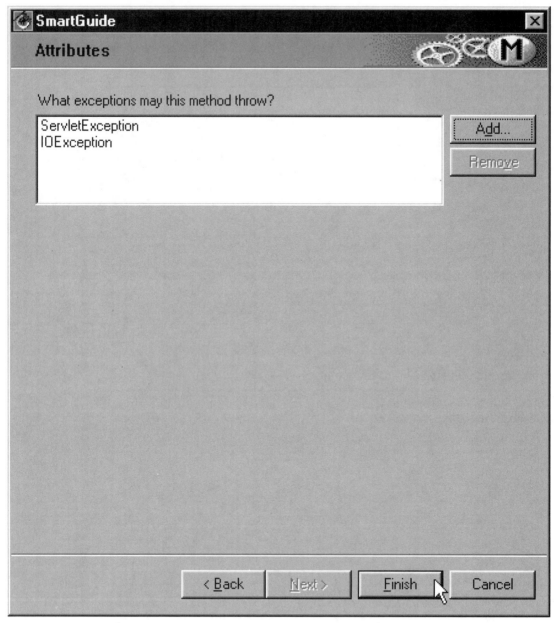

Figure 5.16   *SmartGuide* for Adding Thrown Exceptions on a Method

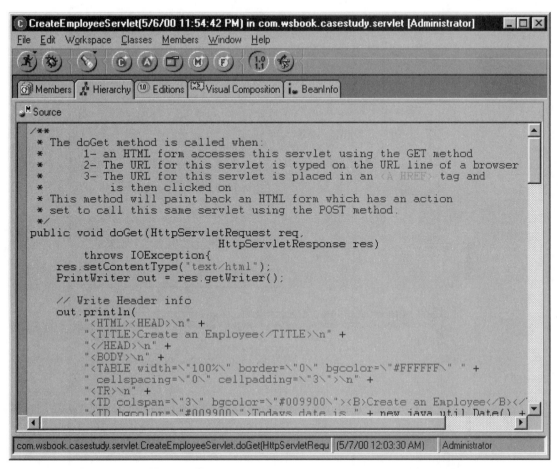

Figure 5.17 Appearance of the Method in a VisualAge for Java Browser

5.2 in order to complete the coding of the doGet() method. When done, your method will appear in VisualAge for Java as in Figure 5.17.

With the doGet() coded, you now need to put the doPost() code into VisualAge for Java by repeating the steps used for the doGet() method. Once you have successfully added both the doGet() and the doPost() methods to CreateEmployeeServlet, it will be time to test the servlet by using the WTE servlet engine.

Configuring the Servlet Engine

Before starting the servlet engine, you must first update its class path to include the new project. Previously when using servlet engine, we did not have

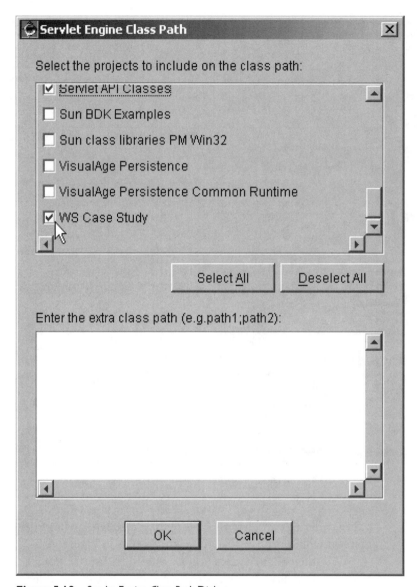

Figure 5.18   *Servlet Engine Class Path* Dialog

to adjust the class path, because HelloServlet was already included in the default class path. In order for our new project, *WS Case Study,* to be a part of the servlet engine class path, we need to add it to the servlet engine class path explicitly. We do this by clicking the *Edit Class Path* button in the *WTE Control Center.* Figure 5.18 shows the resulting dialog.

From this dialog, we need to ensure that the *WS Case Study* is selected. However, the simplest thing to do is to select all the projects and thus not risk missing one. As you build more complex servlets, you will find that you will be using Java code that is spread out across several VisualAge for Java projects. Using the *Select All* button to select all projects is an easy way to ensure that you have all your Java code available to WTE Control Center. Close the dialog by clicking the *OK* button. Now when you run the servlet engine, all the classes in the VisualAge for Java workspace will be available to it. To start a servlet, simply open a Web browser and enter a URL that lists *localhost* as the host name and uses port 8080. To run "CreateEmployeeServlet," enter the following into the URL line of the Web browser:

http://localhost:8080/servlet/com.wsbook.casestudy.servlet.
CreateEmployeeServlet.

If you have not shut down the servlet engine, you will have to click the *Restart Servlet Engine* button to enable the Servlet Runner to find the classes on the new class path. If the servlet engine has been shut down, remember to start it anew before trying the previous URL from your browser.

Summary and Preview

In this chapter, we covered the various ways that the built-in features of VisualAge for Java can be used to create and to test servlets. The WTE's servlet engine allows you to create and to test servlets. We also saw how to start and stop the servlet engine and change its class path to accommodate new projects. In the next chapter, we move outside the WTE and look at using servlets for staging and production.

CHAPTER 6

Using the IBM WebSphere Application Server, Advanced Edition

In previous chapters, we learned how to use the IBM WebSphere Test Environment (WTE) inside VisualAge for Java to create and to test servlets. Now we need to understand how to use our servlets outside a test environment. This can be accomplished by deploying our servlets to the IBM WebSphere Application Server, Advanced Edition (WASAE). The WTE is used at development time, whereas the WASAE is used for staging or production purposes.[1]

The IBM WebSphere Application Server, Advanced Edition, provides the necessary tools to deliver J2EE-based applications. The IBM WASAE allows a machine—more commonly called a *node*—to host multiple application servers. Within each application server, both an EJB container and a servlet engine—known in J2EE parlance as a *Web container*—can exist. Within a servlet engine, multiple Web applications can be defined. Specifically, this chapter covers

- WASAE architecture
- Testing the WASAE installation
- Using the administration console
- Using the XMLConfig tool
- Configuration issues

WASAE is available on Windows, Novell, UNIX, and OS400 platforms. For this chapter, we demonstrate installation only under Windows NT.

---

1. Note that whereas servlets and JSPs can be deployed into WebSphere Application Server, Standard Edition, we discuss the capabilities only of WASAE in this chapter.

However, we point out where configuration steps differ in other environments, such as UNIX.

WASAE Architecture

IBM WASAE, is based on the J2EE specification. Most J2EE products provide a container for each application component type: application client container, applet container, Web component container, and Enterprise Bean container. WASAE provides out-of-the box support for all the containers except the applet container. However, WASAE provides this support, using the IBM Java 1.2.2 Java runtime environment (JRE) with enhancements. We discuss applet deployment issues in a later chapter. Figure 6.1 shows the J2EE architecture.

WASAE is designed for a multinode—multiple-machine—environment. WASAE defines an additional container called a *WebSphere domain,* which consists of a collection of nodes that can be configured and administered together. All the configuration data for all the nodes contained in a WebSphere domain is kept in a single, shared—but, ideally, replicated—repository. This repository, known as the *WAS database,* is kept in an RDBMS.[2] Using a

2. In WASAE version 3.5, the WAS database can be installed in IBM DB/2, Oracle, or Sybase for standalone or networked use or in the Instant DB database for standalone use.

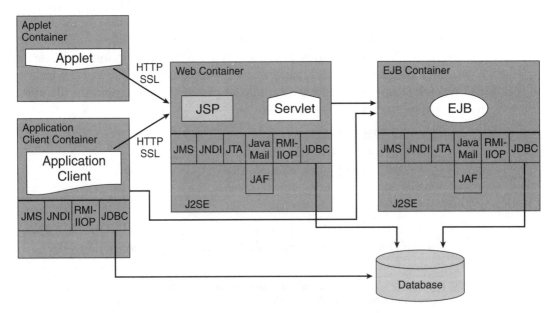

Figure 6.1   J2EE Architecture

single database for all configuration data provides a single point of communication for all nodes and enhances the possible solutions for workload management and balancing, replicated services, and maintenance. Additionally, using a single database for all configuration data greatly decreases maintenance. If each node had its own set of configuration files, you would have to edit the files on each node individually in order to administer it. In WebSphere's model, a shared repository contains all the configuration data, so you can manage the configuration remotely from a desktop because WASAE implements its configuration objects as EJBs, using its own EJB support. Therefore, access to the configuration data by multiple nodes is controlled through the use of the transactional and persistent capabilities of the EJB Entity Beans. This access is done through RMI over IIOP, which allows the configuration to be managed securely over the Internet.

Within each node, WASAE allows multiple application servers to be configured. Each application server may contain a servlet engine—a J2EE Web container—and an EJB container. Both the servlet engine and the EJB container within a particular application server operate within a single shared Java Virtual Machine (JVM). Application servlets and various other Web-based services are defined within the context of the servlet engine. EJBs are deployed within the EJB container. A sample WebSphere domain is shown in Figure 6.2. Note that this domain contains three nodes and that you are shown an exploded view of node 1. Also note that only node 3 contains a Web server.[3]

Because WASAE was designed to work in a multinode environment, you must understand the requirements for each node. Minimally, each node in a WebSphere domain must contain an instance of the WebSphere admin server. The admin server performs many functions, including starting, stopping, and monitoring all configured application servers and providing a location service daemon (LSD), a persistent name server (PNS), and a security server. In addition, the so-called nanny process, a watchdog process, restarts the admin server in case of failure.

In Figure 6.2, node 3 contains a Web server. As is shown, it is not necessary to have the Web server on all nodes. If an HTTP request is sent to node 3, the Web server uses the WebSphere plug-in, possibly with an additional servlet redirector to route the request to the appropriate local or remote application server. The local node then services the request, if possible, or routes it to the proper node, based on the configuration data contained in the EJB Entity Beans using the database.

---

3. WebSphere supports multiple options for separating the Web server from the application server. The configuration and setup of these options is beyond the scope of this book. See [Ueno] for details.

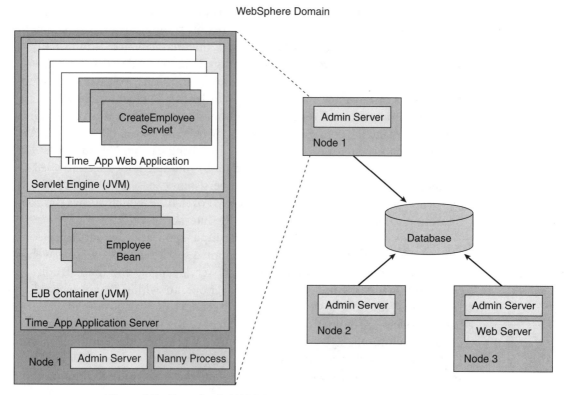

Figure 6.2   Example of a WebSphere Domain

Some Definitions of WebSphere Components

Now that you have seen the overall architecture of WebSphere's process architecture, it's a good time to learn some of the more detailed definitions of the WebSphere components you will use and how they are configured in WebSphere, Advanced Edition. You will learn about the topology view of the WebSphere administrative console, a view arranged as a tree of configuration objects. But before you begin looking at the view, let's examine the following objects you will see:

- Domain: the root of the WebSphere configuration tree. A domain is a set of nodes that all share a single administration database: a single shared WAS database.
- Node: a server machine. Each node is uniquely identified within the domain by its network name, such as its TCP/IP host name. Server processes—called *managed servers* in WebSphere—run within a node.

WebSphere defines two types of managed servers: an application server, a Java process; and a generic server, or any process, such as a CORBA server or an RMI server. All the processes managed on a node by WebSphere may be started or stopped by a single command in the administrative interface.

- Application server: a JVM that is managed by WebSphere. Each application server may contain a servlet engine and an EJB container.
- Servlet engine: a Web container as defined in J2EE. An application server that contains a servlet engine thus has the infrastructure and the classes to execute servlets. A servlet engine contains a set of Web applications, which are isolated logical groups of servlets.
- Web application: a number of common objects brought together into a unified representation of an application. A Web application may contain a group of logically connected servlets and also defines a class path that the servlet class files and associated files are taken from. The Web application also defines a JSP processor that indicates how JSPs will be interpreted, such as using the JSP 0.91 or the JSP 1.0 specification. In addition, the Web application defines a root URI, which will be a part of the URI of all the servlets it contains, indicating the logical grouping within the URL. Finally, the Web application defines a document root path to locate the JSPs used by this Web application.
- Servlet: the servlet at the bottom of this particular branch of the topology tree. Servlets can be accessed in a Web application in one of two ways. The most common, and most maintainable, way is to individually define servlets by specifying the servlet class name and servlet name, as well as a set of URLs that the servlet will be identified by. Servlets may also be defined within a Web application by including a special servlet, called the "Invoker" servlet, which allows servlets to be invoked with a URL containing their fully qualified class name.

Testing the Installation

Once WASAE is installed, you can then test the installation to ensure that everything is functioning correctly. In this section, you will test the installation of the WASAE by using the default server, which can automatically be installed for this purpose.

Before You Start the Admin Server

During the installation of an admin server on a node, the WAS database must be identified. Specifying a JDBC URL and a JDBC driver class identifies the database. This information is stored in the *admin.conf* file, which can be found in the *[ROOT_DIR]\WebSphere\AppServer\bin* directory, where *[ROOT_DIR]* is the root directory where the admin server is installed.[4] For learning purposes, it is best to start with one node before creating a multi-node environment. Here, we will assume that only one node exists in the WebSphere domain and that the WAS database is located on the node itself. If the WAS database is implemented in DB2, using the default database name, you will find the following lines in the *admin.conf* file:

```
com.ibm.ejs.sm.adminServer.dbDriver=COM.ibm.db2.jdbc.app.DB2Driver
com.ibm.ejs.sm.adminServer.dbUrl=jdbc:db2:was
com.ibm.ejs.sm.adminServer.dbUser=userid
com.ibm.ejs.sm.adminServer.dbPassword=password
```

If you want to force the admin server to create the default server application server when it starts, ensure that the *install.initial.config* property is set to true, as in the following line:

```
install.initial.config=true
```

If you have problems because the database becomes corrupted, you may have to drop and recreate the database. To do this, open a *DB2 Command* window and use the following DB2 commands.

```
REM ensure DB2 has the correct computer name
setdb2n.exe %computername%
REM Drop the existing WAS database
DB2 DROP Database WAS
REM create a new WAS database
DB2 CREATE Database WAS
REM increase the application heap size to 256
DB2 UPDATE DB CFG FOR WAS USING APPLHEAPSZ 256
```

At this point, the admin server has been reinitialized. If you ever need to reinitialize the server again, you can perform these same steps. However, you may want to use the XMLConfig tool, described later, to obtain an export of the configuration data so that it can be reimported into the new configuration database.

Starting the Admin Server

Most commonly, the admin server is started from NT services in Windows NT. The service is named *IBM WS Admin Server.* A shortcut to this service is in the *Start* menu of Windows NT under *IBM WebSphere>Application*

---

4. *[ROOT_DIR]* is usually a drive letter under Windows NT or a directory mount point under UNIX.

Server V3.5>Start Admin Server. If you need to debug the admin server, you can also start it from a command line window. You will find a batch file that can be used to start the admin server in *[ROOT_DIR]\WebSphere\AppServer\bin\debug\adminserver.bat,* where *[ROOT_DIR]* is the root directory where the admin server was installed.

Opening the Administrator's Console

The primary tool used to view and to change the configuration of a Web-Sphere domain is the WebSphere administrator's console, a Java-based application that acts as a client to the configuration EJBs that are running in the admin server. In WebSphere 3.5, an administrator's console can connect to any available admin server in the domain. In this chapter, we assume that the default configuration, in which the administrator's console connects to an admin server on the same node, will be followed. To start the administrator's console under Windows NT, choose *IBM WebSphere>Application Server V3.5>Administrator's Console* from the Windows NT *Start* menu.[5]

Starting the Default Server

When the admin server is started, it automatically starts all the application servers that were in the "started" state before the admin server was last shut down. If this is the first time that you have started the admin server, the default server application server will not automatically start. Instead, you must ensure that it is started. In order to start a server, you must open the administrator's console as described earlier. The *WebSphere Advanced Administrative Console* is shown in Figure 6.3.

Select the *Default Server.* To start this application server, click the *Start* button. When the server has started, the dialog shown in Figure 6.4 will be displayed.

Starting the Web Server

The last thing that has to be done is to start the Web server. WebSphere supports a number of Web servers, including IBM's HTTP server, which is supplied with WASAE, and Web servers from Microsoft, Netscape, and the Apache consortium. The Web server will listen, by default, on port 80 for

---

5. If you forget to launch the admin server before opening the administrator's console, you will see a dialog box informing you "The Admin Client failed to connect to the admin server." If this happens, first start the admin server and then try opening the administrator's console.

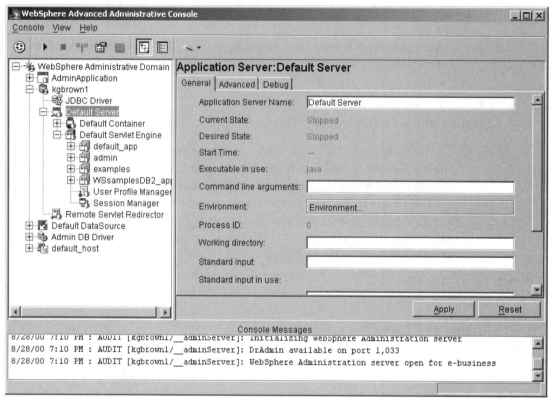

Figure 6.3   The *Administrative Console*

Figure 6.4   The Start Dialog

HTTP requests and will forward any requests for servlets through the Web-Sphere plug-in to the applicable application server. From the *NT Services* panel, select *IBM HTTP Server,* and then start it. If you are using a Web server other than the IBM HTTP server, start it by following the instructions provided by the Web server manufacturer.

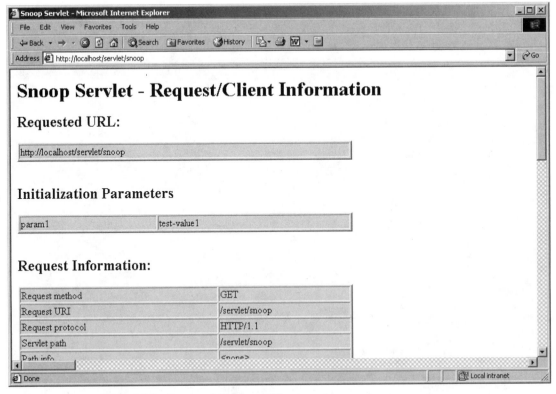

Figure 6.5 Results of the "Snoop" Servlet

Test Using the "Snoop" Servlet

The "Snoop" servlet echoes back to the Web browser the details of the request, the requested server, and the servlet context. This servlet is part of the initial configuration that comes with the default server. In order to invoke "Snoop" servlet, open a Web browser and type http://localhost/servlet/snoop on the URL line of the Web browser. If WebSphere is installed correctly, the "Snoop" servlet will display a response as shown in Figure 6.5

Creating the "EmployeeSys" Application Server

Now that you have verified that the WASAE product is installed correctly, you need to create a new application server for the book's case study. The case study defines an application server named "EmployeeSys" that contains both an EJB container and a servlet engine (Web container). Additionally, the servlet engine defines a Web application with a root URI of */TimeApp*. The

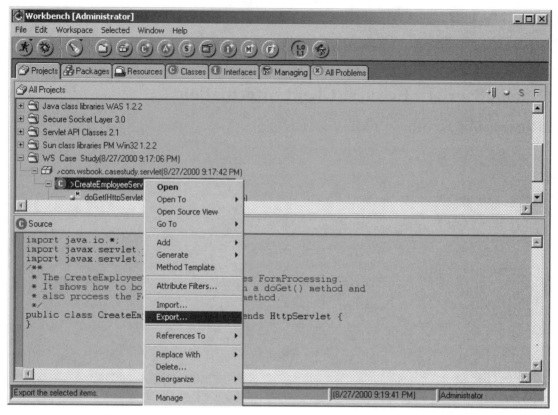

Figure 6.6   Exporting *CreateEmployeeServlet*

steps that follow will help you to export the Java classes from VisualAge for Java and to configure the "EmployeeSys" application server in WASAE.

1. From the *Projects* tab in the VisualAge for Java *Workbench*, select the *CreateEmployeeServlet* class. This class is contained in the *WS Case Study* project and the com.wsbook.casestudy.servlet package. (Remember that you created this project, package, and servlet in the previous chapter.) Using the pop-up menu from the right mouse button, select the *Export* option, as shown in Figure 6.6.

2. When the dialog appears, select the *Directory* radio button and click the *Next* button. When the next dialog appears, type the export directory:

   [ROOT_DIR]\WebSphere\AppServer\hosts\default_host\TimeApp
   WebApp\servlets

   as the export directory. Click the *Finish* button to start the export. (See Figure 6.7.) At this point, a dialog will appear informing you

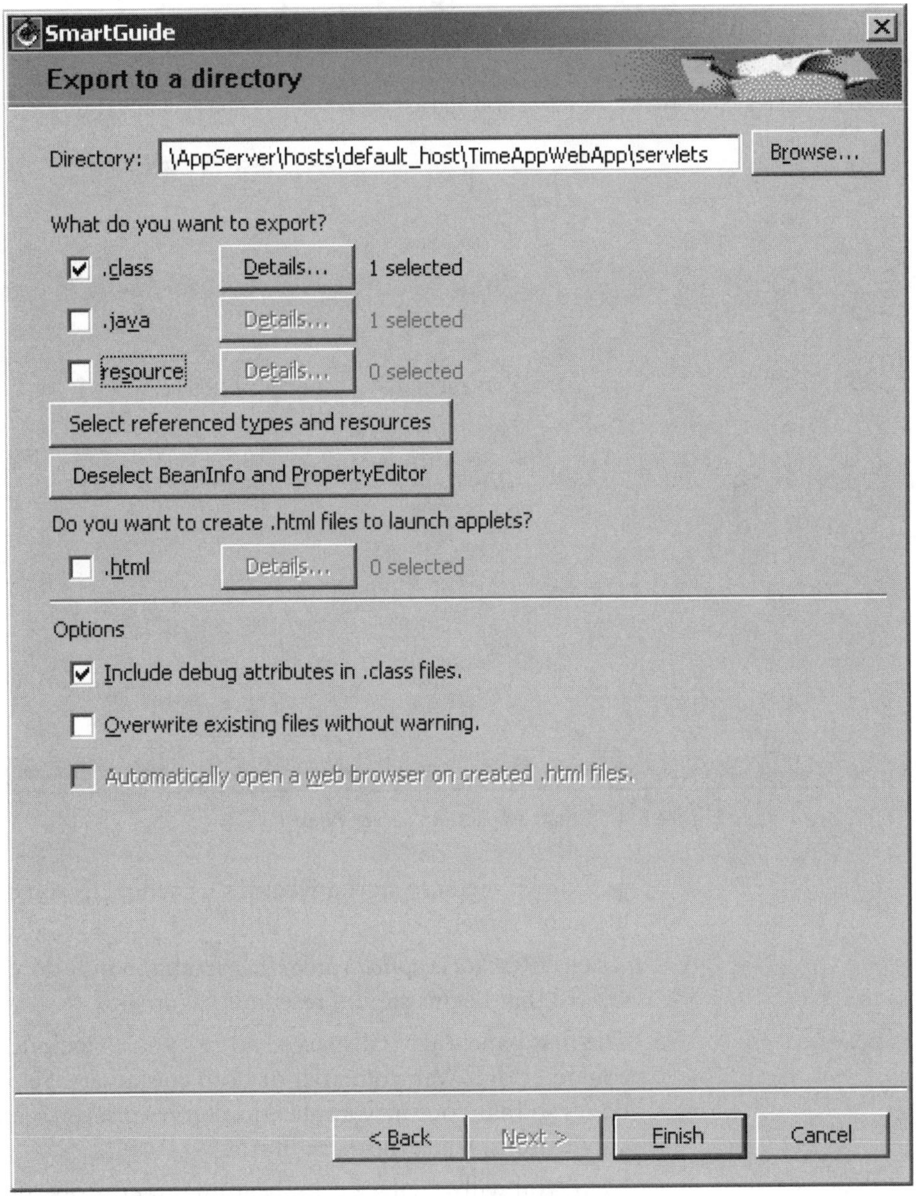

Figure 6.7 Exporting "CreateEmployeeServlet" to WASAE

that this directory has not been created. Click *OK* to let WebSphere create the directory.

3. Ensure that the *IBM WS Admin Server* NT service is still running, and open the WebSphere administrator's console.

4. Inside the administrator's console, you will now use the *Start Wizard*

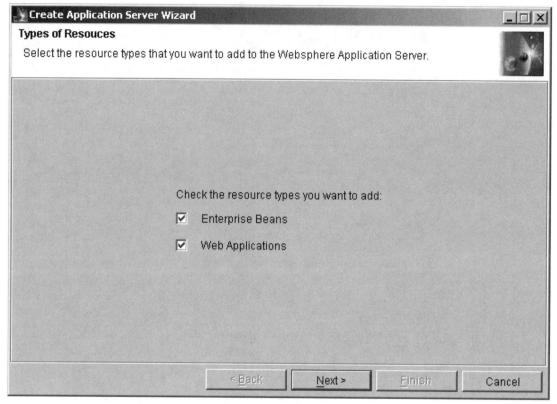

Figure 6.8   Create Application Server Wizard

pull-down menu to start a wizard that will help you create a new application server.

Select *Create Application Server* from the pull-down menu. The wizard that begins should resemble Figure 6.8.

5. The first panel that is displayed allows you to include either an EJB container or a Web container or both containers. Select both check boxes so that your new application server can service EJBs and Web applications. Click the *Next* button.

6. Next, you will specify the application server properties: the application server name, command line arguments, working directory, and standard output and standard error. Type EmployeeSys for the application server name. Change the name of the standard output to empsys_stdout.txt, and change the name of the standard error to empsys_stderr.txt. Click the *Next* button.

7. Specify that the server not be automatically started after creating it. Click *Next*.

8. Select your node from the list of nodes and click *Next*.

9. The next panel allows you to specify Enterprise Beans to be installed on this server. For now, do not make any changes to this panel. Click *Next*.

10. On the *General* tab, accept the EJB container name *EmpSys Container*. Click *Next*.

11. On the *Select Virtual Host* page, select the *default_host* virtual host, and click *Next*. We will not be defining new virtual hosts for this node, so we will use the default host (which refers to the default host name defined for this node in TCP/IP).

12. On the *General* tab of the *Servlet Engine Properties* page, accept the servlet engine name *EmpSysServletEngine*. Click *Next*.

13. On the *General* tab of the *Web Application Properties* page, *do not accept the default Web application name;* instead, type the Web application name TimeAppWebApp. Select *default_host* as the virtual host. Type /TimeApp as the Web application Web path. This path will become the root URI for servlets in this Web application. Select the *Advanced* tab.

14. On this tab, you can change both the document root and the servlet class path. Accept the default document root *[ROOT_DIR]\ WebSphere\AppServer\hosts\default_host\TimeApp\web*. Accept the servlet class path as *[ROOT_DIR]\WebSphere\AppServer\hosts\ default_host\TimeApp\servlets*. Click *Next*.

15. This last page of the wizard allows you to specify system servlets that will be part of the Web application. Uncheck the *Enable File Servlet* check box. Check the *Enable Serving Servlets By Classname* check box.[6] Select *Enable JSP 1.0* so that the JSP 1.0 page compile servlet will be used by the Web application. Click the *Finish* button to create the application server.

16. When the process has completed, drill down to the "EmployeeSys" application server to show the configuration as in Figure 6.9.

17. Select the Web application *TimeApp WebApp* in the administrator's console. Then, using the pop-up menu by clicking the right mouse button, select the *Create->Servlet* option, as shown in Figure 6.10.

18. When the *Create Servlet* dialog appears, type the servlet name CreateEmployee. Type a Web application name of TimeAppWebApp and

---

6. Note that it is a best practice *not* to use the "Invoker" servlet. We will describe these and more best practices later. Nonetheless, we will use this servlet in our example.

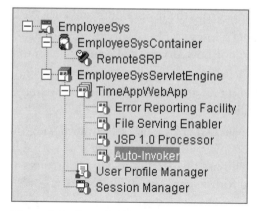

Figure 6.9   Expanded View of the "EmployeeSys" Application Server

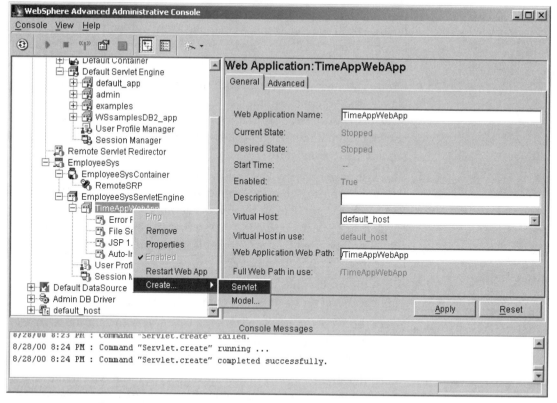

Figure 6.10   Adding a New Servlet

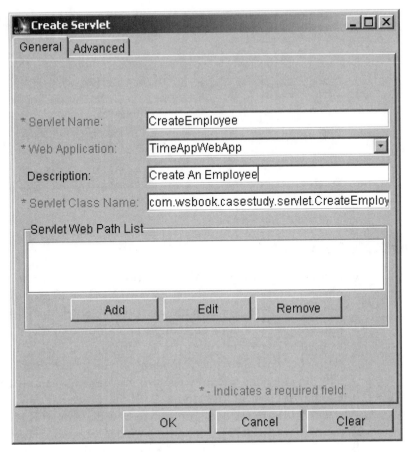

Figure 6.11 Create Servlet Dialog

a description of Create an employee. Type the class name com.wsbook. casestudy.servlet.CreateEmployeeServlet, as shown in Figure 6.11.

19. Finally, add a servlet Web path. Click the *Add* button to display the *Add Web Path to Servlet* dialog. Type a path URI of /TimeApp/ CreateEmployee, as shown in Figure 6.12. Click the *OK* button to close the dialog.

20. Click *OK* on the *Create Servlet* dialog to finish the addition of the servlet to the "TimeAppWebApp."

21. Having configured all the items, start the application server by selecting the application server "EmployeeSys" and then click the *Start* button.

22. To test the deployed servlet, ensure that the Web server has been started, and then open a Web browser on *http://localhost/TimeApp/ CreateEmployee,* as shown in Figure 6.13.

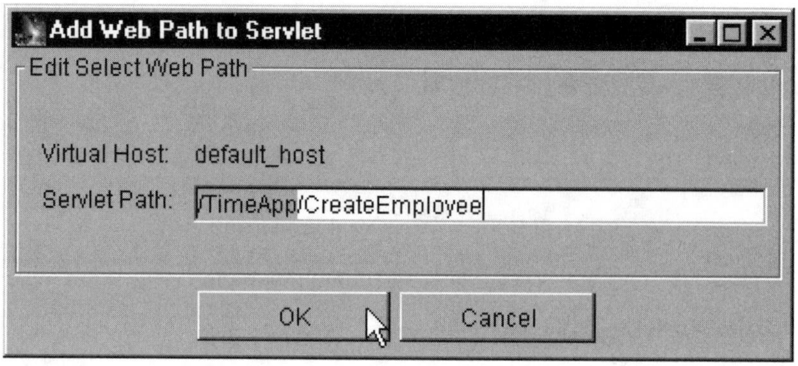

Figure 6.12   Add Web Path to Servlet

Using XMLConfig

In addition to using the administration console to create and to configure application servers, WebSphere offers an XML configuration management tool called *XMLConfig,* which allows you to export a complete or a partial configuration from a node or to import configuration into a node. This tool can be used to create and to restore a configuration backup or to copy a configuration between WebSphere domains. If you have staged your servlets and EJBs on one node and now want to move them to another node, the XML-Config tool is ideal for helping speed this process. You can use XMLConfig to export the entire configuration from a node to an XML file. Change directories to the [ROOT]\WebSphere\AppServer\bin directory and enter the following command to perform the export on the node named *my_node.*

```
xmlconfig -export myNodeConfig.xml -adminNodeName my_node
```

You must then edit the exported file to remove any items that you do not want on the new node and to change most of the tags with action= "update" on them to action= "create." In order to import an XML file containing a WAS configuration, type the following command:

```
xmlconfig -import myNodeConfig.xml -adminNodeName my_node
```

The XML schema that the XML configuration utility uses is quite simple. Its structure mirrors that of the topology view in the administration console. For instance, consider the following minimal XML configuration file template:

```
<websphere-sa-config>
  <node name="nodename" action={"create" | "locate" | "update}>
    <application-server name = "name"
      action = {"create"|"locate"|"update"}>
```

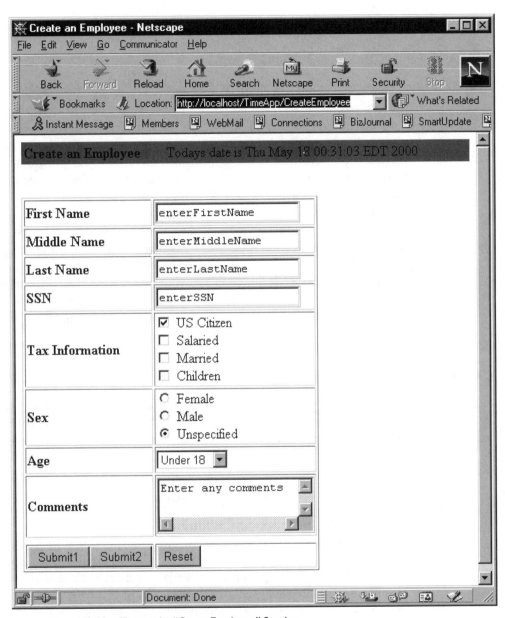

Figure 6.13 Testing the "CreateEmployee" Servlet

```
            ...insert the parts of the application server here...
         </application-server>
      </node>
   </websphere-sa-config>
```

If you wanted to update an application server with a new value—for instance, to change its trace-output file—you would simply insert the appropriate tags into the minimal file. To change the trace-output file, you would insert the tag <trace-output>(ROOT)\mytrace.trc</traceoutput> between the <application-server...> and the </application-server> tags. If you wanted to change the definition of a servlet, you would need to also include the tags defining the servlet engine and Web application, and so on.

The CD-ROM that accompanies this book contains a sample XML file (*employee_sys.xml*) that can be used to configure the "EmployeeSys" application server in the same way that we configured it using the administrator's console. You would configure the new application server by changing the node name in the XML file to match your node name and then running the *xmlconfig* import as shown previously. You can learn more about how to use the XML configuration tool by reading the product documentation and by browsing through this example output file.

Configuration Issues

Earlier, we went through the steps of setting up an application server with an EJB container, a Web application, and a servlet. In this section, we will present some best practices for configuring your application servers and Web applications.

Application Server Versus Web Application

To understand the best practices for using application servers and Web applications, you need to consider a few more facts about Web applications. Each application server contains a single JVM, whereas a Web application is contained within an application server and shares the JVM with other Web applications. However, each Web application has its own class path and document root because a specialized class-loader class enforces isolation between the Web applications. As such, servlets within one Web application cannot directly invoke or directly utilize public static variables from a servlet within another Web application. In effect, having multiple Web applications divides up a JVM such that each Web application acts as if it has its own JVM. The only way servlets in different Web applications can communicate with one another is through the ServletContext object. You might recall that each Web application has its own ServletContext associated with it. The Servlet API allows a servlet to "look up" other servlet contexts,[7] thus allowing communication with servlets in other Web applications.

Earlier, you learned that a Web application is a logical grouping of servlets that share a common root URI. Each Web application also defines a class path; what has not been discussed so far is the fact that each Web application within an application server can be independently "restarted," or made to reload its servlets from the files on the class path. This can happen in two ways. First, a feature called *autoreload* can be set on each Web application. If autoreload is enabled, whenever a file changes on the class path for that Web application, the application server will dump all the current servlet instances and any other objects that were loaded with the servlets and reload the servlets from the new files on the class path. Second, an administrator can force a reload of a Web application by choosing the *Restart Web App* menu option from the menu in the topology tree.

This ability to force a reload of a particular Web application makes it possible to change the files related to a particular Web application while leaving running and unaffected all the servlets in the other Web applications within the application server. Thus, you can administer servlets and their associated classes, such as controllers and domain classes, on an individual Web application basis. The only limitation to this administration ability is that you cannot add or remove named servlets from the Web application unless you shut down the entire application server. These facts are key to making the decision between choosing to create a Web application or an application server.

For example, let's say that we have two logically independent sets of servlets that run within the same intranet, although the same notion applies to different applications running within an Internet portal or application service provider (ASP). We will assume that one Web application contains our time card application—"TimeApp," which was built for the human resources department of our fictional company. We can also assume that another set of servlets was developed for the sales department representing an application for setting and monitoring sales quotas: "QuotaApp." Now let's say that both applications have relatively low utilization rates—no more than five concurrent users at a time total—well within the processor utilization capabilities of a single-processor Windows NT or UNIX server.

If we create two application servers, one for each set of servlets, we will need to either deploy the two application servers on different nodes or equip

---

7. This lookup is through the "ServletContext.getContext(String uri)" method, which returns a Servlet Context for a particular root URI.

our server with a substantial amount of RAM to run the two servers simultaneously. The reason is that each application server has a substantial memory overhead. An empty application server occupies between 30MB and 60MB of RAM—just the overhead to create the JVM and to load the base Web-Sphere classes. If you add more application classes, this figure will grow. However, adding a new Web application to an existing application server will not substantially increase its base memory size. So, to avoid the overhead of a new JVM, you should add a new Web application instead of creating a new application server. Your applications can still remain largely independent of one another through the Web application class path feature, but you will not have the unnecessary extra overhead.

Finally, you need to understand the autoreload feature. Autoreload is a computationally intensive process; WebSphere has a thread for each Web application that will "wake up" every few seconds—set in the reload interval—and scan the class path for changes. Although this is fine for servers with low utilization or that are in a test or quality assurance (QA) environment, it becomes an unacceptable amount of "wasted cycles" when in a higher transaction-volume environment. Therefore, we recommend that you turn off the autoreload feature for production WebSphere servers in all but the least-active server environments.

Some advantages of using a Web application are as follows.

- Servlets within the same application server can use the RequestDispatcher object to forward (transfer control to) or to include the output of other servlets in the same application server.
- A running Web application can be restarted apart from restarting the application server so as to pick up configuration changes.
- Less system resources are needed, as only one JVM is needed for several Web applications.

Some disadvantages of using Web applications are as follows.

- In order to add servlets or to delete servlets from the Web application, the entire application server must be restarted.
- Less isolation between "applications" exists.

When should you use one rather than the other? The general rule of thumb is to use one application server per set of related applications and to apply Web applications as a way to segment the application into subapplications within a larger application. We would caution you to not group several unrelated projects with different delivery schedules into one application server, as you will inevitably force the other Web applications to have to restart when new servlets are added.

"Invoker" Servlet

As discussed earlier, the "Invoker" servlet can find other servlets by their Java class names and then load and/or invoke them on request. Generally, this servlet should be used only during testing and staging. Using "Invoker" can open up security holes. When "Invoker" is used, the HTML contains the class name of the servlet. As such, the user has more information than is necessary for calling a servlet. This small bit of information might lead an unscrupulous user to attempt to break into your system by using that information. Using "Invoker" can also decrease performance. In order for it to find a servlet by its class name, "Invoker" must use the Java Reflection API to find and to load the servlet. This API is generally slower than using a direct reference in Java. Finally, using "Invoker" limits how you can pass parameters to your servlet. You can only supply initialization parameters to a servlet that has been defined in the administrator's console.

Summary and Preview

In this chapter, you have seen how the WASAE can be used to deploy both servlets and EJBs. You learned about how WASAE implements the containers in the J2EE architecture, how to verify a WASAE installation, how to configure an application server in WASAE by using the administrator's console and the XMLConfig tool, and some best practices for configuration. In the next chapter, we look at WebSphere Studio and how it can be used to manage and deploy a Web application's resources.

CHAPTER 7

Using IBM WebSphere Studio

The days of an application being delivered as a self-contained executable, with perhaps only an additional property file or two, is a thing of the past. At least this is true in the case of Web-based applications. We have traded ease of deployment on the client machine—which, for HTTP and HTML-based applications, requires no application deployment at all—for a complicated deployment process on the server. First of all, remember that Web-based applications are installed on server(s) rather than on each client machine. In an application architecture that follows the J2EE Model II design, the installation of multiple resource files for the application is a fact of life.

IBM's WebSphere Studio product provides a solution to the management and deployment of resources making up a Web application. In this chapter, we focus on WebSphere Studio's file management and publishing capabilities. In Chapter 11, we revisit WebSphere Studio to discover more about its page design capabilities.

Rationale for WebSphere Studio

Most Web applications following this architecture contain most or all of the following types of common application resource files:

- JSPs
- HTML
- Image: graphics in such formats as GIF, JPEG, and BMP
- Servlet: application Java servlet in the form of a complied class file
- Class: JavaBeans or EJBs compiled into a class file
- Property: text file with externalized property values used within the application

- XML (Extensible Markup Language) documents
- CSS (cascading style sheets)

An approach to managing these resource files within the context of an application might seem obvious. You could simply set up a directory structure, with a hierarchy reflecting each resource. However, if multiple developers work on different portions of the application, conflicts will inevitably arise. Likewise, if your project has multiple iterations requiring deployment to test and production servers, relying on copying these application resources files using only operating system file management tools can easily become a nightmare. Developers and system administrators will spend an enormous amount of time synching up and locating these resources when deploying to servers.

WebSphere Studio provides a formal view of a developer's environment and streamlines deploying application resources to different stages of development, reducing deployment to a few mouse clicks. In this way, WebSphere Studio helps developers manage the process of resource creation and maintenance.

Developers familiar with the product often refer to it simply as *Studio,* which is a more succinct name. Therefore, we will adopt the name Studio throughout the rest of this chapter.

Studio offers more than just resource management and HTML design capabilities. However, because these capabilities overlap with approaches described in other chapters, we will instead focus on the management and publishing components of Studio in this chapter.

Installing and Starting Studio

Studio is a product separate from the WebSphere Application Server, Advanced Edition, and VisualAge for Java, Enterprise Edition IDE. Studio version 3.5 is packaged in two editions: Professional and Advanced. Both editions include VisualAge for Java Professional edition. WebSphere Studio Professional includes as part of the software bundle WebSphere, Standard Edition, whereas WebSphere Studio Advanced ships with a copy of WebSphere Application Server, Advanced Edition. Studio can be used separately from WebSphere and VisualAge and with other development and application server products but is best used in combination with WebSphere and VisualAge, as you will see later in the chapter. Studio is available only on Microsoft Windows platforms.

Installing Studio is accomplished through a standard installation wizard. The only decision the user must make during this process is which drive path to use for the product location.

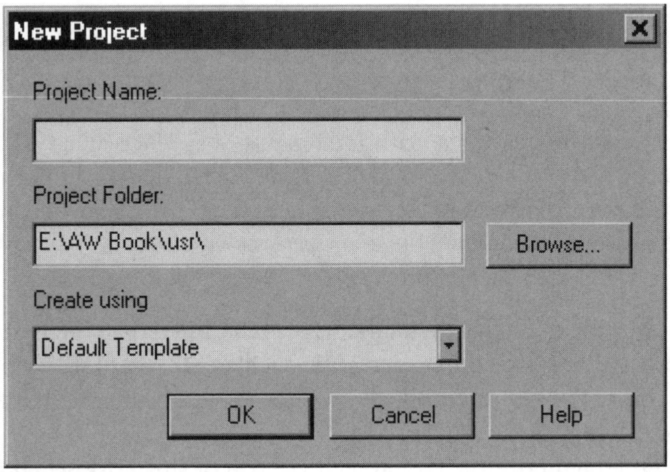

Figure 7.1 Creating a New Project

You start Studio by selecting the menu option under the Window *Start* menu. The menu selection is found under the following menu path: *Start->IBM WebSphere->Studio 3.5 ->IBM WebSphere Studio 3.5*. The first time Studio is started, a dialog will appear, prompting for a new project name, location, and, optionally, a previously defined template (Figure 7.1).

After you click *OK*, Studio's main screen, the *Studio Workbench,* will open. The window will open to a default template if none has been selected from the initial dialog (Figure 7.2).

Project Templates

Templates provide a mechanism to capture a common folder and resource structure for use in the creation of new Studio projects. Templates are defined by simply defining a directory structure and HTML files in the template subdirectory in the location where Studio was installed. Studio's template list consists of subdirectory names defined in a template directory.

A couple of templates are provided as examples. You can create a template by simply copying, or publishing, an existing resource and directory structure to the template directory. The template will appear as a choice in the *New Project* dialog's template choice box for selection. Once a template has been selected, Studio will import the template's directory structure into the project (**.wao*) file and display it in the *Workbench,* ready for editing.

Why use templates? From an organizational standpoint, templates help support a standardized Web application structure. Instead of relying on a developer to create a Studio project file with a structure that conforms to a corporate standard, standardized resources can be defined and will be included in every project. For example, an HTML document defined to display official copyright material or a corporate logo can be defined in a template to be available consistently for every project.

The workbench is divided horizontally into two panels. The left panel lists the project's resource elements, such as HTML, JSP, servlets, images, text files, or just about anything else. Elements can be inserted in a project by using the *Insert* menu option, which can be activated with a right-click or by using the menu option available at the top of the workbench menu bar. The

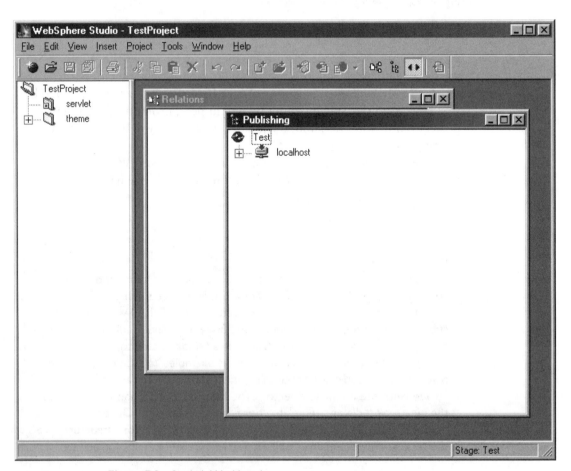

Figure 7.2   Studio's Workbench

Insert option opens a dialog (Figure 7.3) that allows elements to be imported into the project in three ways.

- A new resource can be created by specifying a name and a resource type. Studio will prompt for the specified file type. The new file will be an editable template or a prototype of the appropriate file type.
- An existing resource can be located and imported with the *Use Existing* option.
- Resources can also be imported from other content management systems with the *From External Source* option. This option will be used later in the chapter to import class files from VisualAge.

The workbench *Relations* view provides a graphical view of selected element relationships. If in the left-hand pane you select an HTML file element

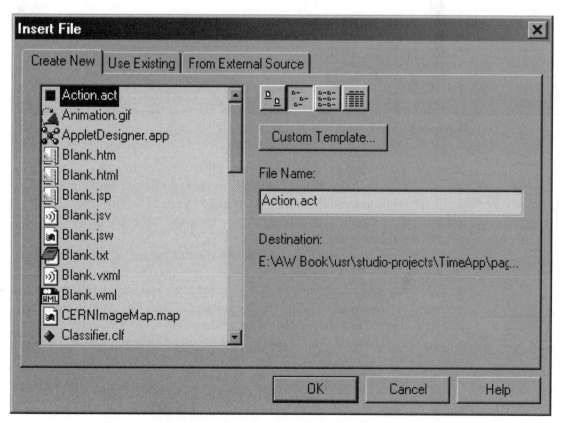

Figure 7.3   Inserting a Resource File into a Project

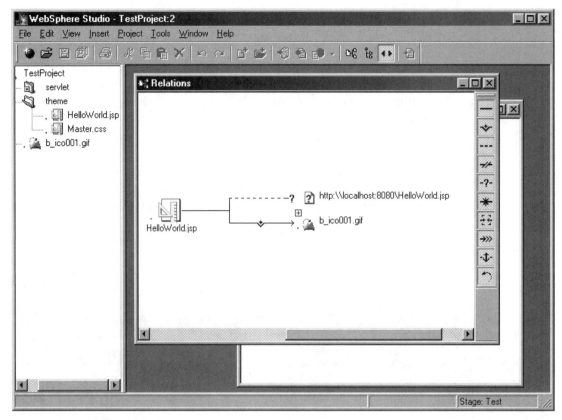

Figure 7.4   *Relations* View

that references other HTML documents, JSPs, or image files, Studio will de-
pict these internal references graphically in the right-hand pane (Figure 7.4).

Each relation from the source file is linked to its associated file with a
meaningful link symbol helping to convey the type of the association. Relation type indicators are shown in Figure 7.5.

An alternative to the *Relations* view is the *Publishing* view, which shows
defined servers and the structure of content for a specific stage. Any number
of publishing stages can be defined; by default, test and production stages are
provided. The workbench displays one stage at a time. Elements in this stage
can be organized independently of the left-hand element view. Folders and
servers can be created and the elements organized differently for each stage.
When a stage is published, Studio automatically produces the proper linking-
document reference tags in the published HTML/JSP files. Therein lies a
powerful management feature of Studio. You can deploy application resources in various ways from a central location. Later sections will discuss
stage and server creation in more detail.

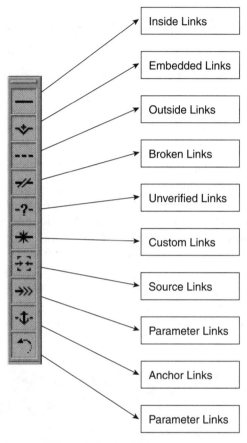

Figure 7.5   Relationship Link Types

What Is Staging?

In a logical sense, a stage represents a particular audience of a Web-based application during its development life cycle. Initial development efforts can be considered the development stage, initial user acceptance of the application the testing stage, and general usage by end users to solve a specific problem space a production stage. Of course, an organization may define additional life-cycle stages to support its internal operations and procedures. Studio relates these logical development life-cycle stages physically as an element of a Studio project definition. Within a project, any number of stages can be defined; within each stage, application resources can be organized and partitioned into any number of files and servers that can vary between stages. Stages can also be used to represent a unique target operating environment. Thus, a project might define multiple production stages for each target environment.

> Studio saves workbench elements and properties in a *.wao* file. Publishing a project to a stage results in exporting these files in their native format to publishing targets defined in the publishing stage. All the references (relations) will be modified to reflect the structure of the defined stage.

Using Page Designer

No one tool has cornered the HTML authoring market. To the contrary, many tools allow HTML documents to be created by using a drag-and-drop metaphor. Studio provides Page Designer, an authoring tool that provides a drag-and-drop mechanism to create complex HTML documents.

Page Designer is invoked when an HTML or JSP resource is double-clicked from the workbench, or when you select *Edit With >> Page Designer* from the pop-up menu. Page Designer allows HTML to be constructed in two ways. You can either use a WYSYWIG feature with drag-and-drop, referred to as the *normal view,* or you can directly input HTML tags into the HTML view, a color-coded HTML editor (Figure 7.6).

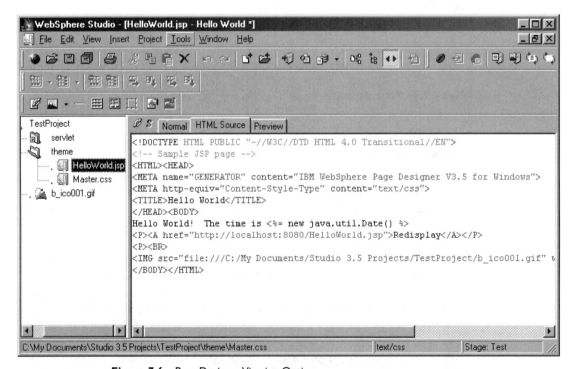

Figure 7.6   Page Designer Viewing Options

Additionally, you can preview how an HTML document will appear in a browser by using the *Preview* button (Figure 7.7). Another distinguishing feature of Page Designer is its awareness of JSP tags that can be used to adorn an HTML document with dynamic content. These capabilities are discussed in detail in Chapter 11.

Page Designer supports all HTML elements, such as frame, form, and table elements. Because these elements are the foundation for laying out most HTML documents, Page Designer allows these elements to be created and placed through drag-and-drop functionality. Table and form elements, among others, can also be inserted into a document by using convenient icons defined in Page Designer's tool bar.

When the table creation option is selected, a dialog appears, prompting for the initial row and column size of the table. These coordinates are used to create and to display a graphical table in Page Designer's *Normal* view (Figure 7.8).

Another convenient editing feature is the way in which table attributes can be further refined. Table, cell, and row attributes can be accessed collectively by selecting any element of the table, right-clicking, and selecting the *Attributes* menu selection. A property dialog will appear, with notebook tabs

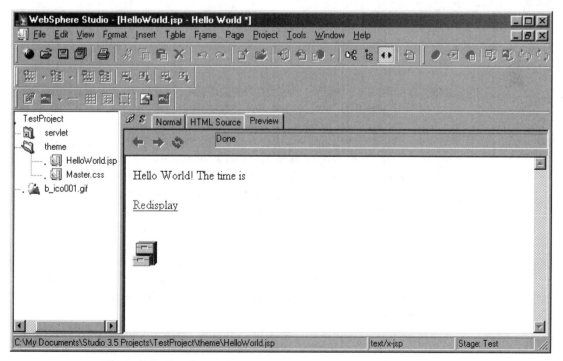

Figure 7.7 The *Preview* View

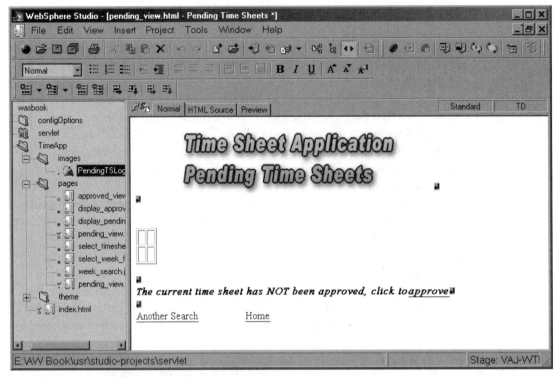

Figure 7.8   The *Normal* View with 2 × 2 Table

that define attribute settings for the table and its elements (Figure 7.9). This prevents the designer from having to attempt to highlight an individual table element, which could be difficult in a complex nested-table implementation.

Before form-input fields, such as push buttons or lists, can be dropped onto the designer's composition surface, a form must be dropped in place. A form is created by selecting the form icon or using the *Insert* menu option. Once a form is in place, Page Designer displays icons for available form-element widgets that can then be dropped within the form. In Figure 7.10, we have deleted the table and replaced it with a new form. Form attributes can be accessed and modified by opening an attributes dialog, which can be accessed from a pop-up menu or from the main menu's *Edit* menu.

Page Designer provides an easy way to partition a document into frame sets. The main menu bar of Page Designer defines a *Frame* menu that defines menu choices to create and modify frames (Figure 7.11).

The *Split Frame* option lets you partition a document vertically or horizontally into frame sets. An open-ended number of frame sets can be de-

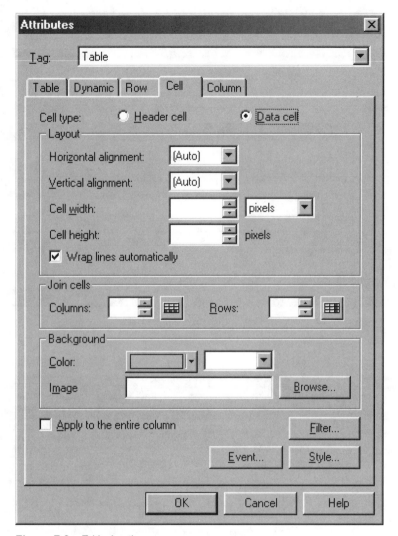

Figure 7.9 *Table* Attributes

fined. Because frame sets result in multiple HTML or JSP document references, Page Designer creates a new document for each frame-set reference. The document in which frame sets are initiated is preserved and is also referenced by a frame-set source attribute. Because the initial document is now partitioned inside a frame set, which document contains the frame-set definitions? Page Designer handles this by prompting for a document name when the designer session is exited; frame-set definitions will be defined in that document.

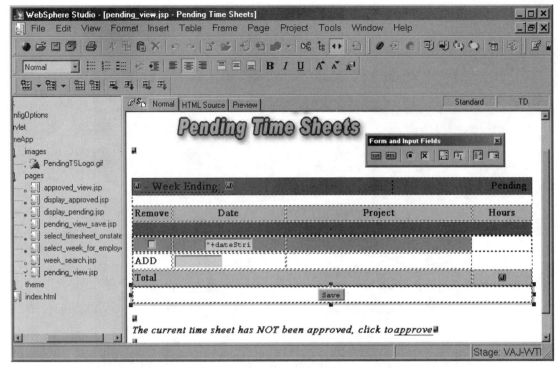

Figure 7.10 *Normal* View with *Form and Input* Fields

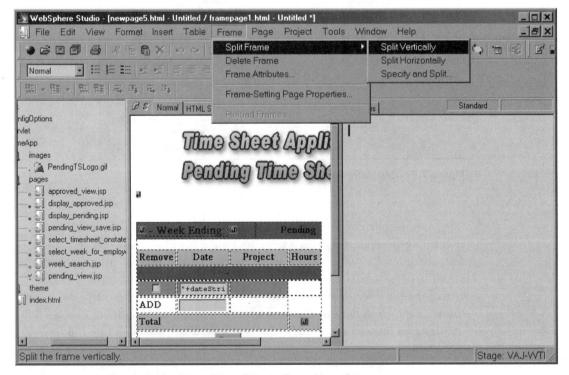

Figure 7.11 *Normal* View Showing *Frame* Menu Options

Managing a Web Site

Studio's workbench allows you to organize and to partition Web site elements into a logical structure. Studio also provides a way to manage the evolving states of a Web application development process.

During application development, HTML and JSP resources are typically published to a Web server test environment. When a developer is working with the VisualAge WebSphere Test Environment, the servlet engine's document root will typically be a directory on the developer's workstation. Thus, the Web resources will need to be published to this local directory. During testing, resources will be published to a test server for QA or usability testing. Finally, as the application moves into production, the resources can be published to the production server(s).

By default, Studio defines two publishing stages: test and production. Within each stage, a default server is defined with a URL address of *localhost*. This is fine during development, especially in VisualAge's test environment, as it also defaults to *localhost*. However, when publishing production stages, the default server URL address will probably need to be modified to the server URL without a port number designation. For all stages, you can specify a port if needed. In the case study Studio project, we have configured the test stage to have a single server, *localhost:8080,* which corresponds to the default configuration we are using in the WebSphere Test Environment. Underneath a stage's server resource, elements and folders exist that initially reflect the folder structure defined in the left-hand pane (Figure 7.12).

New folders may be created in the *Publishing* view. The resources can then be drag-and-dropped into these folders to reflect an independent folder structure. This allows a single set of application resources to be published to different server locations with varying structures. If a publishing structure changes, the change will be reflected only in that stage. When new resource elements are created, they will automatically appear in all the defined stages.

Publishing stages can be created and customized from the workbench by opening the *Customize Publishing Stages* menu option located under *Project Menu*. Choosing this menu option opens a dialog that allows you to modify existing stages and to create additional publishing stages (Figure 7.13).

A publishing stage is published to a server specifically set up for the application. You create a server by selecting the publishing-stage name, right-clicking, and selecting the *insert server* option. The URL used to access the server—the virtual host name and port—can be specified when it is created. If you need to publish application elements to multiple servers, you can add servers and associated URLs to a publishing stage.

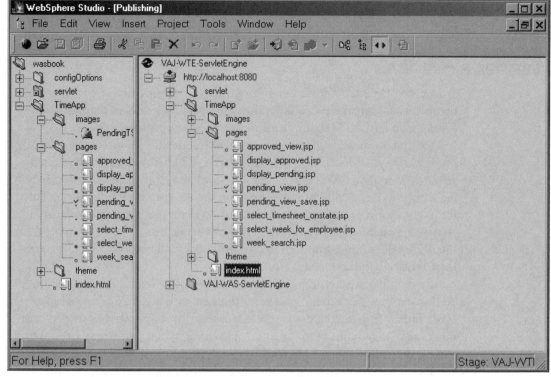

Figure 7.12 Test *Publishing* View: Folder Structure

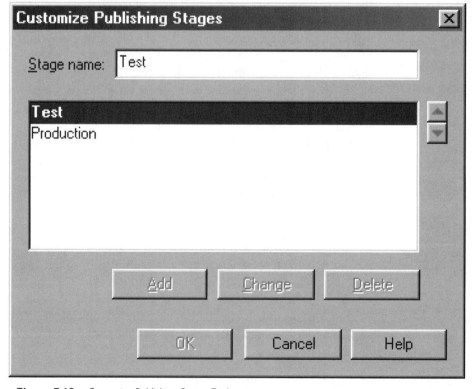

Figure 7.13 *Customize Publishing Stages* Dialog

Assets other than runtime elements can be managed and published from Studio. For the case study, we have defined a publishing stage for each deployment scenario: VisualAge WebSphere Test Environment; and WebSphere via IBM HTTP server (IHS) plug-in. The VisualAge WTE Stage has configuration files associated with it: *default.servlet_engine* and *time_app.webapp*. Each of these files is managed in the same Studio project, with the appropriate versions of the files marked as publishable in the appropriate stage. This way, the configuration is managed concurrently with the application files.

Once you have defined and organized a stage, you can publish workbench elements on an individual, folder, server, or project basis. This is done by selecting the desired elements to publish, right-clicking, and selecting the *publish this...* menu option. A dialog will appear (Figure 7.14), with several publishing options that can be toggled on and off. One publishing option that can be toggled is to publish only modified files, which is good if a large number of documents are defined by a project. Also, prompts can be toggled to warn before overwriting existing files or creating folders. An advanced option allows default publishing-stage options to be defined.

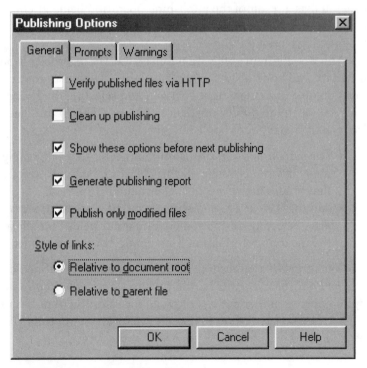

Figure 7.14 *Publishing Options* Dialog

One option that should be addressed is the *Style of Links* option defined on the first page (Figure 7.14). This option indicates how links, or HREFs, defined in HTML and JSP documents will be defined within a published document. Selecting *Relative to document root* causes URL link references in a document to be prefixed with a /, indicating that the linked reference path will start from the document root directory of the server being published to. Selecting *Relative to parent file* generates a link path without the / at the beginning of generated HREFs. Within a Web server–only environment, you would most often select *Relative to parent file*. Within a J2EE application environment with some Web resources being deployed to a Web container that has an associated URL prefix, you will most likely choose the *Relative to document root* option. Further, in this environment, your *Publishing* view will have a folder or folders that represent the application's URL prefix. The net effect for our case study is to have a top-level folder (*TimeApp*) in each of our publishing servers (see Figure 7.12). This reflects the fact that all Web resources are accessed by a URL of the form *http://virtual_hostname/TimeApp/...* Thus, all URLs generated by Studio during the publishing task will contain the Web application URL prefix (root URI) as part of the URL path.

If you opt for it, a browser will appear with a detailed publishing report generated as a result of the publishing operation being attempted. This report is used to determine which files were published, along with why some files may not have been published.

You can configure where a published server or project is physically published to, and how this is accomplished, by selecting a project or a server element defined in a stage, right-clicking, and selecting the *Properties* option. This will open the *Publishing* dialog (Figure 7.15). In this dialog, you can select one of two types of publishing mechanisms.

- *File system publish,* the default, indicates that publishing will occur using a native file system, such as NT or UNIX. Of course, this presumes that Studio has access to the particular drive path.
- Alternatively, *FTP publish* can be used if access to a device is not available. Selecting this option enables input fields that allow port and authentication information for a connection to be defined.

The target of a publishing operation can also be defined by clicking the *Define Publishing Targets* button that appears in the *Publishing* dialog. This option opens another dialog, allowing the selection of publishing paths for HTML and servlet resources (Figure 7.16). These publishing targets can then be associated with folders defined within the server.

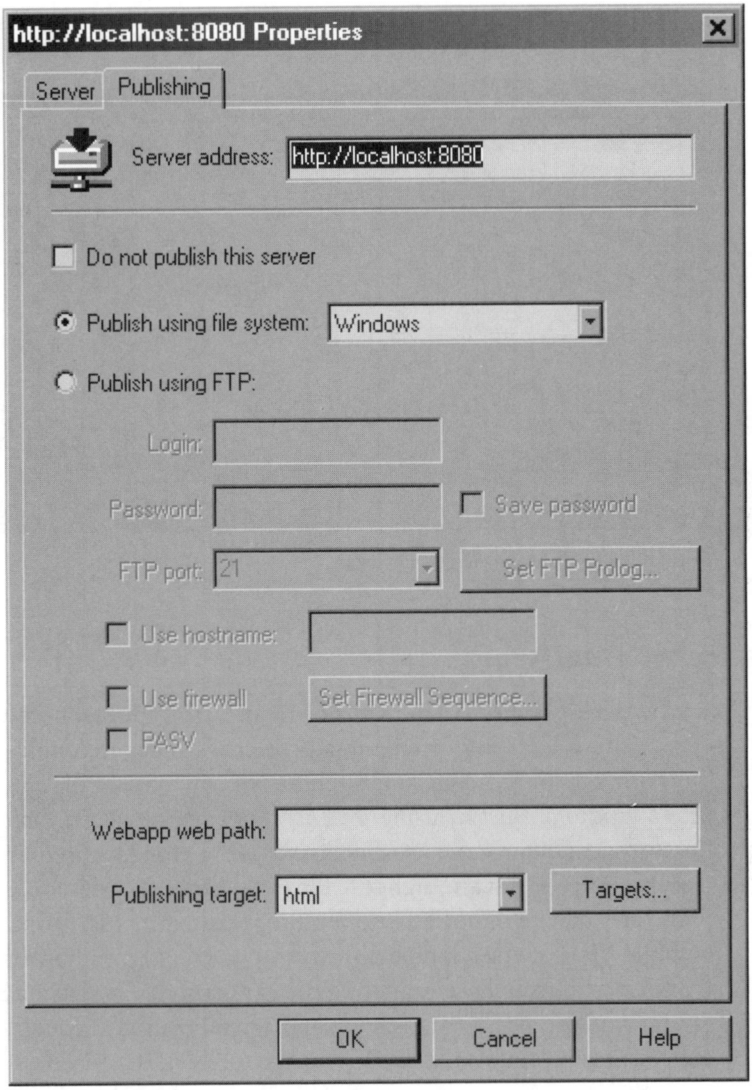

Figure 7.15 *Publishing* Options Dialog

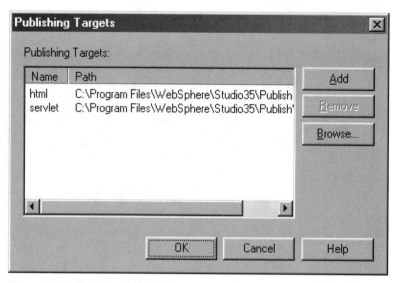

Figure 7.16   *Publishing Targets* Dialog

Importing from VisualAge

Studio manages more than just HTML and JSP type resources; compiled Java classes can also be imported into a project.*wao* file and published together with other resources as a single operation. Any type of file can be imported into a Studio project by using the *Insert* option; however, some nonfile-based development environments, such as VisualAge for Java, require you to first export compiled Java source to a file path. Once the files are exported to a path, they can be imported into Studio by using the *Insert* option. However, compiled Java classes can be directly imported into Studio from a VisualAge workspace, effectively eliminating the export step. Servlets or Beans created in Studio can also be added to the VisualAge repository through the same mechanism. This mechanism is the VisualAge for Java Remote Tool API.

The VisualAge Remote Tool API allows external tool implementation to access classes inside VisualAge. Of course, a tool vendor must incorporate access to this API into its product, as IBM has done with Studio. In order to access a VisualAge repository, a VisualAge workbench session needs to be active on a client. Additionally, the Remote Tool API must be started before Studio or any other tool can access this local workspace. This is accomplished by opening VisualAge's *Options* tree and selecting the *Remote Access to Tool API* option (Figure 7.17).

The Remote Tool API can be started, using the default port, by clicking the *Start Remote Access to Tool API* button. Optionally, the *Use user-*

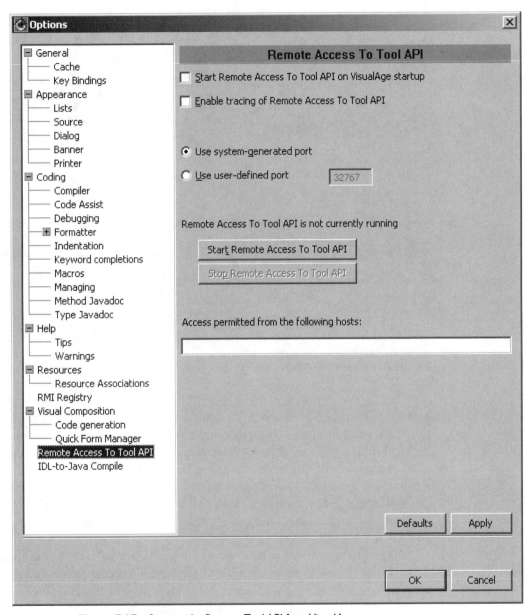

Figure 7.17   Starting the Remote Tool API from VisualAge

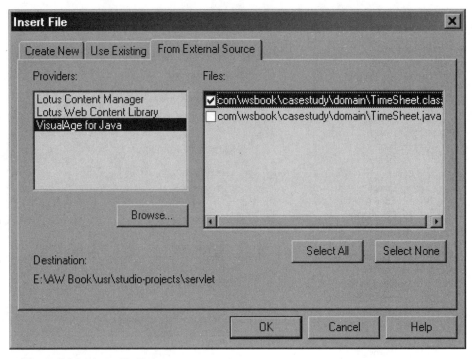

Figure 7.18   *Insert File* Dialog

defined port and host list can be customized. The default port should work
fine for Studio. Inserting Java classes into Studio from VisualAge can now
be accomplished by using the *From External Source* dialog defined in the
workbench's *Insert* option. Selecting the *VisualAge* option and clicking
Browse will open the class-selection dialog defined in VisualAge. Seeking
and selecting a Java type and clicking *OK* will import both the source code
and class file for the class, displaying them for selecting in the dialog's window (Figure 7.18).

Unfortunately, this sequence must be repeated for each type, and the
desired files must also be toggled for selection in the list in order for them
to be inserted into the active Studio workbench folder. Servlet or class files
created in Studio can then be modified in either tool and updated or inserted from Studio by selecting the file in the workbench and then selecting
the *VisualAge for Java* option located in the *Project* menu. Options to send
to and/or update from the repository can be also selected. Sending a class
results in the appearance of a VisualAge project browser prompting for the
VisualAge project into which the class or Java will be inserted the first time;
subsequent inserts will simply create a new edition of the class. Changes

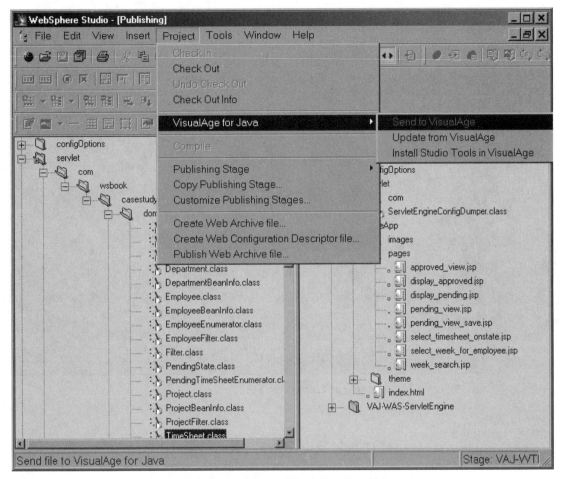

Figure 7.19   Sending and Receiving Classes from VisualAge

made to a class in VisualAge can be updated in Studio by selecting the *Up-date* option (Figure 7.19).

Importing Existing Sites

As well as inserting files for an application, HTML from an entire site can be imported into Studio and then subsequently modified and published. Importing is accomplished by selecting *Import* from the workbench's *File* menu, which will prompt you for a valid URL and is followed by a series of options about how the Web site should be navigated when searching for files to import (Figure 7.20).

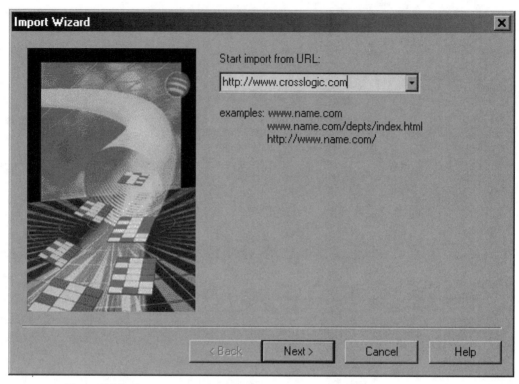

Figure 7.20   Importing an Existing Web Site

Either HTTP links defined in a starting document can be imported, or folders and subfolders can be traversed on the server where the site resides. The latter option requires FTP access. The kinds of files imported can also be determined; only files that are returned to the browser can be parsed into Studio; or, in crawler fashion, files and resources, such as server-side scripts, can be downloaded and imported. This also requires FTP access. How far links should be crawled is another configurable option.

Version Control

Studio does not contain a system for version control. But the Advanced edition does provide hooks for a version control system (VCS). Studio is VCS aware and as such will act as a VCS client for an installed version control system. Example version control systems are

- IBM VisualAge Team Connection
- Lotus Domino Content Manager and Web Content Library

- Microsoft Source Safe
- PVCS
- Rational ClearCase

For more information on configuring WebSphere Studio to work with these version control systems, refer to the product documentation.

Working in a Team

Development teams of more than two or three members must ensure that each team member's efforts do not conflict with those of other developers. The VisualAge team environment helps manage concurrent development of Java code. WebSphere Studio provides a way to manage concurrent access to the static and dynamic presentation aspects of an application by requiring all members of a team to access the same *.wao* file created for the project. This can be facilitated by locating the project file on a network drive. Along with normal production and test stages, additional publishing stages can be created for each developer to reflect the locally installed test structure.

Even if a version control system is not in place, Studio's check-in/out feature can be used to indicate files that are in use. Once a developer is finished with modification, the file can be checked back in. Of course, if a version control system is not in place, the honor system will have to be the enforcement agent.

Summary and Preview

Web-based application development involves myriad different file and resource types. If not efficiently managed, the process of moving from development to test and ultimately to a production environment can result in an endless cycle of regressions, owing to these files being "out of synch." Studio is more than just another HTML authoring tool. It supplies a management and publishing option to large- or small-scale Web-based development, complementing the VisualAge for Java development environment. In the next chapter, we look at one of the major challenges of complex applications: session state management.

CHAPTER 8

Session State Management

Using servlets in complex applications introduces some very interesting challenges to the developer. Possibly the biggest challenge is to maintain an identity with the users as they make multiple trips into your application. The information that is collected and maintained during these "trips" is often called *session data*. The distinction between session data and transaction data is that session data are temporary and for use only across a set of linked pages, whereas transaction data are placed in permanent storage. Session data are often converted into transaction data at various points in the application—for instance, when a user chooses to save profile information or to check out a shopping cart. The maintenance of this type of information creates challenges in our applications.

The first challenge comes from HTTP, used for communication between the Web browser and the Web server. As discussed in Chapter 4, HTTP is based on a request/response model and is stateless. A request is submitted from the client browser to a Web server, and the server acts on the request and sends a response back to the browser. The protocol has no intrinsic method for holding state information about the transaction itself after it is complete.

The second part to this problem comes from the way servlets live in the application server. On a particular application server, a single instance of each servlet class handles all GET and POST requests for its particular URL. In this environment, each HTTP request is handled on a unique thread running the service() method of that instance. Because each servlet instance is a shared resource, you can't effectively store the client session data in the servlet itself. The implication to the developer in this case is that there can be no maintenance of state information in the servlet itself or, more directly, no instance variables! If instance variables are used, there is no guarantee that the state is reliable at any given time. In this chapter, we explore the most common approaches to storing session data and look at the configuration options that are available in the WebSphere Application Server.

Some Client-Side Session Approaches

Before we begin to look at how WebSphere and the Servlet API provide specific support for session management, we need to review some of the existing solutions that Web sites use to convey session information. As we will see later, this discussion is very germane to understanding both how WebSphere's session management works and alternatives to the WebSphere solution.

Cookies

Probably the most common way to store session information in the CGI world is through the use of a cookie. Cookies can be used to send information gathered on the server to the client for storage. This is done by the server attaching information to the HTTP response headers. The browser will then automatically return the cookie on the next request by placing the information in the request header sent to the server. The browser maintains a collection of cookies and groups them by server. The browser will return all cookies that were obtained from a server only to the server from which they were obtained. In other words, a browser will never send a cookie to a server that did not create it.

It is important that cookies be used appropriately. Do not send to the browser cookies that contain sensitive information. It is not a good idea to store passwords, credit card numbers, date of birth, and so on in cookies. This information, if provided by a user, is best kept on the server. If we do not use cookies appropriately, we will not have the luxury of using them at all.

Hidden Fields

Another option for maintaining session data is through the use of hidden fields. This option is very simple to implement and involves the use of standard HTML hidden fields. This solution allows for session sharing between servlets that are linked through the use of HTML forms. Each servlet response that results in HTML form output should write additional input fields into the form. These additional fields should be defined with the type= "hidden" parameter. The net result of this is that the user will not see this field on the form, but the resulting GET or POST will send the value along as a request parameter. The servlet that processes the form information can then obtain the session data through the use of the passed parameters.

URL Parameters

Similar to the idea of hidden fields, information can also be transmitted from the browser to the server in the HTTP header by placing this information in parameters that are passed in as part of the URL that invokes a CGI or a servlet. For instance, if we wanted to pass a user name as part of a URL request, the URL passed to a servlet could look like the following:

http://myhost/servlet/com.ibm.test.TestServlet?userid="Bob Smith"

If this URL was sent from the browser, the target servlet ("TestServlet") could obtain the HTTP parameter named userid by using the HttpRequest. getParameter(name) method. Although URL parameters are useful for passing small pieces of information, they are not appropriate for passing larger sets of information, as there is a limit to the size of the URL.

Servlets and Session State

A framework for saving session state is provided in the Java Servlet API. The API provides an interface designed specifically for maintaining state information in servlet-based applications. This interface is the javax.servlet. http.HttpSession. The HttpSession interface provides a way to store and to manipulate state information that is available to all servlets of the Web application while the session remains valid. In practice, one session is maintained for each user who is interacting with the Web application. This session is established at a point in the application where some state information needs to be maintained, which is typically very early on in the process, such as at login or authentication time. As each session is created, it is assigned a unique identifier. This identifier is then associated with the user and becomes the key that can be used to locate the appropriate session for subsequent requests. The various configurations around which the session identifier can be maintained are discussed later in the chapter. After the session is established, it remains valid until it expires from inactivity, the browser is closed, or is invalidated programmatically. The period of inactivity can be configured in the WebSphere administration client or set programmatically.

The HttpSession interface provides the basic mechanisms for storing and retrieving application state information. First, an instance of an HttpSession must be obtained. This can be done through the HttpServletRequest interface. The interface method that needs to be used here is HttpSession getSession(boolean). The boolean argument, if true, creates a new session if one is not already present for the session ID associated with the request. Conversely, if the boolean argument is false, null will be returned if a session is not already established.

When obtaining a session by using HttpSession getSession(true), it is sometimes desirable to know whether the HttpSession that was returned was a newly created session or one that had been established by a previous call. This can be done by using the HttpSession interface method boolean isNew(). This method simply returns a boolean indicating whether the session ID was delivered in the current HttpServletRequest object.

It may also be desirable to discard a session. The HttpSession interface provides the method void invalidate() for this purpose. This method simply discards the session and gives the assurance that the next call to HttpSession getSession(true) will yield a new session.

The structure of this interface is very simple and can be used to store state data in key/value pairs. We can place objects in a session instance by using the void putValue(String, Object) method and can retrieve objects from the session by using the Object getValue(String). Note that more than one value can be placed in the session object. The HttpSession structure is similar to that of java.util.Hashtable in that any number of elements can be stored by a unique identifier.

In review, the methods of API we have discussed thus far are

- In HTTPRequest:
  ```
  public HTTPSession getSession( boolean param1 );
  ```
- In HTTPSession:
  ```
  public boolean isNew();
  public void invalidate();
  public java.lang.Object getValue(java.lang.String param1);
  public void putValue(java.lang.String param1, java.lang.Object param2);
  ```

(It should be noted that in the Servlet API v2.2, getValue() and putValue() are replaced by getAttribute() and setAttribute(), respectively.) The following example demonstrates the use of some of these methods. Let's say that we want to build an "EmployeeEditor" set of servlets that will allow you to change the attributes of an employee. The user would first enter an employee ID number on an HTML page, which would then be followed by an HTML page showing the current values of the employee's attributes in text fields that can be edited and resubmitted with new values. The first servlet invoked would be "DisplayEmployeeValues," and the code of its doPost() would look like the following:

```
// First servlet will retrieve employee values and place them in
// in the session
```

```
            public void doPost ( HttpServletRequest request,
                                 HttpServletResponse response )
                          throws ServletException, IOException {
        // Obtain the employee id from the parameter
        String id = request.getParameter ( "id" );
        Employee emp = Employee.getEmployeeFor(id)
        // Create a new session
        HttpSession session = request.getSession( true );
        // check to make sure session is new and
        // if a session already exists invalidate it and create again
        if( session.isNew() == false ){
              session.invalidate();
              session = request.getSession(true);
}
session.putValue( "employee", emp );
    // send a response back with a JSP page
    . . .
}
```

That code shows you how to

- Create a session. The true parameter in the getSession() method specifies to create a new session if one is not found in the request object.
- Check to make sure that the session is new.
- Add an object to the session, using a key/value pair.

Let's suppose now that the user has finished editing and now wishes to submit the changes. Clicking the *Submit* button invokes another servlet, which will process the changes. Following is some of the code to do this:

```
// Subsequent servlet being called to process changes to the Employee
public void doPost (
    HttpServletRequest request,
    HttpServletResponse response
    ) throws ServletException, IOException {

    // Look for an existing session
    HttpSession session = request.getSession( false );

    // check to see if session exists, if does not exist handle error
    if( session == null )
        handleError();
    else {
          Employee emp = ( Employee ) session.getValue( "employee" );
          if( emp != null ) {
              // Retrieve the values from the Http Parameters
              // and set them into the Employee instance.
              // Next update the employee in the database.
              // Finally invalidate the user session
              session.invalidate();
              }
```

```
    }
        // send a response
        . . .
}
```

Here, we see how to

- Get an existing session from the request object. The false parameter in the getSession() method specifies not to create a new session if one is not found in the request object. In that case, null is returned.
- Handle the error if the session does not exist.
- Retrieve an object from the session. The getValue() method return type is Object, so the value must be cast to the correct type before using it.

This example also shows invalidating the session. When you are finished using a session—for example, no more servlets will need the session—you should send invalidate() to the session to release the objects held in it. A session timeout value is set in the WebSphere administrator's console such that when the timeout is reached, the session will be invalidated, and all objects within it will be garbage-collected. However, invalidating the session manually is more efficient, because relying on session timeouts will result in objects remaining in memory unnecessarily long.

In addition to the methods used in the previous snippets, the HttpSession interface defines methods to remove a particular name/value pair and to obtain all the names of the values stored in the session. These methods are void removeValue(String) and String[] getValueNames(), respectively.

HttpSession *Binding*

Sometimes, objects may need to be notified when they are stored in or removed from the session. This may be to get an opportunity to do some initialization, cleanup, or another function. Objects requiring this function should implement the HttpSessionBindingListener interface found in the javax.servlet.http package. This interface defines the valueBound() and the valueUnbound() methods. These methods, when implemented, will be called when an object of this type is *put* or *removed* from the session, respectively. Implementing the interface in this way allows for fine-grain control over what happens as a result of storing and removing objects from a session.

How the Session Is Found

So, now that you've seen how the HttpSession API is used, how does it work? When the HttpServletRequest.getSession() method is called, the application

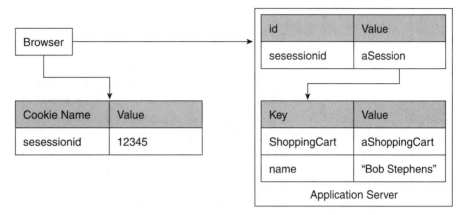

Figure 8.1 HttpSession Lookup Architecture

server determines which HttpSession instance belongs to a particular user by assigning a *session identifier,* which is stored in a special cookie in the user's browser. For sessions to work with the default settings, cookies must be enabled in the browser. Session cookies are not stored persistently and expire when the browser is closed. The HttpSession instances themselves are initially held in memory in an application server's JVM. Only the identifier is stored in the client browser (Figure 8.1).

Retrieving a Session Identifier

The use of cookies provides the simplest approach for maintaining session identifiers. However, although it may be the easiest solution, it is not always the most reliable solution, as you cannot always depend on the cookies being available. This forces the consideration of alternative methods for session management. In order to truly provide the most flexible solutions possible, you must look at providing multiple opportunities for the users to obtain unique sessions.

A popular way to achieve this is to combine techniques in order to obtain the most reliable coverage. The topic of discussion here will be using URL rewriting in conjunction with cookies to provide the most scalable and reliable site possible. The good news in this scenario is that as long as cookies are enabled in the client browser, they will be the vehicle for transporting the session identifier between the browser and the server. This is good news because this technique is very efficient and easy to implement. The bad news, however, is that there must be preparation for the case in which cookies are not available. That is where URL rewriting becomes a useful option.

URL Rewriting

An alternative to using cookies to store the session ID is to use a mechanism called *URL encoding,* or *URL rewriting.* In order to use URL encoding, you need to use the encodeURL() or the encodeRedirectURL() method of the HttpResponse interface. The encodeURL() method is used to append the unique session ID to the URL in any links that your servlet generates. The encodeRedirectURL() method does the same and is used in conjunction with the callRedirect() method. When a user invokes a servlet using this altered URL, the server strips the extra information from the URL and uses it as the session ID to get the session data. The application server must support URL rewriting, and you must also enable that option, when appropriate.

Typically, it is thought that using URL rewriting techniques degrades performance of the Web site across the board. Although this may be a valid argument if you are simply comparing it to the use of cookies, it certainly lacks credibility when you are thinking about the possibility of storing large amounts of data in a back-end data source. Furthermore, the WebSphere Application Server provides some help in this area.

The implementation of session management in WebSphere allows for both options to be configured. In addition, when cookies are enabled in the browser, all subsequent calls to encodeURL(String) are in essence not performed. The method itself results in no operation, thereby removing the performance degradation. As application developers, we have the best of both worlds: the ability to plan for the worst-case scenario while not adversely affecting our performance when the best-case scenario is available.

Third-Tier Session Storage

Up to this point, the discussions of session management have focused mostly on an in-memory storage solution. When HttpSessions are stored in memory, it is very efficient to get to an individual HttpSession instance when it is needed. However, this mechanism becomes a major complication when we need to scale our application to handle more users and we begin using more than one server running the same servlet application. Figure 8.2 illustrates a common setup for a high-traffic Web site.

In most high-traffic Web sites, the total volume of incoming HTTP requests is too great for a single application server to handle. So, a router— either a hardware router or a software router, such as IBM's SecureWay Dispatcher—is used to divide the incoming HTTP requests among a number of application servers. Which server will handle each particular request is chosen by a routing algorithm, such as round-robin routing or random routing. This routing among application servers affects how our application needs to manage session data.

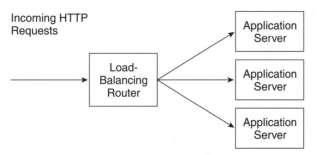

Figure 8.2   Load-Balancing Configuration: Requests Routed to Application Servers

If HttpSessions are stored in memory only on the server that the HttpSession is created on, that server must receive *all* succeeding requests from that client. This requirement is called *server affinity*. This session information will not be available to the servlets running in the other application servers. For some Web sites, server affinity may not pose a problem. However, the way in which routers determine server affinity can pose problems in higher-volume Web sites.

In many routers, a client is assigned to a particular application server by examining the IP addresses on the incoming request and always assigning requests from a particular client address to a particular server. However, the reality of today's Internet is that many Internet service providers (ISPs) have proxy configurations that make it appear to the router that all packets from that ISP are coming from the same IP address. In the worst case, for example, this means that all packets from America Online (AOL), which may make up well over 60 percent of your site's traffic, will end up at the same application server. This defeats the purpose of load balancing, as one server will still end up with the lion's share of the processing. Also, many corporations now assign outgoing IP addresses randomly, so that two requests from the same client are not guaranteed to have the same IP address. In this case, server affinity cannot be guaranteed.

Server affinity may be acceptable for sites that run on very few machines and also where it is acceptable that users may lose their sessions, but it is not normally acceptable. Many router products implement another alternative, content-based routing (CBR), which involves the router software examining the contents of the HTTPRequest to determine which server IP address to route a request to. For instance, an application may place a cookie having a specific value on the user's browser. The cookie value will be examined by the router, which will then route the HTTPRequests for the generating application server back to that server machine. The problem with the CBR solution is that it does not provide for failover. If session data is only in memory, even though requests can be properly rerouted to the generating application server, if that server fails, the set of users being supported by that application server will no longer be able to access their sessions. Also, the current implementation of content-based routing in many products is too slow to be acceptable for many applications.

WebSphere Persistent Session Storage

So, now we see the need to examine how WebSphere solves the problem of server affinity in its HttpSession implementation. The basic solution is the same as how it works with WebSphere's in-memory HttpSession solution. The client-side userid can be used to look up the larger set of data (HttpSessions) needed to join the individual requests together into a coherent application. The difference is that instead of the larger set being held entirely in memory in a single JVM, the set of HttpSessions is instead stored in a third-tier relational database that can be shared by multiple JVMs.

Shared HttpSessions in WebSphere 3.x operate like this: Each use of an HttpSession is a transaction onto a third-tier database. The transaction begins when the HttpServletRequest.getSession() method is called. The transaction ends either at the end of the servlet's service() method or when the special method sync() is called on the class that implements HttpSession in WebSphere.

Figure 8.3 shows the basic outline of how shared HttpSessions work in WebSphere. Note that this is a high-level description of the roles involved, not a description of the way in which the classes function.

As noted in Figure 8.3, the process begins at the getSession() method, where WebSphere's implementation classes begin a database transaction on the shared session database and then retrieve the value of the cookie—called sessionid—used to store the globally unique session ID. The database transaction then uses this session ID to find the appropriate row in the shared session database and retrieves a long binary—or BLOB (binary large object)—column from that row. That column contains, in binary form, the serialized HttpSession implementation object that corresponds to the session ID. WebSphere then deserializes the HttpSession object and returns it to the requesting servlet.

The servlet can then get and set values into the HTTP session. The client transaction remains open until either the sync() method is called or the servlet's service() method ends. In either case, the HttpSession object is serialized back onto the BLOB column in the database row, and then the transaction is committed.

Using WebSphere session storage has some ramifications. First, the amount of user data you can place in any session object has some hard limits.

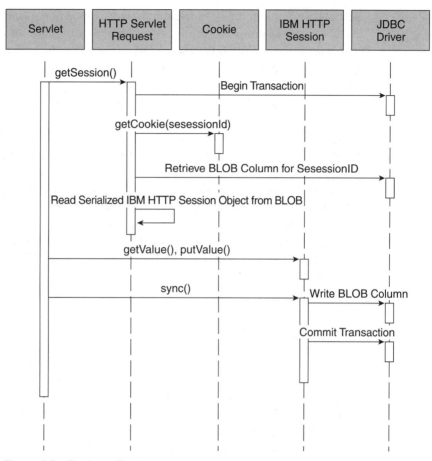

Figure 8.3 Persistent Sessions

The implementation of WebSphere's session storage mechanism can store a maximum of 32K in each row in DB2, where it uses a long varchar data type, and 2MB in Oracle. This means that your HttpSessions can contain no more than this amount of data in each respective database. WebSphere supports another option, called *multirow access,* in which each entry in the HttpSession is stored in its own row, but the total size for each entry still remains the same: 32K and 2MB, respectively.

However, long before you reach this limit, your application performance will probably dictate that you pick a different mechanism for session data or store less data in the HttpSession. In fact, performance studies have shown that the maximum size that an HttpSession can be before it takes too long to marshal and unmarshal into the database is somewhere between 2K and 4K. As a result, you should carefully consider what you place into the HttpSession; don't store everything in your application there. Instead, take a balanced approach, putting only the most frequently accessed data in the HttpSession and placing keys to other data there.

You must also be careful about how you manipulate objects in the session. In this model, if you make changes to an object held in a session, you will need to notify the session of the change by placing it back in the session with putValue(). Some subtle bugs can arise here between development and testing. The getValue() method returns a reference to a real object held in memory. Any changes made to those objects directly modify the object in the session. If you are testing in VisualAge or against a single WebSphere JVM, changes made to the session by modifying the objects contained in it will appear to work. However, those changes are not recorded into the session database unless you send putValue() to the session. Therefore, other WebSphere Application Server JVMs will not be able to retrieve the new value.

Other Session Storage Options

If you cannot use WebSphere's session storage mechanism for either size or speed reasons, the approach it takes can certainly be taken in your own code. You could use either JDBC or SQLJ to store your sessions in nonBLOB fields. This means that you would need to map a database schema to your session data. You could not just serialize your objects. Instead, you would need to write your own marshalling routines to flatten and to rehydrate your session data.

This approach is relatively simple to implement and for most cases is fairly efficient. However, it relies on JDBC to perform the storage and retrieval of the session information. This solution will work fine as long as you have a JDBC driver to the datastore of your choice, but if you want to move the data elsewhere, you will be forced to search for another solution.

Another desirable solution is moving your session data in and out through the use of EJBs. You could effectively store the identifier of an Entity EJBs in a cookie or rewritten URL and then always find the appropriate EJB to retrieve the state. This could potentially provide a more scalable solution, as it does not necessarily depend on JDBC and could use other data sources, such as CICS, to store the session data. However, as the session data becomes more complex, this solution can become problematic, as navigating EJB associations can be expensive. An in-depth discussion of EJBs begins in Chapter 13.

Configuring WebSphere 3.5 Session Support

As one would expect, the WebSphere Application Server provides tools to support the configuration and management of the parameters around which it maintains session information. As with all configuration parameters in WebSphere, this is done through the WebSphere administrator's console.

The basis of configuration centers on a concept called the *session manager,* the object that maintains all the user settings and that is responsible for starting and stopping session-related activities in the application server. The session manager is created automatically during creation of each servlet engine, and a default session manager exists that can be used immediately.

Session management is configured in the *WebSphere Administrative Console* window. Select *Session Manager* under the servlet engine you wish to configure. Five sections of information can be configured.

The Enable *Section*

The *Enable* section, located under *Session Manager,* should be configured first. If you have navigated to the appropriate place, you should see something similar to Figure 8.4.

Several options can be configured on the *Enable* tab. The first and most important is the option *Enable Sessions*. In order to use sessions, this option must be set to *Yes*.

Moving down, you have the option to enable cookies and/or URL rewriting. As we discussed earlier, the configuration of these two items denotes how you wish the session manager to track the session identifier. If you enable cookies, this will be the default, preferred way for the session manager to perform session tracking. If cookies are disabled at any level, URL rewriting can be used to perform this task.

The *Enable* tab also provides the option *Enable Protocol Switch Rewriting*. This option enables the passing of the session identifier on URLs when switching protocols, such as from HTTP to HTTPS.

Finally, you can configure the session manager to persist sessions for maintenance beyond the lifetime of the server itself. This is valuable if you wish to restart the application server while users are interacting with your application. If *Enable Persistent Sessions* is set to *Yes,* session data will be stored in a configurable database for each session transaction.

The Cookies *Section*

The next configurable section is on the *Cookies* tab. As shown in Figure 8.5, this tab has parameters related to how cookies are used in the session

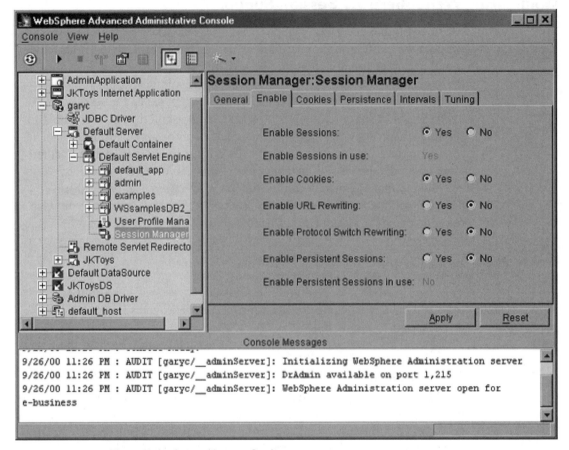

Figure 8.4 *Session Manager* Configuration

manager. The first entry field allows you to specify the name of the cookie that will be sent to the client browser. The default value for this field is *sesessionid*, which if changed should be set to something you can be confident will be unique. Along with the cookie name, a comment can be set here as well. This information may be valuable to the owner of the browser if he or she wishes to see what cookies are being managed and what their purpose is. In no way does the comment affect the performance of maintenance or cookie information in the WebSphere Application Server.

Moving downward, the next field you will encounter is labeled *Cookie Domain*. This field specifies the domain of a session cookie. If you place a value in this field, that value will modify the domain to which the cookie will be sent. This is useful in a clustered server environment to allow the cookie to be sent to any of the servers.

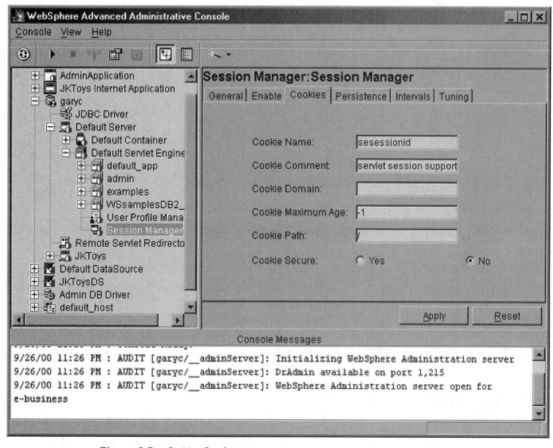

Figure 8.5 *Cookies* Configuration

The next field, *Cookie Maximum Age,* permits the specification of how long a cookie should live on the client browser. This setting is specified in milliseconds and corresponds to the *time to live* value established in the cookie specification. If the value is set to −1, all cookies will be maintained only until the browser is closed.

The *Cookie Path* field can be used to further restrict when a cookie will be sent to a host. This parameter allows you to specify which paths on the host the cookie should be sent to. This allows you to keep the cookie from being sent to certain paths on the server, for example certain servlets or JSPs. If the value is set to the root directory, the cookie will be sent to every request to the server. This is the default and is signified by a blank or a /.

The last setting of the *Cookies* tab is for specifying the *Cookie Secure* option. If this value is set to *Yes,* cookies will be sent only for sessions established over HTTPS.

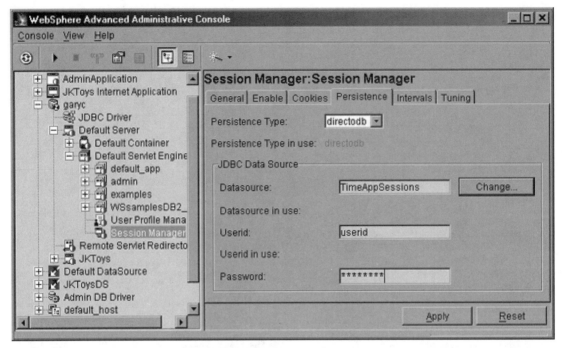

Figure 8.6   JDBC *Persistence* Configuration

The Persistence *Section*

The next tab is used to specify options for persistence of sessions and is enabled only if you set the *Enable Persistent Sessions* to *Yes*. The first option to decide on here is labeled *Persistent Type*. This field has two options: *directodb* and *ejb*. The *directodb* option signifies direct to database. The *ejb* option is intended for use in accessing an HttpSession outside the scope of a servlet. The remaining parameters specify the data source to use to store persistent sessions.

The Intervals *Section*

This section is very brief, containing only one configurable parameter, *Invalidate Time*. This field simply indicates the number of seconds a session remains unused before it is invalidated or removed. This field should be chosen carefully, as you do not want sessions to remain active for longer than makes sense for your application, as this consumes server resources. However, you do not want to invalidate sessions that a user has just left inactive for a period of time but intends to use again, as you will

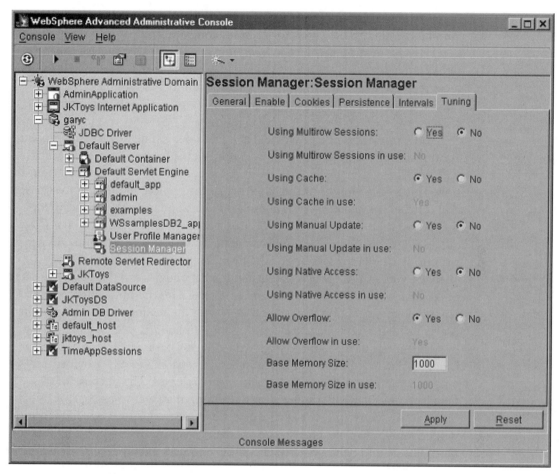

Figure 8.7 *Tuning* Parameters

force the user to reestablish a session. A value of −1 indicates that the session will never be invalidated. The default for this field is 1,800 seconds, or 30 minutes.

The *Tuning* Section

Finally, the *Tuning* tab (Figure 8.7) contains configuration parameters that allow for performance tuning of the persistence options related to session management. The first configurable field, *Using Multirow Sessions,* indicates whether to place each instance of application data in a separate row in the database or to use the same row for all application data. If this value is set to *Yes,* each such instance will use multiple rows, which results in larger amounts of data to be stored for each session.

The next field on the page is *Using Cache.* Setting the value of this field to *Yes* indicates that you want to maintain a memory-resident session for the most recently accessed entities, reducing the number of database accesses needed during normal session tracking. This option is used only if the *directodb* type is selected.

The *Using Manual Update* field is used to determine how session updates are transferred to the database. By default, WebSphere updates the database with any changes made to the session at the conclusion of the session transaction. This transaction begins at the entry of the service() method of the servlet and concludes when service() is completed. This update includes specifying the time of the change and the application data itself. If *Using Manual Update* is set to *Yes,* WebSphere will cache the time of the change and will persist during checks for session invalidation. To persist application data changes, you, as the application writer, must manually call the sync() method of com.ibm.websphere.servlet.session.IBMSession. This method spurs the persistence of any application data maintained with the session itself. This option is also valid only if *Persistence Type* is set to *directodb.*

This brings us up to the *Using Native Access* parameter. This parameter is not used in WebSphere Application Server version 3 and is provided here only as a preview of things to come in future releases. The purpose of this field is to indicate that you wish for the session manager to use native JNI-based SQL written in C to execute persistence session operations. This option will be valid only if the persistence database is configured to be a DB/2 database. The default behavior is to use JDBC to access and update persistent session information.

The next field, *Allow Overflow,* ties closely to the last configurable field on the tab, *Base Memory Size* and is used to specify whether to allow the number of sessions in memory to exceed the value specified by *Base Memory Size,* which indicates the number of sessions you wish to be maintained in memory. If *Enable Persistent Sessions* is set to *No,* this value specifies the number of sessions allowed.

The default configuration for in-memory sessions is specified by *Base Memory Size.* If you don't want to limit the number of sessions, set the *Allow Overflow* value to *Yes.* Although this achieves what you want in terms of allowing an unlimited number of sessions, it opens up potential opportunities for things to go wrong. The first but not least of these things is the chance of consuming all system memory while allocating session space. If an unlimited number of sessions is possible, you run the risk of creating more sessions than you have memory to support. Furthermore, there is a risk of a malicious person programmatically creating sessions until resources are consumed and your application server locks up.

In contrast, the behavior when persisting sessions is that the value of *Base Memory Size* indicates the size of the cache, as well as the amount of updates that are saved when *Using Manual Update* is set to *Yes*. When the number is exceeded, no more sessions are cached and are sent to the database automatically.

The default value of *Base Memory Size* is 1,000. Increasing the value should be done only with careful consideration to the memory constraints of the server and the stack setting of the JVM.

Summary and Preview

In this chapter, we examined the basics of servlet session management. We compared some traditional approaches from the CGI world and saw how WebSphere, Advanced Edition implements the HttpSession interface. This should prepare you to understand some of the more challenging problems that face developers in building applications that must scale across multiple-node and multiple-JVM configurations in WebSphere. Those considerations in servlet design are the focus of Chapter 9.

CHAPTER 9
Servlet Design Considerations

When designing large-scale applications based on Java servlets, many design options need to be considered. Each design decision you make should ultimately enhance the reliability and the scalability of the application as a whole. Furthermore, you should always strive to reduce the complexity of the application and ease the maintenance process. This chapter focuses on a few simple design considerations that can help you achieve some of these goals.

Number of Servlets

The number of servlets you implement can affect several of the stated goals of an effective Web-based application. The design decision here is to determine how many servlets are necessary to most effectively implement an application. Although the answer may seem obvious to some Web programmers, it is certainly not readily apparent to new programmers coming from a traditional windowed user interface background. To begin with, let's examine a simple but often effective approach. To do so, we have to first review the role of the servlet in a layered architecture to understand why this is often a useful approach. We then examine an alternative approach that also has a great deal of merit.

Recall from the discussion of five-layer architecture in Chapter 3 the controller/mediator layer, which is responsible for separating the presentation of information from the domain, or model, that holds the information. The motivation behind this separation is generally to allow more flexibility and reuse when creating or changing the views or presentation or when making changes to the domain layer of the application. Moreover, applying a layered architecture in this fashion allows for a particular domain to be used more flexibly across multiple applications. With this in mind, the servlets that we write in a Web-based application fall into the controller layer of the architecture. Servlets are responsible for taking parameters passed from the presentation layer, contacting the appropriate business logic classes, and passing the processing on to them and then taking the results from those classes and routing the user to the next appropriate screen.

So, taking this into account, what is an appropriate division of labor between servlets? Perhaps the simplest approach is to examine your system's *Go* buttons: the HTML buttons that either submit a form or do a GET on a URL and all links that name servlets. Each unique *Go* button that performs a unique function should have its own servlet. If two or more buttons refer to the same function and have the same set of parameters—or one is a subset of the other—the two buttons can refer to the same servlet URL.

In this respect, a servlet is acting as a filter in a pipes-and-filters architecture [Buschmann]. Data come in, are processed, and go out in a different form. Think about each servlet as filtering a different data stream. Just as you wouldn't attempt to use the same filter to clean both the air and the oil in your car, you wouldn't want to process multiple data streams through the same filter. In this context, you can see why you would want a different servlet, or filter, for each set of input data, or data stream.

Each *Go* button represents one of two things:

- An individual function request to present some data, such as an HTTP GET
- A request to process a particular data stream, such as a set of HTTP parameters from the URL or POST parameters from an HTML form

In the first case, you would want a unique servlet to perform that function in order to determine what set of information the user was requesting. In the second case, the fact that each form or set of HTTP parameters passed on a URL represents a different data stream—with a different format, such as a set of parameters and values—would indicate that you would want a different filter for that data stream and thus a unique servlet.

This is the approach we use in the case study (Chapter 12). You can identify the servlets needed by looking at the links and the HTML forms in your application and then looking for the actions triggered by these forms and links. For instance, an obvious example of this in our case study is "MakeApprovedServlet," triggered from the JSP that displays a list of pending time sheets that have not yet been approved. When a time sheet is chosen for approval, the link invokes this servlet, passing in the information necessary to identify the particular time sheet.

However, as simple and effective as this approach is, it is not always the most appropriate choice. With the role of the servlet clearly defined as a control mechanism in the application, we can quickly identify a very abstract role that it fills. You might even say that every servlet in an application follows a similar design, or pattern. Specifically, the role of the servlet is to take a request made over HTTP, extract any arguments that were passed, initiate a process that is specific to the request, and provide dynamic results based on the processing that was performed. The results returned could fall into one of three types: returning HTML directly, forwarding the request on to a JSP, or redirecting the request on to a new page.

With this said, you can make a valid argument for having only *one* servlet in an application handle all requests and pass the real processing off to a helper class. This argument is strongly based on the fact that each call to a servlet results in a very nearly identical set of processing. Again, the real difference is in the processing that is performed and the results that are returned, but it follows a very simplistic pattern. Here, the key lies in identifying a unique controller for a particular request and can be easily accomplished by using a polymorphic set of controllers, along with the Abstract Factory pattern from [Gamma].

The benefits of using this design technique are twofold. The first benefit is the ability to add new functions to your application without requiring reconfiguration of the application server. This is possible because new functions are not defined in individual servlets but rather by implementing a simple interface or extending an abstract controller class. The second benefit stems from the first and is simply that work is not duplicated between classes; rather, it is leveraged through a simple abstraction. This will ultimately make your applications more extensible and easier to maintain. To understand how this works, let's take a look at some sample code.

The first thing to examine is the concrete servlet implementation. Remember that this servlet will be the only one in our application and must provide a very generic interface for processing HTTP requests and returning customized responses. Let's look at the public and protected method source and then discuss the rest of the interface.

```java
import java.io.*;
import javax.servlet.*;
import javax.servlet.http.*;
import java.util.*;

public class HttpMethodServlet extends BaseServlet {

    public void doGet(HttpServletRequest request, HttpServletResponse
    response) throws ServletException, IOException {
        processRequest( request, response );
    }
    public void doPost(HttpServletRequest request, HttpServletResponse
    response) throws ServletException, IOException {
```

```
      processRequest( request, response );
   }
   protected void handle(Throwable aThrowable, HttpServletRequest request,
   HttpServletResponse response) throws ServletException, IOException {
       RequestDispatcher dispatcher =
   getServletContext().getRequestDispatcher( "error.html" );
       dispatcher.forward( request, response );
   }
}
```

Note that the HttpMethodServlet extends BaseServlet. As you can see, both the doGet() and the doPost() methods simply call a method called process Request(request, response). This private method is shown next.

```
private void processRequest( HttpServletRequest request, HttpServletResponse
response ) throws ServletException, IOException {
   HttpController controller = getHttpController( request, response );
   controller.process();
}
```

As mentioned, this solution uses a unique controller for processing the specific application function. The processRequest() method implies two things. The first is that through the request parameters, you must be able to distinguish the specific controller that needs to be created. This is possible by passing a simple HTTP argument that specifies the application function. Also, the visitor must be expressible as a type named HttpController. The method getHttpController() gives an example of how this can work in the following code.

```
private HttpController getHttpController( HttpServletRequest request,
HttpServletResponse response ) throws ServletException, IOException {
   String controllerClassName = request.getParameter( "CONTROLLER" );
   Class controllerClass = null;
   HttpController instance = null;
   try {
       controllerClass = Class.forName( controllerClassName );
   }
   catch( ClassNotFoundException cnfe ) {
       handle( cnfe, request, response );
   }
   try {
       instance = ( HttpController ) controllerClass.newInstance();
       instance.setRequest( request );
       instance.setResponse( response );
       instance.setServletContext( getServletContext() );
   }
   catch( InstantiationException ie ) {
       handle( ie, request, response );
   }
   catch( IllegalAccessException iae ) {
       handle( iae, request, response );
```

```
        }
        instance.setArguments( getArguments( request ) );
        return instance;
    }
```

The first point of interest in this method is the processing of an HTTP request parameter named controller. The string representation represents the fully qualified class name of the application class that will be instantiated. With closer inspection, you will see that the controllerClassName local variable is used to load a class that is eventually instantiated by using the Class::newInstance() method. In this case, this method is acting as in the Abstract Factory pattern, creating new polymorphic controllers from the information passed in on the HTTP request. Before this new instance of the controller is returned, you see that it has all the request arguments applied to it. This is done as follows:

```
    private Hashtable getArguments( HttpServletRequest request ) {
        Hashtable args = new Hashtable();
        String key = null;
        Enumeration paramNames = request.getParameterNames();
        while( paramNames.hasMoreElements() ) {
            key = ( String ) paramNames.nextElement();
            args.put( key, request.getParameter( key ) );
        }
        return args;
    }
```

That brings us to defining the HttpController interface. This interface is intended to define the methods available to handle the generic servlet operations we defined earlier. This interface (Listing 9.1) is lengthy but should be fairly easy to understand.

Listing 9.1 The HttpController interface.

```
import javax.servlet.http.*;
import javax.servlet.*;
import java.util.*;
import java.io.*;

public interface HttpController {
    void forward( String aPage ) throws javax.servlet.ServletException,
java.io.IOException;
    String getArgument( String aString );
    Hashtable getArguments();
    HttpSession getNewSession();
    HttpServletResponse getResponse();
    ServletContext getServletContext();
    HttpSession getSession();
    void process() throws ServletException, IOException;
    void redirect( String aPage ) throws ServletException, IOException;
    void setArguments( Hashtable args );
```

```
        void setRequest( HttpServletRequest aRequest );
        void setResponse( HttpServletResponse aResponse );
        void setServletContext(ServletContext aContext);
        void writeHTML( String someHTML ) throws ServletException, IOException;
}
```

Let's briefly examine the key points of this interface. It defines method interfaces for getting and setting the HttpServletRequest and the HttpServletResponse. The interface also defines a controller entry point named process(). The other methods worthy of special mention are the three response interface methods: forward(String), writeHTML(String), and redirect(String). These three methods give us the interface to the three most commonly used response mechanisms.

Finally, let's look at how this interface might be implemented in a real situation. One way is to provide a default implementation of the HttpController interface. This could be done in an application-specific manner or in a more abstract manner that would support multiple applications. Listing 9.2 shows the latter.

Listing 9.2 Abstract default implementation of HttpController.

```
import java.io.*;
import java.util.*;
import javax.servlet.*;
import javax.servlet.http.*;
import com.wsbook.servlet.pattern.*;

public abstract class BaseHttpController implements HttpController {

    public Hashtable arguments;
    protected HttpServletRequest request;
    protected HttpServletResponse response;
    protected ServletContext servletContext;

    public void forward( String aPage ) throws ServletException, IOException
    {
        RequestDispatcher dispatcher =
getServletContext().getRequestDispatcher( aPage );
        dispatcher.forward( getRequest(), getResponse() );
    }

    public String getArgument(String aString) {
        return ( String ) getArguments().get( aString );
    }
    public Hashtable getArguments() {
        return arguments;
    }

    public HttpSession getNewSession() {
        HttpSession session = getRequest().getSession( true );
```

```
        if( !session.isNew() ) {
           session.invalidate();
           session = getRequest().getSession( true );
        }

        return session;
    }

    public javax.servlet.http.HttpServletRequest getRequest() {
        return request;
    }

    public javax.servlet.http.HttpServletResponse getResponse() {
        return response;
    }

    public javax.servlet.ServletContext getServletContext() {
        return servletContext;
    }

    public HttpSession getSession() {
        return getRequest().getSession( true );
    }

    public void redirect( String aPage ) throws ServletException, IOException
    {
        getResponse().sendRedirect( aPage );
    }

    public void setArguments( Hashtable args ) {
        arguments = args;
    }

    public void setRequest( HttpServletRequest newRequest ) {
        request = newRequest;
    }

    public void setResponse( HttpServletResponse newResponse ) {
        response = newResponse;
    }

    public void setServletContext(javax.servlet.ServletContext
    newServletContext) {
        servletContext = newServletContext;
    }

    public void writeHTML( String someHTML ) throws ServletException,
    IOException {
        getResponse().setContentType( "text/html" );
        PrintWriter out = getResponse().getWriter();
        out.println( someHTML );
    }
}
```

This class simply gives a default implementation for the HttpController interface. Note that the HTTP request and response arguments are held as instance variables in the class. This allows for the processing of the current function without the need to continually pass these references around. Similarly, the servletContext is held in an instance variable to give access to the Request Dispatcher when forwarding the request on to another page. This can be seen in the forward(String) method, in which a RequestDispatcher is obtained and the request forwarded on the aPage. This provides you with the basis for creating application-specific classes. Merely as an illustration, let's look at few examples.

The first example demonstrates the ability to write simple HTML back to the client in response. The process() method expects an argument called NAME and simply writes the response, using the abstract writeHTML(String) method. This is not a recommended approach to transporting responses back to the client and is shown here only for illustrative purposes.

```
import com.wsbook.servlet.pattern.*;
import javax.servlet.http.*;
import javax.servlet.*;
import java.util.*;
import java.io.*;

public class HTMLExampleController extends BaseHttpController {

public HTMLExampleController() {
   super();
}

public void process() throws ServletException, IOException {
   String name = getArgument( "NAME" );
   writeHTML( "Hello " + name );
}
}
```

The next example performs some processing and then forwards the request on to a JSP for presentation. This is generally the recommended approach to providing the response to the request. Setting up your application in this way gives you the most flexibility for modifying the various layers of the application.

```
import com.wsbook.servlet.pattern.*;
import javax.servlet.http.*;
import javax.servlet.*;
import java.util.*;
import java.io.*;

public class JspExampleController extends BaseHttpController {

public JspExampleController() {
   super();
```

```
        }

        public void process() throws ServletException, IOException {
            String page = getArgument( "PAGETOCALL" );
            forward( page );
        }
        }
```

The final example shows how to redirect the client by using the HTTP redirect method. This is generally done when processing an error condition. Once again, note that this functionality is implemented abstractly and simply taken advantage of in this concrete class.

```
        import com.wsbook.servlet.pattern.*;
        import javax.servlet.http.*;
        import javax.servlet.*;
        import java.util.*;
        import java.io.*;

        public class RedirectionExampleController extends BaseHttpController {

        public RedirectionExampleController() {
            super();
        }

        public void process() throws ServletException, IOException {
            redirect( getArgument( "REDIRECTPAGE" ) );
        }
        }
```

In conclusion, it is important to note the subtle differences between this design pattern and what has been the traditional servlet approach. Traditionally, the number of application functions being supported has determined the number of servlets in an application. In other words, if you need to be able to handle login requests and user profile update requests, you would implement a servlet for each function and configure the application server to recognize both servlets. This solution simply classifies application functions as controllers created in a standard abstract servlet that has the ability to process them abstractly. This provides the ability to add, change, and delete functionality in the application server without the need to administer the configuration of the server itself.

One final advantage of this design is that it makes thread safety less of an issue in servlet development. Because each controller is created individually and will be used only by a single thread, you need not be as careful with thread-safety issues as you must be when the servlet is acting as the controller. This alone is often enough to make developers, especially those who are uncomfortable with multithreaded programming, choose this approach. (However, you still must be careful to consider the use of any shared resources accessed by these controllers.) Although we have not specifically shown the source code for this, it should be noted that this is the design approach used in the Apache *struts* framework. Rather than reimplementing this behavior, we would encourage you to investigate using a pre-buit framework like struts.

State Pattern

One of the principal functions of the controller is to determine the correct application behavior for an incoming client request given the current state of the application. Perhaps the incoming request is to place an order for the items in the current shopping cart. If the shopping cart is populated, the behavior is to create an order and to prompt for payment information. If, on the other hand, the current client session does not contain a shopping cart, as would be the case if the client went directly to a placeOrder bookmark bypassing the shopping activities, alternative behavior is required.

Thus, the controller needs to maintain the application state, include selection logic to respond to requests based on this state, and update the application state as a result of the actions completed. In most Web-based applications, the application state will be represented through values stored in the HttpSession, in hidden fields, and/or in cookies. This state information could be described as indirect state. For complex applications, the controller cannot reasonably interrogate individual state values to determine the appropriate behavior. The better approach is to represent the state directly.

This is where the State design pattern from [Gamma] can be used (Figure 9.1). Each discrete state in the application's state machine is represented by a class, and each class implements a common interface that will define each action—request— as methods. At all times, a single state object is associated with the client's application state. The controller's behavior in response to an incoming request is to obtain the current state object and to invoke the corresponding action method on the state object. Embodied in this method will be the appropriate application behavior for the current request given the current

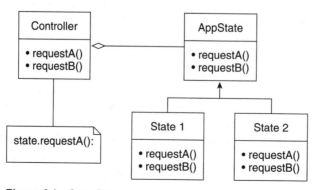

Figure 9.1   State Pattern

application state. Further, each method in each state will update the application's current state object, on completion of the request, to appropriately represent the application state transition.

The key advantage of this approach is very robust applications. You can easily code to ensure that all requests are handled appropriately given the current application state. This is important, as there is little in the way of synchronization between the client view and the server state, given that they are communicating over a stateless request/response protocol (HTTP).

The principal disadvantage of this approach is that a new service (request) results in a new method on the State interface and must therefore now be handled in all State objects. Careful implementation through the use of inheritance that matches substate relationships can minimize this maintenance problem.

Exception Handling

One of the key elements of delivering reliable software is the ability to recover gracefully from unexpected application errors. In Web-based applications, this is key because you do not want the users of your application to see unpleasant HTTP error returns in their browsers. Users who do not understand the meaning of HTTP error codes may be confused.

To ensure that these kinds of errors never reach the client browser, we must have a mechanism in place to intercept any potential application exceptions that are not expected. The following discussion, although brief, provides a simple and straightforward solution to this problem in a way that does not use any application server–specific features. Later, we will examine some WebSphere-specific solutions to the same problem. Which approach you choose is largely a matter of personal preference and concern for portability.

The basis for this solution is an abstract servlet that serves as the root for all your application servlets. This servlet class should be the place where you will implement common behavior across all the servlets in an application. In this case, part of the common behavior is the ability to handle all uncaught exceptions generically. This has proved to be a convenient way to keep the users of your Web-based applications from ever seeing the result of an unexpected server exception. These exceptions, if left unhandled, result in an HTTP Error 500 that is unpleasant and confusing for the user, because it only says "Internal Server Error," giving no indication of what went wrong or why.

```java
import java.io.*:
import javax.servlet.*;
import javax.servlet.http.*;
public abstract class BaseServlet extends HttpServlet {
    public final void service ( HttpServletRequest request, HttpServletResponse
    response ) throws ServletException, IOException {
```

```
try {
    super.service( request, response );
}
catch( Throwable aThrowable ) {
    handle( aThrowable, request, response );
}
}
protected abstract void handle( Throwable aThrowable, HttpServletRequest
request, HttpServletResponse response ) throws ServletException,
IOException;
}
```

The implication of this solution is that extensions of this servlet must not override the service() method, as this will short-circuit the exception-handling functionality. This usually proves to be acceptable, as you usually override specific HTTP request methods, such as doGet() or doPost().

Note also that the handle() method is abstract. This simply means that concrete servlets extending "BaseServlet" must provide an implementation for handling exceptions, which allows for application-specific exception handling. The handle() method in each subclass would probably return a simple error page to the user, indicating what error occurred and providing instructions on how to proceed.

Now that you have seen a generic solution to this problem, we can look at WebSphere-specific solutions. The first solution to examine is the simplest, the one used by the default application—a Web application installed as part of the default server—in WebSphere and thus the WTE in VisualAge. Both of these environments handle errors by directing them to a specific servlet named "ErrorReporter." This servlet will produce a simple error page consisting of an error code, an error message, and then a stack trace of the exception. To use this error page in your own Web applications, which is useful for debugging, you must define a servlet named "ErrorReporter" with the servlet class com.ibm.servlet.engine.webapp.DefaultErrorReporter in your Web application. You must then define the error page in your application to point to the new servlet; for example, the error page must be set to /ErrorReporter.

If you use the "ErrorReporter" servlet, you can take advantage of two error-handling methods in the Servlet API. The Servlet API methods sendError(int) and sendError(int,String) can be used to set the error code and message in the default WebSphere error page.

Although the default error page is useful for debugging and for application development, it is not the kind of error page you want to display to your users. The general solution to this problem is to take advantage of the WebSphere error page feature that will route errors to any named JSP. As long as you have a page compiler for either JSP 0.91 or JSP 1.0 configured in your Web application, you may place a JSP in the error page attribute of the Web application that can handle a Bean of type com.ibm.websphere.servlet.error. ServletErrorReport.

This Bean has methods named getErrorCode(), which returns the error code set by sendError(int); getMessage(), which returns the error string set by sendError(int,String); and getStackTrace(), which can be used to traverse the call stack and find more information on the root cause of the error. A detailed example using this Bean is shown in the *debug_error.jsp file* in the Web directory of the examples *webapp* in the default application server. A very small example of a JSP page that uses this Bean follows:

```
<jsp:usebean id="ErrorReport"
type="com.ibm.websphere.servlet.error.ServletErrorReport"
scope="request"></BEAN>
<HTML><HEAD><TITLE>Application Error</TITLE></HEAD>
<BODY>
<P>An application error has occurred. The error code is
<%= ErrorReport.getErrorCode() %>.<BR>
The text of the error is <%= ErrorReport.getMessage() %>.
Please retry your operation. If this error persists, contact application support.
</BODY></HTML>
```

Servlet Chaining and Filtering

Up to this point, we've seen how to use single servlets to create dynamic content for a Web site. Now we will look at how multiple servlets can work together in content creation. WebSphere has two approaches through which two or more servlets can jointly contribute to a single output stream. Those approaches are servlet chaining and MIME-type filtering.

To use servlet chaining, the simpler of the two choices, you define a set of servlets, called a *chain,* in which the request object and the output stream from the first servlet are passed to the next servlet in the chain. This process is repeated for each servlet in the chain until the last servlet executes, at which time the response is returned to the client. Thus, each servlet in the chain can contribute to the final output by appending to the output stream but cannot overwrite what has already been written to the output stream.

You define a servlet chain in WebSphere by adding an instance of the class com.ibm.websphere.servlet.filter.ChainerServlet to your Web application. You can name this servlet any meaningful Web path, such as /webapp/myapp/ chain. Then, you add the following initialization parameter to the new "chain" servlet in the WebSphere administration console:

chainer.pathlist　　　　*/firstServletWebPath /secondServletWebPath . . .*

Once this is completed, you can invoke your "chain" servlet through its Web path to in turn invoke the remaining servlets defined in the chainer path list in the appropriate order.

Another way in which servlets can cooperate to create dynamic output is through a technique called *MIME-type filtering*. This is similar to chaining except that the output of each servlet is not appended to the output of the previously called servlet in the chain. Instead, the output of each servlet is sent as input to the next servlet. This secondary servlet can then choose to alter, or filter, the input and return its own version of the output. Filter chains are controlled through the use of MIME types. Each servlet specifies what type of MIME it is outputting. The application server monitors the output of each servlet; when a MIME specified as a filtered MIME is sent as output, the server then invokes the appropriate servlet that filters that MIME type.

To help you understand how filtering works, let's consider the following simple example. Let's say that in our Web site, we want to be able to simply build hypertext help files for our application. Further, let's say that these help files come as independent text files from our technical writers. What would be nice is if we could come up with a way to link these files by title so that the title of one file becomes a hyperlink in other files. Filtering is a simple way in which to build this. We can easily build a filtering servlet that can scan an incoming text stream for occurrences of these special reserved words (page titles) and then produce HTML output for the user's browser with these reserved words linked to the appropriate document.

So, without further ado, let's look at the source code of a servlet, "SubstitutionServlet" that can manage this (Listing 9.3).

Listing 9.3 Source code for "Substitution Servlet."

```
package com.ibm.ws.book.example.servlets;

import javax.servlet.http.*;
import javax.servlet.*;
import java.io.*;
import java.util.*;
/**
 * This class is a simple Substitution filter. It surrounds special reserved
 * words in the input file with links to other pages.
 *
 */
public class SubstitutionServlet extends HttpServlet {
    private Properties substitutionList;
    private static final String SUBSTITUTION_FILE = "substitution.properties";
/**
 * SubstitutionServlet constructor.
 */
public SubstitutionServlet() {
    super();
}

/**
 * Initialize this servlet
```

```
 * @return void
 */
public void init() throws javax.servlet.ServletException {
    substitutionList = new Properties();
    try {
        FileInputStream file = new FileInputStream(SUBSTITUTION_FILE);
        substitutionList.load(file);
    } catch (IOException e) {
        System.out.println("No substitution file found");
    }
}
/**
 * This servlet acts as a simple MIME-type filter
 * It takes a document from the input and then substitutes single words
 * it finds with links from the substitution list.
 *
 *@param req javax.servlet.http.HttpServletRequest
 *@param resp javax.servlet.http.HttpServletResponse
 *@exception javax.servlet.ServletException The exception description.
 *@exception java.io.IOException The exception description.
 */
public void service(HttpServletRequest req, HttpServletResponse resp) throws
javax.servlet.ServletException, java.io.IOException {
    resp.setContentType("text/html");
    PrintWriter out = resp.getWriter();
    out.println("<HTML><HEAD>TranslatedOutput</HEAD><BODY>");
    BufferedReader r = req.getReader();
    String value = null;
    while ((value = r.readLine()) != null) {
        StringTokenizer tok = new StringTokenizer(value);
        while (tok.hasMoreElements()) {
            String token = tok.nextToken();
            String matchedValue = (String) substitutionList.get(token);
            if (matchedValue != null) {
                out.print("<A HREF=\"");
                out.print(matchedValue);
                out.print("\">");
                out.print(token);
                out.print("</A>");
            }
            else out.print(token);
            out.print(" ");
        }
        out.println("<BR>");
    }
    out.println("</BODY></HTML>");
    out.flush();

}
}
```

This servlet is not really that complicated. The init() method loads up the
list of properties, such as pairs of reserved words to URLs that will be linked.
The major part of the class is in the service() method. The method begins by

obtaining a BufferedReader from the HttpRequest with getReader() and then cycles through the input, reading each line in the text file with readLine(). Once it has a line of text, the method creates a StringTokenizer on that string and parses it, looking for matches for reserved words held in the substitution list. If it finds one, the method places a hyperlink, such as <A...> </A>, around the word; otherwise, it simply echoes the word to the output.

Now that we've written a filter, how do we set up WebSphere so that files can be directed to it? The first step is to set up this servlet in WebSphere. You can accomplish this by creating a new servlet in an existing Web application, or create your own Web application. Name your servlet "SubstitutionServlet" and set it up to point to our new class: com.ibm.ws.book.examples.servlets. SubstitutionServlet. The next step is to set up the filter for a particular MIME type. This is done in the administration console, on the configuration page for your Web application. After you select the Web application in which you created the "SubstitutionServlet" in the admin console, click on the *Advanced* Tab. You will see a table called *Filter List*. This table is where you define filters. Add the following key/value pair into this table:

```
text/hypertext          SubstitutionServlet
```

Here we are defining a new MIME type (called text/hypertext). Whenever the application server serves up a document having that MIME type, which could be generated from a servlet or from a JSP, "SubstitutionServlet" will be called to filter the output of the target document. To see how this would work, try the following sample JSPs, which contain the text files that would be provided for hyperlinking. The first file *(servlets.jsp)* would be the target of a hyperlink. For instance, it might describe what a servlet is:

```
<% response.setContentType("text/hypertext"); %>
Servlets
```

This file would describe what a servlet is.

The second file *(helpfile.jsp)* would reference the first file:

```
<% response.setContentType("text/hypertext"); %>
Help File
```

This is a help file that would reference the other file about servlets.

The only thing needed now is an example of the properties file that would link the two together. This is a sample *substitution.properties* file used by "SubstitutionServlet" and will work with the two previous example JSPs:

```
# substitution.properties
# Provides connections between reserved words and urls
#
Servlets=http://localhost/webapp/wsbooksamples/servlets.jsp
```

Using XML

With the volume of information that has been written about XML, one might think that it is a well-understood, mature technology and part of every application being developed anywhere in the world. Although it has been around for several years and is a very popular topic of discussion among developers, XML has yet to make its way into everyday application development. However, there is not much doubt that over the next few years, this will change. With this in mind, let's take a brief tour of XML and talk about some design techniques that could be of interest to you.

The first order of business is to understand exactly what XML is. XML is a simplified subset of SGML (Standard Generalized Markup Language). The simple purpose of XML is to place data into a structured format that can be easily shared between organizations and applications. XML is similar in concept to HTML; whereas HTML defines formatting rules for the presentation of data, XML is used simply for placing data into a meaningful structure without regard to presentation format. The following example shows an XML structure for a simple department element.

```
<?xml version=1.0?>
<department>
   <number>A100</number>
   <description>Human Resources</description>
   <employee>
      <id>235</id>
      <name>John Doe</name>
      <email>johndoe@ibm.com</email>
   </employee>
</department>
```

The ability to understand an XML document is dependent on an understanding of the "language" used in the document itself. This language is called the *DTD,* or document type definition, and defines the data model into which the structured data can be parsed. Part of the challenge ahead for XML is to continue to formalize standard DTDs for use in software applications. This is a challenging task, but many well-established DTDs are already available for use. Of course, without agreement on a standard DTD in key industries, XML may never become what it is expected to be. However, this does not mean that it cannot be used effectively in our Web-based application development.

When using XML documents in your applications, it will be necessary to move the data contained in the documents into your application in a consistent and proven manner. Two simple APIs parse XML structures: SAX, or Simple API for XML, and DOM, or document object model. Either of these APIs may be used to parse XML; however, the one you choose may depend on the structure of the data contained and how you plan on using the data. Let's take a look at each of these APIs individually.

The DOM API parses XML into a hierarchical tree structure based on the structure of the XML itself. Once the XML is parsed, you can access the information by interacting with the tree of nodes that was created by the parser. Because XML is hierarchical, this is a very simple process.

The SAX API, by contrast, parses the structure and fires events to indicate significance in the document. Unlike DOM, in which the tree of nodes is built for you, SAX requires you to respond to event notifications by building your own structure. This is typically done by creating a listener that responds to the events of the parser and a custom object model that will be populated by the parsed data.

In general terms, you could use either one of these APIs for a given task. So, you might ask, "Which one should I use within my applications?" That question has no one good answer. The best answer can be determined by looking at the type of data stored in the XML document. Typically, if the data represents Java domain objects and their properties, SAX is usually the better answer. This solution gives you fine-grained control over population of a domain model without the intervention of an intermediary tree structure. Conversely, if you plan to use the DOM to ultimately house the data for your application, SAX is really not necessary and convolutes the issue.

WebSphere Application Server provides support for both SAX and DOM through set of JAR (Java ARchive) files that implement the IBM XML4J parser. This parser is also available from the IBM AlphaWorks Web site, which is the source for information and updates to the XML4J parser. The WebSphere documentation provides extensive examples on how to use both the SAX and DOM APIs with the XML4J parser in your own servlets.

You may now be asking yourself how you can apply XML in your Web-based applications. Although the answers to this question are too numerous to list in full detail, let's explore some of the possibilities XML opens up.

One challenge when developing applications is the integration of data into a structure common to different areas of the business. For example, let's consider a time-tracking application (see the Case Study in Chapter 12). In a typical time-tracking scenario, users of the system need the ability to input their time on a weekly basis, indicating the number of hours worked and to whom the time should be billed. The accounts receivable department then needs to take the inputted time and send out an invoice to the company to which the time was billed. On the surface, this seems like a simple application to build. But think about the implications here to the process in accounts receivable. Although the data are not overly complex, the delivery of the data (invoice) is potentially different for each company being billed. XML can shine here. If a standard DTD can be established for delivering the invoice data, the process is much simplified. The invoice can be sent in a standard format and simply viewed and processed as desired by the receiving company.

Generalizing data and establishing a standard format is one way in which we can use XML. Furthermore, the ability to present this data into a ubiquitous computing world is made much easier when considering XML. The continuing trend is to provide views of your application data for many different end user devices, such as palmtops, pagers, and smart phones. These devices simply read in XML structures and translate the data into device-specific renderings.

Although an in-depth consideration of XML is beyond the scope of this book, we hope that this brief discussion at least whets your appetite for knowledge on this subject. Tool support and overall functionality are still evolving, and other companion technologies, such as extensible style sheets (XSL) are being developed as well. Although it is important not to commit yourself too early, now is the time to familiarize yourself with the features and offerings submitted by XML.

Summary and Preview

We have covered a lot of advanced topics in WebSphere servlet programming in this chapter. We've seen how exception handling can be done in both a WebSphere-specific way and in a generic way, we've examined some design patterns that can be applied to servlet programming, and we've covered some topics related to output processing and XML. In the next chapter, we will wrap up our coverage of servlet and JSP technology in preparation for the detailed case study that is included in the accompanying CD-ROM.

CHAPTER 10

JavaServer Pages Concepts

JSPs is one of a family of technologies known as *server-side scripting*. A competing member of this family is Active Server Pages (ASP) from Microsoft. Both of these technologies share a similar structure, namely, a source file that is a mixture of HTML and script code and runtime processing that occurs on the server. ASP is the older technology.

JSP was developed by a working group under the supervision of Sun Microsystems. Work began on the technology, under its current name, in late 1997 and was announced to the public at the JavaOne conference in March 1998. The first public specification and reference implementation, the 0.91 version, was available in June 1998. One year later, the first true JSP specification, version 1.0, was made public. Version 1.1 became available at the end of 1999. With each release of the specification, Sun Microsystems also released a reference implementation.

The development of JSP specifications and reference implementations has been turned over to the Apache group, under the umbrella of the Jakarta Project; for more information, see *http://jakarta.apache.org*. The Jakarta Project's reference implementation effort for both servlets and JSPs is called *Tomcat*.

IBM WebSphere Application Server Version 3.5 provides runtime support for two versions of JSP: 0.91 and 1.0. with IBM WebSphere version 3.5.3, JSP version 1.1. is also supported.

Most of the content presented to the user as part of a Web application is HTML. These Web pages are most easily created and managed by using page editors, which allow the developer to concentrate on the presentation and content through the use of a wysiwyg, or what you see is what you get, user interface. In previous chapters, we concentrated on the mechanics of the implementation of server-side logic, using servlets. In many of the examples, servlets directly delivered HTML content to the HTTP output stream. Although this gets the job done, few people would consider this a *best practice*.

As an alternative, one could use RequestDispatcher objects to *include* static HTML from files. This frees the servlet developer from having to deal too much with HTML directly but fails to allow a page designer to be able to see a page's layout at design time. The reason is that the page must be maintained and managed as smaller page segments rather than as a complete document. A second disadvantage of this approach is mixing both controller logic and presentation in the same asset, the servlet. It is best to keep the presentation (view) completely separate. This way, the view can be created and maintained by a single individual or team focused only on the presentational concerns of the site or the application.

A better solution to this problem exists in the form of JSP. A JSP is a file that contains extended HTML tags that allow embedding dynamic content, such as Java code and special server-side HTML tags, along with standard HTML. In this way, we can develop the presentation of information by using any standard HTML editor, such as IBM WebSphere Page Designer or Microsoft FrontPage. This not only allows the flexibility to more cleanly separate the back-end generation of dynamic content from the presentation in HTML but also permits the two roles—writing HTML and writing Java—to be split among different team members, each with complementary skill sets. It also makes the process of developing dynamic content simpler, as it is usually much easier to edit and to deploy an HTML page than to change HTML in the Java source code of a servlet and then to recompile and to redeploy it.

Page Templates and Server-Side Scripting

A facility to customize page content on a per request basis is often called a *page template*. The created page template does not completely represent a page delivered to the client but instead represents the form—layout, style—of the page. The template is representative of the page.

To generate a page from a page template requires processing. The processing step executes *instructions* to insert *dynamically* obtained content within the otherwise static HTML stream. For example, consider Figures 10.1–10.3, which show three different views of an extremely trivial JSP.

Figure 10.1 shows a wysiwyg page editor view of the JSP. For the most part, this looks like a simple HTML file. A placeholder, a green *{J}*, is provided as a hint that JSP-specific content has been defined as part of the page.

Figure 10.2 shows the raw, *tag,* view for the page. Here, it is possible to see the JSP-specific content:

```
<%= new java.util.Date() %>
```

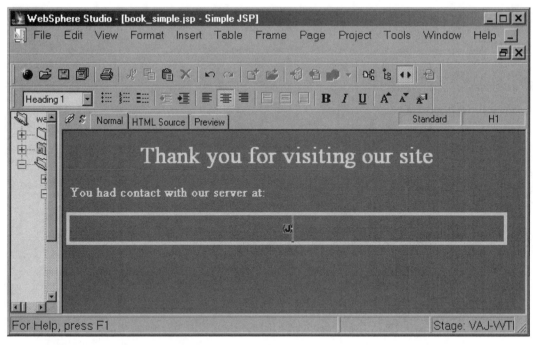

Figure 10.1   Building a JSP

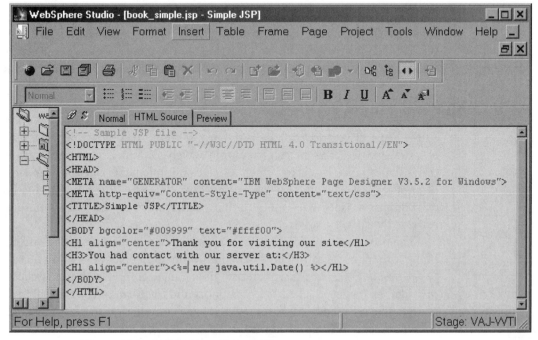

Figure 10.2   HTML Source View of JSP

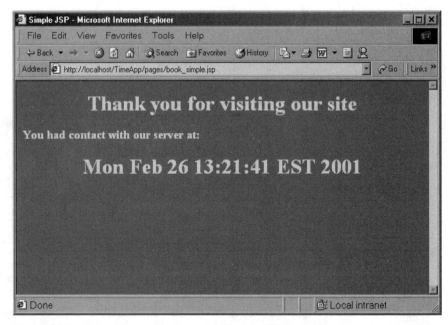

Figure 10.3   Display Sent to the Browser When the JSP Executes

This JSP tag appears as if it were an extended HTML tag. Figure 10.3 shows the rendered page as viewed by a browser. The dynamic content—the time on the server when the request is made—appears seamlessly in the resulting page.

Page Compilation: Runtime View

At the heart of JSPs technology is the process used to convert the JSP source to a runtime object that executes within a Web container. The specification states that a Java class is to be generated that implements the javax.servlet.jsp. HttpJspPage interface. In most cases, this Java class will be a servlet. This Java class defines a _jspService() method that will be called by the Web container to provide the runtime service.

The process of parsing the JSP source, producing the Java class, and compiling it to make it ready to be loaded into the servlet engine is known as *page compilation*. For most Web containers, page compilation is a *service* provided by a servlet. The level of support and the form of the generated code can be selected by choosing which page compilation servlet is installed for a particular Web application.

IBM WebSphere has two page compilation servlets, or JSP enablers, that can be configured within a Web application. One provides JSP v1.0 specification support: com.sun.jsp.runtime.JspServlet. The other one provides backward-compatibility support for JSPs written to the v0.91 specification: com.ibm.servlet.jsp.http.pagecompile.[1]

The parsing task performed by page compilation results in separating the JSP source file into tokens of two categories: JSP tags and everything else. The nonJSP tags need to be tokenized only as individual chunks, or strings, that appear between JSP tags. A typical implementation collects this set of nonJSP tag tokens as an array of strings. This array is then written to a file as a serialized object that is read at runtime by the generated class. These strings get written, unaltered, to the HTTP response stream. During code generation, each JSP tag is converted to the representative Java code, depending on the semantics of the specific tag.

Each page compilation servlet has a number of initialization parameters that you can set, which affects the behavior of the page compilation. One of the most important of these parameters is keepgenerated=true. Setting this parameter ensures that the generated class source code is saved to the file system, not just the compiled bytecode file. This is useful to the developer for debugging and general understanding of how the JSP works.

To learn more aspects of the class that gets generated from the JSP source, consider the Java source code file (Listing 10.1) that is generated for the JSP presented in Figures 10.1 and 10.2.

Listing 10.1 Generated servlet source.

```
public class book_simple_jsp_1 extends HttpJspBase {

    com.ibm.bsf.BSFManager bsf = new com.ibm.bsf.BSFManager();
    static String[] _jspx_html_data = null;

    public book_simple_jsp_1 ( ) { }

    private static boolean _jspx_inited = false;

    public final void _jspx_init() throws JspException {
        ObjectInputStream oin = null;
        try {
            FileInputStream fin = new
                FileInputStream("serialized_array_of_string_filename");
            oin = new ObjectInputStream(fin);
            _jspx_html_data = (String[]) oin.readObject();
        } catch (Exception ex) {
```

---

1. At the time of this writing, a third page compilation servlet for compiling JSPs written to the JSP 1.1 specification was added in WebSphere 3.5 fixpack 2.

```
            throw new JspException("Unable to open data file");
        } finally {
            if (oin != null)
                    try { oin.close(); } catch (IOException ignore) { }
        }
}

public void _jspService(HttpServletRequest request,
                    HttpServletResponse response)
                throws IOException, ServletException {

    boolean _jspx_cleared_due_to_forward = false;
    JspFactory _jspxFactory = null;
    PageContext pageContext = null;
    HttpSession session = null;
    ServletContext application = null;
    ServletConfig config = null;
    JspWriter out = null;
    Object page = this;
    String _value = null;
    try {
        if (_jspx_inited == false) {
            _jspx_init(); _jspx_inited = true;
        }
        _jspxFactory = JspFactory.getDefaultFactory();
        try
        {
            response.setContentType("text/html");
        }
        catch (IllegalStateException ws_jsp_ise){}
        pageContext = _jspxFactory.getPageContext(this, request,
                        response, "", true, 8192, true);

        application = pageContext.getServletContext();
        config = pageContext.getServletConfig();
        session = pageContext.getSession();
        out = pageContext.getOut();
        out.print(_jspx_html_data[0]); //HTML prior to JSP expr
            out.print( new java.util.Date() ); // JSP expr
        out.print(_jspx_html_data[1]); //HTML to end of file

    } catch (Throwable t) {
        if ((!_jspx_cleared_due_to_forward) &&
                        (out.getBufferSize() != 0))
            out.clear();
        throw new
    com.sun.jsp.JspWithNoErrorPageException("book_simple.jsp", t);
    } finally {
        if (!_jspx_cleared_due_to_forward)
            out.flush();
        _jspxFactory.releasePageContext(pageContext);
    }
  }
 }
}
```

The package statement and several import statements were dropped from the file listing. For this simple JSP, everything of interest appears in the _jspService() method. The initial part of this method defines a number of local variables that are later initialized from utility methods on the class PageContext. Immediately after defining the local variables, one-time behavior—calling _jspx_init()—is invoked to read the serialized object file to reconstruct the array of strings that represent the nonJSP content of the original JSP source file. Finally, the following three lines of code represent the behavior of the JSP.

```
out.print(_jspx_html_data[0]); //HTML prior to JSP expr
out.print( new java.util.Date() ); // JSP expr
out.print(_jspx_html_data[1]); //HTML to end of file
```

The first and third lines of code push the static content from the JSP source file to the HTTP output stream. The second line represents the logic of the JSP expression that appears in the source file.

The HttpJspPage interface also defines two methods, jspInit() and jspDestroy(), that can be *overridden* if the JSP needs to perform any one-time initialization or termination behavior. When the generated class is a servlet, the superclass, provided by the page compilation service, will override the service() method of HttpServlet so that its behavior is to call the _jspService() method. Similarly, the init() method of HttpServlet will call the jspInit() method, and the destroy() method will call the jspDestroy() method. In this way, the servlet engine's control model gets mapped to the JSP runtime model, as specified in the HttpJspPage interface.

Page compilation occurs if no servlet class has yet been generated for the target JSP or if the currently available servlet class' creation date (time stamp) is older than the JSP source file. Otherwise, if the servlet class exists, it is invoked if it is already loaded, or it is loaded and then invoked if it is not currently loaded.

Errors can occur during page compilation at two levels. First, the JSP tags can themselves be malformed. This is reported as a syntax error in the JSP. Second, the Java class generated during page compilation may produce Java compilation errors and will be reported as such.

JSP Syntax

The JSP syntax consists of three categories of elements: scripting elements, directives, and action tags. We look at the first two groups of elements in this chapter and consider actions in the next chapter.

Scripting Elements

When writing JSPs, your first interest is in adding code that executes at runtime and that can perform server-side functionality. The most direct way to specify the Java code that appears in the generated class is through the use of JSP scripting elements. The three distinct scripting elements specified for JSP are scriptlets, expressions, and declarations.

Scriptlets

Scriptlets are Java code fragments that are placed as they are directly to the _jspService() method. This is the most direct way to write Java code within a JSP. The syntax for a scriptlet is:

```
<% Java code fragment %>
```

At initial glance, allowing any Java code fragment rather than a statement, collection of statements, or expression probably seems odd. But it should be noted that scriptlets will be intermixed with HTML, and Java "blocks" will frequently need to be split. For example, consider part of a JSP file that will produce a variable-sized HTML table:

```
<Table><Tbody>
<% for (int i=0; i<a.size; i++) { %>
<tr>
<td><% out.print(i); %></td>
<td><% out.print(a[i].getAProperty()); %></td>
</tr>
<% } %> </Tbody></Table>
```

As you can see, the for loop is split across a number of scriptlets. It is quite clear that the preceding JSP code is difficult to read for both HTML page developers and Java programmers. Therefore, we will work hard to minimize scriptlets when developing JSPs. We put forth this goal despite the fact that scriptlets are the most general-purpose scripting element in JSP.

Expressions

A scripting element is frequently required to supply a runtime value, or expression, to the page template. In other words, most of the time, we are trying to place dynamic, or displayable, data to the HTTP output stream. JSP expressions are a short form of scriptlet to be used in these circumstances. The syntax for a JSP expression is:

```
<%= a_Java_expression %>
```

The semantics of this tag is to evaluate the expression; convert the result to a string, if nonprimitive; and output the string, or primitive, to the current output stream. As you will see, JSP expressions are likely to be the most common JSP tag type seen throughout the JSP source file.

Implicit Objects

Both scriptlets and expressions result in code being placed in the _jspService()
method. Several local variables, or implicit objects, are guaranteed to be
available to these scripting elements by the JSP Specification. The implicit objects are shown in Table 10.1.

Both exception and session are present only in particular circumstances.
The exception object is present if the JSP is configured as an error page. (Refer to Chapter 9.) The session object is present if the JSP is configured to be
session aware, which is the default.

Declarations

Scriptlets and expressions permit writing code that appears in the _jspService()
method. Declarations are used to write direct Java code at the class level. The
syntax for a JSP declaration is:

```
<%! Java member definitions %>
```

Declarations can be used to define instance variables and static variables
and to define methods. Defining new methods is useful when complex scripts
are repeated. This repeated script can be encapsulated in a method body, and
the repeated script can be replaced by a repeated method call.

Table 10.1   Implicit Objects in Scriptlets and Expressions

Implicit Object	Java Type	Object Represented by Reference
Request	javax.servlet.http.HttpServletRequest	The request associated with this invocation
Response	javax.servlet.http.HttpServletResponse	The current response object
Out	javax.servlet.jsp.JspWriter	A writer connected to the output stream
Session	javax.servlet.http.HttpSession	The current session object for the requesting client
Page context	javax.servlet.jsp.PageContext	The page context (a utility object) for this JSP
Application	javax.servlet.ServletContext	The servlet context for this JSP
Config	javax.servlet.ServletConfig	The servlet config for this JSP servlet
Page	java.lang.Object	Usually corresponds to this
Exception	java.lang.Throwable	The throwable that resulted in the error page being invoked

More likely, however, declarations will be used to override the jspInit()
and the jspDestroy() methods when needed. An example declaration is:

```
<%!
private static PropertyResourceBundle environment = null;
public void jspInit() {
try {
inputStream stream = getServletConfig().getServletContext().
   getResourceAsStream("/props.txt");
environment = new PropertyResourceBundle.(stream);
} catch (IOException ex) {}
}
%>
```

Directives

Whereas scripting elements map directly to code within the class that is generated, directives represent direction to the page compiler. These requests include
specifying certain properties that the class created is to have, how translation occurs, or how the class will operate during runtime. The three types of directives
are page directives, include directives, and taglib directives. These directives are
very different in what they let the JSP developer specify. We will look at both the
page directive and the include directive here. The taglib directive is part of the custom tag support required in JSP v1.1 and is addressed at the end of Chapter 11.

The page Directive

The page directive is a way to configure a number of operational attributes of
the generated JSP. The page directive syntax is:

```
<%@ page page_directive_attr_list %>
```

Table 10.2 lists items that may be included in page_directive_attr_list.
An example page directive is:

```
<%@ page errorPage="TSErrorHandler.jsp" import="com.workbook.casestudy.
domain, com.workbook.casestudy.mediator" %>
```

A page can contain several page directives. With the exception of the import attribute, no other attribute may be specified more than once. Two of the
attributes, session and isErrorPage, affect the availability of the associated implicit objects for use by scriptlets and expressions.

The include Directive

The include directive allows for the translation-time composition of multiple
files into a single JSP source file. The syntax for the include directive is:

```
<%@ include file="relativeURLspec" %>
```

Table 10.2 The page Directive Attributes

Attribute	Value Range	Description
language	Compliant JSP scripting language	Default value is java.
extends	A Java class that implements HttpJspPage interface	This should not be used without consideration, as it prevents the JSP container from providing specialized superclasses that provide enhanced quality of service.
import	A comma-separated list of fully qualified Java package or type names	The default import list is java.lang.*, javax.servlet.*, javax.servlet.jsp.*, and javax.servlet.http.*. This is the only attribute that may appear in more than one page directive in the page. Multiple import attributes are interpreted as the set union of all listed types and packages.
session	true | false	Indicates whether the JSP is session aware. The default value is true.
buffer	none | size, where size is something like 12K	Specifies the buffering model for the JspWriter opened to handle content output from the page. A specific buffer size guarantees that the output is buffered with a buffer size not less than that specified.
autoFlush	true | false	Default is true. If false and the stream is buffered, an exception is thrown when the buffer overflows. If true, the stream is flushed.
isThreadSafe	true | false	Default is true. If false, the typical implication is that the generated class implements SingleThreadModel.
info	Arbitrary string	This can be retrieved by using the Servlet.getServletInfo() method.
isErrorPage	true | false	Indicates whether the page is used to handle errors. If true, the implicit script variable exception is defined and bound to the offending Throwable from the source JSP in error.
errorPage	a URL	The JSP will catch all exceptions and forward processing to the named target resource.
contentType	Type | Type; charset=CHARSET	The default value for type is text/html; the default value for the character encoding is ISO-8859-1.

Execution of this tag at translation time results in the insertion of the text of the specified resource into the JSP source file. As this is a translation-time include, you will not want to use this directive to include resources that change. If you wish to include *volatile* content, you should use a runtime include mechanism, such as the <jsp:include> action (see Chapter 11 for details).

Roles for JSP

JSP is a broad enough specification to support many programming models and common uses. This potentially broad appeal is both a strength and a weakness of JSP.

With scripting elements, it is possible to write a general-purpose servlet as a JSP. In this role, a JSP consists almost entirely of one or more scriptlets and declarations, providing an opportunity to write an HttpServlet by specifying the content only of the _jspService() method and perhaps other utility methods. For some, this may be a shortcut over using a Java development environment to create the complete class declaration. However, the disadvantage in this approach is that you lose the benefits that such a development environment offers the developer. This loss probably more than offsets the productivity gain from letting the page compiler build the class framework.

At the other extreme, a JSP can play the role of HTML page template only. In this mode, a secondary goal during development is to minimize the Java code that appears in the JSP. JSP-aware HTML page development tools, such as IBM WebSphere Page Designer, support this role.

A third role is a true mix of HTML and Java code. Although more general, this is perhaps the most easily abused role for a JSP to play. For example, when a JSP is used in this way, it plays the role of Controller and View and perhaps part of the Model in the MVC model. In addition to not separating these programming elements, the JSP source itself becomes difficult to maintain. It is difficult to sort out what the runtime behavior is when a lot of complex Java logic is intermixed with HTML tags. Further, there is likely no good development environment to assist in making sense of such a source file.

It is our strong opinion that JSPs should keep to one extreme or the other. No noteworthy tools are available to strongly support the JSP as a faster servlet development mechanism. (For instance, no Java/JSP-based Microsoft Visual InterDev–style tool is on the market.) This leaves us with trying to restrict JSPs to be strictly a page template technology playing the role of the View (or View engine) in our MVC programming model. We revisit this issue while discussing the various JSP programming models in the next chapter.

Summary and Preview

In this chapter, we examined the basics of JSPs and the programming models in which they are best used. In the next chapter, we continue this discussion, examining more JSP tags and discussing what tools support JSP development for WebSphere.

CHAPTER 11

JSP Actions, MVC, and Tools

In the previous chapter, we looked at the basic syntax of JSP. Of the three JSP syntax groups, only actions have yet to be explored. The primary intent of this chapter is to look at the JSP programming models and how the JSP action tags contribute to building effective view engines. We also examine the tool support that WebSphere Studio and Visual Age for Java provide for the JSP programming model and how this tool support can help you in using JSPs effectively.

Programming Models

Two common programming models involve JSPs as display pages. These models, first documented in early JSP specifications written by Sun Microsystems, were known simply as *Model 1* and *Model 2*. We will refer to them as the *direct model* and the *indirect*—through a Controller—*Model*. At first glance, these programming models differ only in which application tier invokes the JSP. The use of JSP programming elements within a *page*, however, is greatly affected by this application architecture.

JSP Direct Model

The first model (Figure 11.1) is directly invoked by the HTTP client. The JSP handles both the incoming HTTP request, handing off the control responsibility to a mediator, and generating the HTTP response stream. The organization is comparable to the most typical interaction model found in Microsoft's ASP. It has the advantage that the view interaction components—both controller and view—are developed in a single asset. The JSP file receives the request, probably builds one or more JavaBeans to encapsulate the

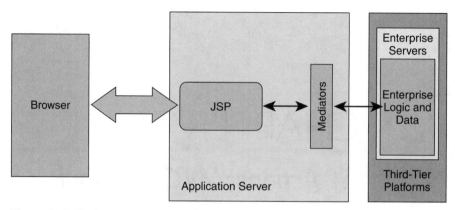

Figure 11.1 JSP Programming: Direct Model

incoming request parameters, and then delegates responsibility to other components. These tasks are frequently characterized by one or more scriptlets, located at the *top* of the JSP file.

Although this model makes file management easier, it does have some drawbacks. One of the problems stems from requests that may result in one of several different responses. In such circumstances, the JSP can include multiple logical responses, selected at runtime by conditional logic (scriptlets). Or, it can either

- Generate the most common response, via the contained page template, and forward to secondary JSPs to handle different responses
- Generate no response directly but contain runtime logic to forward to the appropriate display page JSP.

This latter option identifies the more general JSP interaction model, the indirect model.

JSP Indirect Model

In the JSP indirect model, a JSP is dispatched for the sole purpose of providing a response back to the client. There is no control behavior within the JSP. Figure 11.2 shows the JSP indirect model, the more general of the two interaction models and the one most compatible with the MVC pattern that has been described throughout the book.

The indirect model's organization has several advantages. The greatest of these is the structure of the *display page* JSP itself. As a general rule, this display page can be free from scriptlets. The page can thus be easily generated

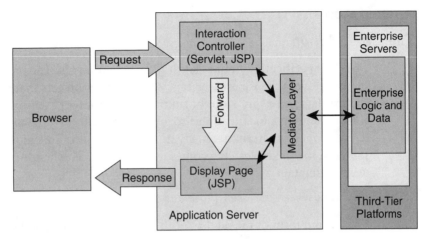

Figure 11.2 JSP Programming: Indirect Model

and viewed by JSP-aware HTML page editors. Without conditional logic, wysiwyg tools will closely show what the JSP will look like at runtime. Also, as we will see later, this style of JSP can frequently be created without the need to write Java code.

By specializing the role of the JSP to display only, the indirect model provides additional advantages. With a JSP-aware page development tool, JSPs can be created alongside static HTML pages by the same developers. In most circumstances, the page development tool produces any Java code that appears in these display page JSPs. Java programming is a task for the role that produces the Controller and/or mediators.

This Model not only helps support separation of development roles but also provides better affinity between development tools and generated assets. Controllers and mediators are pure Java code and will be developed and maintained in a Java IDE-like VisualAge for Java. Display page JSPs are Web page templates and will be developed and maintained in a page development tool, such as WebSphere Page Designer.

By separating the Controller and the View into separate assets, a request can yield several different responses, with each response provided by a separate JSP. Based on the results, the Controller decides which JSP to forward to.

To minimize the coupling between the View and the Model, both programming models will make use of one or more mediator objects. These objects will be packaged as JavaBeans to be friendlier to development tools. The JSP specification provides a direct mechanism for binding to these mediators at runtime.

JSP Standard Actions

The useBean *Action*

The JSP Specification defines six standard action tags. The most involved of these actions is the jsp:useBean tag, which defines objects that are accessible to scriptlets and expressions at runtime. Execution of the jsp:useBean tag results in binding a local variable to an existing object stored in one of four different *scopes* or, alternatively, creating a new object. Like most of our other JSP tags, the jsp:useBean tag comes in two forms. The first form is a self-terminating tag:

```
<jsp:useBean use_bean_attributes />
```

The second form of the tag has both a beginning and an ending tag:

```
<jsp:useBean use_bean_attributes>
   body
</jsp:useBean>
```

The only difference between these two forms is the presence of the conditionally executed body provided in the second form. As noted earlier, the main task of the jsp:useBean tag is to bind a local variable, in the _jspService() method, to an object. This object may have already been instantiated and is being accessed from a named *scope* or is instantiated as a result of execution of the tag.

The attributes for the jsp:useBean tag are:

```
id = "bean_identifier"
scope = "page" | "request" | "session" | "application"
typespec
```

The id, a required attribute, is both a key to access the object in the named scope and the name given to the local variable assigned the reference to the resulting object. The scope attribute defaults to the value of page if it is left unspecified. Each of the four possible scope values corresponds to available implicit objects that provide access to a keyed data structure. Page is the controlling PageContext object. Request is the current ServletRequest object. Session is the current HttpSession object, and application corresponds to the controlling ServletContext object.

The most interesting and complex attribute for jsp:useBean is a set of dependent attributes. The type spec

- Determines the static type of the local variable declared in the _jspService() method. This variable will be assigned the reference to the resulting object.
- Optionally directs how an object is to be instantiated if an existing object is not located in the named scope using the ID.

The type spec, a required element, is a combination of three attributes.

Although they may appear in any order within the jsp:useBean tag, only a limited number of combinations are legal. The legal combinations are

- class="*classname*"
- type="*typename*" class="*classname*"
- type="*typename*" beanName="*serialized_bean_filename*"
- type="*typename*"

To understand the behavior of each of these combinations, we will consider each of the two roles of the type spec separately. The static type of the local variable is the typename, if supplied. If typename is not supplied, the static type of the local variable is classname. A ClassCastException may occur during assignment of the object reference to the local variable.

The rest of the type spec is used if no object is found in the named scope. When this occurs, an object can be instantiated in a manner compliant with the type spec. If classname is present, a new object of type classname will be created. If serialized_bean_filename is present, an object will be instantiated from a serialized instance saved in the corresponding file. In all cases, instantiation may fail, resulting in a ServletException being thrown.

If an object is instantiated, it is then added to the named scope, using the bean_identifier as the key. Also, if present, the body of the jsp:useBean tag is executed only if an object is instantiated. The body is generally used to initialize the newly instantiated Bean. The body may contain any combination of legal Java statements and JSP tags. In particular, the body typically includes one or more jsp:setProperty tags.

Consider the following example useBean action:

```
<jsp:useBean id="TSMediator" scope="session" class="com.wsbook.casestudy.
mediator.TimeSheetMediator" />
```

This simple tag would result in the generation of a block of code within the _jspService() method. Representative code is shown in Listing 11.1.

Listing 11.1 Java code generated for simple useBean action.

```
com.wsbook.casestudy.mediator.TimeSheetMediator TSMediator = null;
boolean _newTSMediator = false;
synchronized (session) {
    TSMediator = (com.wsbook.casestudy.mediator.TimeSheetMediator)
        PageContext.getAttribute("TSMediator",PageContext.SESSION_SCOPE);
    if (TSMediator == null ) {
        _newTSMediator = true;
        try {
            TSMediator =
                (com.wsbook.casestudy.mediator.TimeSheetMediator)
            Beans.instantiate(getClassLoader(),
                "com.wsbook.casestudy.mediator.TimeSheetMediator ");
        } catch (Exception exc) {
            throw new ServletException(" Cannot create bean of class " +
```

```
            "com.wsbook.casestudy.mediator.TimeSheetMediator ");
      }
      pageContext.setAttribute("TSMediator", TSMediator,
                                 PageContext.SESSION_SCOPE);}
  }
      if(_newTSMediator == true) { /* body of <jsp:usebean> tag */
  }
    }
```

In the code, you can see that the local variable, TSMediator, is typed as
com.wsbook.casestudy.mediator.TimeSheetMediator, as specified by the class="..."
attribute. In this particular useBean action, no typename was specified. Next,
aBoolean flag is set to be able to detect whether a new object gets created. This
would be used to trigger execution of the useBean *body*, if present. The common
runtime behavior of the useBean action is fulfilled by the pageContext.getAttribute
(...) call. The getAttribute method is a utility method provided by the PageContext
class. This method allows a common access pattern to objects stored in any of
the four *scopes*. In this particular case, we are looking for the TimeSheetMediator
to be stored in the HttpSession with the key, TSMediator. If the object is located
and no ClassCastException results, the block of code is completed.

If the object is not located in the HttpSession object, an attempt is made to
create a new TimeSheetMediator. In this case, the classname is specified, requiring that a new object be created, using the no-arg constructor. This task is performed by the Beans.instantiate(...) line of code. If this succeeds, the new object
is added to the HttpSession object, using the pageContext.setAttribute(...)
method. The same Beans.instantiate(...) would be used if type="..." and
beanName="..." were specified. In this case, the serialized_bean_filename would
be passed as the second argument in the instantiate method. If only type="..."
were specified in the useBean action tag, no attempt would be made to instantiate the Bean. Instead, a ServletException would be thrown.

Before continuing with the useBean body and other action tags, let's take
a quick diversion and talk about the four scopes available for communicating
JavaBeans to a JSP. These storage scopes are summarized in Table 11.1.

Storage Scopes

The useBean action tag has an attribute that names the storage *scope* for accessing a JavaBean. Each scope corresponds to a particular runtime object in
the context of the executing JSP. Each scope differs in the lifetime of the corresponding runtime object and thus the maximum lifetime of the available reference. This lifetime effects the level of sharing that can take place across
different server-side runtime objects.

The *page* scope has the shortest lifetime. The object reference is stored in the PageContext object associated with the current JSP. The reference is discarded on completion of the current page body for the current request. An object stored in the page scope is unavailable via this reference to any other JSPs or servlets. The page context becomes particularly important in JSP 1.1, in which custom actions place newly created objects into the page context, where they are then available to JSP scripting elements and other JSP actions.

The next scope, in increasing lifetime, is *request*. The object reference is stored in the HttpServletRequest object: the current request. The reference is discarded on completion of the current HTTP request. An object stored in the request scope is available to all JSPs and servlets participating in this request. This scope is very useful for the standard servlet-mediator-JSP configuration. If the mediator(s) that encapsulate dynamic content for the JSP display page need to be consumed only by the JSP for this request, the servlet/controller places a reference to the mediator in the request scope prior to forwarding to the JSP. When the request completes, the mediator can be garbage-collected.

When an object is client specific but can be used several times over the life of the HttpSession, the best storage scope to use is *session*. To discard the reference prior to the invalidation of the HttpSession, the mediator needs to be explicitly removed from the session.

The final scope, *application,* refers to the ServletContext associated with the Web application. This scope permits sharing among all assets of the application for all clients. The lifetime of this scope is typically the lifetime of the underlying JVM. To discard a reference, this scope must be explicitly removed from the ServletContext.

Before leaving the discussion on storage scopes, remember that the default storage scope for the useBean action is *page*. This is generally not very useful. As a rule, prefer to use the storage scope with the most limited, shortest lifetime applicable for the reference being stored.

Table 11.1 Summary of Storage Scopes

Scope	Lifetime	Shared by
Page	Execution of the page only	Elements within the page
Request	Duration of the HTTP request	JSPs and servlets participating in the request
Session	Until removed from the session or the session is invalidated	JSPs and servlets participating in requests on behalf of the same client
Application	Life of the Web application	Shared by JSPs and servlets configured as part of the Web application

The getProperty *and the* setProperty *Standard Actions*

With the declaration of a JavaBean's presence within a JSP, it is possible to treat it specially. The JSP specification defines two standard actions to directly manipulate the properties of a JavaBean. The first of these actions, getProperty, provides a means to access the properties of a Bean made available via the useBean action or, perhaps, custom action tags. The syntax for the getProperty action is:

```
<jsp:getProperty name="bean_id_name" property="property_name" />
```

The behavior of the getProperty action is to retrieve the corresponding property, convert it to a string, and display that string by placing it into the response stream, using the implicit object out. This tag is limited to nonindexed properties of the Bean. Tags defined in earlier versions of the JSP specification and various custom tags have the same goal as the getProperty action but enable both nested and indexed properties. Most JSP scripters would be generally advised to use JSP expressions or tool-specific metatags rather than the getProperty action.

The second of these standard actions, setProperty, is particularly useful for initializing the properties of a newly instantiated Bean. The setProperty action has the following syntax:

```
<jsp:setProperty name="beanName" prop_expr />
```

The prop_expr is of the form:

```
property="*" | property="propertyName"|
property="propertyName" param="parameterName"|
property="propertyName" value="propertyValue"
```

The setProperty action permits easy initialization of Bean properties and is optimized to initialize properties from the ServletRequest parameters, such as provided via an HTML form. In fact, each of the first three forms of the prop_expr is related to the task of initializing Bean properties from ServletRequest parameters.

- The first form, where the prop_expr is property="*", is backward compatible to previous versions of JSP, in which a different tag syntax was used to include a JavaBean within the page. This form uses runtime introspection. The semantics for this prop_expr is to find all parameter names associated with the current ServletRequest and all property names for the JavaBean. When a parameter name corresponds to a property name, the generated code will set the property value to the value of the corresponding request parameter. Using this form of prop_spec has two disadvantages, however: (1) the runtime overhead associated with introspection and (2) the possibility that some properties of the JavaBean will be unintentionally "set" as a result of the presence of unexpected ServletRequest parameters.

- The second form of the prop_expr generates code that sets the property value with the value of the same-named request parameter, if such a parameter exists.
- If parameter names and property names don't completely agree, the third form of the prop_expr can be used. Here, the value of the specified property is set with the value of the specified parameter.

The final form of the prop_expr allows Bean properties to be initialized from sources other than request parameters. Here, the specified property is set with the specified value. The value can be an explicit value, provided as a string, or a JSP expression.

Listing 11.2 shows some examples of the setProperty action with their corresponding useBean action. Note that setProperty is not required to be placed within the body of the useBean action; however, it most often will appear within the body and must appear after the corresponding useBean action is defined.

Listing 11.2 Examples of setProperty actions.

```
<jsp:useBean id="newEmployeeRequest"
      class="com.wsbook.casestudy.domain.Employee" scope="session">
    <jsp:setProperty name="newEmployeeRequest" property="id" />
    <jsp:setProperty name="newEmployeeRequest" property="name"
                                         param="empName" />

</jsp:useBean>

<jsp:useBean id="changeRequest"
      class="com.wsbook.casestudy.domain.ChangeRequest" scope="session">
    <jsp:setProperty name="changeRequest" property="timestamp"
                                value="<%= new java.util.Date() %>" />
...
</jsp:useBean>
```

Don't forget that the body of the useBean action is executed only when a new object is created or instantiated as a result of the execution of the useBean action. If you want to use the setProperty action to change the property value of an existing Bean, the action must appear outside, following the body of the useBean action.

The Rest of the Standard Action Tags

Three additional standard actions are defined in the JSP specification: include, forward, and plugin. The first two permit easy access to the corresponding operations on a RequestDispatcher and provide a way for JSP to temporarily transfer control to another object available within the Web container.

The include Action

The include action permits adding static or dynamic content in the same context as the current JSP. The action names a resource to be included, using a relative URL that is interpreted in the context of the current ServletContext (Web container). An included page cannot set headers and has access only to the JspWriter object. The syntax for the include action is:

```
<jsp:include page="included_page" flush="true" | "false" />
```

In JSP 1.1, an alternative form is defined:

```
<jsp:include page="included_page" flush="true" | "false" >
   { <jsp:param name="name" value="value" />* }
</jsp:include>
```

In both cases, the page and flush attributes are mandatory. The included_page is a relative URL. In both JSP 1.0 and JSP 1.1, the only legal value for flush is true. The flush attribute declares whether the JspWriter is flushed prior to the include, or forward. Some examples are:

```
<jsp:include page="/pages/top_level_navigation_bar.html" flush="true" />
<jsp:include page="/TSMakePending" flush="true" >
{ <jsp:param name="department" value="<%= curDeptValue %>" /> }
</jsp:include>
```

The param action permits augmenting the request parameters for the scope of the include operation.

The forward Action

The forward action allows the JSP to dispatch to a static or dynamic resource, such as a URI, available in the same context. Forwarding effectively terminates the current execution, purging the JspWriter and passing control to the resource forwarded to. This action will most likely be used by a JSP acting in the capacity of controller, or JSP as an easier servlet. This action could also be used in the context of error handling within the scope of the JSP, but this will usually be handled by the errorPage attribute in a page directive. The syntax for the forward action is:

```
<jsp:forward page="forwarded_page" />
```

In JSP 1.1, an alternative form is defined:

```
<jsp:forward page="forwarded_page" >
   { <jsp:param name="name" value="value" />* }
</jsp:forward>
```

Like the include action, the existence of one or more param actions within the body of the forward tag allows for the augmentation of the current request object's parameter list.

The plugin Action

The plugin action is a convenience tag to generate the appropriate HTML, either <object> or <embed> tag, to execute an applet or JavaBean component within the Java plugin on the client. The appropriate tag structure and content will be generated based on the User-agent for the current HttpRequest.

The syntax is:

```
<jsp:plugin type="bean|applet" code="objectCode" codebase="objectCodebase"
    {align="alignment"} {archive="archiveList"} {height="height"}
    {hspace="hspace"} {jreversion="jreversion"} {name="componentName"}
    {vspace="vspace"} {width="width"} {nspluginurl="url"}
    {iepluginurl="url"} >

{<jsp:params>
    {<jsp:param name="paramName" value="paramValue" /> }+
</jsp:params> }

{ <jsp:fallback> arbitrary_text </jsp:fallback> }
</jsp:plugin>
```

The parameters correspond to the <param> tags used with the <Applet> tag. The text specified in the <fallback> tag is displayed when the plugin fails to load within the browser.

At this point, we have completed the JSP syntax with the exception of the details of custom actions defined in tag libraries. We also have yet to look at the specification of making JSP files more XML compliant. Both of these items will be covered at the end of this chapter. Now, it is time to look at development tools to build JSP.

JSP Development Tools: WebSphere Page Designer

Before jumping too far into the discussion of development tools for JSP, we should once again visit the developer roles that may participate in the development and maintenance of JSPs. Many early JSP developers were Java programmers who needed a way to purge their servlets of string literals representing HTML text. For these individuals, any scripting tool or text editor permitting direct editing of the HTML/JSP tags is sufficient.

When the Java programmers in an organization build JSPs, the development process typically observed has the static content of the JSP developed by the Web page developers. These pages, developed to have consistent look and feel with the rest of the Web site, are then handed off to the Java developers to add in the scripting code. The final JSPs are then usually returned to the Web page development team for maintenance.

The MVC programming style, particularly the wrapping of dynamic content in one or more JavaBeans, provides the opportunity for a different development model. When page developers are building JSPs, the only activity they have difficulty performing is placing dynamic content within the page. This difficulty stems mainly from the lack of accessibility to the JSP syntax.

JavaBeans, Introspection, and Contracts

The key problem of building JSPs in an MVC environment is communication. When a team is divided into one set of individuals who develop Web pages and another set of individuals who are middle-tier, server-side Java developers, lack of communication can create challenges.

Web developers are aware of what content should appear on the page. They must communicate to the middle-tier developers that certain dynamic content should be displayed on that page. This dynamic content is generally data that result from a client request, whether successful or unsuccessful. It is also possible for the middle-tier developer to communicate to the Web developer what dynamic content is available for display at any point.

Formalizing the packaging of the dynamic content represents the contract between the JSP developer and the Bean providers. Defining one or more types that expose the dynamic content as properties specifies most of this contract. These types are reified as JavaBeans. JavaBeans have the advantage of being very tool friendly. It is very easy for a tool to introspect on a JavaBean class and/or an accompanying BeanInfo class and to present to the developer the available properties, events, and methods. For our *display page* JSPs, these JavaBeans need only deliver dynamic content as properties.

The rest of the contract involves the location of the JavaBeans at runtime. In other words, what information must be supplied in the useBean action to make it possible to locate the JavaBeans; in what scope and under what ID will the Bean be found?

A typical JSP development tool feature permits browsing a set of JavaBeans to select a property for display on the page. Complexities arise in dealing with indexed properties, primarily with specifying the context for indexing, and *nested* properties. Nested properties arise when the structure of the dynamic data is complex. For example, consider our TimeSheet object. This object represents a collection of TimeSheetEntries. A TimeSheetEntry contains properties for date and project, neither of which is primitive data. If one wants to display the project name for a particular TimeSheetEntry, the JSP expression would look like:

```
<%= TimeSheet.getEntry(index).getProject().getName() %>
```

This could also be specified by walking the Beans and their properties and selecting the leaf property *name* (TimeSheet, entry(index), project, name). For a tool to facilitate *walking* nested JavaBean properties, each property must be available in a nontype-hiding manner. For instance, in the preceding scenario, it is possible to get at the collection of TimeSheetEntries via the method getEntries() on the TimeSheet object. This returns a vector of TimeSheetEntry objects. A vector, however, hides the type information of its contents. All accessors to the contents of the vector guarantee only that they return a Java object. A tool will not be able to expose the properties of the Java type stored in the vector, only the limited properties of java.lang.Object. By supplying the indexed property *entry* in the TimeSheet Bean, it is possible to perform recursive introspection and make the project name visible to a developer.

WebSphere Studio and Page Designer

IBM WebSphere Page Designer represents a new breed of Web page assembly tools. It is tightly integrated with the IBM WebSphere Studio workbench and has strong support for developing JSPs. Page Designer is launched from the Studio workbench. Page Designer grabs some key context information from the currently loaded Studio project. In particular, Page Designer picks up the desired JSP version from the project's advance properties and adds the current project's servlets folder to its Java class path.

IBM WebSphere Page Designer is a powerful wysiwyg page editor that includes usual menus and tool bars to add and to modify HTML within a page. Figures 10.1–10.3 showed the three views provided for a simple HTML page within Page Designer. The common wysiwyg page development view is called the *normal* view (see Figure 10.1.) Within the same tool, it is possible to work directly on the raw tags, via the *HTML source* view; see Figure 10.2. For pages that are true client pages, a built-in *preview* shows the page as rendered by Microsoft's Internet Explorer.

Page Designer has very strong support for building JSPs. All JSP tags can be generated via menu items and tool bar buttons. As with many page development tools, elements that appear on the page have attributes that can be edited via attribute dialogs. When an element is selected to be dropped on the page, such as a text field being placed in an HTML form, the corresponding element (text field) attribute dialog is displayed. An HTML page is usually split into two major sections: the *head* and the *body*. When operating in *normal* mode, you view only elements declared within the HTML body. Items that are typically placed in the body of the HTML <HEAD> tag are entered through the *Document Properties* dialog. One of the tabs in the *Document Properties* dialog is for adding JSP tags that must appear in the head of the

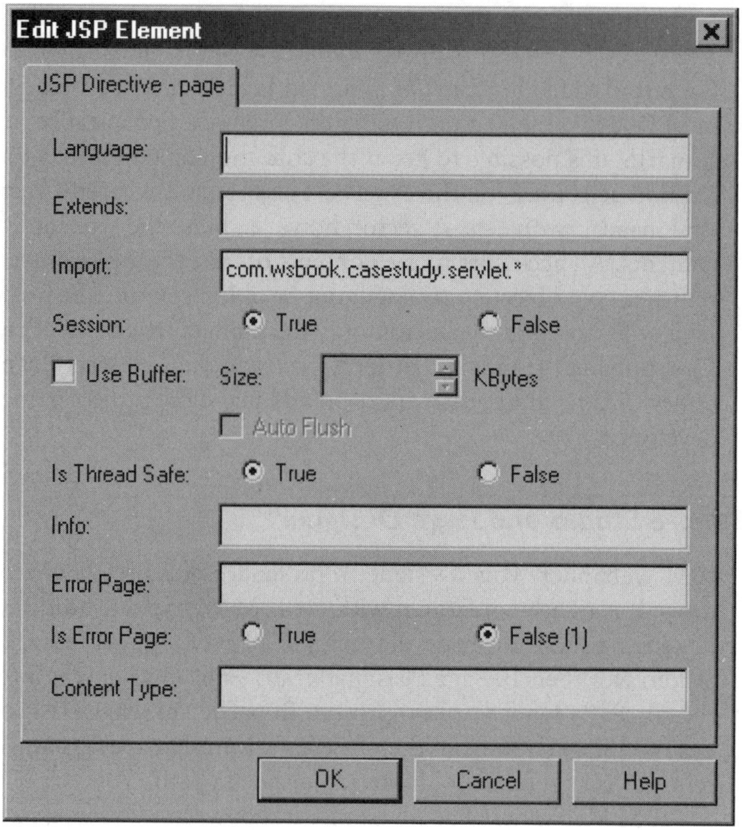

Figure 11.3 Add page directive

JSP file or tags that have page scope and you would just as soon not declare them in the HTML body. This is the only place where the tool lets you insert a JSP page directive from the normal view. The resulting *JSP Directive=page* attribute dialog is shown in Figure 11.3.

A useBean action tag can also be created from the selection list within the *Document Properties* dialog. In general, however, useBean actions just need to be declared before they are used. A more user-friendly approach to creating a useBean action on your JSP is to drag a JavaBean class *(.class)* file from the *Contents Manager* frame onto the JSP. Then, Page Designer introspects the JavaBean class file, partially filling in a useBean action attribute. This occurs if the tool's *Edit* option is configured to create a useBean action in response to dropping a Java class onto the page. (Other configurable responses to a dropped Java class are creating an applet tag, a servlet tag, or a hyperlink.) The useBean *Attribute* dialog is shown in Figure 11.4.

Using the useBean attribute dialog, you can configure all the elements of the useBean action tag. If this is prefilled after dropping a Java class onto the

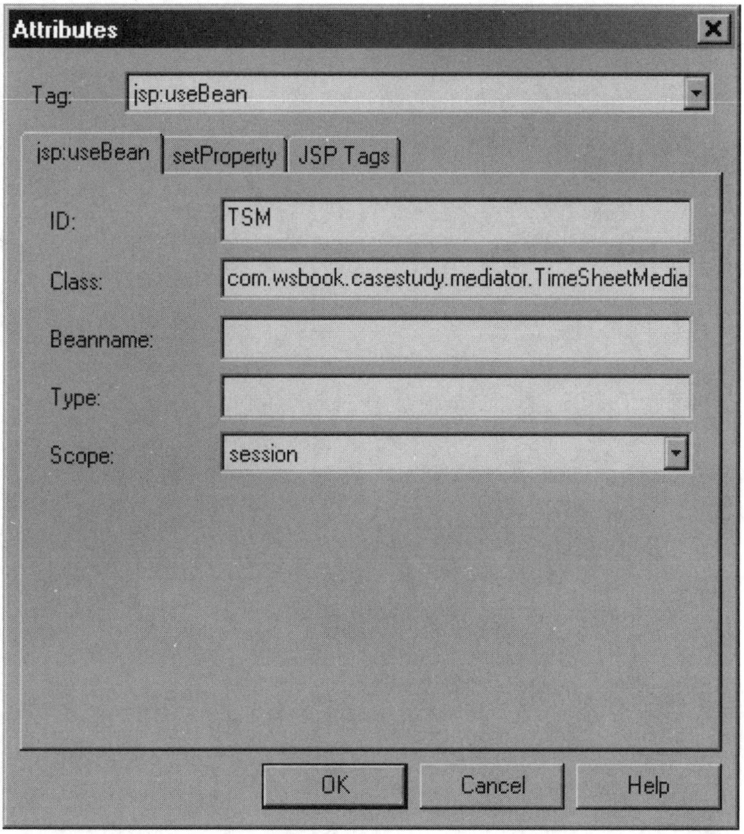

Figure 11.4 Drop a JavaBean on JSP

page, the Java type will be inserted into the class element, a default string will be inserted into the ID field, and the scope will be set to *default,* which, of course, is the page scope. The *setProperty* button on the useBean attribute dialog makes it very easy to add setProperty actions within the body of the use-Bean action tag. Should you want to add a scriptlet to the useBean tag body, you would need to use the HTML source view.

Dropping Java classes on the page makes writing useBean action tags a little easier, but the real benefit is the manner in which the tool treats these new *explicit* objects when manipulating other elements on the JSP. Earlier, when we were discussing the useBean action, we indicated that the JavaBeans are delivering dynamic content to the JSP via Bean properties. Page Designer has defined a number of dynamic elements that can be added to a JSP. The simplest of these is *Property Display.* When adding a *Property Display* element onto the page, the page developer is presented with the attribute dialog shown in Figure 11.5.

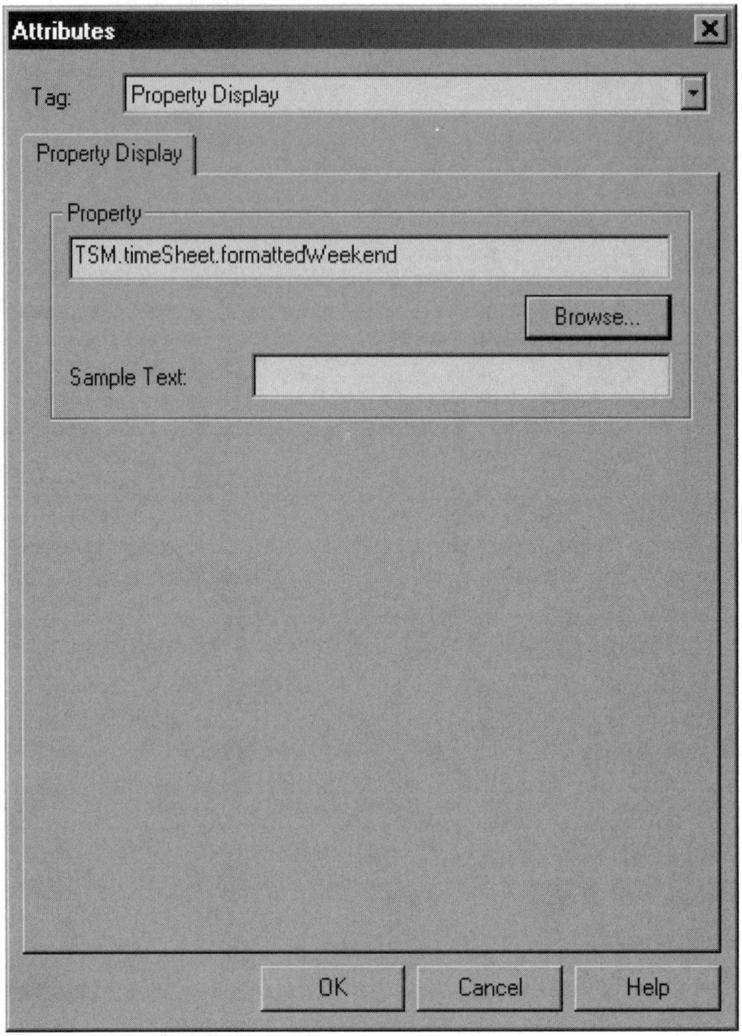

Figure 11.5 Dynamic Element *Property Display*

The purpose of *Property Display* is to insert the string representation of the named object property. As you can see from Figure 11.5, the dialog presents the developer with a *Browse* button. Clicking this button brings up a *Bean Property Selection* dialog (Figure 11.6) that presents all known objects to the developer in a simple tree view.

At the top level, all implicit objects and JavaBeans declared in useBean action tags are displayed. Expanding an object reference exposes all direct properties of the Bean. If a property itself is a Java object, its properties are

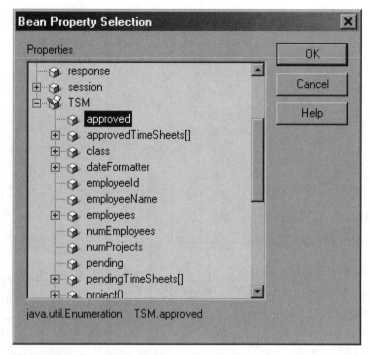

Figure 11.6 *Properties* Browser

available as *nested properties*. For example, in Figure 11.6, you can drill down from *TSM* (the TimeSheetMediator Bean), to its indexed property approved TimeSheets. An instance of this indexed property is a TimeSheet object that has properties approved by employee, entries, state, timesheet, and weekend. If one selects the *approved* property of *TSM,* Page Designer inserts the equivalent of the JSP expression: <%= TSM.getApproved() %>.

To accomplish its tag generation, Page Designer inserts a comment, or metatag. The "page" generator within WebSphere Studio then handles this "private" tag when the JSP is published to a target server. An extensible style sheet language (XSL) style sheet drives this page generation. A different style sheet is used, based on the target application server and the selected JSP enabler, such as version 0.91 or 1.0. This makes the "raw" JSP files, as viewed in the HTML source view of Page Designer, more convoluted. On the positive side, the tool, in conjunction with Studio, will be able to generate the next level of JSP, when it is supported by Studio, without modification of the JSP source.

In addition to directly placing the value of properties—dynamic content— into the HTML stream, dynamic content is often used as runtime expressions

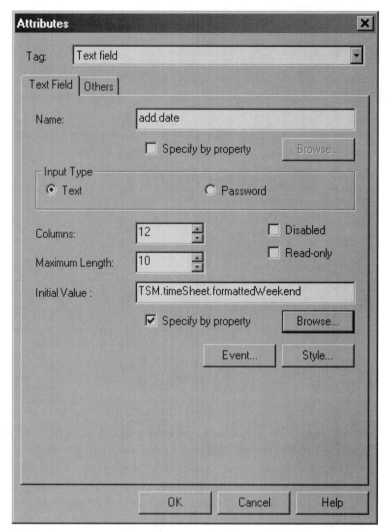

Figure 11.7 Properties as Runtime Expressions in Standard HTML Tags

within other HTML elements. Figure 11.7 shows the support for this provided by Page Designer. Most attributes of HTML tags for which runtime expressions are reasonable are provided with a check box to have the attribute
specified by property. Checking this feature and clicking the associated
Browse button brings up the same *Properties* browser shown in Figure 11.6.

A number of HTML tags displays a collection of items (*Table, Lists, List
Box,* and *Option Menu*). In Page Designer, the attribute dialog for these tags

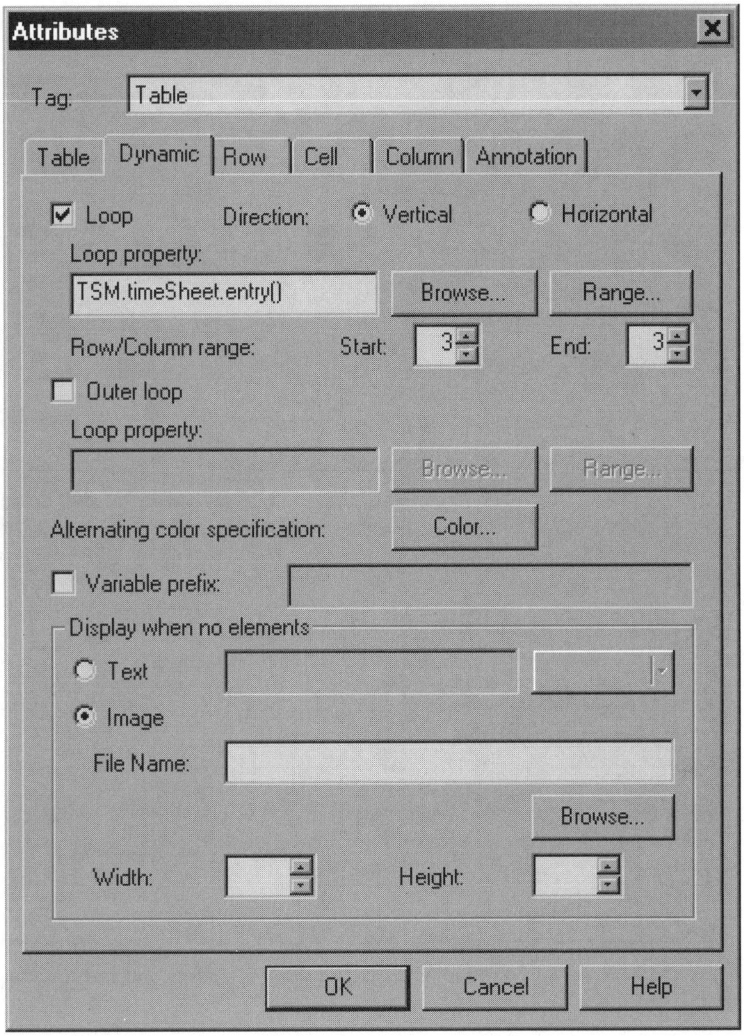

Figure 11.8 Indexed Properties Used to Control Loops in Tables, Lists, and Choices

has a dynamic page where indexed properties can be selected to act as loop control over this collection. Figure 11.8 gives an example of this.

In Figure 11.8, the indexed property, *entry()*, of the TimeSheet object represents all TimeSheetEntries associated with that TimeSheet. Here, we are looping on the third row in *Table*. The first two rows contain fixed information. In each cell in row 3, we would drop *Dynamic Property tags* for each property of a TimeSheetEntry that is to be displayed. Then, if the TimeSheet contains three

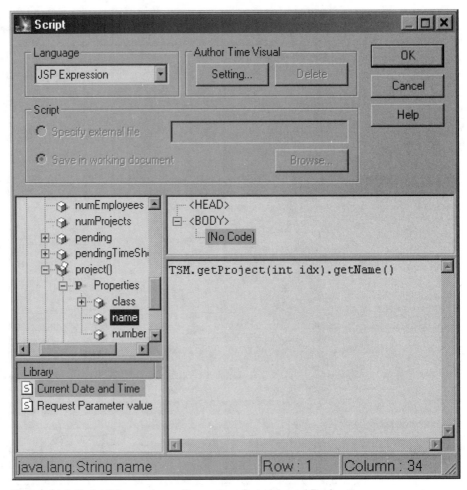

Figure 11.9 Script Editor to Insert Expressions, Scriptlets, and Declarations

TimeSheetEntries, the loop will generate three rows (3, 4, and 5) in the table. If the TimeSheet is empty (no TimeSheetEntries), there will be no "third" row.

This is a very handy feature of the Page Designer in support of JSP. When using JSPs only as display pages and encapsulating all dynamic content in JavaBeans, one of the only reasons to include any scriptlets within the JSP is to handle loop management. For these common HTML tags, which may need looping, this built-in loop control handles many of those cases. One of the remaining cases for looping, displaying repeating text, is supported by two special elements, found on the *Insert>Dynamic Elements* menu. These elements are *Dynamic Loop* and *Dynamic Text*.

Although we strive to eliminate scriptlets in our display pages, Page Designer provides a nice script editor to make this task very easy. (See Figure 11.9.) (*Hint:* Use this to write your JavaScript.) The script editor is accessed when you insert JSP expressions or scriptlets. Like the *Properties* browser, the script editor has a tree view of all available objects. Unlike the *Properties* browser, this tree view provides access to both properties and methods of Beans. Select a method or property, drag it to the script composition pane, and the corresponding (access) code will be written for you.

Testing JSPs

With your splashy JSP written, it is time to turn our attention to deploying and testing. Back in WebSphere Studio, you can check in your JSPs and publish them just like any other Web resources. During development, you will likely want to publish to a stage configured for your test environment running within VisualAge for Java. Before cranking up your test environment, you can run a simple syntax check within WebSphere Studio. When you select the JSP and select *Compile* from the context-sensitive menu, Studio will run the JSP file through the page compiler. Studio will flag both JSP syntax problems and Java compilation errors that result from compiling the generated servlet. This static checker is just that. No artifacts are kept during the process other than error messages. In other words, this is not a true JSP batch compiler.

Configuration of JSPs in the WebSphere Test Environment

Before deploying JSPs to the VisualAge WebSphere Test Environment (WTE), you may first need to perform some configuration of the WTE. For instance, by default, the WTE is configured to work only with JSPs written to the JSP 1.0 specification. If you want to debug a JSP written to the older, configuration, JSP 0.91, you must change the WTE configuration files. This process is described in detail in the product documentation.

By default, the servlet generated from a JSP is imported into the VisualAge for Java workspace and executed from there. The class is imported into a special project named *JSP Page Compile Generated Code.* This can sometimes cause problems in executing JSPs in the WTE. If, for some reason, the generated servlet cannot be imported into the workspace, execution will fail. (This most often occurs when the current workspace owner is not a group member for the package the class is being imported into.)

This behavior of importing the generated servlet into the workspace can be modified. This is one of the options on the page in the *WTE Control Center* associated with the JSP Execution Monitor tool.

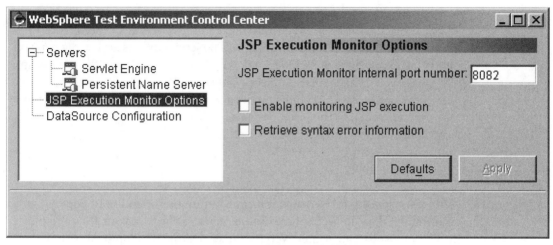

Figure 11.10 Configuring the JSP Execution Monitor

JSP Execution Monitor

JSP is an odd technology when testing and debugging. The source is not directly translated to runtime code but instead is used to generate a Java class file that then is translated to runtime code. VisualAge for Java ships with a nice little tool that helps bridge that gap, particularly for developers who are new to JSP. This tool is called the *JSP Execution Monitor*.

The Execution Monitor has several features that can be enabled or disabled. You access them through the *JSP Execution Monitor Options* page of the *WTE Control Center* (Figure 11.10). To access this page, select the *Workbench>Tools>WebSphere Text Environment...* item of VisualAge for Java's menu, and then select *JSP Execution Monitor Options* in the *WTE Control Center*.

The JSP Execution Monitor provides a simultaneous view on the JSP tag source, the generated Java servlet source, and the resulting emitted output stream created by executing the JSP. These views are shown in Figure 11.11.

The Execution Monitor can be used for two purposes. First, it can be used to locate syntax errors, either JSP tag syntax errors or syntax errors in the generated Java code, usually the result of syntax errors in a scriptlet. This feature is enabled through the check box labeled *Retrieve syntax error information* in the *Execution Monitor Options* page. When a JSP is page compiled and a syntax error is detected, the JSP source and, if applicable, the generated Java servlet are displayed with the lines of code in error highlighted (see Figure 11.11). This makes it very easy to track down and correct errors in your JSP.

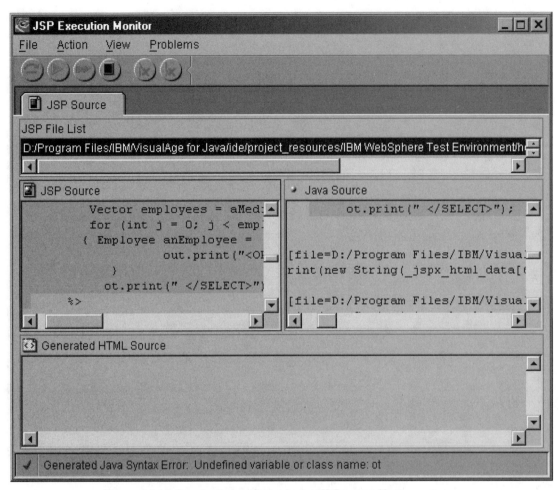

Figure 11.11 Showing Syntax Errors in the *JSP Execution Monitor*

The second use of the Execution Monitor tool is to watch the execution behavior of the resulting servlet. This feature is enabled through the check box labeled, *Enable monitoring JSP execution* in the *JSP Execution Monitor Options* page. With this feature enabled, when a JSP is executed, the Execution Monitor is loaded with both the JSP source and the servlet source, and execution is paused—like a breakpoint—at the entry to the _jspService() method of the JSP servlet. A breakpoint, marked by the "ball" in the left margin, is set on the second visible line of JSP source in Figure 11.12.

The Execution Monitor has controls to single-step, run, fast-forward, and terminate. It is possible to set breakpoints so that you can quickly run through to a particular point in the code and then single-step. You cannot

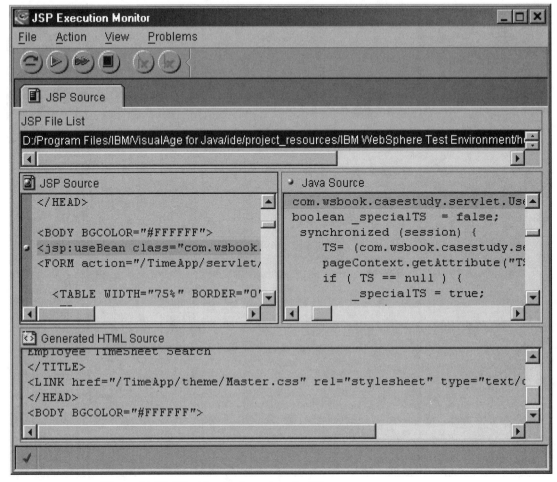

Figure 11.12 Watching the Execution of a JSP

perform any debugging tasks within the monitor other than viewing the execution. However, for certain sequencing errors, this can be a valuable tool. It is also a terrific illustration of what is happening when a JSP is executed.

For solving serious execution problems, you need a complete debugging environment. The WTE also facilitates this. As was discussed earlier, the typical behavior of executing JSPs in the WTE is to have the generated servlet imported into the VAJ workspace in a special project called *JSP Page Compile Generated Code*. During execution, if the *WTE Control Center* has this project on its class path, the servlet class loaded in the workspace will be executed. This means that one can simply place breakpoints in this code, triggering the VAJ debugger when executing the JSP.

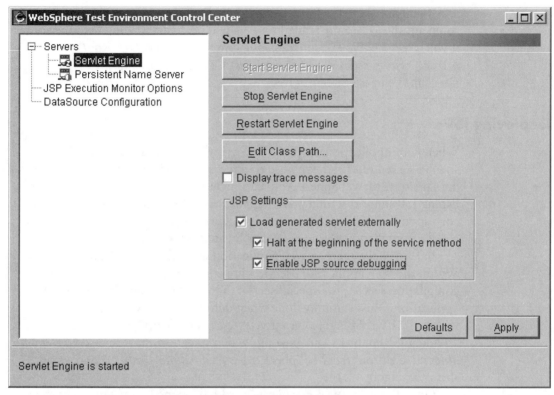

Figure 11.13 *JSP Settings* on the *Servlet Engine* Page

To initialize the debugging of a JSP this way requires running the test case twice. The first time through will cause the JSP servlet to be loaded in the workspace. Then you can go to the *JSP Page Compile Generated Code* project, locate the source, and set a breakpoint. The next runthrough will pick up the breakpoint and drop you into the debugger. Although you can change code and variables in this environment, it is the JSP source that you ultimately need to update when correcting your errors.

When running many JSPs within the test environment, you may want to disable the Execution Monitor and/or have the generated JSP servlet loaded externally. Externally loading the JSP prevents loading the class into the workspace and, more important, the repository. If you don't have need to debug the JSPs, you can minimize the number of editions added to the repository by selecting to load these generated servlets externally. You do this by changing the *JSP Settings* configuration options on the *Servlet Engine* page of the *WTE Control Center,* as shown in Figure 11.13.

If you are using the JSP 1.0 page compilation servlet within the test environment, the externally loaded servlets will be created, along with the source if you select *Enable JSP source debugging,* in the *<VA Java Root>/ide/ project_resources/IBM WebSphere Test Environment/temp/JSP1_0/ <webapp_name>* directory tree.

Deploying JSPs

When your application is operating correctly, you are ready to deploy to a staging server. But first, you need to understand the tasks involved in deploying JSPs to IBM WebSphere Application Server. The starting point is establishing JSP support within a *Web application.* Recall that Web applications correspond to the *Web container* abstraction in J2EE. The Web application is a collection of cooperating resources located via a common URL prefix.

In IBM WebSphere, a Web application is hosted by an application server. Within the Web application, servlets are configured. A JSP enabler, a page compilation servlet, is a special servlet that can be configured within a Web application. This is usually done when defining a new Web application within IBM WebSphere; alternatively, it can be performed as a separate task. To add a JSP enabler to an existing Web application, start the *Add a JSP Enabler* wizard from the WebSphere *Advanced Administrative Console,* as shown in Figure 11.14.

Once the *Add a JSP Enabler* wizard has opened, you can select the level of JSP support to add, in the first page of the wizard, and select the Web application you wish to add the JSP enabler to. The wizard is shown in Figure 11.15.

The JSP enabler associates the corresponding page compilation service with the URL, *<web_app_virtualhost>/<web_path>/*.jsp.* Although JSPs look and feel like HTML pages, they are resolved and handled by the Web application services of a running application server. Within WebSphere, each Web application has a *document root* property, which is used to locate and to resolve JSP files. In general, your HTML files and all the other embedded resources, such as images and audio files, will be resolved and served by the Web server and its collection of document roots, aliases, and so on. To correspond to this distribution of responsibility, you will probably want to deploy, or publish, your JSPs to a document root that is unique for your Web application and that is not visible to your Web server.

The effect of the previous scenario is to have a minimum of three publishing targets defined for a Web site in a tool like WebSphere Studio. The targets represent the (1) Web components served by the Web server, (2) JSP

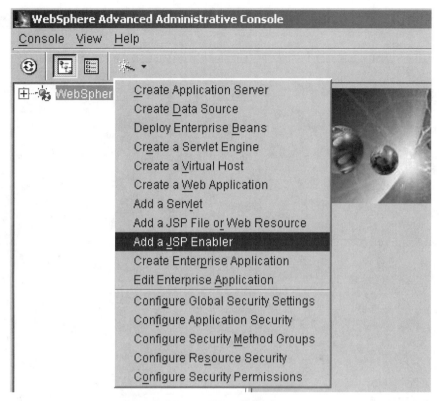

Figure 11.14 Adding a JSP Enabler to a Web Application

source pages, and (3) servlets and support classes. The page compiler will use the Web application's class path when compiling a JSP. Thus, all support classes (JavaBeans) of the JSP must be deployed to a location that is on this class path. The compiled class, the serialized arrary of strings, and, optionally, the "kept" servlet source can be found in the *<WebSphere_Root>* */temp/<virtual_hostname>/<webapp_name>* directory tree.

One of the optional features of IBM WebSphere Application Server's JSP support is the batch JSP compiler. Use of this feature enables faster responses to the initial client requests for the JSPs on your production Web server. Batch compiling saves system resources on the application server and is useful during application development as a fast way to resynchronize all the JSP files for an application after changes are made to one file. It is best to batch compile all the JSP files associated with an application. Once the compiled files are placed on the system, the application server still monitors the JSP source file for changes, prompting recompile and reload.

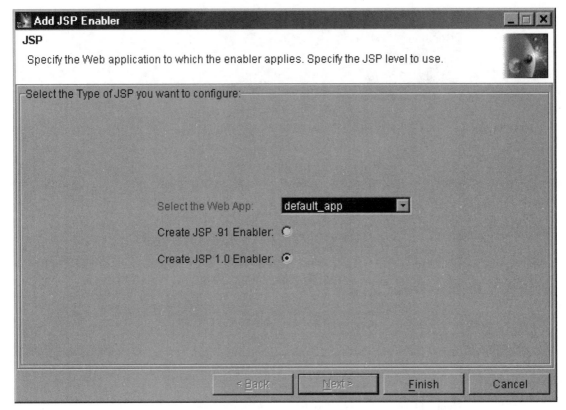

Figure 11.15 The *Add JSP Enabler* Wizard

For information on naming the JSP batch compiler, refer to the product documentation.

Support for taglib and XML

We will wrap up the JSP discussion by looking forward to the current JSP 1.1 specification and support for custom action tags and interoperability with XML data formats. JSP is intended to be a flexible specification that strongly supports tool vendors in supplying high-end productivity tools. Toward that goal, it is clear that no fixed set of tags can fully meet this requirement. In particular, as tools offer more design-time controls to be dropped on JSPs with specific functionality, it would be nice if that could be supported both by a static tag and the corresponding runtime services.

This flexibility is provided by the tag library support in JSP 1.1. A tag library abstracts functionality through the definition of custom actions. The inclusion of custom action tags within a JSP requires identifying the tag library that supplies the corresponding functionality. This is accomplished with the taglib directive. The syntax for the taglib directive is:

```
<%@ taglib uri="taglibraryURI" prefix="tagPrefix" %>
```

The taglibraryURI identifies the descriptor (tag library descriptor) for the corresponding tag library. The tagPrefix is used to qualify each defined action within the JSP. For example, consider the xyzTagLibrary referred to in the following directive, and assume that it defines a tag call Loop.

```
<%@ taglib uri=/xyzTagLibrary prefix="abc" %>
```

When appearing within the associated JSP file, the Loop tag would be written as <abc:Loop>. The tag library descriptor, an XML file, specifies the various tags and their formats available in the library. Each declared tag has a corresponding Java class to handle the request-time behavior—it implements the javax.servlet.jsp.tagext.Tag interface—and, optionally, a Java class to handle part of the translation-time effort: a class that implements the javax.servlet.jsp.tagext.TagExtraInfo interface.[2]

XML Compliance

The future of JSP is to permit JSP source to be transmitted—and emitted by tools—as XML documents. A number of JSP tags needs to have an alternative syntax to support this direction. More is involved than just defining XML-compliant JSP tag syntax, but for now, that is the most important area of concern for JSP developers. Both the JSP directives and JSP scripting tags need an alternative form.

For the directives, the XML-compliant syntax is:

```
<jsp:directive.directivename directive_attributes />
```

An example is <jsp:directive.page isErrorPage="true"/>.

The scripting elements are block tags. They are:

```
<jsp:declaration> declaration goes here </jsp:declaration>
<jsp:scriptlet> code fragment goes here </jsp:scriptlet>
<jsp:expression> expression goes here </jsp:expression>
```

As the JSP Specification moves forward and Web container support for XML increases, emphasis on the creation of JSPs as XML documents will increase.

---

1. For more information on using tag libraries in WebSphere 3.5 with Fixpack 2, refer to the product documentation.

Summary and Preview

JSP offers an extremely productive tag language to develop server-side Java logic. Its greatest value is in the development of Web pages that include dynamic content. JSPs make it possible to eliminate the need for servlets to ever write content to an HTTP response stream. By factoring all business logic and data translation out of both servlets and JSPs through the use of JavaBeans as mediators, the resulting set of server-side assets have a very clean division of responsibility. Servlets are simple controllers, JSPs are simple page templates, and everything else is facilitated by the remaining server-side layer(s) in the application.

With JSP-aware page development tools, such as WebSphere Page Designer, it is further possible to easily develop and maintain JSPs within these tools. This allows developers in the right roles and using the right tools to produce the right assets for the enterprise application.

Having completed our discussion of servlet and JSP technology, we are ready to present this book's case study. In Chapter 12, we present a Web-based entry system for time sheets and show how to apply servlets and JSPs.

CHAPTER 12

Servlet and JSP Case Study

In the past several chapters, we have shown how servlet and JSP technology should be used in a layered application architecture. Now, in this chapter, we will present a reference implementation of a Web-based time-sheet entry system to show how to apply the best-practice approaches and the technologies—specifically, servlets and JSPs—discussed in previous chapters. For instance, Figure 12.1 shows the five-layer application architecture discussed in Chapter 3. Also, the HTML interface for the application is built using servlets and JSPs, as described in Chapters 4–11. Throughout this book, we have selectively taken, and will continue to take, implementation examples from the case study in this chapter to illustrate particular points. Here, we examine an application using these technologies in depth in order to show how they fit into application development.

IBM's VisualAge for Java 3.5 development environment and WebSphere 3.5, Application Server, Advanced Edition, provide the context for the examples in this chapter. However, the case study has been written using 100% Pure Java and conforms to the JSDK 2.1 and JSP 1.0 specifications, so in theory, it should be possible to deploy the case study into any conformant application server.

The sections in this chapter do not have to be read in any particular sequence. If you are interested simply in loading the case study into the VisualAge WebSphere Test Environment (WTE) and reading the code, read the first two sections, which describe this process and document how to use the example application. The other sections delve into topics in analysis and design and some implementation specifics of the case study.

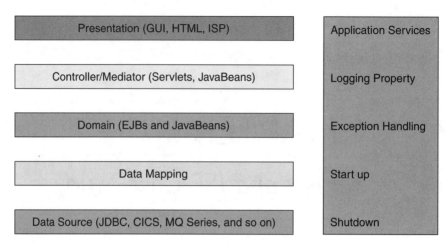

Figure 12.1 Five-Layer Architecture

Executing Test Scripts

Earlier, we described as a best practice defining test scripts to help verify the application implementation and behavior. Only domain model behavior is exercised in test scripts. We have not included test scripts to test our presentation layer, but the goal is that it should be simple enough to let you eyeball it and determine whether it is working correctly. As simplistic as they might seem, our test scripts provide value beyond just testing domain logic. They provide a way to validate the function of the domain logic in case it is extended or refactored, making it easy for you to experiment with changes to these classes.

In our case study, we have implemented test scripts to create and to retrieve time sheets and their associated objects and then to report the results to the Java console. We have defined these test scripts as Java classes in a package specifically created for that purpose and containing only test scripts. Each test script is named, using a meaningful class name derived from the name of the class under test and the type of test being performed. We have made our test scripts executable by defining the test operations in a main() method.

The case study test script classes can be executed from VisualAge by selecting a test script and then performing the run operation. Figures 12.2 and 12.3 display the results.

Loading the Case Study into the WebSphere Test Environment

The following instructions explain how to load the case study into VisualAge 3.5, Enterprise Edition, and test its operation by using the VisualAge WTE.

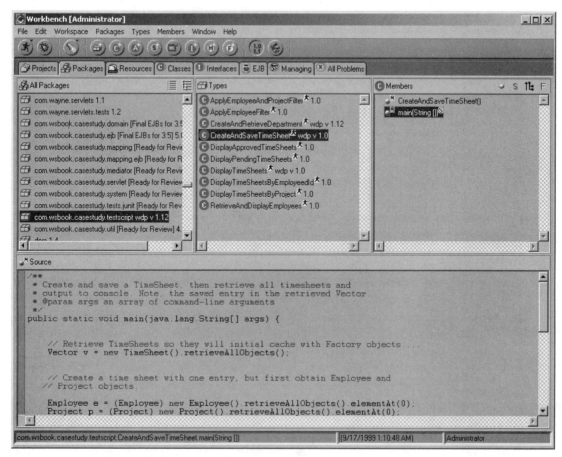

Figure 12.2 Case Study Test Scripts

Step 1: Import the *WebSphereCaseStudy.dat* file from the CD-ROM accompanying this book. Start the import process by selecting *File>Import* from the VisualAge for Java workbench. The dialog in Figure 12.4 will then appear.

Select *Repository* as the source from which you will import into VisualAge. The difference here is that VisualAge allows you to import source code or *.class* files from not only a directory or a *.jar* file but also from a VisualAge repository *(.dat)* file that contains metainformation about version numbering, visual composition, and EJBs. After you select *Repository,* click *Next>* to see the next dialog (Figure 12.5).

In this dialog, you will need to use the *Browse* button and standard file dialog to locate the *WebSphereCaseStudy.dat* file from the CD-ROM. After selecting the file, choose *Projects* from the *What do you want to import* radio

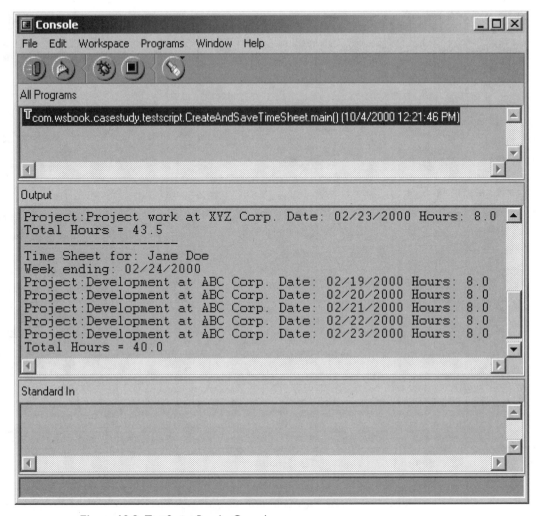

Figure 12.3 Test Script Results Console

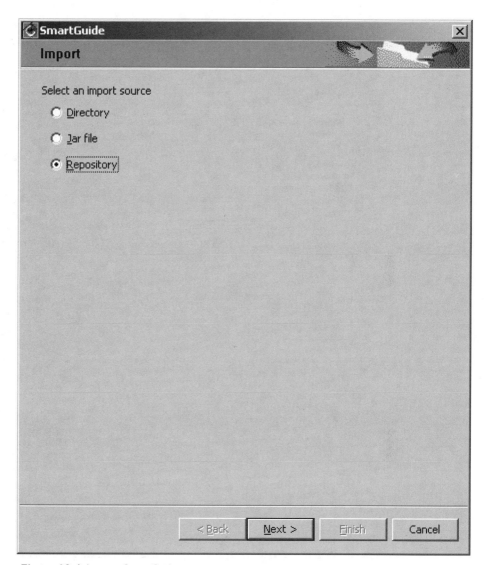

Figure 12.4 Import *SmartGuide*

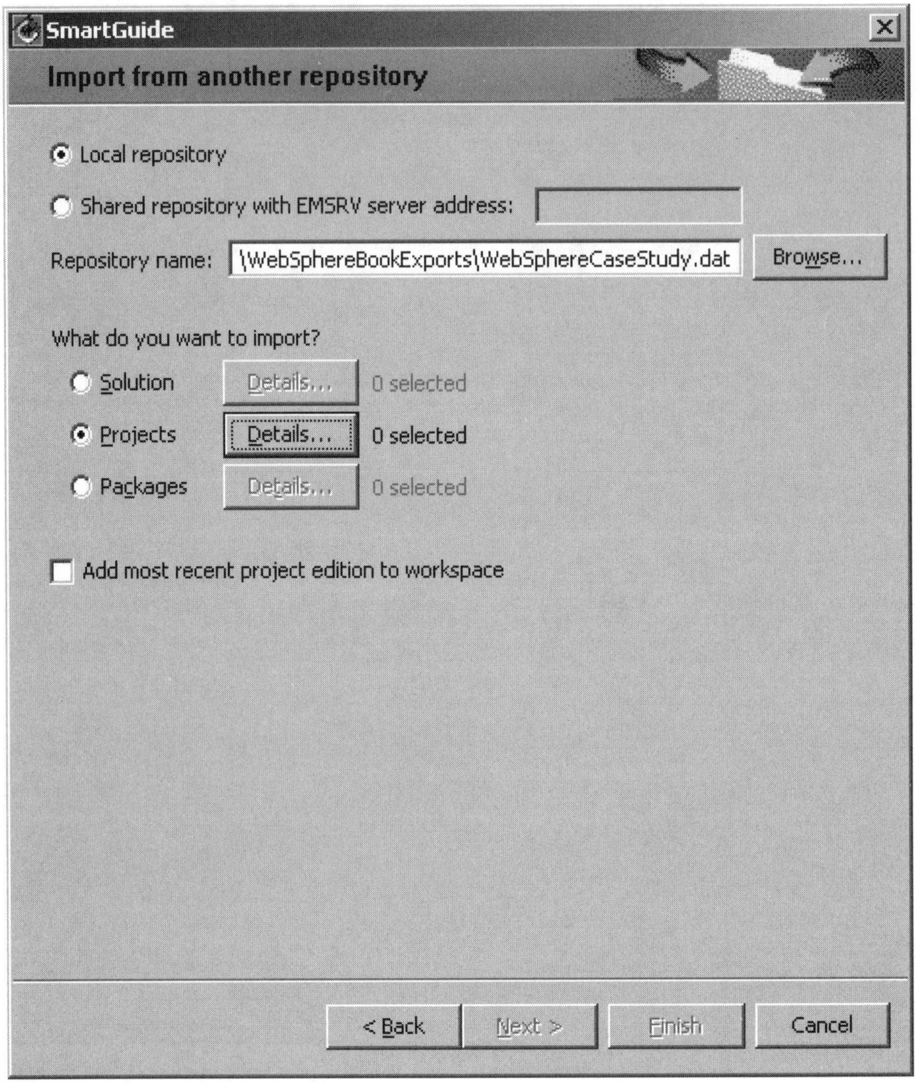

Figure 12.5 Import from *Repository* Page

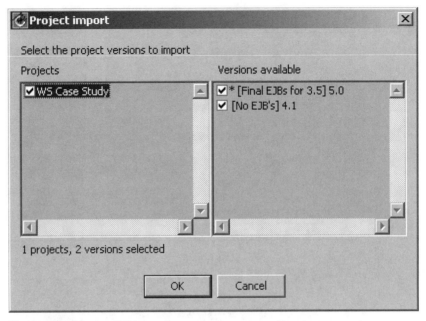

Figure 12.6 Versions Dialog

button group. Then click the *Details...* button to bring up the versions dialog (Figure 12.6).

Select both versions and click *OK* to dismiss this dialog. Before completing the import process by clicking *Finish*, make sure that you uncheck the *Add most recent project edition to workspace* radio button. The reason is that two versions of the case study project are in this repository.

- *[No EJB's] 4.1* contains the version of the case study that does not include any EJBs. This version implements the servlets and JSPs but does not store or retrieve time-sheet information from EJBs, instead using default in-memory collections.
- *[Final EJBs for 3.5] 5.0* contains all the EJBs that you will see being constructed in the next few chapters. Please don't load this version until later, when you are ready to examine how these EJBs work.

Step 2: Copy the HTML and JSP files from the CD-ROM's *vahtml* subdirectory to the test environment's document root. This directory will normally be *[VAJ Install Root]/ide/project_resources/IBM WebSphere Test Environment/hosts/default_host/ default_app/web*.

Step 3: Go to the VisualAge for Java *Workbench* and select *Projects*. Open the right-button mouse menu. Select *Add Project*, as shown in

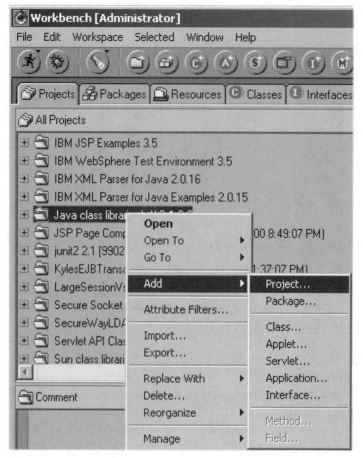

Figure 12.7 *Add* and *Project* Menus

Figure 12.7. Choosing this menu option will display the *Add Project Smart-Guide,* shown in Figure 12.8. Select the *Add projects from the repository* radio button and choose *WS Case Study* in the *Available project names* list box. Choose *[No Ejb's] 4.1* from the *Available editions* list box. Finish adding the project to your workbench by clicking the *OK* button.

Step 4: Open the *WTE Control Center* and set the class path properties to include the *WS Case Study* project. (Details on how to do this are given in Chapter 5.)

Step 5: Start the servlet engine, as described in Chapter 5.

Step 6: Open a browser and type in the following URL: *http://localhost: 8080/index.html.*

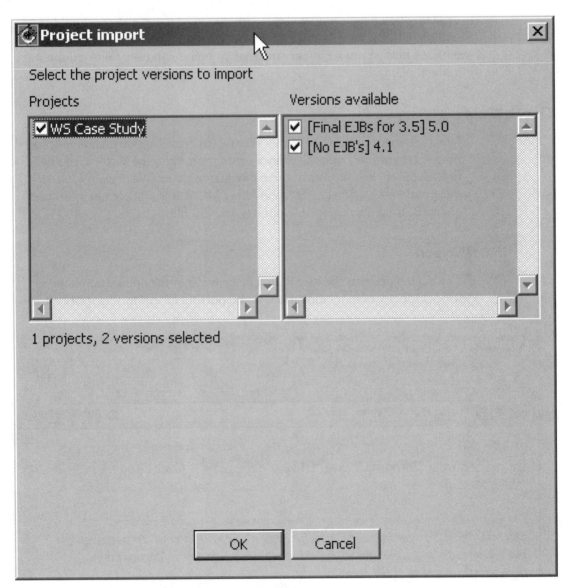

Figure 12.8 The *Add Project SmartGuide*

Note: Instead of following step 2, an alternative is to publish the HTML and JSP files from WebSphere studio. In that case, the URL in step 6 will be: http://localhost:8080/TimeApp/index.html

Once you have completed these instructions, your browser should contain the initial screen described in the next section. If instead you see an error message in the browser, make sure that you have carefully followed the steps, and try again.

User's Guide

Our time-sheet application allows the user to create, modify, and report on time-sheet entries. From the primary entry point into the Web-based application, the user can take any of three navigation paths. We explain each of these paths by showing the generated HTML as it is rendered in a browser and indicating the responsible servlets and JSP files.

Initial Screen

This screen presents the user with a description of the application links to time-sheet creation, modification, and reporting functions (Figure 12.9).

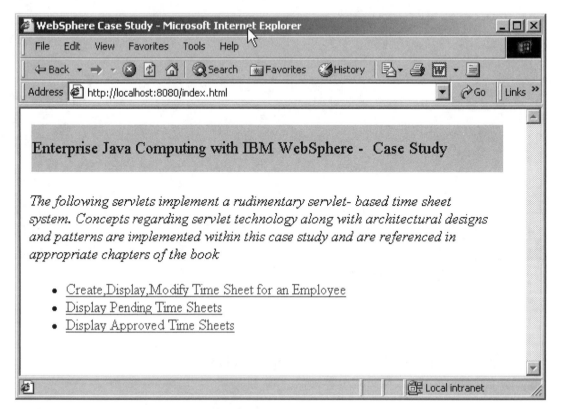

Figure 12.9 Case Study Initial Screen

Create, Display, and Modify Time Sheet for an Employee

This action searches for and displays a time sheet based on an employee name and week-ending date. If the date is not found, a list is displayed of all currently defined time sheets for the selected employee; a particular time sheet can then be selected. Also, the entered date is displayed and can be selected to create a new time sheet (Figure 12.10).

If a time sheet for a week-ending date exists for the named employee, the time sheet is displayed. Only pending, not-approved time sheets can be edited. The date, project, and hours for each time-sheet entry can be modified. Time-sheet entries can be marked for deletion, and new entries can be added (Figure 12.11).

If a time sheet for the specified week-ending date is not found, a list of week-ending dates is displayed. Also, a link for creating a new time sheet for the specified week-ending date appears (Figure 12.12).

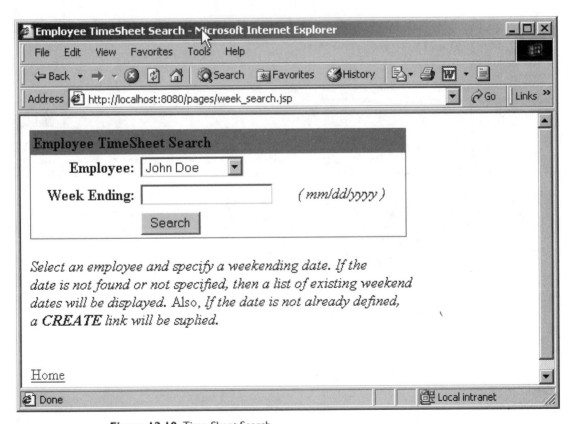

Figure 12.10 Time-Sheet Search

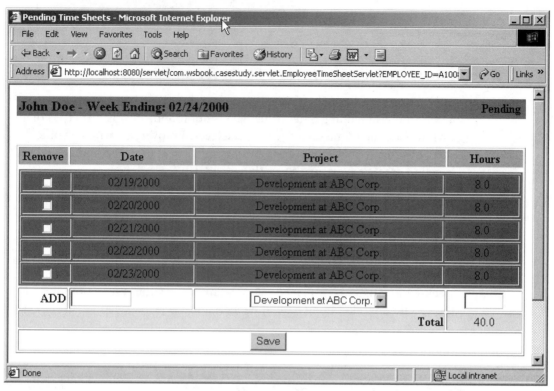

Figure 12.11 Pending Time Sheet

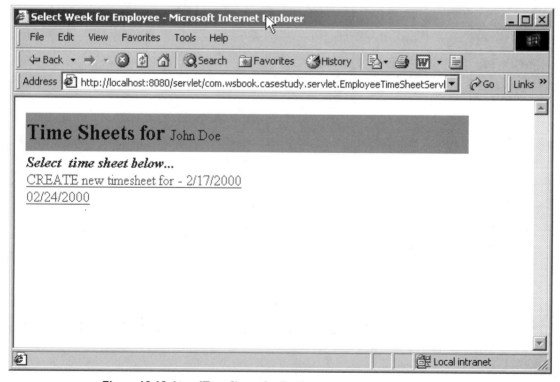

Figure 12.12 List of Time Sheets for Employee

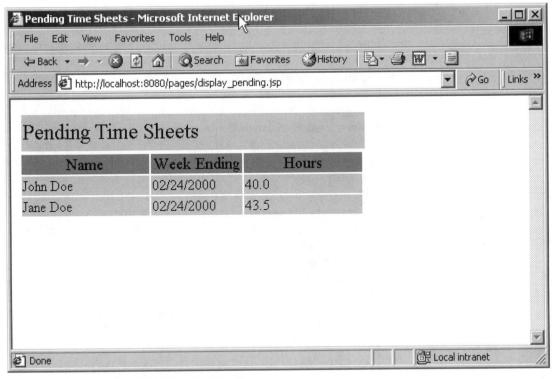

Figure 12.13 Pending Time Sheets

Display Pending and Approved Time Sheets

In this screen, all pending and approved time sheets for an employee are displayed, respectively, depending on which link is accessed (Figure 12.13).

Case Study Analysis and Design Artifacts

In this section, we present some of the key analysis and design (A&D) artifacts produced during the development of our case study. Although this book is not an appropriate place to discuss all the ramifications of performing a detailed analysis and design of a Web-based application, we hope to convey at least a sense of the kind of process that is followed and some of the artifacts that can be produced. In designing our application, we use a simple use case driven approach, compatible with that described in [Fowler]. We show the analysis and design artifacts, using UML[1] notation, again as described in [Fowler].

---

1. Unified Modeling Language as defined by the Object Management Group standard.

What Type of A&D Process Is Appropriate for Web Applications?

One question we are commonly asked in our consulting practice is how to go about setting up a development process for Web applications. The problem is that Enterprise Java applications can be approached from two sides: the Web-up and the Enterprise-down sides.

In the Web-up approach, a Web site built by using ad hoc, seat-of-the-pants development methods must suddenly be rearchitected to scale up to thousands or millions of users to meet new demands. In this case, we see that often no development process is in place, as it has not been necessary in the small-team environment that most Web shops still have. In the other approach, a traditional information systems (IS) organization finds that it must reinvent itself to address the needs of customers and partners on the global Internet. In this case, a set of development practices is often in place, but they probably do not apply to the development tools, techniques, and time scales that Web development necessitates.

We have found that most groups doing Enterprise Java development can lie in a happy medium between these two sides. We often recommend that our clients begin by looking carefully at two books: *Extreme Programming Explained,* by Kent Beck [Beck], and *UML Distilled, Second Edition,* by Martin Fowler [Fowler].

Extreme programming (XP), the subject of the first book, is a radical revisiting of some old theories about software development. The book proposes a very rapid, highly productive development cycle characterized by continual testing, minimal up-front design, and tight control of software iterations. We have seen several cases in which small teams of three to ten programmers, which is about the limit of what XP can handle, can produce high-quality software in a very short time using this process. On the other hand, there is often a need for some slight formalism in A&D artifacts, specifically when developers are learning new technologies and need to be able to see, at a glance, where they fit into an overall picture of a software system. For this purpose, we often recommend that an XP-like process be combined with some, but not all, elements of UML (Unified Modeling Language, the standard notation for OO A&D). Because many Web programmers, coming from both sides, are very visual people, they may take better to a more diagrammatic approach to rapid design than to the text-based approach suggested by [Beck]. So, we often recommend XP plus UML. We often take this approach ourselves and recommend it for most small teams beginning to learn Enterprise Java technologies.

However, some cases require a larger scale approach. If a team has more than about 15 people or must produce specific requirements and design documentation to fit an existing corporate or governmental process, a more elaborate technique, such as the Unified Software Development Process, described in [Jacobson 99], may apply. Although the Unified Process is both well understood and complete, we feel that it is overkill in many cases, as it does not accmmodate itself well to either Web time scales or Web team sizes. However, it must be chosen for some cases. You must consider carefully your time scales and the size of your team before you begin either process.

Problem Statement

All analysis and design must start with a statement of the problem to be solved. This can be as simple as the user stories defined in [Beck] or as complex as a traditional functional specification. Ours is simple and is more like a user story than a functional specification.

Sample Problem Statement

Corporate personnel perform various activities throughout a given business day. These activities are most often dictated by assigned projects. As such, time spent on project-specific activities is tracked and reported on a specified basis. Summary information can then be compiled and reported on project and personnel and applied against project and budgetary plans.

Ensuring that time is entered for projects is accomplished through a time-sheet approval process. Authorized employees have been given the ability to preview pending time sheets and to mark them as being approved. Additionally, employee time sheets can be given automatic approval.

The system will be used frequently for short periods of time on a daily basis. Therefore, quick and convenient access to the time-entry portion of the system is required.

System Tasks

Another part of design is to specify the tasks that a user must perform in order to use the system. These tasks can be in the form of user stories. [Beck] explains how to enter these on "task cards" that can be used to partition development and to prioritize the order in which functions will be developed and delivered. [Fowler] describes these tasks as scenarios that can be used to build use cases. Our system tasks are specified as follows.

1. Employees can enter half-hour time increments against any available projects.

2. Employees can enter time-sheet information on a weekly basis.

3. Managers can ask for summary reports that include the details of hours charged against any given project.

4. Managers can ask for summary reports that include the details of hours charged for any given employee.

5. Both employees and managers should be able to access the system from any corporate-standard Web browser with intranet access.

6. Employees can modify entered time sheets before they are approved.

7. Authorized personnel can view and approve time sheets on a department or a project basis.

8. Authorized personnel can define projects, employees, and departments.

Use Case List

In a more formal process than the XP process described in [Beck], use cases can be used to specify user interactions with a system or system-to-system interactions, which can be useful in specifying business-to-business (B2B) applications. The following list of use cases is derived from our user tasks. We then show the UML diagrams and use case writeups for these use cases.

1. Employee enters daily time entries against project(s).

2. Employee creates a new time sheet for a week-ending date.

3. Employee updates a time sheet that is not yet approved.

4. Manager approves employee time sheets.

5. Manager unapproves employee time sheet.

6. Manager requests a report of pending time sheets.

7. Manager requests a report of approved time sheets.

By examining our list of use cases, we discovered that two actors participate in our use cases.

• Employee: enters daily time associated with projects
• Time-sheet authorizer (manager): authorizes employee time sheets

Figure 12.14 shows the use cases and relationships with our defined actors.

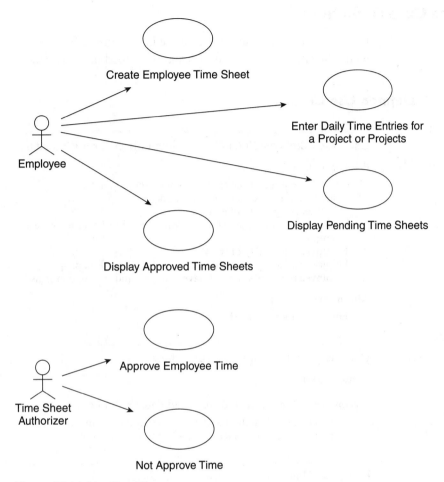

Create Employee Time Sheet

Employee

Enter Daily Time Entries for
a Project or Projects

Display Pending Time Sheets

Display Approved Time Sheets

Approve Employee Time

Time Sheet
Authorizer

Not Approve Time

Figure 12.14 Use Case Diagram

Use Case Definitions

Here, we show the use cases that we have defined for the case study. We are using the simplified use case format described in [Fowler].

Defined Use Cases

Use Case Employee Enters Daily Time Entries for a Project(s)

Primary course:

1. Employee requests time sheet for a week-ending date.
2. System checks for existence of time sheet.
   a. If it exists, present to employee.
   b. If it does not exist, see Create Employee Time Sheet use case and present to employee.
3. Employee selects day of week.
4. Employee selects project and enters hours worked on project.
5. Employee requests system to save changes, and system confirms.

Alternative course:

5a. Employee aborts time sheet entry.

Use Case: Create Employee Time Sheet

Primary course:

Precondition: Employee and week-end date are known.

1. System creates time sheet and associates employee and week ending.
2. System puts new time sheet in pending state and commits.

Use Case: Unapprove Employee Time Sheet

Primary course:

1. Authorized employee selects time sheet for employee and week end.
2. System for and displays pending time sheet.
3. Employee toggles time-sheet state to pending.

Alternative course:

2a. If not found, display available time sheets.

Use Case: Approve Employee Time Sheet

Primary course:

4. Authorized employee selects time sheet for employee and week end.
5. System for and displays pending time sheet.
6. Employee toggles time sheet state to approved.

Alternative course:

2a. If not found, display available time sheets.

Use Case: Display Pending Time Sheets

Primary course:

1. System displays list of pending employee, week end, and totals for pending time sheets.

Use Case: Display Approved Time Sheets

Precondition: Approved time sheet for employee exists

Primary course:

1. System displays list of approved-time-sheets employee, week end, and total hours.

Time-Sheet Domain Model

Now we are ready to show part of the outcome of the analysis and design process: the class diagram of the domain model of our system. Figure 12.15 shows the class diagram in UML notation.

Class Listing

As an adjunct to the UML class diagram of the example domain model presented previously, we show a list of definitions and purposes of the classes in this model:

- TimeSheet–defined on a week-ending basis for each employee. References a collection of time-sheet entries.
- TimeSheetEntry–project and hours applied for a time increment.
- TimeSheetState–abstract class representing the current state of a TimeSheet. Concrete states implement behavior state transition behavior.
- Pending–concrete implementation of TimeSheetState. Models initial state of a TimeSheet. Pending time-sheets transition into an Approved state.
- Approved–concrete implementation of TimeSheetState modeling a TimeSheet that has been approved by an authorized user.
- TimeSheetContainer–references a list of TimeSheets that can be iterated over, based on project or employee.
- EmployeeEnumerator–implements ability to enumerate over TimeSheets objects, ordered by employee.
- ProjectEnumerator–implements ability to enumerate over TimeSheets objects, ordered by project.
- Filter–interface defining a contract for filtering behavior. Filters apply match method to an enumeration of TimeSheet objects.
- ProjectFilter–filter TimeSheets for a project.

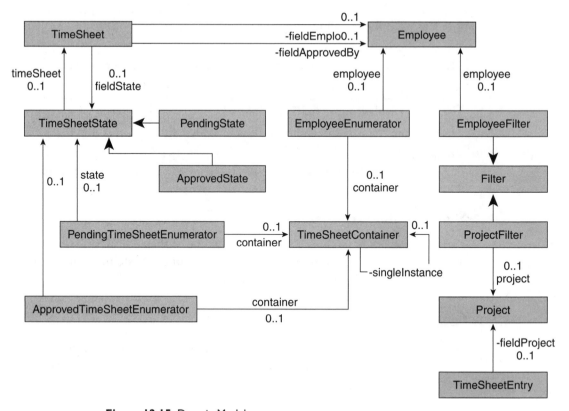

Figure 12.15 Domain Model

Collaboration Diagram

The time-sheet domain model is exercised be using servlets and JSP. Application functions are defined as JSP/servlet combinations that interact with a TimeSheet mediator for specific application functions. The collaboration diagram shown in Figure 12.16 depicts message flow for the application's time-sheet search function.

Mediator

The EmployeeMediator in this message flow holds on to the entered employee ID and week-end date (Figure 12.17). With these values set, the mediator provides a convenience method to return a matching TimeSheet instance. If this instance is pending, control is transferred to the pending_view.jsp. Otherwise, the approved_view.jsp is dispatched. It is worth noting that a single mediator instance is maintained throughout this messaging activity.

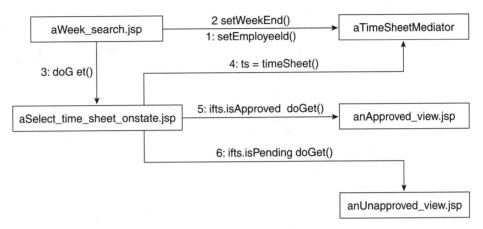

Figure 12.16 Time-Sheet Mediator Collaboration Diagram

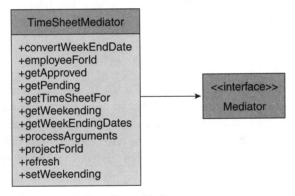

Figure 12.17 TimeSheet Mediator

Another interesting behavior the mediator implements is the processArguments() method. This method accepts a hash table of arguments that are extracted, transformed to their proper type, and set associated mediator attributes.

Mediators also provide a useful session management mechanism. For a more detailed discussion of how mediators help support session management, see Chapter 8.

Domain

The application domain is implemented in the form of JavaBeans. Persistence is implemented by requiring all domain classes to implement from TsObject,

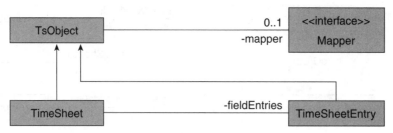

Figure 12.18 Base Object and Mapper Design

where persistent operations, such as save() or delete(), are forwarded to a mapping class (Figure 12.18).

The time sheet's primary intent is to model a time sheet and its entries. Therefore, it does not implement a lot of behavior, barring simple summing-type operations to obtain total hours for a specific time sheet. However, a design that models enumeration behavior filtering on project, employee, or week ending, has been created.

Enumeration

This enumeration design is implemented with an abstract class named TimeSheetEnumeration that implements the java.util.Enumeration interface. Along with the required enumeration methods, the TimeSheetEnumeration abstraction defines an abstract init() method with the intent of providing concrete implementations with the ability to initialize themselves (Figure 12.19).

Filtering

Filtering enumerations on such values as Employee or Project has been captured in the case study domain in the form of an abstract Filter type. This abstraction generalizes the extraction of domain objects matching the filter criteria. Filters are established by extending from the abstract Filter class (Figure 12.20).

Concrete filters are required to implement a match() method that accepts a TimeSheet as an argument and returns a true is the time sheet argument is a match. Each filter implementation is responsible for determining whether the supplied TimeSheet instance "matches" this filter. Filters will define attributes that reference objects used by the matching operation to determine match. The match method for the EmployeeFilter compares the current employee reference to that held on to by the supplied TimeSheet argument, as follows:

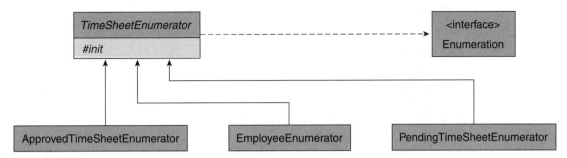

Figure 12.19 Enumeration Hierarchy

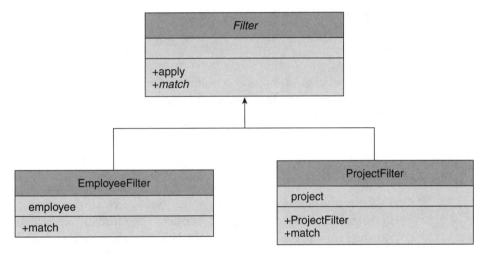

Figure 12.20 Filter Hierarchy

```
/**
 * Return true if supplied Timesheet employee matches
 * filter employee.
 */
public boolean match(TimeSheet aTimeSheet) {
if (employee.getId().equalsIgnoreCase(aTimeSheet.getEmployee().getId()))
    { return true; }
return false;
}
```

Container

Enumerations are used by a TimeSheetContainer implemented by using the
Singleton design pattern from [Gamma] (Figure 12.21). The primary

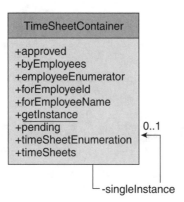

Figure 12.21 TimeSheetContainer Singleton

responsibility of this singleton is to define a centralized place where enumerations of domain objects can be obtained. Because enumeration objects are created and returned from container methods and these references are not held on to by the container, no more than one instance is needed in runtime memory.

Time Sheets

The problem domain centers on the notion of creating and maintaining time sheets for employees on a project basis. Therefore, the design process established a number of types representing the elements of a real time sheet. Of course, the most obvious type, and the apex of the design, is the TimeSheet type. An Employee is associated with a TimeSheet, and any number of TimeSheetEntries can be added to the TimeSheet. Also, each entry will reference a Project type (Figure 12.22).

Time-Sheet State

Every TimeSheet instance is in either a pending or an approved state. Instead of reflecting state as a simple attribute that is assigned a primitive value, the State pattern (from [Gamma]) is used (Figure 12.23).

The advantage of this design is that new states can be added by simply adding a subclass to the state hierarchy. Also, even though the case study has not taken advantage of the State pattern's ability to place state transition logic in each state type, states have a back reference to a TimeSheet, so this could be done if more states are introduced.

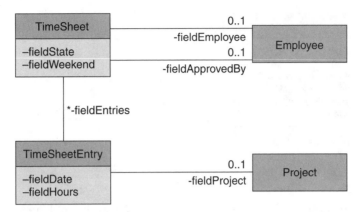

Figure 12.22 Time-Sheet Model

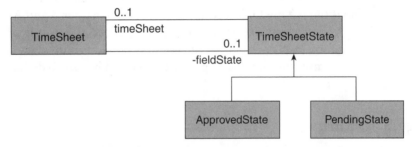

Figure 12.23 TimeSheet State Pattern

Mapping

Persistent operations are forwarded to a Mapper class defined for each do-main object class. The Mapper type is defined as a Java interface. Mapping in-stances are obtained from TsObject, using a naming convention of appending Mapper to the end of the receiving instance's class name and making sure that it is defined in a package with the same name as the domain class but with the domain segment replaced with mapping. This design allows various types of Mappers to be installed at any time, at a class level.

```
// Domain class Project...
com.wsbook.casestudy.domain.Project

// Mapper for Project...
com.wsbook.casestudy.domain.ProjectMapper
```

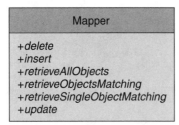

Figure 12.24 Mapper Interface

To support the iterative process, the case study implements an object mapper that emulates some simple mapping operations. In later chapters, we will replace this "emulated" version with a version that uses Enterprise JavaBeans for persistent data storage and retrieval. For a more detailed explanation, see the Object Mapper sidebar in Chapter 3 and Appendix A.

Persistent requests sent to TsObject types are aware only of type Mapper. Therefore, Mappers can be created and installed for any data type. Of course, a class implementing the Mapper interface still has to be defined. (See Figure 12.24.)

Package Structure

The Java classes defined in the case study application are partitioned into packages that reflect architectural elements discussed in Chapter 3. These package names reflect a commonly used naming convention that helps enforce a Java class namespace across virtual machines, organization, applications, and layers within applications.

Packages should begin generally and become more specific to provide a unique namespace for classes. Also, it is commonplace to define the complete package name in lowercase.

The first section of a package name is generally made up of one of the following abbreviations:

- com–commercial
- edu–educational
- org–not-for-profit organization
- mil–military

The second section of a package name should be enterprise specific, such as abci–ABC Incorporated—or com.abci....

Subsequent sections can be used to designate department/areas of an enterprise. Enterprise-wide classes can omit this section.

- acct–Accounting, or com.acbi.accounting...
- com.acbi.common.... (enterprise-wide classes)

Next, the package name should define an application-specific name. Classes that exist across the enterprise and applications can be defined in a package named common.

- gl–general ledger
- common–application/enterprise-wide, such as com.acbi.accounting.gl....

The final package-name section should reflect the architectural-layer class services:

- domain–domain-layer classes
- mediator–mediator-layer classes
- panel–panels in presentation-layer classes
- system–system classes used to provide services to all layers
- testscripts–test scripts used to drive domain
- mapping–mapping-layer classes
- controller–controller-layer classes
- applet–applet(s) defined for application
- frame–frame defined for standalone applications
- util–utility classes that are architecturally independent of any layer

Following this convention, the case study packages are as follows:

- com.wsbook.casestudy.domain
- com.wsbook.casestudy.servlet
- com.wsbook.casestudy.mediator
- com.wsbook.casestudy.system
- com.wsbook.casestudy.util
- com.wsbook.casestudy.testscript

Summary and Preview

In this chapter, we examined some A & D techniques and showed how they are applied in our case study. The primary purpose of this chapter is to introduce the design and implementation of the case study in depth so that you can learn how to implement similar applications yourself. To this end, we demonstrated the process by which we built the case study, and we discussed various trade-offs and design decisions that were made in its development.

This chapter forms the midpoint of this book. From now on, we will build on the tools and techniques you have seen in this and the previous chapters and will introduce a new set of technologies (EJBs) that can make enterprise application development more manageable. In the next chapter, we look at the architecture of EJBs.

CHAPTER 13

Enterprise JavaBean Architecture

So far in this book, we've demonstrated how you can effectively use Java servlets and JSPs with JavaBeans to build a server-side MVC architecture that can solve a variety of real-world programming problems. Now we are ready to take an in-depth look at the last of the major J2EE technologies that make up the heart of the WebSphere Application Server: Enterprise JavaBeans.

The first question you have to ask is, "Why do I need yet another Java API?" After all, you've already seen that standard Java classes and JavaBeans can be effective in acting as the Model layer in an MVC architecture, and you've also discovered how you can write persistence and other application services for Java in a layered architecture. The answer is that although we can write classes that can do these things for us, better ways to do them exist.

Java is a general-purpose language that you can use to build just about anything. However, when you start facing the problems of building a robust, distributed, persistent application, you begin to notice that some problems are more difficult than others. To understand why we need EJBs, let's focus on the following four problems:

- Distribution
- Persistence
- Transactions
- Security

In this chapter, you will learn that the goal of EJBs is to manage these problems in a standard way and to do so without requiring the developer to spend time explicitly programming these aspects of enterprise-level programming.

Object Distribution

The first of the problems addressed by EJBs is that objects in an enterprise-scale system need to be *distributed*. In short, this means that parts of your program should be able to be deployed to as many different physical machines and in as many separate operating system (OS) processes as appropriate to achieve your system's performance, scalability, and reliability goals. Another reason to distribute objects is to take a system that is logically layered and implement the layering as physical tiers. In this way, a set of distributed objects can be accessed from multiple, independently developed systems so long as those objects provide a single, common, networked API for the new systems to build on.

In the Java world, two distribution technologies stand out as especially widespread and important. Not coincidentally, those two form the core of the distribution solution for EJBs. The two are the Object Management Group (OMG's) CORBA object distribution model and Sun's Java RMI protocol. Because this book is not about either CORBA or RMI, we refer you to other works, such as [Orfali], that provide a more detailed overview of these technologies.

However, we do need to look at a couple of the pros and cons of each technology to understand why the EJB model has evolved in the way that it has. Along the way, we will point out areas that we will cover in more depth as we begin to examine the EJB distribution model.

CORBA Overview

CORBA was developed by the OMG, a consortium of companies, during the early 1990s to provide a common language and vendor-neutral standard for object distribution. CORBA has been well accepted since its inception, with a number of products and vendors supporting the CORBA standard and a long history of successful projects developed using it.

The heart of CORBA is the idea of a special-purpose piece of software, an object request broker (ORB), that facilitates communication between object spaces. The CORBA model requires an ORB on both ends of the distributed system. The ORB marshals parameters from outgoing method invocations to a CORBA proxy, receives messages on the other end of a conversation, and turns them into local messages to a CORBA "stub" that can then act on the received message and return a response to the calling object.

The CORBA model has two more major pieces: IDL (interface definition language), which defines CORBA interfaces, and CORBA services, which provide standard ways for CORBA objects to interact. CORBA services include such things as naming and transactions, which are major parts of building a distributed system. By default, CORBA uses the Internet-Inter ORB Protocol (IIOP) for low-level communication between ORBs.

CORBA, a robust and complete set of technologies that are both mature and well understood, has the following advantages.

- CORBA is a standard interface. This makes it possible for multiple vendors to implement their own products based on the standard and makes it possible for these products to interoperate.
- CORBA is computer language neutral. CORBA clients and servers can be written in a variety of computer languages, including Java, C++, C, Smalltalk, and Ada. The only requirement is that the remote interfaces for CORBA-distributed objects be written in CORBA IDL, which is translated into classes in the target implementation language through a postprocessor, a CORBA compiler.

However, the technology cannot be all things to all people. Using CORBA to build distributed systems in Java has the following disadvantages.

- CORBA programmers must write in two languages: IDL and Java.
- Interoperability of services is very spotty. For example, CORBA naming services are not interoperable.
- Very few vendors implement all the optional services, such as security and transactions, making it difficult to buy a complete infrastructure.
- Purchasing the ORBs and tool suites necessary to use CORBA can be expensive.

As a result, CORBA has not made the great inroads into corporate IS departments that its originators had hoped. Instead, developers started to look for simpler solutions, ones that perhaps were not as flexible and powerful. Out of that search grew the interest in Java RMI.

RMI Overview

Java RMI is a standard part of the Sun JDK 1.1 and the Java 2 platform. As an all-Java distribution solution, RMI's primary advantages are that it (1) features a very simple programming model that does not require programming in two languages, Java and IDL, and (2) does not require you to purchase an additional ORB and CORBA tools.

RMI's programming model is very simple. It has the notions of a Remote object and a Remote interface as its two primary constituents. A Remote object has methods that can be invoked from another JVM, potentially on a different host. A Remote object is described by one or more Remote interfaces, which are Java interfaces that declare the methods of the Remote object. *RMI* is the action of invoking a method of a Remote interface on a Remote object. Remote interfaces are standard Java interfaces that extend java.rmi.Remote. Remote objects can be any class of objects that implement a Remote interface, although more often than not, Remote objects extend java.rmi.server.UnicastRemoteObject.

An advanced feature in RMI that is not in CORBA is distributed garbage collection. Another feature that is not directly supported in CORBA is the notion of pass-by-value objects. In RMI, any Java object that implements java.io.Serializable can be passed as a method parameter to a Remote object and will be serialized on the client end and deserialized on the server end, allowing the server to operate on a local copy of the parameter.[1]

Although RMI is very powerful, it doesn't support multiple languages and does not support all the services that CORBA does. For instance, RMI includes a naming service but not other CORBA services, such as transactions or persistence.

Also, systems using RMI have a perceived lack of security. RMI includes a security manager that allows applets to use RMI, but its lack of authentication and other security protocols and the lack of support for RMI in corporate firewall systems have made its introduction more problematic than that of CORBA. These reasons lead us to the combination of the two technologies (RMI over IIOP).

RMI over IIOP combines the best features of RMI and CORBA. Like RMI, RMI over IIOP allows developers to develop purely in Java, rather than in both Java and IDL. Like RMI, RMI over IIOP allows developers to write classes that pass any serializable Java object as remote method arguments or return values. However, RMI over IIOP uses IIOP as its communication protocol, so it is interoperable with other CORBA applications. The combination of these two technologies forms an unbeatable combination of power and ease of use.

Remaining Problems

Although RMI makes distributed programming a much simpler proposition for Java programmers and RMI over IIOP gives programmers the ease of use of RMI combined with the interoperability of CORBA, many difficult problems remain in building distributed systems. In particular, RMI did not include direct support for a common distribution idiom that had initially

---

1. Java serialization is a technology that is often poorly understood. For an explanation of serialization, see [Horstmann].

emerged to circumvent a drawback for CORBA but that had found wider acceptance. One of the CORBA services that had been proposed in part to deal with the fact that CORBA had no facilities like distributed garbage collection was the CORBA life-cycle service. At the heart of this service specification was the idea of a *Factory*[2] object that served as a source of other distributed objects. The Factory created new objects and retrieved existing instances where appropriate. Most CORBA systems had evolved into using this idiom, even where the life-cycle service was not fully implemented.

Object Persistence

Of all the problems of object-oriented programming, few have generated as much interest, or as much confusion, as the problem of object persistence. When reduced to its bare essentials, object persistence is not a difficult problem to understand; making an object persistent means that its state, the values of its variables, can be preserved across multiple invocations of a program that references that object. This can be accomplished in any number of ways, the easiest of which for Java programmers is probably the Java serialization mechanism that is part of the basic JDK.

However, it's not persistence per se that gives programmers and architects nightmares. The problem is not that people want objects to be persistent but that they want to store the information in the objects in a particular format. In most cases, this format is a relational database. Unfortunately, objects and relational databases have a serious impedance mismatch.

The relational (table) model is a simple model, built on a sound mathematical foundation that has been its key strength. It is a technology that has been used very successfully for a number of years and is consequently well understood. Because new applications are seldom built in a vacuum, relational technology is commonly used in new applications, for the following reasons.

- Information often exists in legacy databases that must be used by new systems.
- Relational databases have strong query and report-writing capabilities. Even in the brave new world of Web interfaces, people still want to see paper reports.
- Relational technology provides built-in data integrity constraints in the form of database transactions and integrity rules.

---

2. A Factory is simply an object that creates other objects. The Factory Method and the Abstract Factory design patterns [Gamma] are specializations of this more general pattern.

- As a mature technology, relational technology has well-known procedures for backing up and restoring databases after catastrophic failures. This level of safety provides a great deal of comfort and peace of mind to the customers who pay for new systems development.

Nonetheless, using a relational database with an object system has some drawbacks.

- Relational databases have limited modeling capabilities. Behavior, object containment, and inheritance are not easy to define in a relational database when compared to Java or an object database.
- True Java object identity cannot be represented in a relational database. When programming in an OO language, such as Java, you must interact with an object that contains a *copy* of the persistent data. Two "spaces" are always at work in a problem: the "data" space in the relational database and the "object" space in Java.
- Java and SQL have a semantic mismatch. SQL data types do not exactly match Java data types, leading to conversion problems.

In many cases, up to 50 percent of application code bulk is devoted to the mechanics of connecting application objects with the relational database. Considerable care and diligence are required to ensure a good design and implementation when combining the two architectures. Luckily for Java programmers, many commercial persistence frameworks have evolved to fill the gap and provide a mapping between an object model and a relational database. The disadvantage to this is that each vendor's API is proprietary, and the capabilities of these solutions are not standardized. However, as we will see, even this is not the whole story.

Objects and Transactions

Even die-hard Java persistence programmers begin to roll their eyes when the subject of object transaction management comes up. After all, persistence frameworks have solved the difficult part of object-to-relational mapping, so what could be so difficult about transactions? This attitude stems more from the experience of the majority of Java programmers than from a close examination of the details of large-scale Java systems.

Most Java systems that use a database read or write data only to databases provided by a single database vendor. Although a Java program may use many database tables, an application usually will use *one* of Oracle, Sybase, or DB2 but not all three together or even two of three. Even experienced Java programmers have seldom worked with multidatabase systems.

However, the small minority of programs that do use multiple persistence stores can cause a disproportionate number of headaches for the programmers who build them.

To illustrate this problem, let's take a quick glance at JDBC, the Java API that is at the heart of most persistence schemes. In JDBC, the primary point of contact between the Java program and the database lies with an interface named java.sql.Connection. Each Connection represents a "live" conversation with a *single* database, be it an Oracle database, a DB2 database, or whatever. Connections are obtained from a connection Factory and are used to create SQL statements, to query metadata—for example, table structure—and to perform other functions, primarily the execution of a transaction against a database.

The class java.sql.Connection has three methods that relate to transactions.

```
public abstract void setAutoCommit(boolean autoCommit) throws SQLException
public abstract void commit() throws SQLException
public abstract void rollback() throws SQLException
```

The first method, setAutoCommit(), toggles the connection between autocommit mode—which means that each individual SQL statement is executed in its own transaction—and nonautocommit mode. In nonautocommit mode, a transaction is "opened" when the Connection is obtained, and another transaction is "opened" at the end of the current transaction.

When a Connection is sent setAutoCommit(false), the SQL statements will all execute, but the transaction will not commit until the message commit() is sent to the Connection. At that time, all the statements will either commit or roll back if any of them cannot commit for some reason. If rollback() is sent to the Connection, all the statements roll back, and the database remains unchanged from the state that it was in before the transaction began.

The problem is that each Connection object represents a *single* database. Say that you are building a system that uses both DB2 and Oracle. This is common in enterprise systems in which one group manages a local, workstation-based departmental database and another group manages a global, enterprise-wide mainframe system. So how can you build a system with JDBC such that all SQL statements are either fully committed or fully rolled back to *both* databases at once?

The short answer is that you can't, not without adding another layer of software. Synchronizing multiple data sources like this is a complex problem. Solving this problem has historically been the role of a system called a *transaction processing (TP) monitor,* such as IBM's CICS or Encina products. As Java becomes more prevalent in this kind of system, some of the roles of a TP monitor must be absorbed into our enterprise programs. Understanding how this works is key to understanding some of the more complex and powerful features of EJBs.

Security in Enterprise Applications

Another consistent problem in building enterprise applications in Java has been the lack of a set of common APIs that enable developers to handle the basics of application security. Simply put, the problem of application security lies in determining

- Who should be allowed access into a system and how to verify their identity (authentication)
- What access to the different parts of a system should be granted to which individuals (authorization)

CORBA defines a security model, but ORB vendors rarely implement it. Java RMI does not even contain any provisions for application-level security. As a result, most distributed-object programmers have ended up creating a "roll-your-own" security model, resulting in a plethora of incompatible implementations with varying capabilities.

EJB Definition

We've seen that neither CORBA nor Java RMI solved all the problems of the enterprise Java programmer. However, we will now see the core concepts of the EJB specification and how they are meant to address these concerns. In the process, we will see how the EJB model makes distributed programming in Java manageable. For additional perspective on this complex issue, you may want to consult [EJB] or a book like [Monson-Haefel].

Some of the key core concepts of the EJB specification are as follows.

- EJBs use RMI over IIOP. This means that there is a well-defined, standard mapping of EJB interfaces to CORBA IDL, thereby ensuring the interoperability of systems written in an EJB-compliant server to external CORBA systems. In addition, systems, such as firewalls, that have evolved to support CORBA can support EJB systems.
- EJBs take the RMI approach of insisting only that the programmer define a simple Java interface that declares a remote object's "external face" to the rest of the world. In EJB terminology, this Remote interface declares the externally accessible methods the Remote object will implement.
- EJBs also take a page from the CORBA book in that they subscribe to the Factory idiom for creating objects. An EJB programmer creates a Java interface, called a Home interface, that defines the ways in which remote objects are created. An EJB Factory that implements these

interfaces—whose implementation is provided by the container—is called an EJB *Home.*

- Clients locate EJB Homes through a standard naming service that supports the JNDI (Java Naming and Directory Interface) API. JNDI is simple to use, like the RMI naming service, but supports many of the advanced features of the CORBA naming service, such as support for directory-structured names.
- Standard, well-defined ways exist for making EJBs persistent through both vendor-provided frameworks—the container-managed persistence (CMP) model— and a user-developed persistence mechanism— the Bean-managed persistence (BMP) model.
- A standard transaction model for EJBs is provided by the services offered through the JTA APIs. The underlying transaction service allows applications to update data in multiple data sources with a single, distributed transaction.[3]
- EJBs are built on a security model that allows the person deploying the EJB to determine what access should be granted at an EJB or method level and to whom.

An EJB is a component that implements business logic in a distributed enterprise application. An EJB *container* is where EJBs reside; multiple EJB classes can be contained in a single EJB container. The EJB container is responsible for making the EJB classes available to the client. EJBs are deployed into EJB containers and run on EJB servers (EJS). Application developers can use two types of EJBs to build applications: *Session* Beans and *Entity* Beans.

Containers

The EJB container provides the client view of the EJB. The container is transparent to the client. The EJB container provides

- Security
- Concurrency
- Transaction support
- Memory management, swapping unused EJBs to secondary storage

---

3. Although JTA supports distributed transactions to any resource manager, WebSphere supports only a limited number, owing to limitations in the level of technology. See Chapter 18 for details.

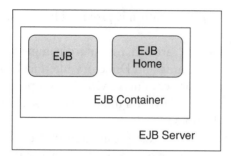

Figure 13.1 EJB Containment Hierarchy

An EJB container can hold EJBs of multiple EJB classes. The EJB container is responsible for making the EJB classes available to the client. An EJB container can

- Create EJB objects
- Remove EJB objects
- Get the EJB information to allow loose client/server binding and scripting

A client's view of an EJB object is the same, regardless of the implementation of the EJB and its container. This ensures that a client application is portable across all container implementations. An EJB container is where EJBs reside. The EJB container provides Home interfaces that allow clients to create, look up, and remove EJB objects. An EJB server may host one or multiple EJB containers. There is no client API to manipulate the container, and there is no way for a client to tell in which container an EJB is found. This structure is shown in Figure 13.1.

Session EJBs

A Session EJB is a nonpersistent object that implements some business logic on the server. A client accesses a Session EJB through an implemented Remote interface. Therefore, a Session EJB is a Remote Java object accessible from a client.

Session EJBs can be either stateful or stateless. Stateful Session Beans exist for the duration of a single client/server session. Likewise, the client has a reference to a stateful Session Bean that is potentially valid for the lifetime of the client.

However, a client that has a reference to a stateless Session Bean is not necessarily holding a reference to a *particular* Session Bean. The EJB container may pool stateless Session Beans to handle multiple requests from mul-

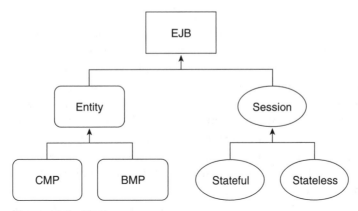

Figure 13.2   EJB Types

tiple clients. At any given moment, a stateless Session Bean executes on behalf of only a single client.

A typical Session EJB object

- Executes methods on behalf of a client
- Does not directly represent shared data in the database, although it may
- Can direct and participate in transactions

Entity EJBs

An Entity EJB is a persistent object that represents an object view of information stored in a persistent data store or an entity that is implemented by an existing enterprise application. Entity EJBs contain persistent data that can be saved in various persistent data stores. Each Entity EJB carries its own identity. Entity EJBs that manage their own persistence are called *BMP Entity Beans*. Entity EJBs that delegate their persistence to the EJB container—for example, use a vendor-provided persistence framework—are called *CMP Entity Beans*.

A typical Entity EJB

- Represents data in a database—is persistent
- Can participate in transactions
- Allows shared access from multiple users

An EJB server, such as WebSphere, provides a scalable runtime environment for a large number of concurrently active Entity EJBs. The hierarchy of EJB types is shown in Figure 13.2.

Need for EJBs

Although EJBs provide a complete, scalable solution for large-scale Java programming, the technology is not appropriate for every project. We can now complete our look at the architecture of EJBs by considering some questions that project teams may ask if they are considering moving to EJBs from other technologies or considering a new project that may use EJBs.

Let's begin by examining some questions that can be used to determine whether EJBs are an appropriate technology for your situation. If you can answer yes to any of these questions, EJBs may be appropriate. On the other hand, if these questions do not apply, other technologies may be more appropriate.

Is there an architectural push toward a standard, portable, component-based architecture? For many forward-looking developers, the key issue is how to achieve platform, vendor, and application server implementation independence. The EJB architecture, which is an industry-standard component architecture, can help achieve these goals. EJBs developed for WebSphere can usually be deployed on competitors' application servers, and vice versa. Although this promise has not been completely achieved, this is a strategic direction that many customers choose to take. Although in the short-term, it is often easier and faster to take advantage of features that may precede standardization, standardization provides the best long-term advantage.

Also, customers must consider the increasing availability of tools and optimized implementations of the EJB standard that they would not get with home-grown managed object frameworks. Because most customers are not in the middleware business, their efforts can be more effectively targeted at activities that are more directly related to their businesses.

Is there a need for access to enterprise data and shared business logic from multiple client types? Whenever an application needs to be used from multiple client types, such as HTML browser; pervasive devices, such as cell phones and PDAs; and Java client applications, EJBs are often good solutions to provide a common platform for shared business logic and data. EJBs provide a distributed infrastructure on which multiple client applications written using a number of technologies—servlets and JSPs, Java clients, and even Visual Basic and CORBA clients—can be layered.

Is there a need for concurrent read and update access to shared data? Traditional, fat client solutions require the application to manage access to shared data at the database level. This often results in highly complex schemes to deal with database locking and concurrency or, alternatively, loss of data integrity when these issues are not considered.

EJBs automatically handle these complex threading and simultaneous shared-data issues. As mentioned previously, the EJBs control the access to the back-end data and manage the current transactions and database locking internally. This reduces the total programming effort by reducing the amount of effort spent in writing database control logic and ensures the consistency and validity of the data.

Is there a need to access multiple disparate data sources with transactional capabilities? Many applications require the ability to access multiple data sources. For instance, a program may use data in both a middle-tier Oracle database and a mainframe CICS or IMS system accessible through MQ Series. The key is that some applications require that this access be fully transactional: that data integrity be maintained across the data sources. For example, an application may demand that placing a user order will consist of storing the detailed order information in an Oracle database and simultaneously placing a shipment order with a CICS system through MQ Series. If either the database update or the MQ enqueuing fails, the entire transaction should roll back.

In the past, the only choices to build systems like these were transaction monitors, such as Encina, CICS, or Tuxedo, which used nonstandard interfaces and required development in COBOL, C, or C++. EJBs in Web-Sphere Application Server 3.5 support multiple concurrent transactions with full commit and rollback capabilities across multiple DB2 and Sybase data sources in a full two-phase commit-capable environment. WebSphere supports other data sources (Oracle, MQ Series, CICS) with one-phase commit transaction support.

Is there a need for method-level object security seamlessly integrated with security for HTML documents, servlets, JSPs, and client logins? Certain types of applications have security restrictions that have previously made them difficult to implement in Java. For instance, certain insurance applications must restrict access to patient data in order to meet regulatory guidelines. Until the advent of EJBs, there was no way to restrict a particular user's access to an object or a method. Previously, restricting access at the database level and then "catching" errors thrown at the JDBC level or by restricting access at the application level by custom security code would have been the only implementation options.

However, EJBs now allow method-level security on any EJB or method. Users and user groups can be created that can be granted or denied execution rights to any EJB or method. In WebSphere, these same user groups can be granted or denied access to Web resources (servlets, JSPs and HTML pages), and the user IDs can be seamlessly passed from the Web resources to the EJBs by the underlying security framework.

Is there a need for multiple servers to handle the throughput or availability needs of the system? Over the past several years, customers have found that fat client systems simply do not scale to the thousands or millions of users that Web-based systems may have. At the same time, software distribution problems have led to a desire to "trim down" fat clients. The 24-hour, 7-days-a-week nature of the Web has also made uptime a crucial issue for businesses. However, not everyone needs a system designed for 24×7 operation and able to handle millions of concurrent users. We should be able to design a system so that scalability can be achieved without sacrificing ease of development or standardization.

What customers need is a way to write business logic that can scale to meet these kinds of requirements. WebSphere's EJB support can provide this kind of highly scalable, highly available system. It does so by using the following features:

- Object caching + pooling: WebSphere automatically pools stateless Session EJBs at the server level, reducing the amount of time spent in object creation and garbage collection. This results in more processing cycles being available to do real work.
- Workload optimization at server: WebSphere Application Server features EJB server cluster management. You can create server groups that span nodes. In addition, you can create "models"—abstract representations of a server—that are then "cloned" into multiple JVMs. Customers can configure clones to run on any of the server machines in the cluster. In addition, multiple clones of a single server can run on a single machine, taking advantage of multiprocessor architectures. Likewise, the clones can administer an entire set of "clones" as a single group. This improves availability and prevents a single point of failure in the application server.
- Cloning supports automatic failover. With several clones available to handle requests, it is more likely that failures will not damage throughput and reliability. With clones distributed to various nodes, an entire machine can fail without producing devastating consequences.

All these features happen without specifically being programmed into the system. No changes to the server-side code are necessary to take advantage of this kind of scalability.

Note that WebSphere supports distribution, cloning, and automatic failover of other server-side Java technologies, such as Java servlets and JSPs. However, these more presentation-oriented technologies serve as a complement to EJBs rather than as a competitor to EJBs. When uptime and scalability are key, EJBs should be a part of the overall solution.

Summary and Preview

In this chapter, you've gained a glimmering of understanding about EJBs. You've seen how the EJB standard has evolved from RMI and CORBA and how it has been written to address some of the most difficult problems in building large-scale business systems using distributed objects. You've also seen some qualification criteria that help you decide whether EJBs are right for your particular project. In later chapters, you will learn more about EJBs and how they are deployed in WebSphere Application Server, Advanced Edition and developed in VisualAge for Java, Enterprise Edition.

CHAPTER 14

Building Basic EJBs in VisualAge for Java

Now that you've seen the basic outline of what EJBs are and how they work, you are ready to begin learning how to apply them to a business problem and how the various parts of the EJB specification are used to build a single, unified software component. We will walk through an example of how EJBs are built in VisualAge for Java, Enterprise Edition and deployed into WebSphere Application Server, Advanced Edition. As with most new programming environments, the simplest way to illustrate this is with a *Hello World* program.

The Simplest EJB

As distributed Java components, EJBs have a remote part that executes business logic and a client stub that allows a client to invoke methods on the remote object and to receive results. Remote methods are declared in a Remote Interface, such as the following:

```
package com.ibm.ws.book.example.ejbs;
/**
 * This is an Enterprise Java Bean Remote Interface
 */
public interface HelloWebSphere extends javax.ejb.EJBObject {

/**
 * Return a String containing a message to the client
 * @return java.lang.String the message returned
 * @exception RemoteException throws RemoteException.
 */
java.lang.String getMessage() throws java.rmi.RemoteException;
}
```

All EJBs must declare a Remote interface, regardless of the type of EJB (Entity or Session) being built. All Remote interfaces must extend javax.ejb. EJBObject or another interface descended from javax.ejb.EJBObject. Methods declared in the Remote interface follow two conventions.

- All arguments and return types must follow the rules of Java RMI.[1]
- Methods declared in a Remote interface may be declared as throwing java.rmi.RemoteException.[2]

Both of these conventions apply because you are declaring how your EJB will "look" to the outside world. The argument restriction applies because the declared object types are the ones that can be "marshaled," or put into a form for transmission over the network. Likewise, the exception rule applies because of the possibility that a Remote call may fail, as when the network goes down or something goes wrong on the server side. The RemoteException describes a common way to declare that a client must be able to handle things going wrong in this way.

Bean Implementation and Life Cycle

Now that you've seen the Remote interface for the *HelloWebSphere* EJB, you're probably starting to wonder what the implementation of that interface looks like. To understand how that works, you need to remember some of the context of an EJB. An EJB is a software component that lives within a defined life cycle. An EJB runs within the context of an application server like WebSphere, which means that WebSphere is responsible for creating it, destroying it, and handling how the Bean is moved in and out of working memory.

Each EJB type has its own life cycle defined in the EJB specification. Most of the time, you don't need to be concerned with all the details of the life cycle. If you are, or if it becomes a problem, you can refer to the specification to obtain the details. The parts of the life cycle can be summarized in the following way:

- *Creation:* The application server is responsible for creating EJBs. A method named ejbCreate() defined in each EJB represents a "hook" for user code to execute when the EJB is created. In stateful Session Beans and Entity Beans, the ejbCreate() methods are rather like constructors,

---

1. In practice, this means that they should be primitives, serializable objects, or other Remote interfaces.
2. Remote interface methods can throw additional exceptions as well.

with each EJB possibly implementing multiple ejbCreate() methods, each with a different set of arguments. Stateless Session Beans can implement only one ejbCreate() method, with no arguments.

- *Activation and passivation:* EJBs can be passivated or stored to secondary storage, and activated, or returned to working memory, by the application server. The EJB specification defines two hook methods that allow an EJB notification of this process. The ejbPassivate() method is called immediately before an EJB is passivated, allowing it to prepare itself for being serialized, perhaps by closing and removing JDBC connections or other objects that are not serializable. Likewise the ejbActivate() method is called immediately after the EJB is returned back into memory to reconstruct any state that was changed or removed for passivation.

- *Removal:* As for creation, the application server is responsible for the deletion of EJBs. The ejbRemove() method is a hook that allows the EJB to do any necessary cleanup immediately prior to the EJB's being removed from the system.

Having seen the EJB life-cycle methods, you can understand why the following implementation class is the minimal class that can implement the EJB Remote interface that was defined earlier.

```
package com.ibm.ws.book.example.ejbs;

import java.rmi.RemoteException;
import java.security.Identity;
import java.util.Properties;
import javax.ejb.*;
/**
 * This is a Session Bean Class
 */
public class HelloWebSphereBean implements SessionBean {
    private javax.ejb.SessionContext mySessionCtx = null;
    final static long serialVersionUID = 3206093459760846163L;

/**
 * ejbActivate method comment
 * @exception java.rmi.RemoteException The exception description.
 */
public void ejbActivate() throws java.rmi.RemoteException {}
/**
 * ejbCreate method comment
 * @exception javax.ejb.CreateException The exception description.
 * @exception java.rmi.RemoteException The exception description.
 */
```

```
public void ejbCreate() throws javax.ejb.CreateException, java.rmi.Remote
Exception {}
/**
 * ejbPassivate method comment
 * @exception java.rmi.RemoteException The exception description.
 */
public void ejbPassivate() throws java.rmi.RemoteException {}
/**
 * ejbRemove method comment
 * @exception java.rmi.RemoteException The exception description.
 */
public void ejbRemove() throws java.rmi.RemoteException {}
/**
 * This method returns a message to the user.
 * @return java.lang.String
 */
public String getMessage() {
    return "Hello World!";
}
/**
 * setSessionContext method comment
 * @param ctx javax.ejb.SessionContext
 * @exception java.rmi.RemoteException The exception description.
 */
public void setSessionContext(javax.ejb.SessionContext ctx) throws
java.rmi.RemoteException {
    mySessionCtx = ctx;
}
}
```

Pay particular attention to the heart of this EJB, the implementation of the getMessage() method that was defined in the Remote interface:

```
/**
 * Return a message String.
 * @return java.lang.String
 */
public String getMessage() {
    return "Hello World!";
}
```

Note that nothing is unique or unusual about the implementation of this method. It doesn't have to throw any special exceptions, such as java.rmi. RemoteException; nor does it have to include special logic so that its result will be sent across the network. This is the key to the way in which EJBs handle distribution: The application server handles the details, leaving the programmer to worry only about what business logic needs to be written.

One more programming element needs to be written to complete the *HelloWebSphere* EJB. This is the Home interface, which describes the way in which an EJB is created, found, and destroyed.

EJB Home **Interfaces**

The Home interface for the *Hello WebSphere* EJB is incredibly simple:

```
package com.ibm.ws.book.example.ejbs;

/**
 * This is a Home interface for the Session Bean
 */
public interface HelloWebSphereHome extends javax.ejb.EJBHome {

/**
 * Default create method for a session bean
 * @return com.ibm.ws.book.example.ejbs.HelloWebSphere
 * @exception javax.ejb.CreateException
 * @exception java.rmi.RemoteException
 */
com.ibm.ws.book.example.ejbs.HelloWebSphere create() throws javax.ejb.
CreateException, java.rmi.RemoteException;
}
```

A simple correspondence here is worth pointing out. Note that a single create() method is defined in the Home interface and takes no arguments. Likewise, a single ejbCreate() method, with no arguments, is implemented in the HelloWebSphereBean class and a corresponding ejbPostCreate() method. These three methods always come together. If you define a create(String arg) method in a Home interface, you must have a corresponding ejbCreate(String arg) method implementation in the Bean implementation class and an ejbPostCreate(String arg) also. The same is true of any argument list.

Remember from the previous discussion about the ejbCreate() method that stateless Session Beans, such as this *Hello WebSphere* example, define only a single create() method, with no arguments. If you were building a stateful Session Bean or an Entity Bean, you would define other create() methods specifying the initial set of values with which the EJB would be initialized. We will revisit the subject of EJB Home interfaces when we examine Entity Beans in depth, as only in Entity Beans are some of the more complex parts of the Home interface exercised. We will also revisit the ejbPostCreate() method in more depth in later chapters.

Building EJBs in VisualAge

Now that you've seen the classes and interfaces that go into building a simple EJB, let's see how you can take advantage of the features of VisualAge for Java, Enterprise Edition to build this EJB so that it can be deployed into WebSphere.

You will follow these steps in implementing our simple example in VisualAge for Java:

1. Install the EJB Development Environment feature into VisualAge for Java.
2. Create a project to organize the example code.
3. Create a Java package for the EJB code.
4. Use the *Create EJB Group SmartGuide* to create an EJB group.
5. Use the *Create EJB SmartGuide* to create the *HelloWebSphere* EJB.
6. Create the getMessage() method with the *Add Method SmartGuide*.
7. Fill in the implementation of the getMessage() method.
8. Promote the getMessage() method to the Remote interface.

Step 1: Install the EJB Development Environment. To install this feature, open the *Quick Start* window, in VisualAge by either selecting *File Quick Start* from the workbench menu or pressing the F2 key inside the workbench. This window is shown in Figure 14.1.

In the *Quick Start* window, select *Features* in the left-hand pane and then select *Add Feature* in the right-hand pane. Click the *OK* button, which will

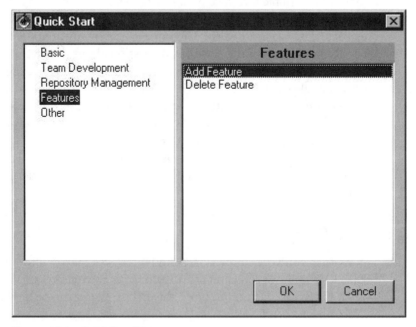

Figure 14.1   *Quick Start* Dialog

bring up a feature-selection dialog. Select *IBM EJB Development Environment 3.5* and click *OK* to dismiss the dialog. A progress dialog shows that the feature is being installed. When the progress dialog disappears at the end of the installation, your workbench will contain a new tab, *EJB,* which is shown in Figure 14.2.

Step 2: Add the *WS Case Study* example code project. (*Note:* This step assumes that you have loaded the case study repository file into your Visual-Age repository, following the instructions described in Chapter 12. If you have already added the [No EJBs] version of the case study in Chapter 12, you may skip to step 3.) Now you must complete two tasks in the *Projects* tab of the VisualAge for Java workbench. Switch to the *Projects* tab and open the right-button mouse menu. Select *Add Project,* as shown in Figure 14.3.

Choosing this menu option will display the *Add Project SmartGuide,* shown in Figure 14.4. In this *SmartGuide,* select the *Add projects from the*

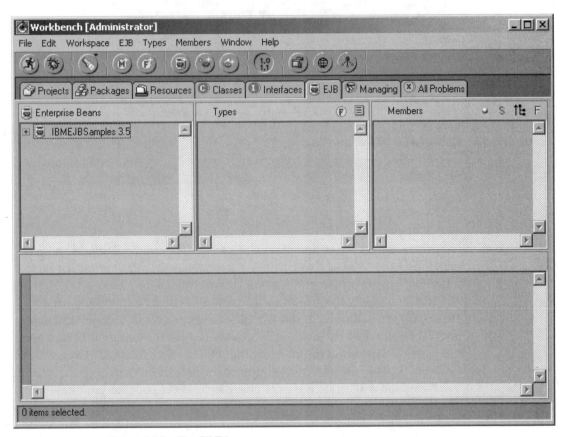

Figure 14.2 The *EJB* Tab

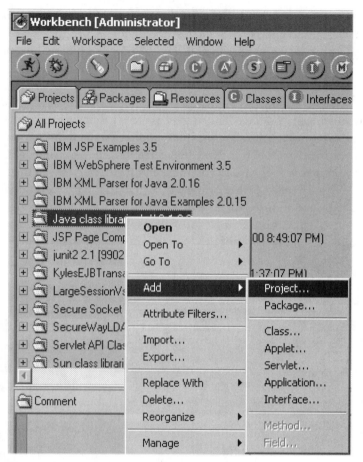

Figure 14.3   *Add>Project* Menu

repository radio button, and choose *WS Case Study* in the *Available project names* list box. Choose *[No EJB's] 4.1* from the *Available editions* list box. Finish adding the project to your workbench by clicking *OK*.

Step 3: Prepare the project for the new EJB code. First, we will need to create an "open edition" of the *WS Case Study* project in order to add new packages and classes to it. Select *WS Case Study* in the workbench, and open the right-mouse-button menu. From that menu, select *Manage>Create Open Edition*. This will create a new edition of the project in VisualAge.

Next, you will create a Java package to hold the code for your new EJB. The process for creating a package in VisualAge for Java is similar to that for creating a project. Begin by selecting your new project—*WS Case Study*—in the *Project* pane. Then, again bring up the right-mouse-button menu and

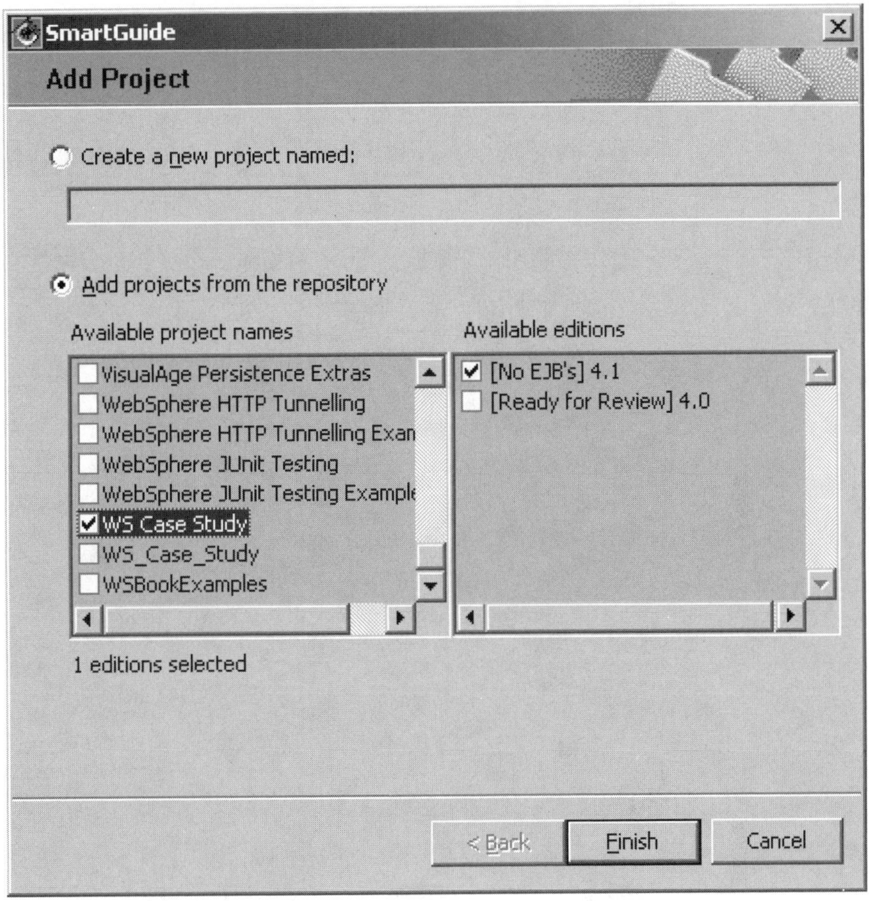

Figure 14.4   The *Add Project SmartGuide*

select *Add>Package* from the menu. Selecting *Add Package* results in the appearance of the *Add Package SmartGuide*, shown in Figure 14.5.

In this *SmartGuide*, select the radio button labeled *Create a new package named:* and type com.ibm.ws.book.example.ejbs in the accompanying text field. Finish creating the package by clicking *OK* to dismiss the dialog. A warning dialog (Figure 14.6) will be displayed.

This dialog appears because the repository contains this package in the completed case study that you can compare your code to. Select *Do not show this message again* and click *OK* to continue working your way through the example. Once this process is complete, you should see your package available as a tree selection in the projects pane beneath your newly added project.

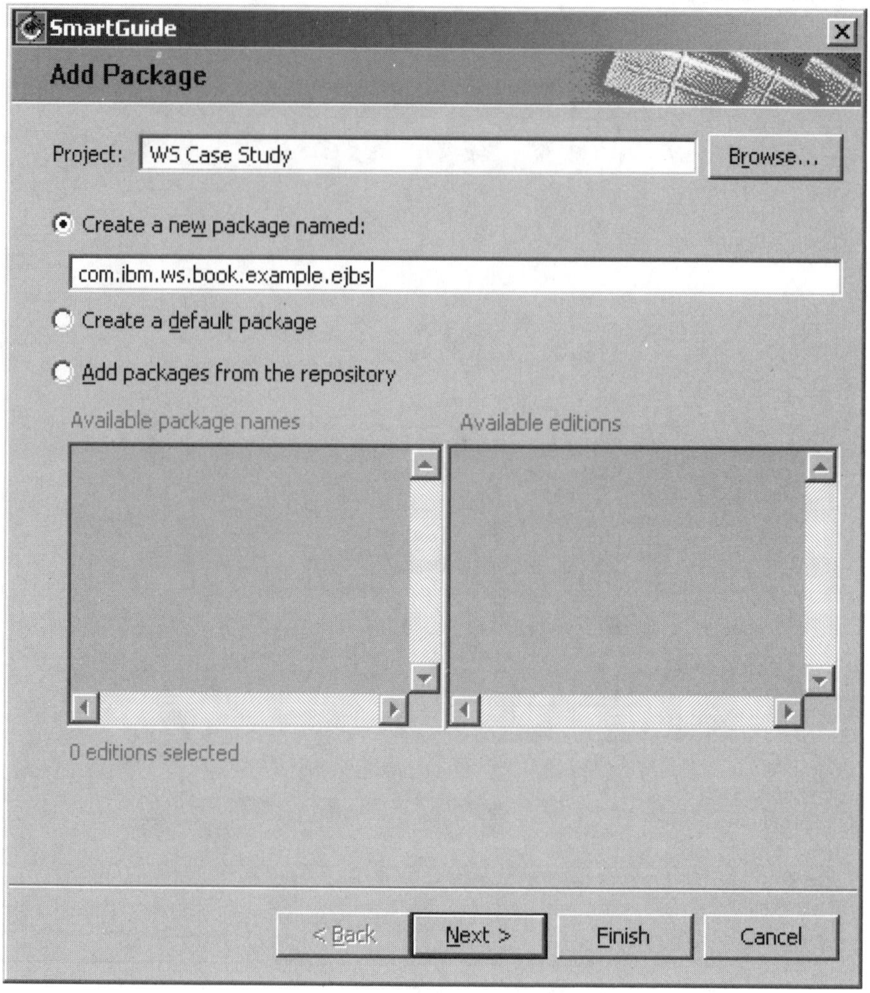

Figure 14.5 *Add Package* Dialog

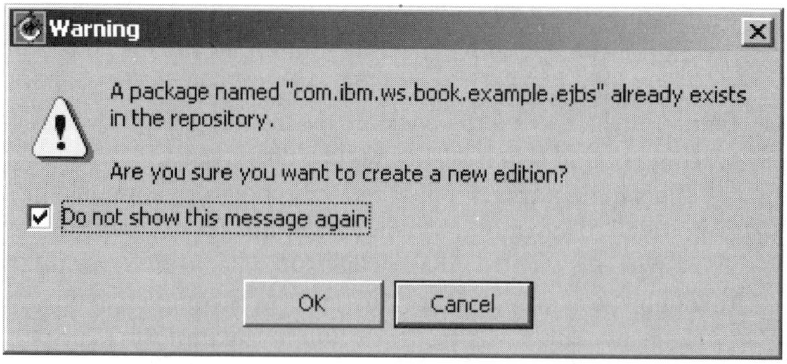

Figure 14.6 Warning Dialog

Step 4: Use the *Create EJB Group SmartGuide* to create an EJB group. This step requires you to use the *EJB* tab for the first time. The *EJB* tab, shown in Figure 14.7, consists of several panes.

- The upper-left pane, *Enterprise Beans,* allows you to manage groups of related EJBs—an EJB group, in VisualAge terms—and manage all the individual classes and interfaces that make up a particular EJB as a single entity.
- The top-middle pane, *Types* and *Fields,* shows the various classes and interfaces that make up an EJB selected in the *Enterprise Beans* pane.
- The top-right pane, *Members,* allows you to select individual field and method declarations.
- The bottom pane, *Source,* is an editor for viewing and modifying the source code corresponding to the selections made in the previous panes.

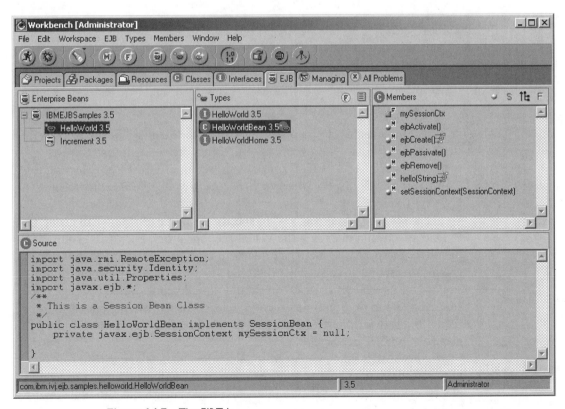

Figure 14.7   The *EJB* Tab

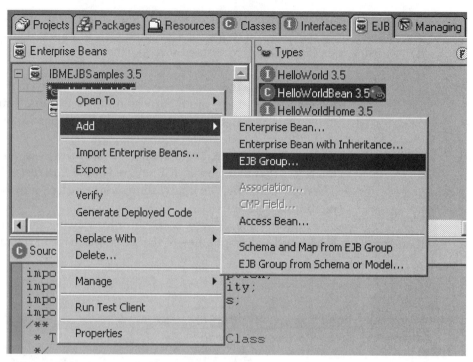

Figure 14.8   The *Add EJB Group* Menu

To complete this step, you will need to use the menu in the *Enterprise Beans* pane to create a new EJB group. Open the right-mouse-button menu and select *Add>EJB Group,* as shown in Figure 14.8. Selecting this menu option will display the *Add EJB Group SmartGuide,* shown in Figure 14.9.

This *SmartGuide* allows you to specify the name of a new EJB group or to load an existing one from the VisualAge repository. Each EJB group is a member of a specific VisualAge project. In fact, you will see that the EJB group corresponds to a special "reserved" package in the project with the same name as the EJB group. You should not add code to this package outside the *EJB* tab or attempt to version, release, or remove the package directly. To carry out these tasks, use the corresponding operations on the EJB group in the *EJB* tab instead.

In this *SmartGuide,* you need to select the *Create a new EJB Group named:* radio button and type in the name of the EJB group. For our example, type WebSphereBookSamples in the text box beneath the radio button. Then click the *Finish* button.

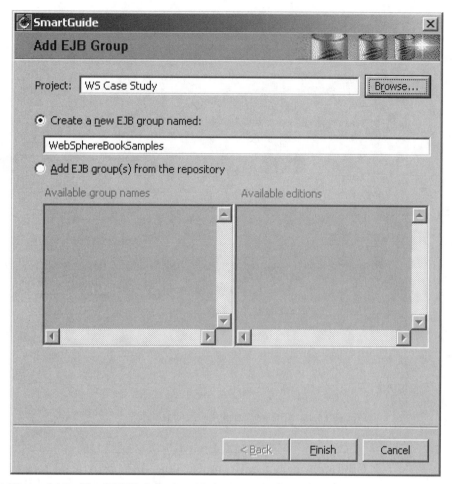

Figure 14.9   The *Add EJB Group SmartGuide*

What's an EJB Group?

We did not discuss EJB groups in our previous overviews of the EJB specification or WebSphere because EJB groups are an organizational device specific to VisualAge. We will see in later chapters how EJB groups are used to group related EJBs when you generate EJB associations and inheritance. You will also see that EJB groups are not carried outside of VisualAge when you deploy EJBs into WebSphere.

Step 5: Use the *Create EJB SmartGuide* to create the *HelloWebSphere* EJB. Now you will begin to see some of the power of the VisualAge for Java

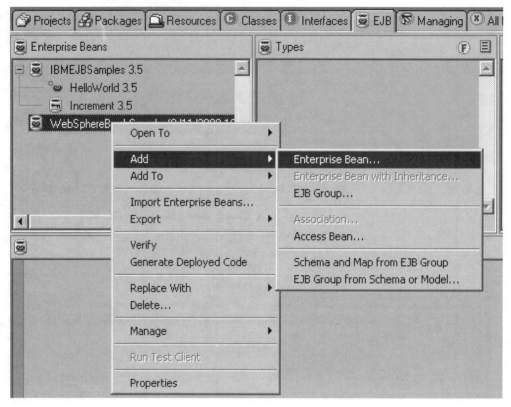

Figure 14.10   The *Add Enterprise Bean* Menu

EJB Development Environment. VisualAge provides a comprehensive set of *SmartGuides* to automate most of the standard tasks in EJB development. Possibly the most useful *SmartGuide* is *Create EJB,* which you will use in this step to automatically create all the interfaces and implementation classes necessary to create an EJB.

Go back to the *EJB* tab, select your new EJB group, and bring up the right-mouse-button menu in the *Enterprise Beans* pane. This time, select *Add>Enterprise Bean* from the pop-up menu, as shown in Figure 14.10. Selecting this menu item displays the *Create EJB SmartGuide,* whose first page is shown in Figure 14.11.

This *SmartGuide* can be used in three ways, corresponding to the three following scenarios.

- You want to create a new EJB from scratch. If you are building a new program using EJBs, this will be the most commonly used option and corresponds to the two settings *Create a new Enterprise Bean* and

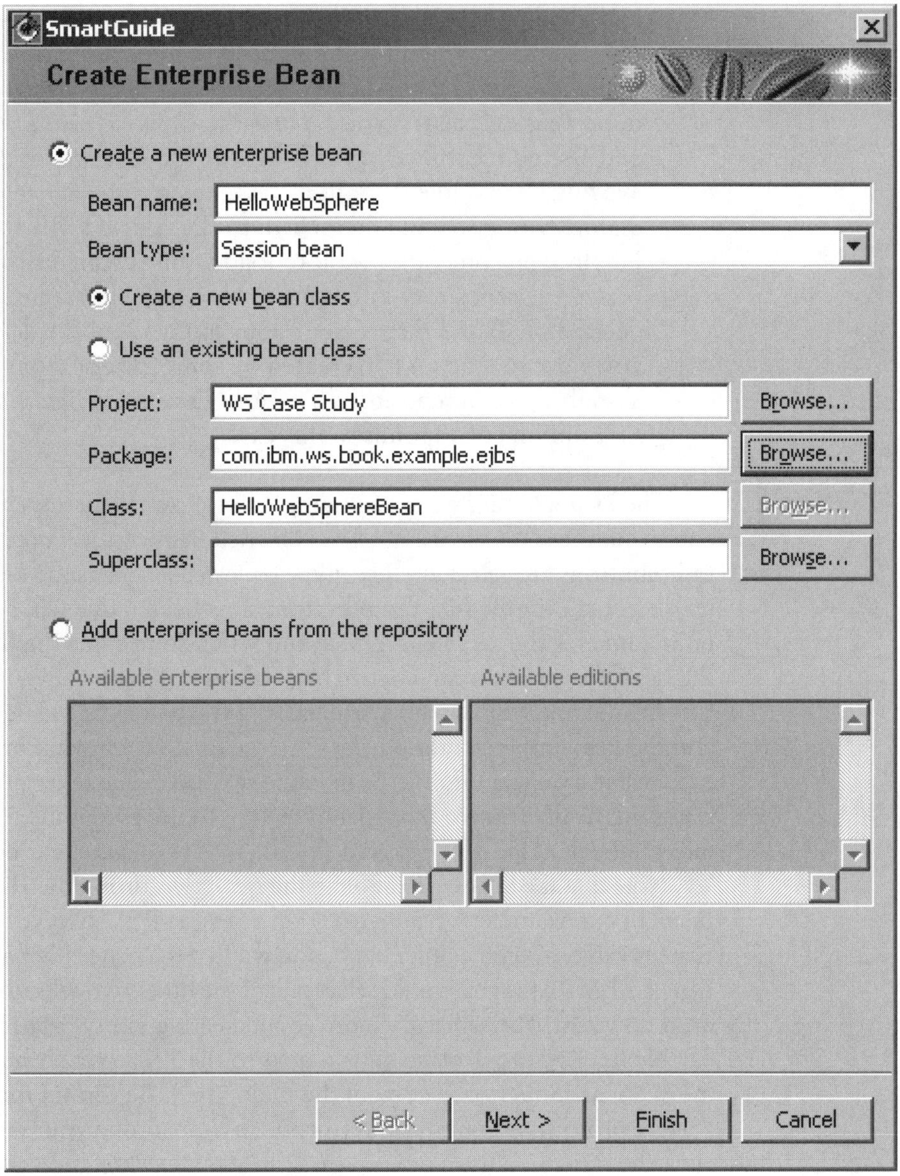

Figure 14.11 The *Create Enterprise Bean SmartGuide*

Create a new Bean class in the *Create EJB SmartGuide*. VisualAge for Java also supports creating EJBs that are subclassed from other EJBs. You would also use these two selections in this case, but you would select a different superclass for the EJB.

- Sometimes, you want to edit an EJB whose Home and Remote interfaces and EJB implementation class were created outside of VisualAge for Java. In that case, you will first need to import the classes into the VisualAge for Java repository, using the standard import dialog. After importing the classes, you can use the *Create a new Enterprise Bean* and *Use an Existing Bean class* selections. You would then select the existing Bean implementation class, Home, and Remote interfaces in this dialog. Doing so will add the EJB to the selected EJB group.

- Finally, you sometimes want to load a fully created EJB from the VisualAge repository into your workspace. This can occur when you delete an EJB and then change your mind about the deletion or when you want to load an EJB created by someone else from a shared VisualAge team repository. The *Add Enterprise Beans from the repository* option corresponds to this case.

The example that we are building will follow the first scenario. Begin by confirming that the *Create a new enterprise Bean* and *Create a new Bean class* radio buttons are selected. Next, type HelloWebSphere as the Bean name in the text box beneath the first radio button. This Bean name will become the default name for the Remote interface and will also become the JNDI name for the Bean's Home. You can change both of these defaults later, if you choose. The Bean name will also form the basis of the names of the Home interface and the Bean implementation class. To see this, watch what happens as you type HelloWebSphere into the Bean name text box: The text HelloWebSphereBean is automatically formed by appending Bean to the end of the text that you type into the Bean name text box and entered into the *Class:* text box.

Note that the default selection in the *Bean type* drop-down list is *Session Bean.* In our example, we want to create a Session EJB, so leave the selection at its current value. If, on the other hand, you wanted to create either a CMP Entity EJB or a BMP EJB, you would select one of the other two selections from this drop-down list. You will learn more about creating Entity Beans in a later chapter.

Next, click the *Browse* button next to the *Project:* text box, and select the *WS Case Study* project from the dialog box. Be certain that you select the correct project, or you may have problems versioning your code later. Finally, click the *Browse* button next to the *Package:* text box, and select *com.ibm. ws.book.example.ejbs.* Again, be sure that you have selected the correct package for your code. One of the most common mistakes in creating a new EJB is not selecting the correct package, which results in code being generated into a package you did not intend to use.

Once you have completed this part of the *Create EJB SmartGuide,* click the *Next>*button to see the second page of the *SmartGuide,* which allows you to specify more information about your EJB. The second page is shown in Figure 14.12.

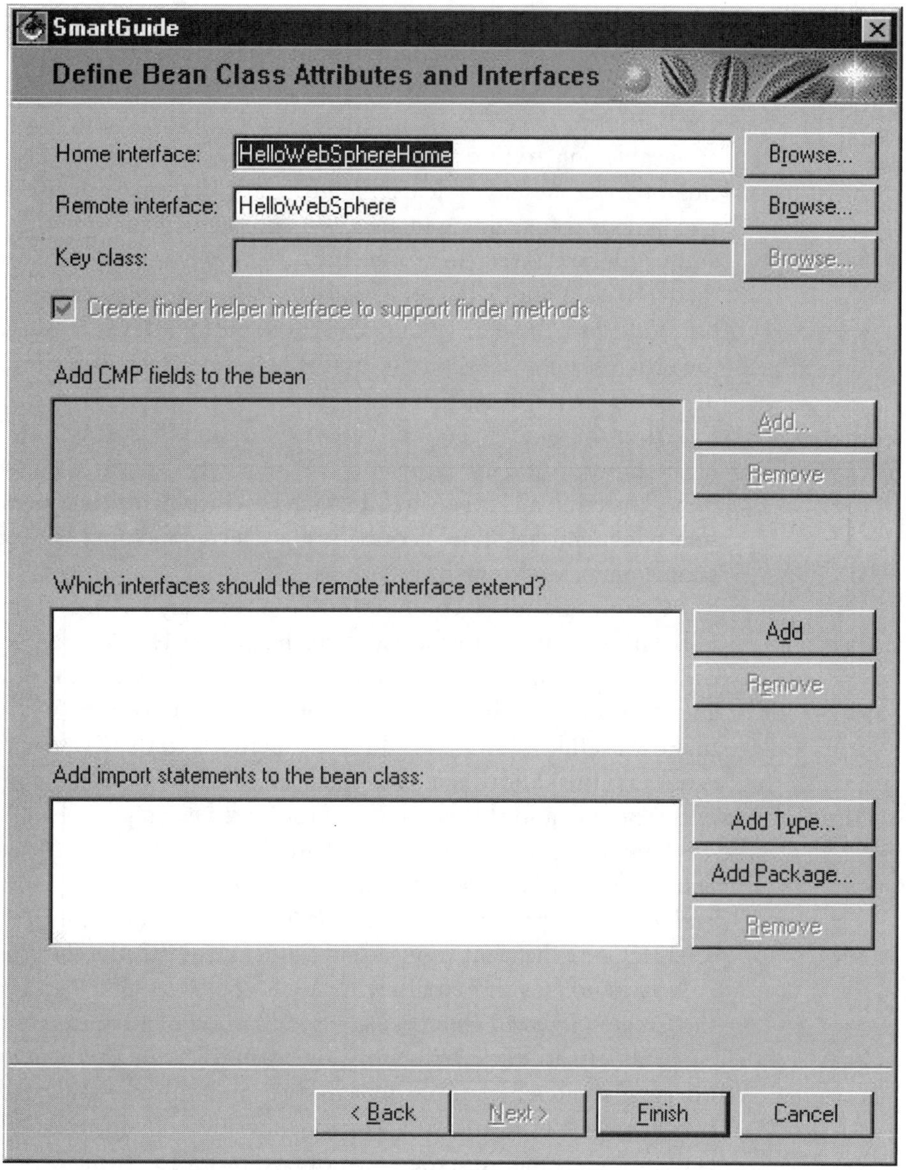

Figure 14.12 Second Page of *Create EJB SmartGuide*

At the top of this *SmartGuide* page, in the *Home interface:* and the *Remote interface:* fields, are the names that were formed automatically from the Bean name you typed in the previous page. If you wanted to use a different name for these two interfaces, you could simply edit the text in the text boxes. If you were importing a Bean from code created outside VisualAge, you would use the *Browse* button beside the text boxes to select appropriate Home interface and Remote interface classes for your Bean.

Next, you will see that the fields *Create finder helper interface* and *Add CMP fields to the Bean* are unavailable for selection (grayed out), as they are applicable only to Entity Beans. Because you are creating a Session Bean, you cannot select these two fields. Finally, at the bottom of the page, you will see two list boxes for adding interfaces for the Remote interface to extend and for adding import statements to the Bean class. We do not need to use either of these boxes in our example, so finish out the *SmartGuide* by clicking the *Finish* button. A progress bar will appear at the bottom of the *SmartGuide,* indicating the progress with the generation of the classes; at the end, the *SmartGuide* will disappear.

After the generation is complete, you can select your new Enterprise Bean in the *Enterprise Bean* pane and see the newly generated classes in the *Types* pane. Selecting a class or an interface will display its members in the *Members* pane, and the source code for the selected member will be shown in the source pane, as shown in Figure 14.13.

Congratulations! You have now successfully written your first complete EJB. Granted, it's not very useful at this point: The generated code contains only the basic life-cycle methods, such as ejbCreate(), but it is already a fully specification-compliant EJB that could be deployed into WebSphere. Now to make it useful, we need to add some methods to the EJB to perform some work and then allow access to those methods in the Remote interface of the EJB. You will add this behavior in the next few steps.

Step 6: Create the getMessage() method with the *Add Method SmartGuide.* Select the *HelloWebSphere* Bean in the *Enterprise Beans* pane; then select the *HelloWebSphereBean* class in the *Types* pane to view its methods (Figure 14.13). Open the right-mouse-button menu for the *Members* pane, and select *Add>Method,* as shown in Figure 14.14. Selecting this menu option will open the *Create Method SmartGuide,* which is shown in Figure 14.15.

This versatile *SmartGuide* allows you to create constructors, main methods, and standard methods by simply typing the method signature in the text box provided. Alternatively, you can add methods from the repository, which is useful when merging the work of two or more people or when you change your mind about a method deletion. To create the new getMessage() method, ensure that the *Create a new method* radio button is selected; then type the method signature (public String getMessage()) in the text box beneath the set of creation radio buttons. Complete this step by clicking *Finish* to generate the method and to dismiss the *SmartGuide.* If you prefer, you can type only a partial method signature—leaving off, for instance, the privacy level—and fill in the rest of the method signature by using the radio buttons on the second page of the *SmartGuide,* which you reach by clicking the *Next>*button.

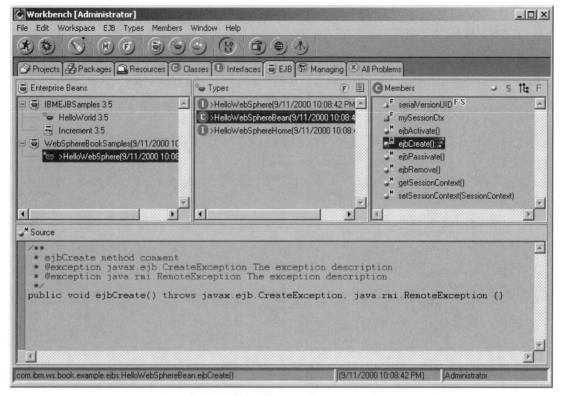

Figure 14.13 *HelloWebSphere* EJB

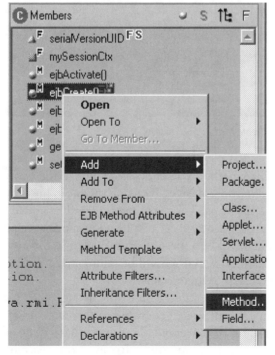

Figure 14.14 The *Add>Method* Menu

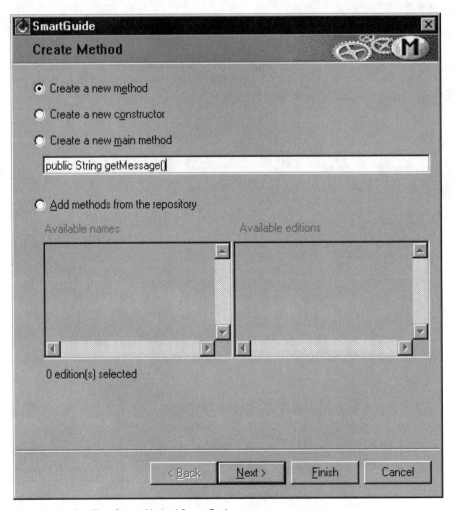

Figure 14.15   The *Create Method SmartGuide*

No matter which method you choose—typing in the full method signature or a partial signature followed by using the radio buttons on the second page—the result is the same. Your new method will be added to the *Members* pane, and the method's code will be displayed in the *Source* pane. Note that all that will be added will be a method stub: The only code inside the brackets following the method signature will be return null;. You will need to add the code in the next step of this exercise.

Step 7: Fill in the implementation of the getMessage() method. Simply select the return null; in the code generated in the previous step and replace it with the code return "Hello World!";. This is standard code editing and shouldn't pose a challenge to anyone. However, the last part of this step

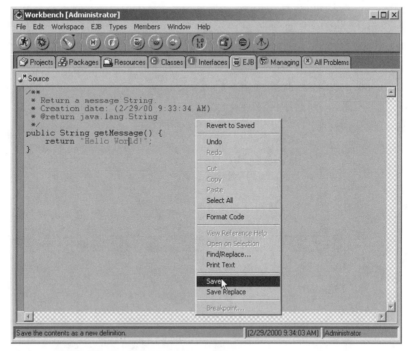

Figure 14.16   The getMessage() Source Code

may deserve some discussion. After changing the code, you have to inform
VisualAge for Java that you are finished editing the method. This is different from other Java IDEs), in which any code change is immediately accepted or you have to explicitly save code at a class level before compiling
the code. VisualAge for Java features an incremental compiler: Once you
indicate that you are finished with a method, the compiler will compile
and link the method in a single step, allowing that method to be used immediately in a running process in the VisualAge debugger. You indicate
that you are finished with a method to VisualAge for Java by choosing the
Save option from the middle-mouse-button menu of the *Source* pane, as
shown in Figure 14.16.

(You can switch between the full-screen code view seen in Figure 14.16
and the four-pane view seen in the previous figures by double-clicking on the
divider next to the *Source* label.) Note the two *Save* selections: *Save* and *Save
Replace*. The distinction between the two is subtle and may cause confusion
to someone new to the VisualAge environment.

Save means that VisualAge should compile the contents of the *Source*
pane as a method, regardless of their semantics. This means that if you
change the method signature of a method—by changing its name or the

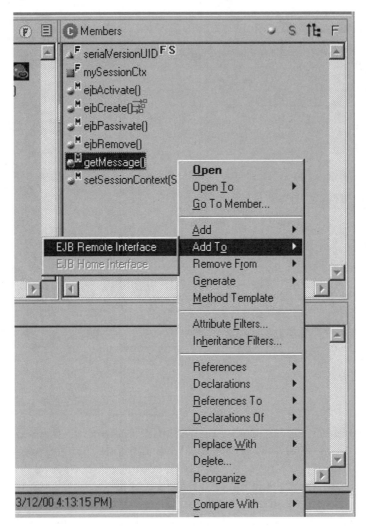

Figure 14.17   *Add to>EJB Remote Interface*

number or type of parameters—it assumes that this is a new method and that the old method should be unchanged.

Save Replace means that only the previously selected method should be changed. If you change the method signature and then choose *Save Replace,* the old method is replaced by this one, which is equivalent to saving the new method and deleting the old one.

Step 8: Promote the getMessage() method to the Remote interface. To see how this very simple Visual Age process works, open the right-mouse-button menu in the *Members* pane and select *Add To>EJB Remote Interface,* as shown in Figure 14.17.

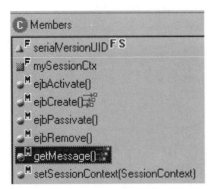

Figure 14.18   Promotion Icon Added to getMessage() showing

Note that the *Add To* submenu has two potential choices. VisualAge determines whether a method can be added to either the Home or the Remote interface by its method signature. If a method is an ejbCreate(...) method or a finder method implementation (ejbFindXXX), VisualAge will allow the method to be added to the Home interface. All other methods signatures will be available to add to the EJB Remote interface.

Once you have selected the getMessage() method and added it to the Remote interface, you will see a change in the way the method is displayed in the *Members* pane: A promotion icon—three arrows terminating in blocks—has been added to the right of the method name, as shown in Figure 14.18. The color of the three arrows indicates whether the method has been promoted to either the Remote or the Home interface. If the arrow on top is red, the method is part of the Remote interface. If the arrow on the bottom is red, it is part of the Home interface.

Summary and Preview

In this chapter, you have seen what the code for a simple Session EJB's Remote interface, Home interface, and Bean implementation class looks like. You have also seen how they can be created in VisualAge for Java's EJB Development Environment. This should give you enough information to begin creating simple Session EJBs on your own. We will examine more parts of the EJB Development Environment in the next chapter, which will focus on testing and debugging your new EJB.

CHAPTER 15

Testing and Debugging EJBs in VisualAge for Java

In the previous chapter, you saw how to use the VisualAge for Java EJB Development Environment to build the various parts of an EJB: a Home interface, a Remote interface, and a Bean implementation class. In this chapter, you will find out how to generate deployment code for your EJBs and how to test and debug EJBs in VisualAge for Java.

Overview of the Testing Process

To proceed with testing EJBs, you will need to learn about some of the built-in testing tools in VisualAge for Java's EJB Development Environment. Just as you can develop EJBs by following a step-by-step approach, you can test and debug your EJBs by using a similar kind of approach. In short, the steps necessary to test simple EJBs are as follows.

1. Generate the EJB deployment classes.
2. Add an EJB server process.
3. Start the naming service.
4. Start your EJB server process.
5. Test your EJB with the generated test client.
6. Debug the EJB code, if necessary, in the integrated debugger.

You must return to the EJB Development Environment in VisualAge for Java to begin working your way through this process.

Step 1: Generate the EJB deployment classes. Before you can begin this step, you need to understand what happens in this step. An EJB is a *software component,* and in the previous chapter, you developed the user-developed part of an EJB: the Home and Remote interfaces and the Bean implementation class. However, an EJB also consists of container-provided classes that handle the distribution, transaction, thread safety, and, optionally, persistence aspects of the EJB. We call these classes *deployment* classes, as generating them is part of the EJB deployment process that is outlined in the EJB specification. Table 15.1 lists the classes and their purposes that WebSphere generates for a Session EJB.

Now that you have seen all the classes that must be generated and learned why they must be generated, you are ready to understand the first step in the process of testing EJBs in VisualAge for Java. Starting the code generation is simple. First, select either the *HelloWebSphere* EJB or the *WebSphereBookSamples* EJB group in the *Enterprise Beans* pane. Next, open the right-mouse-button menu in the *Enterprise Beans* pane and select *Generate Deployed Code,* as shown in Figure 15.1.

Table 15.1　EJB Deployment Classes

Class group	Purpose
• _\<beanname>_Stub	• The RMI-IIOP stub class that is used as a proxy on the client side.
• _\<beanname>_BaseStub	• The superclass of \<beanname>_Stub.
• EJSRemote\<beanname>	• The EJB object that the container uses to control access to an instance of the Bean implementation class.
• EJSRemote\<beanname>_TIE	• The CORBA internal class that translates IIOP requests from the ORB into messages to the EJSRemote object.
	These four classes make up the backbone of the Remote interface and handle distribution for Remote instances.
• _\<beanname>Home_Stub	• The RMI-IIOP stub for the Home.
• _\<beanname>Home_BaseStub	• The superclass home stub.
• EJSRemote\<beanname>Home	• The EJB object for the home Bean.
• EJSRemote\<beanname>Home_TIE	• The _TIE class translates requests, as does the corresponding class for the Remote interface.
• EJSRemote\<beanname>HomeBean	• The implementation of the EJB Home generated by VisualAge for Java to implement the Home interface. This class is ultimately responsible for creating, finding, and deleting instances of the EJBs.

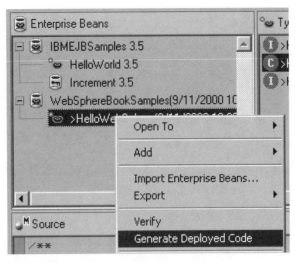

Figure 15.1 *Generate Deployed Code* Menu Option

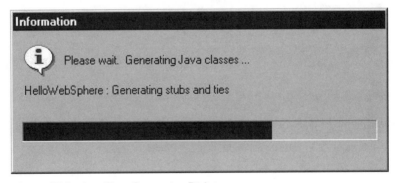

Figure 15.2 Java Class Generation Dialog

The resulting process can take anywhere from a few seconds to several minutes, depending on the speed of your processor and the number of EJBs selected. VisualAge is capable of generating deployed code for either an individual EJB or an entire EJB group at once. Once you have made the menu selection, the progress dialog shown in Figure 15.2 will appear.

The text label directly above the progress bar tells you what classes are being generated or compiled. When the generation process finally completes, you will be able to view the generated classes by clicking on the "full-view" button *(F)* in the upper-right corner above the *Types* pane. (This view appears as a few lines, indicating that you are viewing only a subset of the full set of

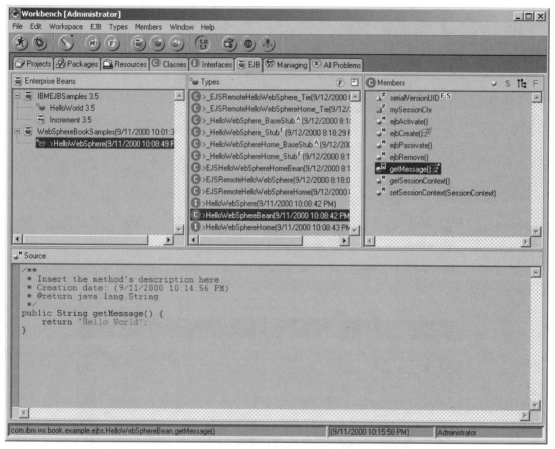

Figure 15.3   Deployed Code Tree View for *HelloWebSphere* EJB

classes. The "partial-view" button consists of multiple lines extending to the bottom of the button and indicates that you are viewing the entire set of types available.) The full set of classes for the *HelloWebSphere* example is shown in Figure 15.3.

Step 2: Add an EJB server process. The *EJB Server Configuration* window is your view onto the processes that make up the runtime portion of the WebSphere Test Environment (WTE). To open this window, you can begin by adding the EJB group you created in the previous chapter as a new server. To do this, select the *WebSphereBookSamples* EJB group in the *Enterprise Beans* pane, and open the right-mouse-button menu. Select *Add To>Server Configuration,* as shown in Figure 15.4.

Choosing this menu selection adds a new server for this EJB group. The *Server Configuration* window will also appear when you make this selection.

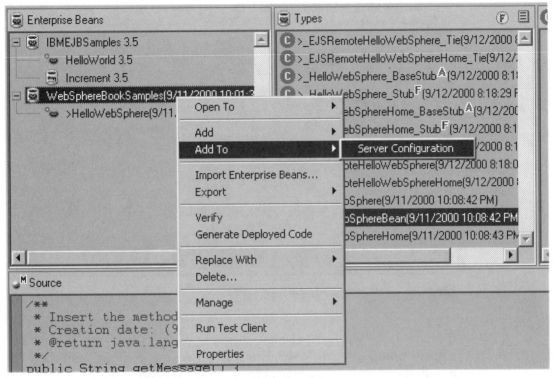

Figure 15.4 *Add To≥Server Configuration* Menu

To view the *Server Configuration* at other times, select *Open To>Server Configuration* from the previous pop-up menu or from the *EJB* menu in the menu bar. Once you take a look at the *Server Configuration* window, the explanation of what has been done above will become clearer. This window is shown in Figure 15.5.

Note that one entry is in the *Servers* pane of the *EJB Server Configuration* window. In VisualAge, each EJB group is individually added as a "server" to this pane. The closest analogy to this in WebSphere is an EJB container, which in fact a server is. Each server is a separate JVM, started by the VisualAge master process, that acts as a self-contained EJB runtime environment. In a later chapter, you will examine some of the properties and settings of the EJB servers.

Step 3: Start the naming service. In order to use your EJB classes, you have to start the helper processes that make up the WebSphere EJB Test Environment, just as you had to start the servlet engine to test your servlets. The first process you must start is the persistent naming service (PNS). VisualAge uses the PNS to register objects, such as EJB Homes and data sources. PNS is

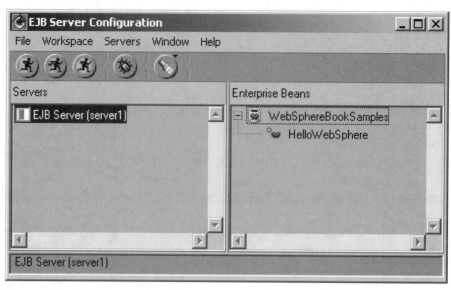

Figure 15.5   *EJB Server Configuration* Window

the same as the WebSphere Naming Service, which is part of the WebSphere administration server. In WebSphere, this service is part of the WebSphere administration server; in effect, you are starting a miniature subset of the WebSphere admin server inside VisualAge.

To start the PNS, you need to open the *WebSphere Control Center* by selecting *Workspace>Tools>WebSphere Test Environment,* just as you did in previous chapters. The difference here is that you select the *Persistent Name Server* branch of the tree and then click the *Start Name Server* button, as shown in Figure 15.6. When the name server has started, the icon beside the *Persistent Name Server* tag will change from two red semicircles to four blue-and-white quarter circles.

Step 4: Start the EJB server process. Now you can start your new EJB server. To start a server, select the server in the *Servers* pane of the *EJB Server Configuration* window, and then select either the *Run* button at the upper-left corner of the *Server Configuration* window—the button with the "runner" icon—or *Run* from the right-mouse-button menu.

Note: You need to be certain that the PNS startup has completed before you start your EJB server. The reason is that one of the first things an EJB server attempts to do is create an instance of each EJB Home in the server and then register that Home with the PNS. It may take a few minutes for the PNS to start. If you attempt to start another EJB server too early in the process, before the PNS initialization has completed, the EJB server will fail

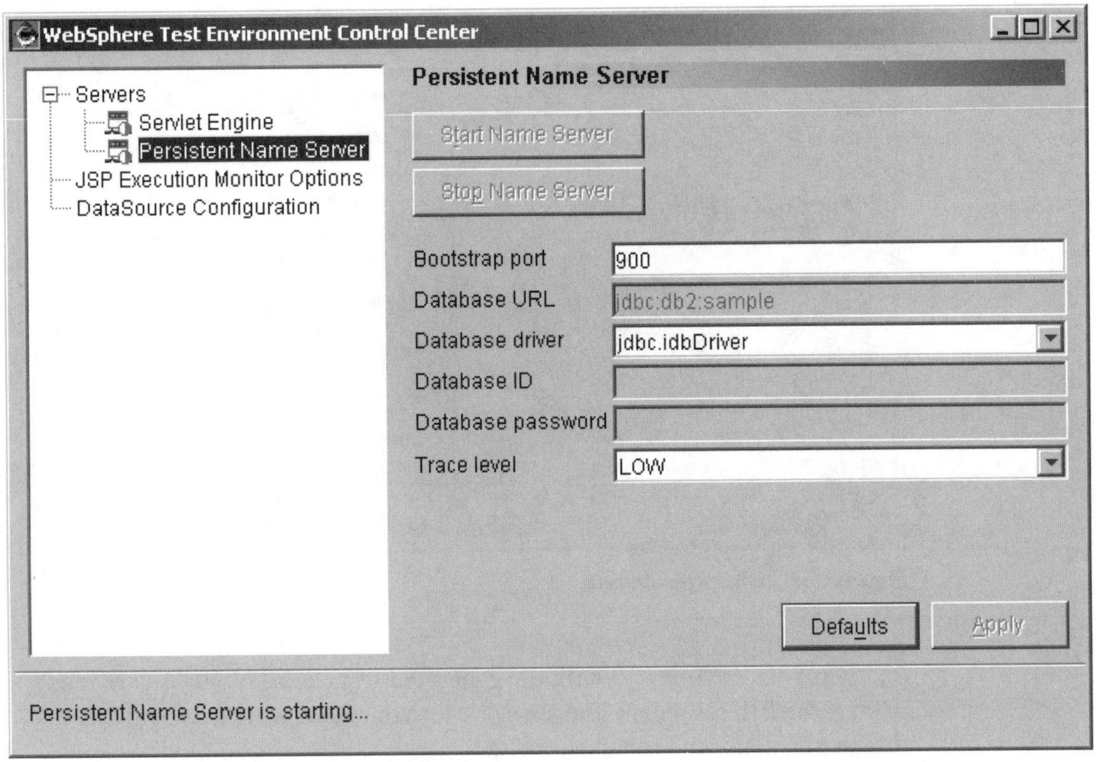

Figure 15.6 Start *Persistent Name Server*

to start. To avoid this from happening, watch for completion of the PNS startup cycle before attempting to start any EJB servers. If you look in the VisualAge console, you will see that a set of messages indicates the status of the PNS startup cycle being written to the console. (The VisualAge console separates its output lists by process; you will have to select the PNS process to view its output.) In the console, the last message, indicating successful PNS startup, will be:

[timestamp]<hex value> EJServer **"E Server open for business."**

Once this message has appeared, you are guaranteed that it is safe to start the EJB servers without the possibility of failure because of the PNS not being available. Note that if you do start a server too early, simply restart it after letting the PNS complete its startup cycle; the server will begin to function the second time you start it. When you have successfully started your EJB server process, you will see a "running" icon next to the process name in the *EJB Server Configuration* window, as shown in Figure 15.7.

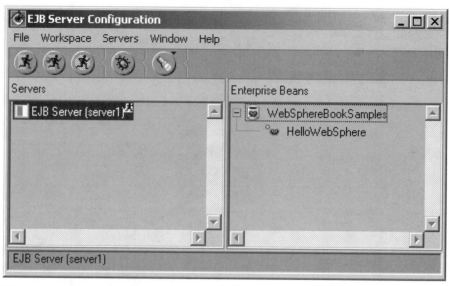

Figure 15.7   EJB Server Started

Step 5: Test your EJB with the generated test client. Now you are ready to start the EJB test client and see whether your hard work has paid off. In this step, you use the test client to

- Obtain a reference to the EJB home for your *HelloWebSphere* EJB
- Create an instance of the *HelloWebSphere* EJB
- Send the getMessage() to the new instance

To begin this step, go back to the *EJB* tab of the workbench. Select the *HelloWebSphere* EJB and open the right-mouse-button menu in the *Enterprise Beans* pane. Select *Run Test Client* from this menu, as shown in Figure 15.8. Selecting this menu option will open the *EJB Test Client,* which will look like Figure 15.9.

The test client uses a multiple document interface (MDI) paradigm. You can select which window you wish to view by selecting the *Window* drop-down menu. In most circumstances, you will want to use the test client like a *SmartGuide* and let the client lead you between the windows as you complete the action on each window in the foreground, as you will see in this example.

The first window you see, *EJB Lookup,* contains the following parts.

- The URL of the PNS is shown in the *Provider URL:* text box. The default for this is *IIOP://localhost:900/,* which is equivalent to port

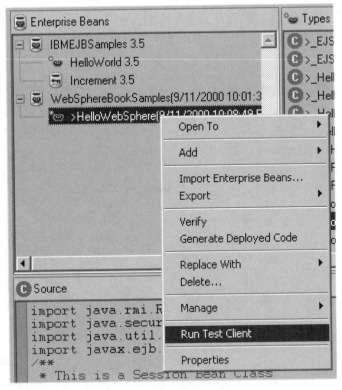

Figure 15.8   The *Run Test Client* Menu

900 on the local machine. You can set this to another value if you
wish, for example, to test an EJB running on another machine.
- The name of the InitialContextFactory class is shown in the *Context factory:* text box. You would change this name only if you were going to
  test an EJB deployed to WebSphere Enterprise Edition.
- The JNDI name of the EJB, which by default is the same as the fully
  qualified class name of the EJB, as was explained in the previous chapter, is shown in the *JNDI Name:* text box.

In this example, you will leave all these fields with their default values.
Click the *Lookup* button to attempt to obtain a remote reference to the
HelloWebSphere EJB Home by performing a JNDI lookup of the Home object. The test client will inform you of the progress of this action by updating
the status bar. When the reference is obtained, a new window for your EJB
will open, as shown in Figure 15.10.

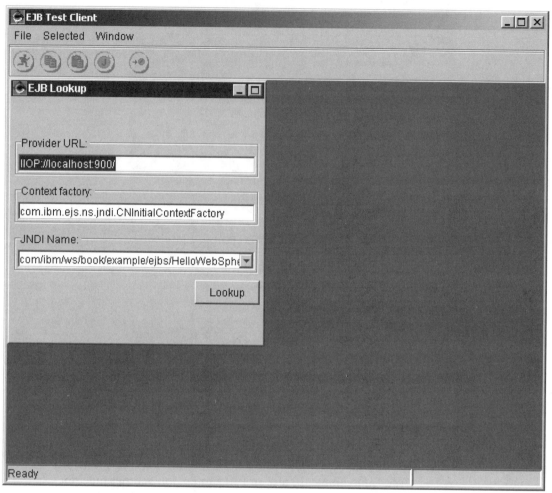

Figure 15.9   The *EJB Test Client* (*EJB Lookup* Window)

This window also deserves a few moments of inspection to understand its parts. This window has two tabs: *Home* and *Remote,* corresponding to the two interfaces in the EJB. At this moment, only the *Home* tab will be operable, as you have not yet created any EJB instances.

At the left-hand side of the *Home* tab is a tree view listing the methods defined in the Home interface (the *Methods* pane). At the right-hand side of the tab is a tree view that can contain the details of what is selected in the left-hand tree view. This could include parameters of the selected method in the *Methods* pane or an inspector on objects returned from the create methods.

To create an instance of your stateless Session Bean, you will need to send

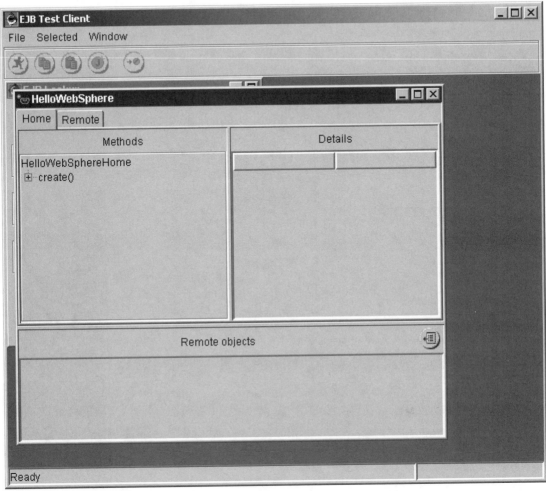

Figure 15.10   *EJB Test Client* Opened to *HelloWebSphere* Window, *Home* Tab

a create() message to the EJB Home. Select the create() method in the *Methods* pane. Because the default create() method has no parameters, the *Details* pane has nothing for you to select. Instead, simply click the *Run* button: the one with the "runner" icon. The progress of this operation will be indicated in the status bar in the lower-right corner. Once the Bean creation has completed, the *HelloWebSphere* window in the test client switches to the next tab, *Remote,* shown in Figure 15.11.

This tab has a structure exactly like that of the Home interface page. The only difference is that the methods of the Remote interface are shown rather than the methods of the Home interface. You can complete the example by

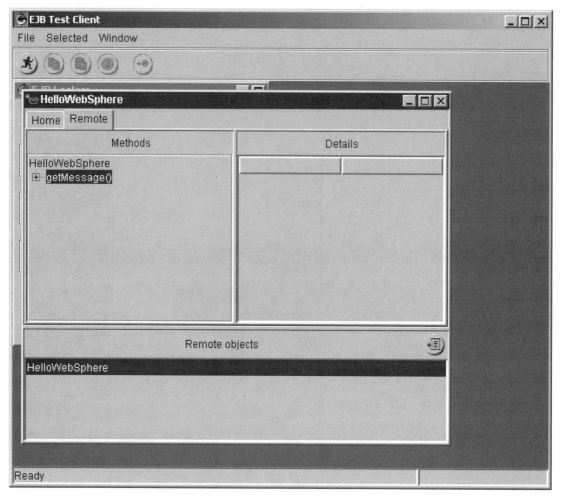

Figure 15.11   *Remote* Tab in Test Client

selecting the getMessage() method in the *Methods* pane and clicking *Run* again. If everything works correctly, you will see the result—"Hello World!"—displayed in the *Details* area next to the getMessage() method.

Debugging EJBs in VisualAge for Java

One of the greatest advantages that VisualAge for Java has over its competitors is that it allows you to debug EJBs that are developed in the EJB Development Environment in place in the WTE that is part of VisualAge. You can use the standard VisualAge debugger to

- Set and clear breakpoints in EJB code and client code
- Step over code, step into code, or jump to the next breakpoint
- Examine values of variables in EJB code and client code and change the values while the code is running
- Change EJB code or client code directly in the debugger and resume the paused process at the beginning of the current method, without losing any of the state of your application

You never need to leave the VisualAge environment to do any of these things. You do not have to perform a separate deployment or compilation or debug step to run the debugger. If you set a breakpoint and run the EJB server as described in the previous step, the debugger will halt the currently running thread at the breakpoint you set and wait for your intervention to continue.

Teaching all the features of the VisualAge for Java debugger is beyond the scope of this book. However, you can get a taste for how easy it can be to debug your EJBs through the following exercise. We will change the code of the getMessage() method so that we can investigate how to set breakpoints, step through code, inspect variable values, and change code in the debugger. You need to begin by returning to the *HelloWebSphere* Session EJB in the *Enterprise Beans* pane of the EJB Development Environment. Select the *HelloWebSphereBean* class in the *Types* pane, and then edit the text of the getMessage() method in the *Members* pane to match the following implementation.

```
/**
 *This method returns a message to the user.
 *Creation date: (3/11/00 10:00:23 PM)
 *@return java.lang.String
 */
public String getMessage() {
    String message = "Hello World";
    return message;
}
```

Now you need to set a breakpoint at the first line of the method, such as the one declaring the string variable message. Setting breakpoints is easy. Simply place your cursor on the line you want to set a breakpoint on, and then press CTRL-B. (Or, alternatively, choose *Breakpoint* from the pop-up menu in the *Source* pane.) This will bring up a window that allows you to choose what kind of breakpoint you want to set, as Figure 15.12 shows.

This window allows you to specify whether you want to set a breakpoint only in specific threads or processes, on an iteration, or on a particular expression. In our case, we want the simplest case, which is setting a breakpoint on the default expression, true. To set this, simply click the *On expression*

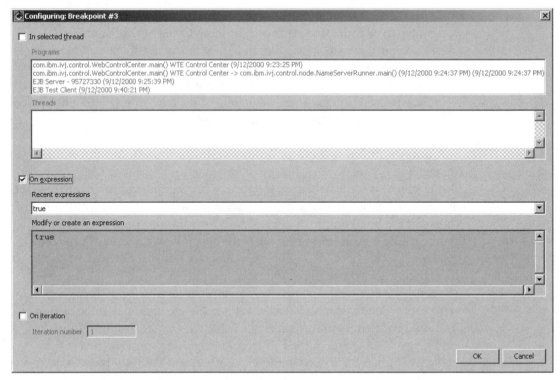

Figure 15.12   Breakpoint Configuration Window

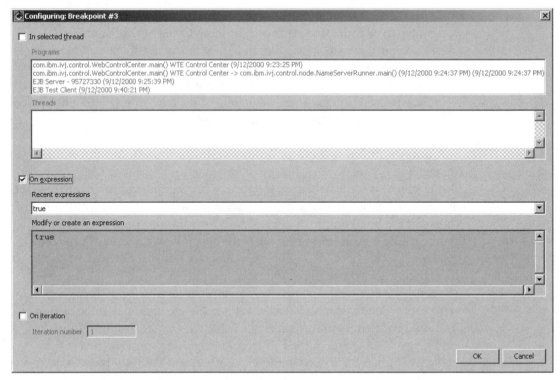

Figure 15.13   Breakpoint Set

check box and click *OK*. Once a breakpoint is set on a line, the line will have a small blue-and-white ball to the left of the method text in the source pane, as shown in Figure 15.13.

Once you have set the breakpoint, you are ready to find out how the debugger operates. If you have shut down the EJB server and the naming ser-

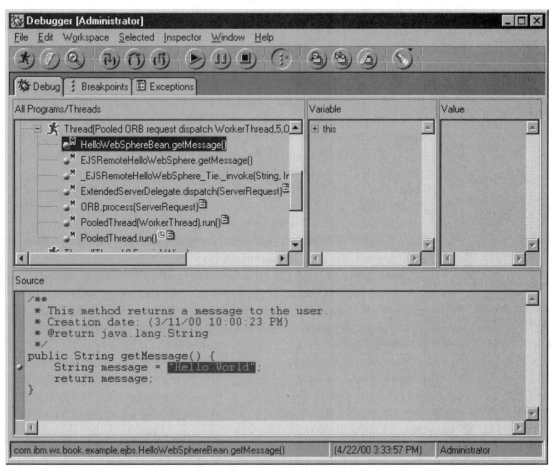

Figure 15.14   Debugger on getMessage() Method

vice, restart them, being careful to start the naming service first. Next, you
need to follow the procedure outlined in the previous section for opening a
test client for the *HelloWebSphere* EJB, walk through the steps of connecting
to the naming service and obtaining a home reference, and then create an instance of the *HelloWebSphere* EJB by sending the create() method to the
Home. Things will start to be different only when you try to use the *Send*
button on the Remote interface page to send the message getMessage() to the
EJB. When you click *Send* at that step, the VisualAge debugger will appear
(Figure 15.14).

We should state again that we can't cover all the features of the Visual-
Age for Java debugger in this book. For a complete coverage of these features, you should read the product documentation or [Jakab]. We do want to
introduce a few features of this window, though.

The debugger has three tabs. The most commonly used tab, *Debug*, is selected by default when a breakpoint is encountered. The other two tabs show the breakpoints set in your program and a list of exceptions that will suspend execution at the throw point. For our purposes, we will focus on the *Debug* tab. When this tab is selected, you see four panes in the window. The upper-left pane *(All Programs/Threads)* shows a tree view of the currently running processes in the VisualAge environment. When you select a process, the tree will expand to show the threads that are running as part of that program. In this way, you can simultaneously debug multiple programs, such as a servlet acting as an EJB client and the EJB itself.

When a breakpoint is encountered, the debugger automatically opens to the proper process and thread. As you can see, when a thread is selected, the tree opens to show the call stack of that thread. The top of the call stack, which is what will be selected, shows the currently running method, which is where the breakpoint was encountered.

The pane to the right of *All Programs/Threads* is the *Variable* pane, which shows the list of variables currently in scope. Selecting a variable in this pane will show its value, such as the value of a primitive or the result of sending toString() to an object, in the *Value* pane. Finally, the source of the method selected in the methods pane is shown in the bottom text pane, *Source*.

To find out how to handle a breakpoint, examine the row of buttons at the top of the window. A group of three buttons shows red arrows and black braces: {}. The first button, showing an arrow entering a set of braces, is the "step-into" button. It will step the execution of the program into the next method ahead of the execution cursor and change the selected method to be the new method. The second button, showing an arrow bypassing the set of braces, is the "step-over" button. That button will execute the next method without changing the focus of the debugger into that method. The remaining button in this group is the "run to return" button, which executes the current method until the end of the method.

To the right of the previous set of buttons is a set of three buttons that look like VCR or tape-deck controls. The first button, with the universal "play" symbol, is the "resume" button, which means resume execution of the program until the next breakpoint or the end of the program. The button to the right of that, with the universal "pause" symbol, is the "suspend" button, which suspends the currently running thread at the next opportunity. The final button in the group, with the "stop" symbol, is the "terminate" button, which terminates execution of the selected thread.

Now that you know what the controls in this window are, you are ready to debug your program. Click the "step-over" button twice to complete execution of the first line of code. After you have stepped over the first line of code and the selection is set to the second line, you will see that the *Variable* pane now contains a selection for the message variable. If you click on the message variable, you will see its value displayed in the *Value* pane. After you've examined the value, go ahead and click the *Resume* button to finish execution of the method. When you return to the test client window, you should see the same value displayed in the *Result:* field.

The next exercise will really show the power of the VisualAge for Java Development Environment. It is something that you can't accomplish in any other Java IDE. Return to the test client window and again click the *Send* button to send the getMessage() method to the *HelloWebSphere* EJB. This time, when the debugger window appears, select the static string *Hello Web-Sphere*, and type Hello Nobody. Then bring up the right-mouse-button pop-up menu and select *Save*. This will change the source text of the method and automatically recompile and relink the new method into the currently running thread. You will then need to double-click *Resume:* once to restart execution to the beginning of this method and once to resume execution. When you examine the new value in the test client, you will see that the returned value was indeed Hello Nobody.

This will give you a taste of what you can do with the VisualAge for Java debugger. The tool is worth spending time to get to know, as using it can save immense amounts of time. Feel free to continue to experiment with the debugger, adding more complex code into the method or experimenting with different types of variables to get a feel for how to examine variable values in the *Variable* pane.

Summary and Preview

In this chapter, you've learned how to test EJBs by using the VisualAge for Java EJB Development Environment. You've discovered how to start and stop servers and run test clients. Finally, you've learned a little about how to use the powerful debugging tools built into the VisualAge for Java environment to debug your EJBs. In the next chapter, we will proceed to the next step: writing simple EJB clients.

CHAPTER 16

Writing Simple EJB Clients

Prior to EJB technology, as we have discussed previously, Java objects were distributed via RMI or CORBA ORBs providing Java bindings. The EJB specification takes a page from each of these technologies, which you can see as you examine the client-side interface to EJB components.

EJB Client Steps

The EJB architecture formalizes how EJB clients obtain and affect remote references and local object (nonremote) instances from the server. Client access to EJB object consists of the following steps:

1. Obtaining an initial naming context
2. Looking up an EJB Home from the initial context
3. Using the Home interface (creating, finding, or removing EJBs)
4. Manipulating EJB references

Obtaining a Home *Interface*

Clients can create, remove, and obtain references to EJBs of a specific type by obtaining a Home instance from a container using JNDI. Figure 16.1 shows the JNDI API.

JNDI

Directory services are a convenient way to organize and to partition information about users, resources, networks, machines, security information, and, in the case of Java, objects. In an attempt to make access to specific directory

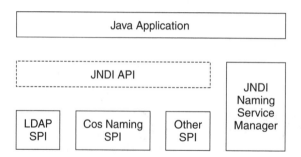

Figure 16.1   JNDI API

services independent of a specific service implementation, Sun and other leading industry vendors defined the JNDI specification and reference implementation. Version 1.2 of the specification is available for download at the Java software Web site.

The JNDI implementation provides a standardized access API to directory service into a JNDI naming manager, which controls access to specific directory service implementations, such as RMI, CORBA Object Services (COS) naming, or (Lightweight Directory Access Protocol) LDAP.

The JNDI service provider interface (SPI) allows directory/naming implementations supplied by different providers to be installed and accessed from Java in a neutral fashion. Java developers commonly access directory services through the interfaces defined in the javax.naming package. Context, a core interface in this package, provides operations to maintain name-to-object bindings. The javax.naming.directory package supplies the ability to create directory objects and attributes objects that can be examined through the use of the DirectoryContext interface. For more information about the JNDI specification, visit the *http://java.sun.com/jndi* site.

Container vendors are responsible for providing an interface to their particular distribution solution through JNDI. WebSphere's SPI uses an underlying CORBA naming service to store references to Home objects in a relational database. In fact, these remote reference/name pairs are stored in a table in the shared administration database for the WebSphere domain, so the names are persistent. If an admin server fails, WebSphere's nanny process will automatically restart the admin server and allow it to pick up the values of the registered Home objects from the database when it comes up.

When you are writing an EJB client, you are responsible for creating a JNDI InitialContext that will work together with a remote instance of the WebSphere naming service running in an admin server. To do this, you need to provide two pieces of information:

- The location—host name and port—of the remote WebSphere naming service
- The name of the InitialContext Factory: for example, the object that will create an InitialContext that connects to the naming service

You have to provide the name of the InitialContext Factory because a program may use multiple JNDI SPIs. For instance, you might want to use both the WebSphere naming service and an LDAP repository. An example of code that obtains an InitialContext for the WebSphere naming service follows:

```
java.util.Properties properties = new java.util.Properties();
properties.put(javax.naming.Context.PROVIDER_URL, "iiop://localhost:900/");
properties.put(javax.naming.Context.INITIAL_CONTEXT_FACTORY,
"com.ibm.ejs.ns.jndi.CNInitialContextFactory");
InitialContext initialContext = new InitialContext(properties);
```

Two things in particular are important about this code. First, the information is provided to the constructor of the InitialContext as a java.util.Properties. The keys to this Properties object are constants from the class javax.naming. Context. Note what we have used for the values of the properties, though. In the first instance, where the key was PROVIDER_URL, we have used the string "iiop://localhost:900/". This string is shorthand for saying "find the naming service at the standard port on the local machine." The general form of the PROVIDER_URL string is iiop://hostname:port/. The value of the second property, INITIAL_CONTEXT_FACTORY, is the class name of the WebSphere naming service Factory, com.ibm. ejs.ns.jndi.CNInitialContextFactory. You will always use this class name when obtaining an InitialContext for the WebSphere naming service in WebSphere Application Server, Advanced Edition or VisualAge for Java, Enterprise Edition.

JNDI Contexts and the WebSphere Naming Service

In the previous example, we used the string iiop://localhost:900/ to find the naming service running on the local machine. We have found that many people don't realize that they can use *any* admin server in a WebSphere domain to create an InitialContext. Programmers with experience in other application servers often worry that client code needs to know a "magic" name server host to hook into WebSphere. In fact, any host in the

WebSphere domain will suffice, as a copy of the WebSphere naming service runs in the administration server of every node running the WebSphere Application Server. This is possible because all the names in that naming service are obtained from the shared database used by all admin servers in an administrative domain. Because our clients often are servlets also running in the WebSphere domain, they can safely use their local name server; hence, iiop://localhost:900/.

Obtaining Home *References*

The Bean developer is responsible for creating a Home interface for the Bean, which is usually generated by container development tools. Home objects are the apex for obtaining and affecting EJBs occupying a container. Remote Home objects for a type are obtained from a container using JNDI. In the previous chapter, we introduced the *HelloWebSphere* EJB that defined a Home interface named HelloWebSphereHome. A client can obtain a reference to a remote Home instance by using the following source:

```
Object initialReference = initialContext.lookup("HelloWebSphere");
HelloWebSphereHome helloWebSphereHome = (HelloWebSphereHome)
javax.rmi.PortableRemoteObject.narrow(initialReference,HelloWebSphere-
Home.class);
```

The obtained Home instance can be used to create, locate, and remove EJBs from the server's container. The final step necessary here is to use the utility class PortableRemoteObject to "narrow" the reference obtained from the InitialContext. This step can be thought of almost as a "cast"; it takes a generic RMI-IIOP reference and returns an instance of the proper class (HelloWebSphereHome).

Creating

Creating objects is accomplished by invoking the Home interface create(args...) method. A single Home class can implement multiple create() methods by specifying different argument combinations for each create() method. A remote instance of a Session or an Entity Bean is returned that has been initialized with the argument values of the create() method. The following code shows how you obtain a reference to a *HelloWebSphere* EJB from a Home reference.

```
// using the create method
HelloWebSphere object = helloWebSphereHome.create();
```

Removing

Session Bean instances are removed from the server by sending the remove() method directly to a Session Bean instance, or the remove(Handle aHandle) method can be invoked against the javax.ejb.Home interface. Entity Bean instances are removed with the Home interface's remove(Object primaryKey) method.

When you are finished with the *HelloWebSphere* EJB, you could remove it with the following code:

```
object.remove();
```

Using the EJB

Now that you've seen how to obtain an EJB proxy, you are ready to start using it. This is the simplest part of the EJB mechanism. Simply start sending the EJB client stub methods from the EJB Remote interface. For instance, you can try out our *HelloWebSphere* EJB by trying the following messages:

```
// object is an EJB stub obtained in the previous step
String result = object.getMessage();
System.out.println("The message received was " + result);
```

We have left out a few details from this example: Each of the methods we have looked at could throw a different set of exceptions. So, you have the choice of wrapping them in individual try..catch statements or putting a single try...catch block around the entire set of statements. Usually, that is the better option, as it results in less code that is more easily read.

EJBObject **and Remote Proxies**

Remember that clients never directly access EJB instances; instead, they are provided with a Remote interface that acts as a proxy to the real instance, which resides in the server's container. Typically, the implementation classes that reside on the server are produced by using an EJB tool. Methods available to both the Session Bean implementation and the remote, sometimes known as a proxy, are defined in an interface implemented by both client remote proxies and server-side implementations.[1] This allows the session Bean to be treated as the same type on the server and the client side (Figure 16.2).

---

1. In fact, as we have seen, the Bean implementation class does not implement the Remote interface directly (through the implements keyword) but instead indirectly implements the methods of the Remote interface by providing methods that match the method signatures in the Remote interface.

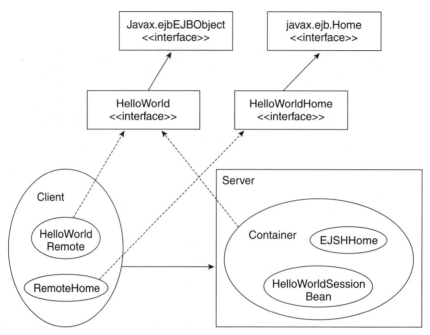

Figure 16.2   EJBObject Interface

VisualAge for Java Access Beans

As you have seen, the entire process of obtaining an InitialContext, looking up a Home interface, and then creating an EJB can be a bit complicated. VisualAge for Java avoids this complication by generating EJB-specific Access Beans. VisualAge can generate an Access Bean that encapsulates the EJB access protocol, making it appear to be a simple JavaBean class. In effect, the Access Bean will "wrap" the EJB stub inside itself. This approach is a useful way to use EJBs in the visual composition environment or from a JSP.

To see how to generate Access Beans, select the *HelloWorld* Bean in the *Enterprise Beans* panel; then right-click and select the *Add>Access Bean* option. The *Access Bean SmartGuide* will appear (Figure 16.3).

Click *Finish*, as the default information should be sufficient. The *HelloWorldAccessBean* will be created in the same package as the EJB interfaces and generated code: in this case, com.ibm.ws.book.example.ejbs.

Testing EJB Code in the Scrapbook

Access Beans cut through a lot of the complexity of EJBs and allow you to run simple EJB tests in the *Scrapbook*. You open the *Scrapbook* by selecting

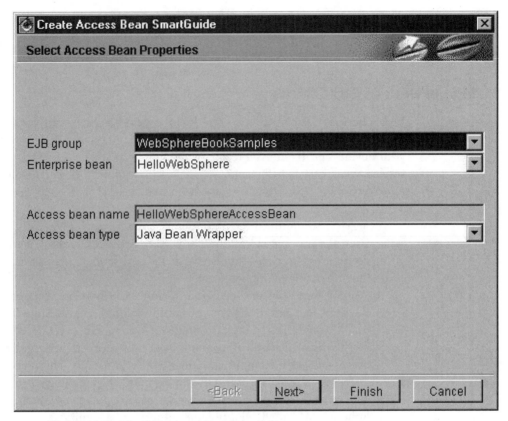

Figure 16.3 The *Create Access Bean SmartGuide*

the *Window>Scrapbook* menu option from the workbench. To see how this works, type the following code into a *Scrapbook* page:

```
com.ibm.ws.book.example.ejbs.HelloWebSphereAccessBean bean =

new com.ibm.ws.book.example.ejbs.HelloWebSphereAccessBean();
bean.getMessage();
```

First, make sure that all the EJB server processes in the *Server Configuration* window are running. Once you have typed this code into the page, select all the text and then pop open the right-mouse-button menu and select *Display.* This will run the client code and print the result after the final message. (You will see "Hello WebSphere" or, possibly, "Hello Nobody," depending on where you left off from the last chapter.)

This type of testing is a useful feature, allowing you to quickly test a single line of code or a few lines of code independent of a fully running program, but it does not replace more formal testing. Although this would normally be challenging with an EJB client because of the number of things that must happen to connect to an EJB, Access Beans make this a possibility. Still, don't rely on *Scrapbook* testing for all your testing needs. We will examine how to write more formal test classes in a later chapter.

Using Servlets as EJB Clients

WebSphere is possibly being used to its fullest extent when your application uses both servlets and EJBs together to bring the full power of J2EE to bear on your business problem. As a result, WebSphere is really designed to make servlets work best as EJB clients; whereas a Java application can also be a client to a WebSphere EJB, servlets are the preferred client type, for several reasons.

- Servlets communicate to end-client browsers through HTTP. More firewalls support HTTP than any other protocol, making it easier to configure your corporate network to use a servlet client than an IIOP client like a Java application.
- WebSphere's EJB stubs have been optimized to avoid network calls when the EJB client and the EJB are physically colocated in the same Java Virtual Machine (JVM). If you configure a WebSphere server to have both a servlet engine and an EJB container, the calls between the servlet EJB clients and the EJBs in the container will be local calls. This is considerably faster (about 20 percent less overhead) than when making a network call.
- You must distribute a fairly large set of JAR files that contain the WebSphere RMI-over-IIOP implementation and a significant part of the underlying WebSphere CORBA ORB with Java application clients. The total set of JAR files that you must distribute adds up to approximately 3MB of code. Another restriction is that you must use the IBM JDK and JRE (on platforms where it is available), because only it contains the appropriate level of *.dll* files for RMI over IIOP. (We will cover this in more detail later.)

So, as you can see, it is easiest to build your clients as Java servlets. This is the approach we take in our case study, and it should be encouraged whenever possible. So, now that you understand the reasons why we want to build servlet EJB clients, you are ready to see an implementation of the simplest EJB client. We will call this one *HelloWebSphereEJBServlet*. Its source code follows (Listing 16.1).

Listing 16.1 Source code for *HelloWebSphereEJBServlet.*

```
package com.ibm.ws.book.example.clients;
import java.io.*;
import javax.ejb.*;
```

```
import javax.naming.*;
import javax.servlet.http.*;
import java.util.*;
import com.ibm.ws.book.example.ejbs.*;
/**
 *This class is a simple EJB Servlet Client
 *@author: Kyle Brown
 */
public class HelloWebSphereEJBServlet extends HttpServlet {
/**
 *HelloWebSphereEJBServlet Constructor
 */
public HelloWebSphereEJBServlet() {
    super();
}
/**
 *This service() method handles all HTTP requests.
 */
public void service(HttpServletRequest req, HttpServletResponse resp) throws
javax.servlet.ServletException, IOException {
    try {
        Properties properties = new Properties();
        properties.put(javax.naming.Context.PROVIDER_URL, "iiop://local-
        host:900/");
        properties.put(javax.naming.Context.INITIAL_CONTEXT_FACTORY,
        "com.ibm.ejs.ns.jndi.CNInitialContextFactory");
        InitialContext initialContext = new InitialContext(properties);
        Object initialReference = initialContext.lookup("com/ibm/ws/book/
        example/ejbs/HelloWebSphere");
        HelloWebSphereHome helloWebSphereHome = (HelloWebSphereHome)
        javax.rmi.PortableRemoteObject.narrow(initialReference, HelloWebSphere-
        Home.class);
        HelloWebSphere object = helloWebSphereHome.create();
        String result = object.getMessage();
        PrintWriter out = resp.getWriter();
        out.println("<HTML>" + "The message is " + result + " </HTML>");
    } catch (Exception e) {
        System.out.println("Exception caught in service() " + e);
    }
}
}
```

As you can see, the servlet simply contains the client code that we've outlined before inside the service() method. The servlet takes the result from the
getMessage() call and then simply places it on the output PrintWriter to return
the message to the client browser that makes the request.

Testing this servlet inside VisualAge for Java is extremely simple. First,
you simply need to ensure that all the EJB server processes are running as
they were in the previous examples. Then, start the servlet engine and type
the URL *http://localhost:8080/servlet/com.ibm.ws.book.example.clients.*
HelloWebSphereEJBServlet in your browser. The more interesting question is

then how to deploy this servlet to WebSphere and test it there; how that is done will be answered in a later chapter.

Some Design Points about Servlet Clients

One of the easiest traps to fall into for a developer new to servlets or EJBs is to assume that how a simple example is built is the way all programs using that technology *should* be built. Ideally, we've been able to convince you in this book that this is not true; you need to plan your architecture ahead of time to deal with issues of scalability, performance, and maintainability. The following general points about the last example explain what you should *not* do in your own EJB client code.

- Don't always create a new InitialContext for every Home lookup. Creating an InitialContext is a fairly slow operation. Although an InitialContext cannot be shared among multiple threads of execution–at least according to the Sun specification—you should try, at the very least, to limit the number of InitialContexts you create.
- You don't want to create and drop an EJB Home reference after one use. Unlike InitialContexts, Home references can be shared among multiple object types or threads of execution, so you should consider using the Singleton pattern (see [Gamma]) to share them. Creating and dropping these objects is not only slow but also generates a lot of objects that must be unnecessarily garbage collected.
- Try to avoid generically catching Exception. Your code should usually trap and handle each potential exception type individually. Often, you will want to do something different for each type of exception that may occur. Resort to catching Exception only when the total code bulk of trapping each exception type becomes too unwieldy or when you really do want to do the same thing no matter what exception is thrown. If you have too many of your own exceptions, consider making them descend from a special MyException class for your project or company and trapping that instead.
- Don't try to do all the client steps—obtaining the initial context, getting the Home, creating the EJB, sending messages, and so on—in a single method. Use functional decomposition to split these steps into multiple methods so that each method does only one thing. This will make maintenance and debugging simpler.
- *Don't do everything in one class.* Follow the MVC architecture, which splits the responsibility for presentation, user request handling, and model behavior into different classes. The same layering principle applies to EJB clients as well. In a later chapter we will

describe how to build layered systems that hide the EJB implementation details from the objects manipulated by the servers. Access Beans are a step in this direction, so you can consider using them for simple applications.

Java Application Clients

We will close this chapter by considering what you need to do to use and to deploy a nonservlet (Java application) client. Take a look at the following source code:

```
package com.ibm.ws.book.example.clients;
import com.ibm.ws.book.example.ejbs.*;
import java.util.*;
import javax.ejb.*;
import javax.naming.*;
/**
 *This is a simple application client.
 *@author: Kyle Brown
 */
public class HelloWebSphereEJBClient {
/**
 *HelloWebSphereEJBClient constructor comment.
 */
public HelloWebSphereEJBClient() {
    super();
}
/**
 *Starts the application.
 *@param args an array of command-line arguments
 */
public static void main(java.lang.String[] args) {
    try {
        Properties properties = new Properties();
        properties.put(javax.naming.Context.PROVIDER_URL, "iiop://local-
        host:900/");
        properties.put(javax.naming.Context.INITIAL_CONTEXT_FACTORY,
        "com.ibm.ejs.ns.jndi.CNInitialContextFactory");
        InitialContext initialContext = new InitialContext(properties);
        Object initialReference = initialContext.lookup("com/ibm/ws/book/
        example/ ejbs/HelloWebSphere");
        HelloWebSphereHome helloWebSphereHome = (HelloWebSphereHome)
        javax.rmi.PortableRemoteObject.narrow(initialReference, HelloWebSphere-
        Home.class);
        HelloWebSphere object = helloWebSphereHome.create();
        String result = object.getMessage();
        System.out.println("The message is " + result);
    } catch (Exception e) {
        System.out.println("Exception caught in service() " + e);
    }
}
}
```

The only truly special thing to mention about this code is that it's not a servlet but rather a standard Java class with a main() method. Also, you might want to consider that normally in an application client, the PROVIDER_URL will not be the default iiop://localhost:900/ that we have used in our servlet clients. You would normally obtain a URL from a properties file that would indicate which naming service instance to connect to.

If you want to follow along with this example, you can either type this code into a VisualAge project or import the code from the CD-ROM. Of course, all the previous design points about servlet clients apply to application clients, too, so please take this as an example only. The interesting part of this comes in testing it both inside and outside VisualAge for Java.

Testing Application Clients in VisualAge

Inside VisualAge for Java, you will need to set the project path of this class to help it locate the classes it needs to execute. This is analogous to setting the Java class path on the command line, which we will see next. To set the class path, select the class in the *Projects* tab of the workbench and right-click to bring up the *Properties* dialog (Figure 16.4).

To set the project path, click the *Compute Now* button on this dialog. When the new project path has been computed, click *OK* to dismiss the dialog. Once this is done, you can run the main() method on the client class by selecting the class and either clicking the *Run* button or right-clicking and selecting *Run>Run main* from the menu. When the main() method completes, you will see the message in the console.

Running Application Clients Outside VisualAge

Although it is interesting and useful to know how to test application clients within VisualAge, the real goal is to run a client outside VisualAge. Luckily, you need not master a lot of additional concepts to understand how this works. As we mentioned earlier, you need to deploy a number of .*jar* files with your client code to run an application client from the command line. The .*jar* files and their purposes are listed in Table 16.1.

The .*jar* files listed in the table are originally found in the /*WebSphere/ AppServer/lib* directory. If you are distributing a client application to other computers that do not have WebSphere installed on them, you must distribute copies of these JAR files with your application. You must also ensure that the client machines have the IBM JRE installed on them; only the IBM JRE contains the special files necessary to communicate via RMI over IIOP.

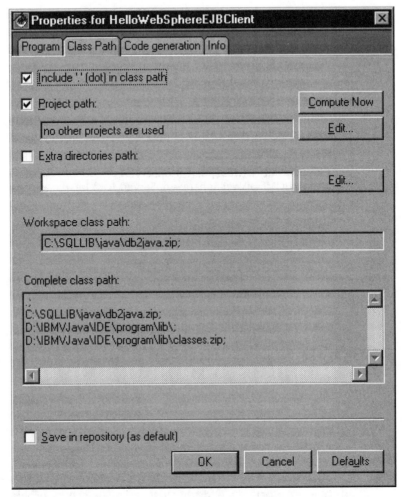

Figure 16.4 *Properties for* Dialog *HelloWebSphereEJBClient*

Table 16.1 JAR Files

JAR file	Purpose
EJS.JAR	Contains a number of IBM-specific classes, such as the connection pool classes, and a number of utility classes used by classes in *UJC.JAR*.
UJC.JAR	The universal Java client (UJC) contains most of the base OMG and Sun classes for RMI over IIOP, as well as IBM EJB-specific classes.

Finally, you need to have all the EJB classes—both the interfaces and the RMI over IIOP stub classes—on the class path of your application. The easiest way to do this is to export a client JAR file from VisualAge for Java for your EJBs and then place that file on the class path. (We cover client JAR files in more depth in a later chapter.) A simple way to ensure that all the *.jar* files are on the class path of your JVM is to execute your program from a batch file or a shell script. An example batch file for starting our client program under Windows NT follows:

```
rem setup the classpath
SET WAS_HOME=I:\WebSphere\AppServer
SET JAVA_HOME=I:\WebSphere\AppServer\JDK\Jre
set WAS_CP=%WAS_CP%;%WAS_HOME%\lib\ejs.jar
set WAS_CP=%WAS_CP%;%WAS_HOME%\lib\ujc.jar
set WAS_CP=%WAS_CP%;%JAVA_HOME%\lib\classes.zip;
set WAS_CP=%WAS_CP%;hellowebsphereclient.jar;
rem start the client program
%JAVA_HOME%\bin\java -classpath
%WAS_CP%;%JAVA_HOME%\lib\rt.zip.com.ibm.ws.book.example.clients.
HelloWebSphereEJBClient
```

As you can see, this batch file ensures that the two *.jar* files described previously are on the class path of the JVM started on the last line. Writing start-up files like this is a good "best practice" for invoking client EJB applications, as it can help eliminate problems caused by class-path differences on different machines.

Why Can't You Use an Applet as an EJB Client?

We have explicitly not discussed using an applet as an EJB client. Although this is a supported option in WebSphere 3.5, it is a complicated endeavor that is probably not worth the effort in most cases. The central problem is the RMI-over-IIOP communication and the dependence on the IBM JRE.

First, only the IBM JRE is supported as a way to run applet or application clients. This means that you must install the IBM JRE on each machine and install it as a plug-in into your browser. Second, some of the classes in the RMI-over-IIOP implementation make native method calls into C routines and also communicate with a socket to an external machine. Unfortunately, both of these requirements violate the applet sandbox security model. So, the calls will fail. The ways around this are very drastic. To get around the sandbox restrictions, you must sign the applet and install special security configuration files to allow the applet to make native method calls. These procedures are so difficult to roll out over a large set of clients that we recommend that you not use applets as an EJB client type for WebSphere.

Summary and Preview

In this chapter, you have learned the basics of writing simple clients that access EJBs. You've seen how to use wrapper Access Beans to simplify your clients and learned how servlet and application clients can be written to use WebSphere EJBs. The next chapter, on CMP Entity Beans, will introduce new concepts that you need to know to begin building complete applications with WebSphere EJBs.

CHAPTER 17

Simple Container-Managed Persistence Entity Beans

In an earlier chapter, we identified two types of Enterprise JavaBeans supported by WebSphere: Session Beans and Entity Beans. You have already learned a lot about how Session Beans work and how they are written in VisualAge for Java for deployment into WebSphere. Now it is time to discover the other part of the puzzle: how Entity Beans work and how they provide access to persistent data stored in a relational database.

Some Entity Bean Basics

Earlier, we discussed how Entity EJBs can provide access to data sources, such as a DB2 relational database, MQ Series messaging, or a CICS or IMS transaction processing system. The two basic types of Entity EJBs are

- Bean-managed persistence (BMP) Entity Beans, sometimes called *self-managed persistence* EJBs
- Container-managed persistence (CMP) Entity Beans

CMP Entity Beans handle the details of the mapping between the object representation of your data—the EJB attributes—and the way in which your persistent data is stored—for example, as columns in a relational database table. They can accomplish this feat because they are generated by a toolset that has knowledge of both the data source that you want to use and the structure of the data in that data source (like a table schema). Because they handle this mapping themselves, they are easier to build, as most of the work is done by generated code. The trade-off for this ease of use comes in the fact that each EJB container, such as WebSphere, can support only a few data sources. For instance, in WebSphere 3.5, CMP Beans support only Oracle, Sybase, and DB2.

BMP Entity Beans make handling the details of mapping to a particular data source the responsibility of the Bean developer. The BMP specification provides a set of "hooks" for user-defined code. The developer of a BMP Bean is guaranteed that these methods will be called at particular points in the EJB life cycle but is responsible for providing the implementation of these methods, which will store and retrieve data from the persistent store. As a result, BMP Beans can be written to retrieve data from and store data to any data store that is available through Java but at the cost of more effort spent in programming by the Bean developer.

As EJBs become more mature, tools will become available to support a wider variety of data sources through CMP. So, a valid design decision is to use a mix of the two approaches in an application, knowing that in the future, Beans that today must be implemented as BMP Beans can later be implemented as CMP Beans.

CMP in WebSphere and VisualAge for Java

Part of the "magic" of CMP comes from the fact that tools for code generation can take advantage of knowledge of the structure of both the persistent data and the objects that map to that data to generate mapping code. However, with that sophistication come some difficult choices in tool implementation. Not everyone can define a sophisticated object-relational mapping. It requires a high level of knowledge in both relational database technology and object design to make the mapping work in the best way.

The EJB specification defines three roles that are applicable to the development of an EJB.

- The Enterprise Bean provider, who designs the EJB interfaces and writes the business logic in the EJB
- The application assembler, who combines EJBs into applications and subsystems to meet specific user requirements
- The deployer, who deploys the Enterprise Beans in a specific operational environment

IBM has developed a suite of tools to provide the most flexibility to developers acting in each of these three roles. You have to understand all three roles in order to understand how IBM's tool strategy for CMP EJBs works.

For instance, an EJB deployer is expected to have knowledge about a particular operational environment, including what relational databases are available to store EJB data. On the other hand, an Enterprise Bean provider or an application assembler is expected to have much more detailed information about what database schemas exist that may need to be mapped to EJBs. To address these two roles and their different goals and expectations, IBM has provided two ways of developing CMP EJBs.

- WebSphere provides a simple CMP implementation that maps an Entity EJB to a single relational database table with a straightforward column-to-attribute mapping.
- VisualAge for Java provides tools that allow more complex CMP mappings from columns in multiple relational database tables to a single Entity EJB and also supports modeling inheritance and association relationships between Entity EJBs as relations between tables in a database.

In an environment requiring only a very simple Entity Bean mapping, WebSphere's basic CMP Entity Bean support is adequate. An Enterprise Bean provider can deliver an EJB-JAR file containing only the basic parts of the Entity Bean: the Remote and Home interfaces, the Bean implementation class, and the key class. The deployer can then take this JAR file and use WebSphere's built-in deployment tools to automatically generate the necessary persistence code and also automatically create a database table to contain the Bean information.

In a more complex environment requiring multiple-table mappings, associations, or inheritance, the Enterprise Bean provider or the application assembler will have to work within the VisualAge for Java tool suite to provide a mapping between the EJBs and the relational database tables that the EJB's data will be stored in. The developer will then deliver a deployed JAR file to the deployer, who will then simply "install" it, without having to generate the deployment code, as the code will already contain the information necessary to perform the complex mapping. That code must be generated within VisualAge for Java in order for the mapping to succeed.

In this and the following chapters, you will learn about both simple and complex mappings. You will also learn how WebSphere and VisualAge for Java interoperate to make CMP Beans work.

The Parts of an Entity Bean

To understand how Entity Beans work, you need to review what the EJB specification says about Entity Beans. Entity Beans and Session Beans have some significant differences, so first examining some of these differences can help in understanding the examples that follow.

Remote *Interfaces*

As part of implementing our case study, you will need to create a way to store information on the different departments in our company. A department consists of a unique integer, departmentNumber and a name, such as Engineering or Consulting. The Remote interface for the DepartmentEJB example doesn't look significantly different from the other EJB Remote interfaces you have seen:

```
package com.wsbook.casestudy.ejb;

/**
 *This is an Enterprise Java Bean Remote Interface
 */
public interface DepartmentEJB extends javax.ejb.EJBObject {

/**
 *Getter method for departmentNumber
 *@return int
 */
int getDepartmentNumber() throws java.rmi.RemoteException;
/**
 *Getter method for name
 *@return java.lang.String
 */
java.lang.String getName() throws java.rmi.RemoteException;

/**
 *Setter method for name
 *@param newValue java.lang.String
 */
void setName(java.lang.String newValue) throws java.rmi.RemoteException;
}
```

This Remote interface defines two types of methods: Getter methods return the value of an attribute of the EJB, and Setter methods allow clients to change the value of an EJB attribute. Attributes that have both types of methods are called EJB *properties*. The only thing even slightly unusual about this Remote interface is that departmentNumber has no Setter method. The reason is that departmentNumber is treated as a special *key field,* as you will see later.

Home *Interfaces*

Like Session Beans, Entity Beans also must define a Home interface that describes the Factory responsible for creating them. However, Entity Home interfaces must define some additional features that Session Beans do not define. For example, look at the following Home interface, which defines a DepartmentEJBHome interface.

```
package com.wsbook.casestudy.ejb;

/**
 *This is a Home interface for the Entity Bean
 */
public interface DepartmentEJBHome extends javax.ejb.EJBHome {

/**
 *create method for a CMP entity bean
 *@return DepartmentEJB
 *@param argDeptNumber int
 */
DepartmentEJB create(int argDeptNumber) throws javax.ejb.CreateException,
java.rmi.RemoteException;
/**
 *
 *@return DepartmentEJB
 *@param argDeptNumber int
 *@param argName java.lang.String
 */
DepartmentEJB create(int argDeptNumber, java.lang.String argName) throws
javax.ejb.CreateException, java.rmi.RemoteException;
/**
 *findByPrimaryKey method comment
 *@return DepartmentEJB
 *@param key DepartmentEJBKey
 */
DepartmentEJB findByPrimaryKey(DepartmentEJBKey key) throws java.rmi.
RemoteException, javax.ejb.FinderException;
}
```

This simple EJBHome defines two create() methods that differ in two ways from the create() methods in the example stateless Session EJB that was covered earlier. First, create() methods for Entity EJBs—and stateful Session EJBs, by the way—can take arguments. These arguments will be used by the EJB's ejb-Create() methods to set the values of the EJB's attributes when it is created. Second, note that we have defined two create() methods, each with a different number of arguments. In this respect, create() methods are like class constructors in Java: You can have as many as you like, so long as they differ in parameter type and/or order. This allows you to create your EJBs in different ways, depending on the situation. You will learn more about why you would want different create() methods later, as we work through the details of this example.

The next thing to note about this Home interface is the presence of a new type of method: a finder method. You can identify one in a Home interface because it always begins with the lowercase letters find. This example has a single finder method, findByPrimaryKey().

```
DepartmentEJB findByPrimaryKey(DepartmentEJBKey key) throws java.rmi.RemoteException, javax.ejb.FinderException;
```

Clients use finder methods to locate an existing instance of an Entity EJB or a set of existing instances. Correspondingly, finder methods can return either a single instance of the EJB, as the preceding findByPrimaryKey() method does, or can return an enumeration, which can be iterated over by the client to obtain the set of instances.

The findByPrimaryKey() method is special. Every Home interface for an Entity Bean must define a findByPrimaryKey() method. The argument to this method is always an instance of another class that must be specially defined for this Entity Bean: a *primary key* class. Understanding why this method and this class must be defined deserves a little explanation. Remember that an Entity Bean represents persistent data. This means that there must be a way of matching a particular EJB instance with the corresponding data in the data store. The primary key class contains an attribute or set of attributes that the container will use to perform this matching. In a relational database, these attributes correspond to the key columns of the database table(s) that the Entity Bean will be stored in.

Other finder methods can take different sets of arguments; those methods aren't required to take the primary key class as an argument. Such finder methods are often called *custom finders*. Later, you will see how VisualAge and WebSphere implement custom finder methods that take other arguments.

Key Classes

Now you are ready to examine the key class for our example:

```
package com.wsbook.casestudy.ejb;

public class DepartmentEJBKey implements java.io.Serializable {
    public int deptNumber;
    final static long serialVersionUID = 3206093459760846163L;

/**
 *Default constructor
 */
/*WARNING: THIS METHOD WILL BE REGENERATED. */
public DepartmentEJBKey() {
    super();
```

```
}
/**
 *Initialize a key from the passed values
 *@param argDeptNumber int
 */
/*WARNING: THIS METHOD WILL BE REGENERATED. */
public DepartmentEJBKey(int argDeptNumber) {
    deptNumber = argDeptNumber;
}
/**
 *equals method
 *@return boolean
 *@param o java.lang.Object
 */
/*WARNING: THIS METHOD WILL BE REGENERATED. */
public boolean equals(java.lang.Object o) {
    if (o instanceof DepartmentEJBKey) {
        DepartmentEJBKey otherKey = (DepartmentEJBKey) o;
        return (((this.deptNumber == otherKey.deptNumber)));
    }
    else
        return false;
}
/**
 *hashCode method
 *@return int
 */
/*WARNING: THIS METHOD WILL BE REGENERATED. */
public int hashCode() {
    return ((new java.lang.Integer(deptNumber).hashCode()));
}
}
```

The only requirement the EJB specification places on a key class is that
it must be serializable. However, the container WebSphere and VisualAge
uses puts a few more restrictions on the key class. The class must implement
the methods equals() and hashCode() so that instances of the class can be
compared.

Finder Helpers

The last new type that must be introduced is a FinderHelper interface.[1] The Web-
Sphere EJB container requires that every CMP Entity Bean also defines a special

---

1. Note that FinderHelpers are not part of the EJB specification but are a WebSphere-specific implementation detail.

interface named <ejbname>FinderHelper. The container uses this interface to build the SQL statements that implement the custom finders described earlier. Here, with no custom finder methods, an empty interface declaration will do:

```
public interface DepartmentEJBBeanFinderHelper {
}
```

Bean Implementation Classes

In order to understand the code that follows for the DepartmentEJBBean implementation class of the DepartmentEJB, you will need to review a few concepts that are true about all EJBs.

- All EJBs must implement ejbActivate() and ejbPassivate(), which are hooks for special behavior that needs to happen when a Bean is swapped to or retrieved from secondary storage.
- All EJBs must implement the ejbRemove() hook method, which is called before the EJB is destroyed, so that you can execute any necessary cleanup code.
- All EJBs must implement a set of ejbCreate() methods that correspond to the create() methods on the Home interface of the EJB. For each create() method defined in the Home interface, a corresponding ejbCreate() method will match it in number, type, and order of parameters.

A few life-cycle methods that you haven't seen before are specific to EntityEJBs.

- The methods getEntityContext(), setEntityContext(EntityContext e), and unsetEntityContext() handle the management of the EntityContext. This object provides access to some of the underlying EJB framework features, such as the transaction framework and the EJBObject, which manages much of the transaction, threading, and distribution scut-work for your Bean implementation. The previous stateless Session Bean had a corresponding setSessionContext() method, but the EntityContext is much more often used.
- The methods ejbLoad() and ejbStore() are hooks that will be called before the data in your EJB is written to a persistent store by the container and after new data has been read in, respectively. These methods are useful if you need to do any conversion from data types that cannot be stored in a relational database to those that can.
- The method ejbPostCreate(), which is a hook called after any ejbCreate() method is called. You can use this method to do any additional generic

setup that must be done before a Bean instance is ready for use. The EJB object itself—for example, the object that controls transaction and thread safety—is not available until the ejbPostCreate() method, so you do not want to invoke Remote business methods as part of EJB creation until that point.

The final methods needed to complete the EJB are those that implement the Remote interface. Now you are ready to examine the implementation of the class as a whole. Afterward, we will revisit some of the methods to point out some salient features of the implementation.

Listing 17.1 Implementation of the CMP Entity Bean class.

```
package com.wsbook.casestudy.ejb;

import java.rmi.RemoteException;
import java.security.Identity;
import java.util.Properties;
import javax.ejb.*;
/**
 *This is an Entity Bean class with CMP fields
 */
public class DepartmentEJBBean implements EntityBean {
    public int deptNumber;
    public java.lang.String name;
    private javax.ejb.EntityContext entityContext = null;
    final static long serialVersionUID = 3206093459760846163L;
/**
 *ejbActivate method comment
 *@exception java.rmi.RemoteException The exception description.
 */
public void ejbActivate() throws java.rmi.RemoteException {}
/**
 *ejbCreate method for a CMP entity bean
 *@param argDeptNumber int
 *@exception javax.ejb.CreateException The exception description.
 *@exception java.rmi.RemoteException The exception description.
 */
public void ejbCreate(int argDeptNumber) throws javax.ejb.CreateException,
java.rmi.RemoteException {
    // All CMP fields should be initialized here.
    deptNumber = argDeptNumber;
    name = null;
}
/**
 *ejbCreate method for a CMP entity bean
 *@param argDeptNumber int
 *@param argName String
 *@exception javax.ejb.CreateException The exception description.
 *@exception java.rmi.RemoteException The exception description.
 */
```

```java
public void ejbCreate(int argDeptNumber, String argName) throws javax.ejb.
CreateException, java.rmi.RemoteException {
    // All CMP fields should be initialized here.
    deptNumber = argDeptNumber;
    name = argName;
}
/**
 *ejbLoad method comment
 *@exception java.rmi.RemoteException The exception description.
 */
public void ejbLoad() throws java.rmi.RemoteException {}
/**
 *ejbPassivate method comment
 *@exception java.rmi.RemoteException The exception description.
 */
public void ejbPassivate() throws java.rmi.RemoteException {}
/**
 *ejbPostCreate method for a CMP entity bean
 *@param argDeptNumber int
 *@exception java.rmi.RemoteException The exception description.
 */
public void ejbPostCreate(int argDeptNumber) throws java.rmi.RemoteException {}
/**
 *ejbPostCreate method for a CMP entity bean
 *@param argDeptNumber int
 *@param argName String
 *@exception java.rmi.RemoteException The exception description.
 */
public void ejbPostCreate(int argDeptNumber, String argName) throws
java.rmi.RemoteException {}

/**
 *ejbRemove method comment
 *@exception java.rmi.RemoteException The exception description.
 *@exception javax.ejb.RemoveException The exception description.
 */
public void ejbRemove() throws java.rmi.RemoteException, javax.ejb.Remove
Exception {}
/**
 *ejbStore method comment
 *@exception java.rmi.RemoteException The exception description.
 */
public void ejbStore() throws java.rmi.RemoteException {}
/**
 *getEntityContext method comment
 *@return javax.ejb.EntityContext
 */
public javax.ejb.EntityContext getEntityContext() {
    return entityContext;
}
/**
 *Getter method for name
 *@return java.lang.String
```

```
  */
 public java.lang.String getName() {
    return name;
 }
 /**
  *setEntityContext method comment
  *@param ctx javax.ejb.EntityContext
  *@exception java.rmi.RemoteException The exception description.
  */
 public void setEntityContext(javax.ejb.EntityContext ctx) throws java.rmi.
 RemoteException {
    entityContext = ctx;
 }
 /**
  *Setter method for name
  *@param newValue java.lang.String
  */
 public void setName(java.lang.String newValue) {
     this.name = newValue;
 }
 /**
  *unsetEntityContext method comment
  *@exception java.rmi.RemoteException The exception description.
  */
 public void unsetEntityContext() throws java.rmi.RemoteException {
    entityContext = null;
 }
 }
```

Now that you've seen the class as a whole, you can take a closer look at some of its individual features. First, many of the methods in the class have an *empty* implementation: They don't do anything. This is true of ejbPost Create(), ejbActivate(), ejbPassivate(), ejbRemove(), ejbLoad(), and ejbStore(). The reason is that this class is simple enough that hooks to perform special processing are not needed. In general, most of the life-cycle methods in your EJB implementation classes will be empty. The method hooks must be implemented because they are defined as abstract in the superclass of your Bean class, but they don't have to do anything unless you require them to. Although this may seem like a waste of programming effort, you always want to have the option to implement these methods to deal with unusual circumstances when the time comes. In the meantime, you have two good options for implementing all these empty method bodies.

- VisualAge for Java will automatically generate the empty method bodies when you create an Entity EJB in the EJB Development Environment. This way, you don't have to worry about doing the typing yourself.

- If you aren't using VisualAge for Java to develop EJBs for WebSphere, you can take advantage of an idiom, defined in [Monson-Haefel], called BeanAdapters. The BeanAdapter class extends javax.ejb.EntityBean or javax.ejb.SessionBean that provides default do-nothing implementations of the EJB life-cycle methods. Your classes will subclass this class and thus inherit the method implementations. This way, you will need to override a life-cycle method only when you need the additional implementation details.

A few life-cycle methods must not have an empty implementation. In particular, the methods managing the EntityContext must set or return an instance variable of the type EntityContext. The container uses this instance in managing the life cycle of the Bean, so it is important that you remember to implement these methods accordingly. The implementations shown here give you all the information you need to implement these methods in your own Beans. Again, if you are using VisualAge for Java to write your Beans, these methods implementations are automatically generated for you.

This leaves only two sets of methods to examine: the ejbCreate() methods and the methods that implement the Remote interface. To understand the implementation of these methods, first take a look back at this fragment of the definition of the class:

```
public class DepartmentEJBBean implements EntityBean {
    public int deptNumber;
    public java.lang.String name;
    private javax.ejb.EntityContext entityContext = null;
...
}
```

This example declares two public instance variables: deptNumber, which is the key field of the class, and name. All instance variables that are going to be managed by the container—those whose values are to be persistent—must be declared *public*. Most of the remaining method implementations you need to examine will manage the state of these two public variables. For instance, consider the following ejbCreate() method:

```
public void ejbCreate(int argDeptNumber, String argName) throws javax.ejb.
CreateException, java.rmi.RemoteException {
    // All CMP fields should be initialized here.
    deptNumber = argDeptNumber;
    name = argName;
}
```

This method shows how you initialize the values of the EJB properties from the arguments of a create() method. Different create() methods provide different ways of initializing the variables. For instance, often you will have a create() method that does not take in arguments corresponding to all the properties of a Bean, and you will instead set some of them to a default, or calculated value, as shown in the other create() method:

```
public void ejbCreate(int argDeptNumber) throws javax.ejb.CreateException,
java.rmi.RemoteException {
    // All CMP fields should be initialized here.
    deptNumber = argDeptNumber;
    name = null;
}
```

This example has nothing more that we need to examine from a code perspective. The variable Setters and Getters for the properties are simple and work exactly as they would in any Java class. Instead, now is the time to examine how to create and test Entity EJBs in VisualAge for Java and how to deploy them in WebSphere.

Summary and Preview

In this chapter, you have learned about some of the differences between CMP and BMP Entity EJBs. You have also learned a little about the structure of CMP Beans in WebSphere and VisualAge for Java. Finally, you've walked through a code example showing the classes that a Bean provider must write to implement a CMP EJB. In the next chapter, we turn our attention to EJB transactions.

CHAPTER 18

EJB Transactions

One of the most difficult parts of the EJB specification for people to grasp is how to use EJB transactions. Relatively few Java programmers have ever become concerned about the details of database persistence and thus transactions. Even fewer programmers have ever dealt with a TP monitor and understand the background from which the transaction aspect of the EJB specification derived. In this chapter, we introduce some of the parts of the EJB specification that deal with transactions and show you how they apply to almost every type of program that may be written with EJBs. In later chapters, we will examine some example programs that use the various types of EJB transactions.

Transaction Defined

Unless you come from a database background, you may not be familiar with the concept of transactions. Simply put, a *transaction* is *a sequence of processing steps—called a unit of work—that is treated as a unified whole to satisfy a request.* The standard definition of a transaction uses the acronym ACID to characterize a unit of work, which should be

- Atomic: If this unit of work is interrupted by failure, all effects are undone. (This is called *rolling back* a transaction.)
- Consistent: The effects of a transaction preserve the integrity of modified resources. This means that the affected objects, or database rows, move from one consistent state to another.
- Isolated: What happens within the scope of one transaction should not affect any objects involved in any other transaction or be visible until completion of the transaction. Any intermediate states are transparent, and the unit of work therefore appears to execute serially.

- Durable: The effects of a completed transaction are permanent and are never lost.

A more rigorous definition of a transaction is found in [Elmasri].

So, what does this mean for EJBs? In simple terms, an EJB transaction is a group of methods during the execution of which the state of EJBs in memory and the state of the data in a transactional data source follow the ACID rules. As we will see, this is crucial when dealing with Entity EJBs, as our programs depend on both the state of the EJBs and the database being correct.

Transactions and Two-Phase Commit

One of the key implementation features of database systems and transaction processing systems, such as WebSphere, is a special feature called *two-phase commit* (2PC). This feature allows multiple databases to be updated in a single transaction or to be returned to their pretransaction states if an error occurs. To understand how 2PC works, we need to provide a few more definitions.

- *Transactional object:* An object whose behavior is affected by being invoked within the scope of a transaction. Transactional objects update resource managers by changing attributes managed by them.
- *Resource manager:* An object that manages a single data source, such as a relational database, or an IBM MQ Series connection, and that participates in a managed transaction.
- *Transaction manager:* An object that takes care of managing the details of transactions behind the scenes, for example, determining when to instruct individual resource managers to commit their transactions to permanent storage or when to roll back to the previous state.

In IBM WebSphere, EJBs are transactional objects. Database drivers act as resource managers, while part of the WebSphere infrastructure acts as a transaction manager.

Some of the interactions between these object types are illustrated in Figure 18.1.

These object types are tied together through the 2PC protocol, which involves two sets of messages from the transaction manager to the resource managers. Each resource manager initially temporarily stores database changes. The transaction manager then issues a precommit, or "Are-you-ready?" message to each of the resource managers. If each of the resource managers responds back with an acknowledgment saying that it can commit, the transaction manager sends the final "commit" message to the resource managers.

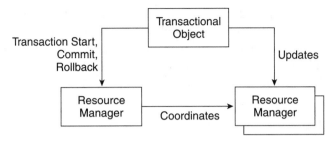

Figure 18.1 Transaction Interactions

The promise of 2PC is one of the main drivers behind the adoption of EJBs and the development of EJB servers, such as WebSphere. In fact, the promise is still somewhat unattained. WebSphere Advanced Edition version 3.5 supports 2PC only for Oracle, DB2, and Sybase. The reason is partly a lack of Java database drivers that support the X/Open XA standard, which is the standard way of issuing the 2PC protocol messages, and partly owing to complexities in making XA work in distributed systems. This situation will improve in the near future, as this is one of the key features targeted by the WebSphere development team for intensive future development and testing. In addition, WebSphere also provides 2PC for MQ Series messaging.[1]

EJBs and Transactions

How does this set of definitions relate to EJBs? An EJB is a transactional object. A single transaction can involve multiple objects and multiple operations. So, EJBs operate within the scope of a transaction context. A transaction context represents a transaction scope shared by a set of participating transactional objects. A transactional object can be associated with only one transaction context at any time. Transaction contexts are usually automatically propagated to transactional objects as they are used, so they follow the call tree: If one EJB calls a method on another, the transaction context is passed along to the receiver EJB. Transaction contexts are used to synchronize affected transaction objects at transaction commit or rollback.

The usual scenario works like this: A client, either another EJB or an EJB client, begins a transaction, and a new transaction context is associated with the client thread. Then, the client calls operations on objects. These transactional objects are implicitly associated with the client's transaction by sharing the same transaction context.

---

1. This support was added in WebSphereAE, ptf 3.

When it is finished, the client issues a commit to the transaction manager. The transactional objects associated with context are now told to commit; thus, both the resource managers will commit, and special "hook" methods may be called in the transactional objects themselves so that they can participate in the commit.

Starting a Transaction

The EJB specification defines three ways of starting a transaction.

- *Client demarcation:* In this case, the programmer of a client uses explicit programmatic transaction management. The methods of the interface javax.jts.UserTransaction are used to start, commit, or roll back the transaction.
- *Container demarcation:* In this case, the programmer does not define when the transaction starts, commits, or rolls back; instead, this is defined by the EJB container. The behavior of this object in a transaction is based on information in the *transaction attribute* deployment descriptor.
- *Bean demarcation:* Here a Session EJB with the transaction attribute set to TX_BEAN_MANAGED can explicitly control a transaction by using the methods of javax.jts.UserTransaction.

By far the preferred way of managing a transaction—for example, determining when it starts and how it terminates—is through container demarcation, or declarative transaction management. Declarations in the deployment descriptor tell the container when to start and commit the transaction. To understand how this works, let's examine what values the transaction attribute can take on. Transaction attributes can be set on either the Bean or the method level. (Setting them at the method level overrides Bean-level settings, if any.) The values of the transaction attribute are

- TX_BEAN_MANAGED: The EJB will programmatically start and stop the transaction as described previously. In WebSphere, only Session Beans may be marked as being TX_BEAN_MANAGED, which follows the EJB 1.1 specification.
- TX_MANDATORY: The client of this EJB must create a transaction—either programmatically or declaratively through container demarcation— before invocation of a method. If a transaction context is not present, a TransactionRequiredException is thrown. The execution of the EJB method will be associated with the client transaction (for example, this object will participate in the transaction context associated with the calling thread).

- TX_NOT_SUPPORTED: Transactions are not supported by this EJB or method. If a client provides a transaction, it is ignored, and methods will always execute without participating in the transaction context. However, the transaction will be propagated to other objects called in this thread.
- TX_REQUIRED:The EJB requires that methods be executed within a transaction. If a client transaction is provided, it is used, and the execution of the method is associated with it. If no transaction context exists, a new transaction is created for this thread at the start of the method, and it commits when the method has completed.
- TX_REQUIRES_NEW: The EJB requires that a method be executed in a *new* transaction. If a client transaction is provided, it is suspended for the method execution.[1] A new transaction is always created at the start of the method, and it commits when the method has completed.
- TX_SUPPORTS : The EJB supports execution of a method in a transaction but does not require it. If this thread is associated with a transaction context, method execution will be associated with that transaction. If this thread is not associated with a transaction context, the method executes without a transaction.

Table 18.1, derived from [EJB], shows how transactions are propagated or passed by Beans with different settings of this attribute. Note that on the

---

1. The EJB specification [EJB] describes support only for "flat" transactions and does not include support for "nested" transactions. Only one transaction may execute within an object at a time.

Table 18.1 Transaction Attribute Settings

Transaction attribute	Client transaction	Transaction associated with Bean method
TX_NOT_SUPPORTED	None	None
	T1	None
TX_REQUIRED	None	T2
	T1	T1
TX_SUPPORTS	None	None
	T1	T1
TX_REQUIRES_NEW	None	T2
	T1	T2
TX_MANDATORY	None	Error
	T1	T1

TX_REQUIRED line, a transaction, T2, is created because the client does not have an existing transaction and the transaction attribute is TX_REQUIRED. Also, note that in TX_MANDATORY, an error is produced because the client does not have an existing transaction when calling the method. Careful use of the transaction attributes can help to enforce application-defined transactional integrity within a set of EJBs.

How do you start a transaction programmatically either in an EJB client or in a Bean, using the TX_BEAN_MANAGED transaction attribute? Let's look at the following methods defined in the interface javax.jts.UserTransaction.[2]

- begin(): Creates a new transaction and associates it with the current thread.
- commit(): Completes the transaction associated with the current thread. When this method completes, the thread is no longer associated with a transaction.
- rollback(): Rolls back the transaction associated with the current thread. When this method completes, the thread is no longer associated with a transaction.
- setRollbackOnly(): Modifies the transaction associated with the current thread such that the only possible outcome of the transaction is to roll back the transaction.

How does a client obtain an object that implements this interface? The EJB specification indicates that clients should be able to obtain this by looking it up through JNDI.[3] The following code fragment indicates this:

```
UserTransaction tranContext = (UserTransaction) initContext.lookup("jta/
usertransaction");
tranContext.begin();
// get and manipulate EJBs
tranContext.commit();
```

Participating in a Transaction

You've seen how transactions are started and rolled back, but what do you have to do to your EJB code to make this work? The answer depends on the type of EJB you are writing. For Session EJBs, the answer is usually nothing. Session EJBs are functional objects that direct the action of Entity EJBs or other data sources, such as JDBC. In most cases, a Session EJB will simply

---

2. For a more complete listing of the messages in this interface, refer to the JTS (Java Transaction Service) specification [JTS].

3. Session EJBs using the TX_BEAN_MANAGED attribute may also find this transaction by using the method EJBContext.getCurrentTransaction().

originate or propagate a transaction through declarative transaction management.[4] Likewise, for container-managed Entity Beans, you do not have to explicitly write anything to participate in a transaction. In this case, the generated persistence code handles persisting changed data to a database when a transaction commits. In BMP Entity Beans, however, you do have to write code within the "hook" methods ejbLoad() and ejbStore() to load data from a database or to store updated data to a database, respectively, in response to a transaction commit or rollback.[5] (We cover this topic in more detail in Chapter 21, on BMP.)

A Session Bean can participate in a transaction that is sometimes useful in one more way. Stateful Session Beans may store intermediate state in databases and must therefore be synchronized with an EJB transaction. These Beans can be made aware of transaction synchronization by implementing the interface javax.ejb.SessionSynchronization. This interface provides hook methods to a stateful Session EJB that allows it to read or write its internal fields to or from external database storage. Likewise, the Session Bean could also force a rollback, using sessionContext.setRollBack-Only(), if necessary. You should become familiar with the three methods in this interface:

- afterBegin(): Receipt of this method notifies a Session Bean instance that a new transaction has started. Subsequent business methods on this instance will be invoked within the context of the transaction.
- beforeCompletion(boolean): This method notifies the Session Bean instance that a transaction is about to be committed. The value of the Boolean tells the instance whether the transaction has been committed or rolled back.
- afterCompletion(boolean): This method notifies the Session Bean instance that a transaction commit protocol has completed. The value of the Boolean tells the instance whether the transaction has been committed or rolled back.

Why would you need to implement this interface? Simply put, some data sources are not able to participate in an EJB transaction because they cannot roll back. If you needed to, say, use FTP in an EJB transaction, you could do so in the afterCompletion() method, being assured that the rest of the data in this transaction has been committed.

---

4. An exception to this would be through the use of the SessionSynchronization interface for stateful Session Beans, as described later.
5. These methods are also defined in CMP Beans, but you usually do not do anything in them. (The method implementations contain no code.)

Setting Transaction Attributes

To wrap up all this information into some recommendations for setting transaction attributes on our EJBs, let's consider some architectural considerations. Our first rule of thumb should be: Don't allow nonEJB clients to directly access Entity EJBs. Entity EJBs should not be directly accessed from nonEJB client code, for two reasons. First, if a client directly accesses an Entity EJB, either each individual method call to get or set a variable will be a unique EJB and database transaction. This also means that at least one SQL SELECT or UPDATE statement will be executed for each method call.

Second, with each call being an individual transaction, it is possible to leave a database half-updated if one variable is updated while another update fails. In the common example of a bank account transfer, this means that one account could be debited for an amount while the corresponding account would not be credited for the same amount, making money appear or disappear.

The solution to this problem is to perform all reads and updates from an Entity EJB as part of an overarching transaction started by a Session EJB. This common practice is discussed in depth in [Monson-Haefel] and [Brown 99].

You can now consider transactions in the context of at least two types of objects: (1) controlling Session Beans and (2) Entity Beans and other Session Beans that are closer to the data. In this case, transactions that are read-only should use TX_REQUIRED, which can be set on the Session Bean or the Entity Bean or both. If it is on the Entity Bean and not the Session Bean, you must understand that each method call from a Session Bean to an Entity Bean or Entity Bean Home will run as a separate transaction. This can become costly, as we discussed previously. Therefore, for your Entity Beans, you might want to consider TX_MANDATORY.

Many read/write transactions can also rely on this same combination of TX_REQUIRED and TX_MANDATORY. However, complex transactions that are read/write might consider not relying on TX_REQUIRED semantics, because a commit might fail, but not all failures are equally bad. If a commit fails, the exception will bubble up and leave the EJB client with the responsibility of making a decision about what to do next. In most cases, this decision requires code that should be done inside of a Session Bean, because the error *might* be at least partially recoverable. Therefore, in particularly complex updates, you should consider using a TX_BEAN_MANAGED Session Bean with TX_REQUIRED or TX_MANDATORY Entity Beans. Here, the Session Bean can put in logic to do retries or to return information that can be given back to the client for reposting back to the end client.

Transactions and Concurrency

The next issue to address is how to deal with concurrency. We must balance the need to keep transactions isolated from one another with the need for performance when the strictest isolation policy—one that locks out all access to EJBs participating in a transaction—might be too restrictive. The EJB specification tries to define ways of balancing speed versus consistency. Unfortunately, the specification does not fully define the interaction between the EJB server (transaction manager) and the database driver (resource managers), leaving a lot of room for vendor interpretation.

EJB Caching

One of the easiest ways to gain more performance in an application is to cache, or store, data in memory rather than always going to a back-end store, such as a database, for the data. Unfortunately, caching schemes are always susceptible to problems with stale data, as when the data in the back-end store is changed, but the data in the cache remains the same. Determining how to balance these two issues—speed versus accuracy—in setting up your Entity EJBs is a key system design decision.

The EJB specification defines three kinds of Entity EJB caching that can occur: in Option A, EJB state is read once and then held in the object space of the application server between transactions. In Option C, state is reread into each object at the beginning of each transaction. Option B is similar to Option A, but is not implemented in WebSphere, so it is not relevant to our discussion. To choose an option for a particular EJB class, change the *Database Access* setting in WebSphere. This setting is available in the WebSphere administrator's console on the *General* tab of the *EJB* page. Each Entity EJB deployed into WebSphere can be set individually. The default option is *Shared*. If you change the state of the database access setting to *Exclusive*, the first option is used.

If you use cached Entity Beans (Option A), you are not guaranteed the correctness of Bean data, because of updates made by other processes. Therefore, you want to cache Entity Beans only if you know that the container has exclusive access to the database used by the Entity Bean—and therefore has the only copy of a Bean's persistent state—or that the Bean's data is accessed read-only at all times. By the way, "other applications" includes other WebSphere Application Servers in a cluster. The first option should be used only when you are certain that only one clone can access a particular table.

Introduction to Isolation Levels

Regardless of the caching policy you select, the Websphere EJB server does not provide transaction isolation and concurrency management on its own but instead provides directives, called *isolation levels,* that are "hints" to the database as to what policies should be used. The database is responsible for providing these services to your EJBs and other applications. The isolation levels defined for an EJB are as follows:

- TRANSACTION_READ_UNCOMMITTED: The transaction can read uncommitted data, that is, data changed by a different transaction still in progress.
- TRANSACTION_READ_COMMITTED: The transaction is not able to read uncommitted data from other transactions. However, *nonrepeatable reads*—for example, the first read in a transaction gets one result, whereas the second gets a different result, owing to the data's being updated by another transaction or program—can occur. Likewise, *phantom records* can occur; records can be inserted while the transaction is in progress of which this transaction may be unaware.
- TRANSACTION_REPEATABLE_READ[6]: The transaction is guaranteed to always read back the same data on each successive read. Phantom records can still occur.
- TRANSACTION_SERIALIZABLE: All transactions are serialized, or fully isolated from one another. All rows touched during the transaction are locked for the duration of the transaction.

The isolation levels determine what concurrency mechanism will be used. For instance, consider what happens when you use TRANSACTION_ SERIALIZABLE. If you open a transaction and do a select (find) on an EJB, all the rows found by that find (select) are locked, so no other applications can change the rows being used, because they are locked. Note that in any case, changes are not recorded to the database until the transaction commits, at which point, the EJB's methods write the data out with a set of UPDATE statements and then commit the transaction, releasing the lock.

As mentioned previously, the problem is that the effect the isolation levels have on your applications is determined by the locking mechanisms available in the database and how WebSphere's transaction manager uses them. Therefore, each database driver supported by WebSphere could have different external semantics with regard to locking.

---

6. This is the default setting for EJBs in WebSphere Advanced Edition, version 3.5.

WebSphere-Specific Transaction Settings

One thing to carefully note is that using TRANSACTION_SERIALIZABLE can result in a deadlock condition. If two transactions both read the same row (entity), they both acquire a read-lock on it. If one then tries to write the entity, it acquires a write-lock, which must wait to complete until all read-locks are released. If the other transaction also tries to write to the entity, deadlock will occur. Therefore, WebSphere includes the *Find for update* option. This option specifies whether the container should get an exclusive lock on the Enterprise Bean when the find-by-primary-key method is involved. If it is set to false, it will instead acquire exclusive locks on find-by-primary-key methods, and the deadlock condition will not occur. For more information on handling deadlock conditions in WebSphere and DB2, see [Ivanov].

Another way to improve the performance of your applications is to consider which methods are read-only, or do not modify data in an EJB, and which methods are not. The EJB specification does not describe any way for the container to find out whether a Bean's state has changed during a transaction. The specification implicitly assumes that all Beans used during a transaction are "dirty" and must have their state written back to the backend store at the end of a transaction. WebSphere goes beyond the EJB specification to address this issue. WebSphere defines a *read-only* method flag in the deployment descriptor of Entity Beans, allowing the EJB developer to tell the container which methods are read-only, that do not change the state of the Bean.

WebSphere will look for the setting of this flag whenever a method is invoked. If only methods having this flag set are sent to a Bean in a transaction, WebSphere will not assume that the Bean is "dirty" and will not execute a SQL UPDATE statement when the transaction is committed. By default in WebSphere, methods are not read-only, so an UPDATE statement will be issued regardless of whether the data in the Bean changed. Therefore, it is to your benefit to carefully consider which methods are read-only and to mark them accordingly.

Also, WebSphere will use the "read-only" flag in determining the locking policy in an attempt to reduce deadlocks, although this depends on the database used. For more information on this, see [Ivanov].

A final WebSphere setting that affects transaction behavior and of which you must be aware is found on the Database Driver configuration window in the WebSphere Administrator's console. The pulldown labeled, "JTA Enabled" indicates that this database driver should use the JTA protocol. If you intend to use more than one database in the application (e.g., both Oracle and DB2), be certain that this is set to "yes".

Summary and Preview

In this chapter, we have examined how WebSphere interacts with databases to manage transactions and how EJBs act as transactional objects. We have investigated what the EJB specification says about EJB transactions, and we have seen a few of the special features that WebSphere has for managing concurrency and reducing the occurrence of deadlock. In the next chapter, we look at some of the differences in building Entity Beans and Session Beans.

CHAPTER 19

Building Entity Beans in VisualAge and WebSphere

You've seen how Entity EJBs are structured and how Session EJBs are built and tested in VisualAge for Java. Rather than carry you step by tedious step through the entire process of building Entity EJBs in VisualAge, this chapter merely points out some of the differences between building simple Entity Beans and building Session Beans and introduces a few new concepts and tools along the way.

Also, although we show you examples from our case study, we won't walk through every step of the process. Instead, you can load the final edition of the VisualAge project that represents the case study and follow along by examining the code as it has already been written. At the end of this chapter, after introducing the procedures for building and testing Entity EJBs, we indicate all the Entity EJBs in the case study that were built in this way, so that you can examine them more thoroughly later.

Creating an Entity Bean in VisualAge

When you build an Entity Bean in VisualAge, the first difference you notice is that the procedure for using the *Create Enterprise Bean SmartGuide* is slightly different from that in building Session Beans. Remember, you enter this *SmartGuide* by choosing *Add>Enterprise Bean...* from the *Enterprise Beans* pop-up menu. In our case study, we will add these Enterprise Beans to a new EJB group named *TimeSheetGroup* and a new package named com. wsbook.casestudy.ejb.

Look at Figures 19.1 and 19.2. Then think about some of the differences between these examples and the examples on building Session Beans.

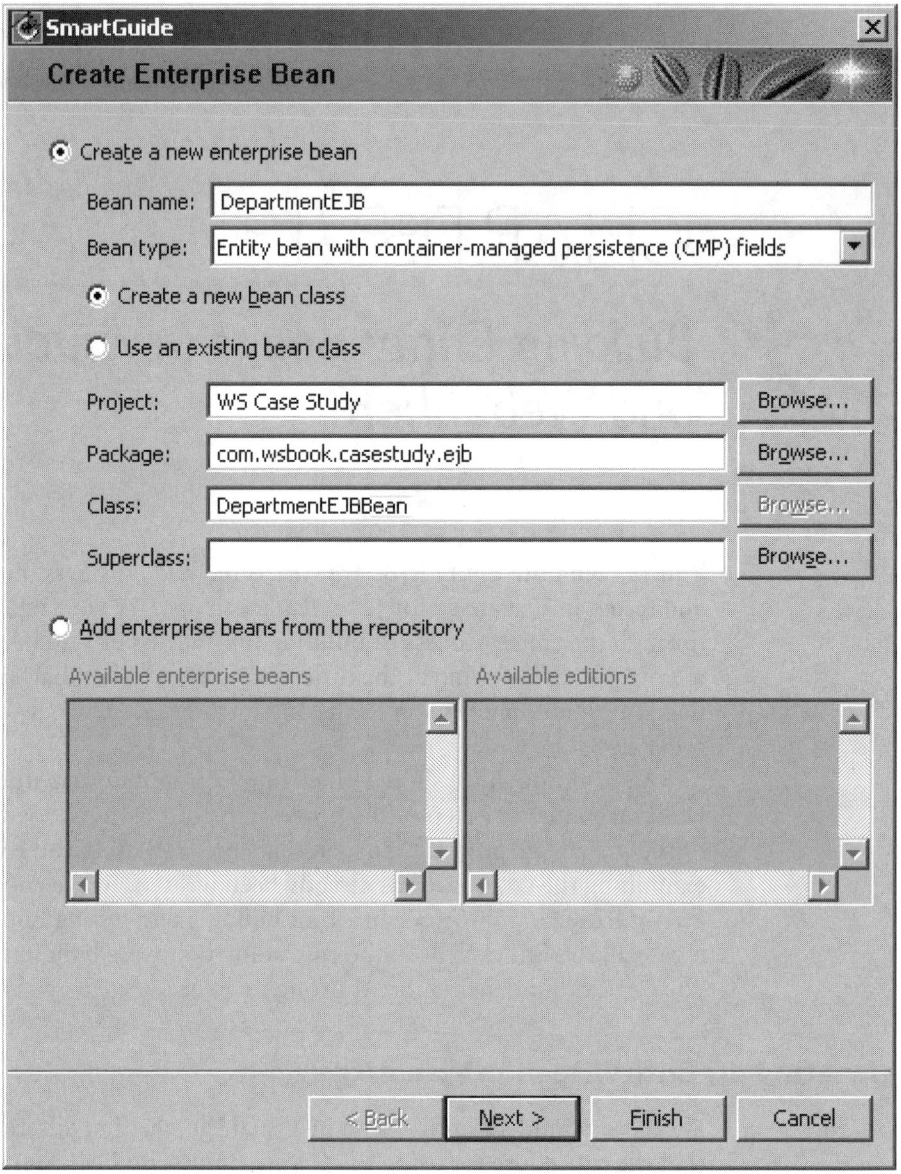

Figure 19.1   Creating a CMP Bean

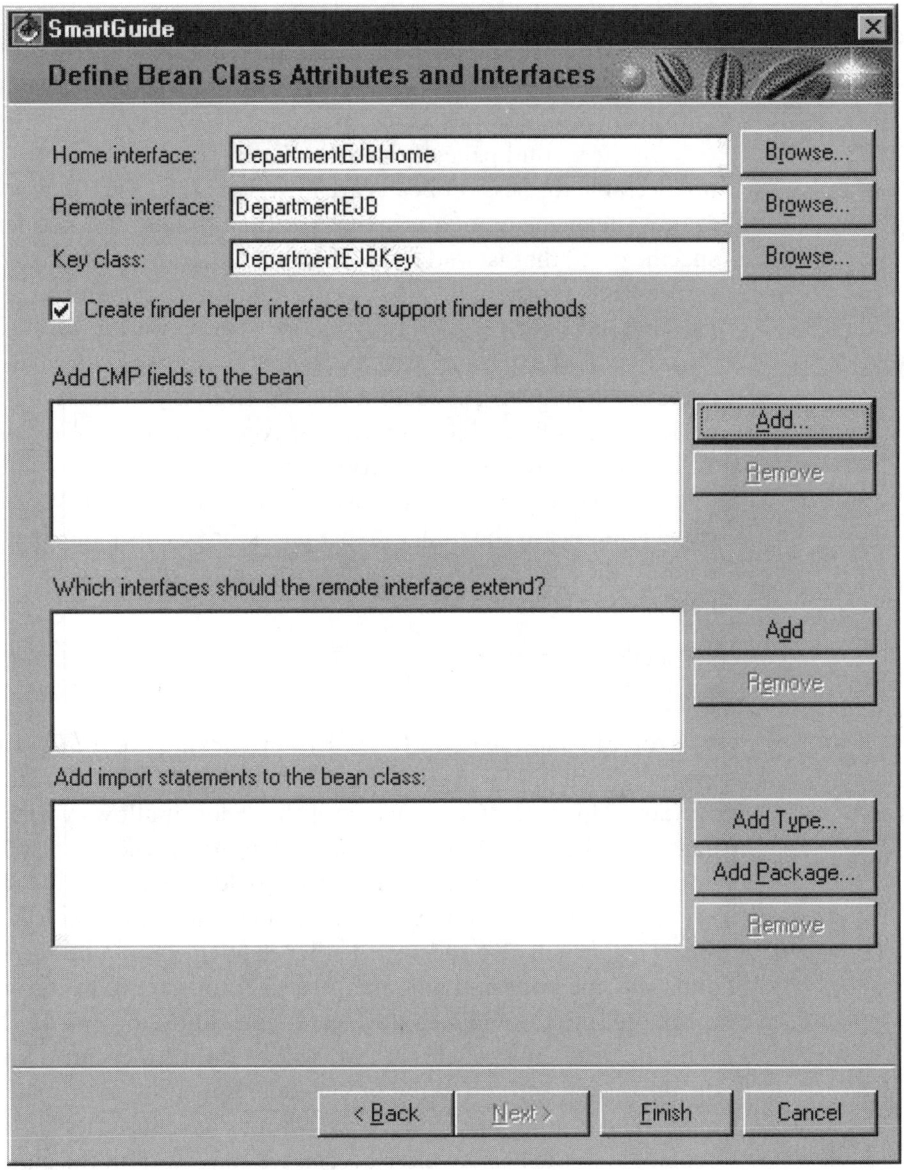

Figure 19.2 Second Page of EJB *SmartGuide*

This time, the Bean type selected is *Entity Bean with container-managed persistence (CMP) fields.* Other than that, everything else is the same on this page. Things start to look different, however, when you click the *Next>* button and move to the second page.

On the second page of the *SmartGuide,* two of the sections previously unselectable for Session Beans are now available. The first, and most important, is the inclusion of a primary-key class, a special class, defined in the EJB specification, that is used by the EJB container to distinguish one EJB instance from another and also as a mechanism to represent the key parts of an EJB that have not yet been fully loaded. The second is the check box marked *Create finder helper interface to support finder methods.* This interface is necessary to implement custom finders. Even if you don't define any custom finders, you still need this interface if you intend to deploy your Beans into WebSphere, so retain the selection.

The second panel that is now available is the *Add CMP fields to the Bean* panel underneath the finder helper check box. This panel is where you add fields to the EJB. As we saw earlier, the *DepartmentEJB* example has two fields:

```
int departmentNumber
String name
```

You can add the fields to the EJB by clicking the *Add* button next to the list box. Each time you click the *Add* button, the *SmartGuide* in Figure 19.3 appears. This *SmartGuide* accomplishes a lot. It allows you to define the name and the type of the field and to determine whether it is a key field. Each Entity EJB must define at least one key field; the key fields become part of the Key class that the container will use to identify individual EJB instances. This *SmartGuide* will also specify whether the field should be accessed by getter and setter methods and whether these methods are to be automatically added (promoted) to the Remote interface. If you choose *Key Field,* the option to generate getter and setter methods will be disabled because VAJ wants to handle the setting and retrieving of key fields specially. In this particular case, the name field is not a key field, so we want to have its accessors generated and promoted to the Remote interface, so we can select all the check boxes.

At this point, you can now click the button labeled *Create a CMP field and continue. . .* and create the field named departmentNumber. This field should be of type int and should have the *Key Field* check box marked. When you have specified this field, click *Finish.*

After adding the departmentNumber field in the *Create CMP Field SmartGuide,* you can complete the EJB. Clicking *Finish* on the original *SmartGuide*

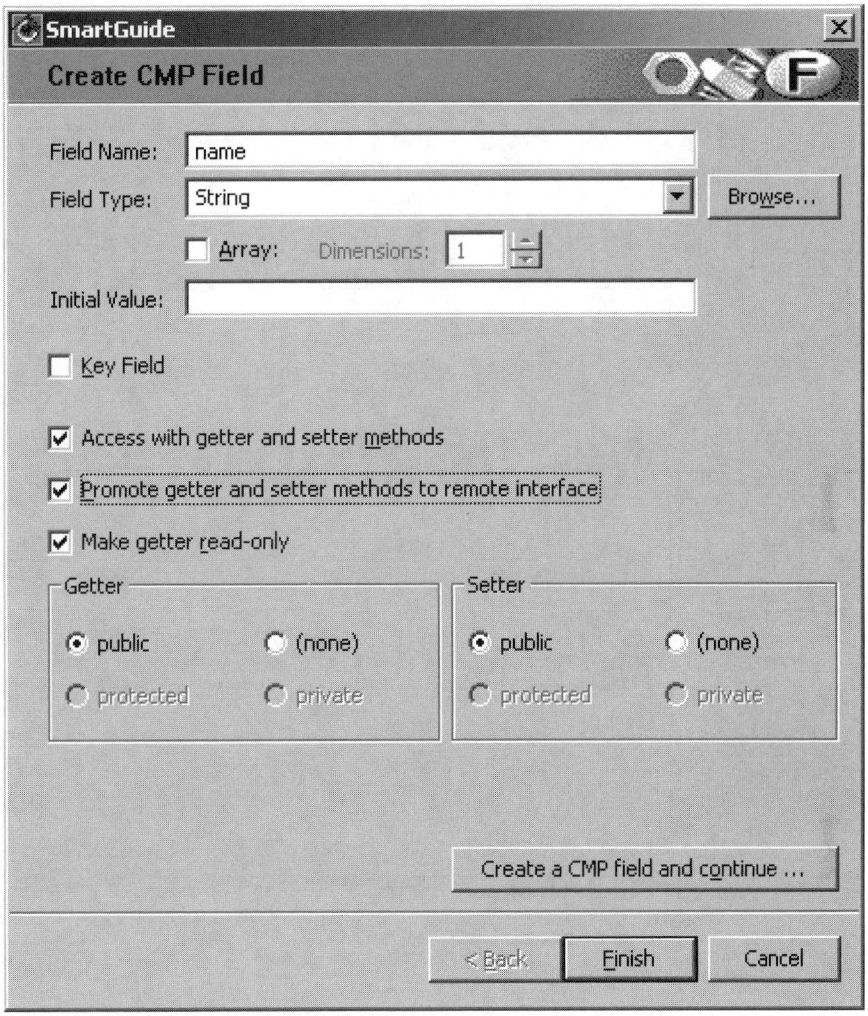

Figure 19.3 Creating CMP Fields

will begin the code-generation process and show you the progress of the generation, as shown in Figure 19.4.

Now that you've seen how the process of defining a new Entity EJB works in VisualAge, you can see how the rest of the Entity EJBs in the case study will be built. Table 19.1 shows the other EJBs that are defined for the case study, along with the fields that they contain.

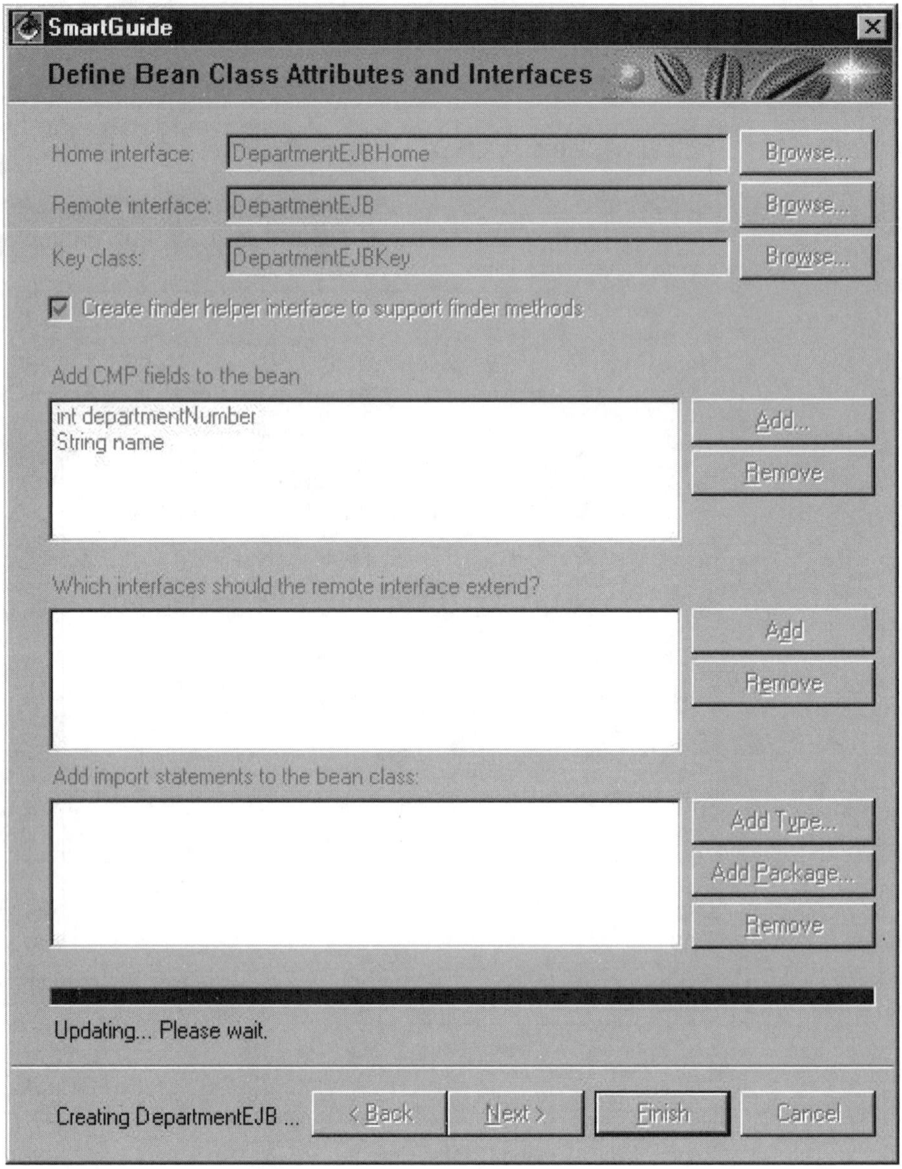

Figure 19.4 Creating the CMP Bean

Table 19.1 Case Study EJBs and Fields

EJB	Basic CMP fields
ProjectEJB	int projNumber *(key)*, String name
EmployeeEJB	int empId *(key)*, String name
TimeSheetEJB	int timeSheetId *(key)*, String state, String weekend
TimeSheetEntryEJB	int entryId *(key)*, String date, double hours

Schemas, EJBs, and Table Maps

You've discovered what the basic object model of our EJB example looks like, so you're now ready to look at how that compares with the representation of those objects in the database. First, however, you need to take a step back and review some basic relational-technology terminology.

In a relational database, data is stored in *tables* as *rows* and *columns*. A table is a single entity that represents a particular record layout. You define a table by stating the names, data types, and, optionally, sizes of the columns that make up the table. The definition of a set of database tables and the relationships among them is called a database *schema*.

We need to define how our objects, Entity EJBs, map to a set of database tables. In other words, we will be defining a mapping between our EJBs and a database schema. To do this, you need to be able to view and to manipulate both the database schema and the object model. VisualAge for Java contains a set of tools that allow you to do precisely this. In VisualAge for Java, you can define a database mapping to an EJB model in one of three ways.

- A top-down mapping automatically creates a new database schema from a set of Entity Beans by following some simple mapping rules.
- A bottom-up mapping creates a new set of Entity Beans matching a set of database tables by reversing the rules followed in a top-down mapping.
- A meet-in-the-middle mapping allows you to create a set of Entity Beans and a database schema separately and then to define the mapping between the two.

We will walk through an example of how to do a top-down mapping, the simplest of the three. Along the way, you will see how the other two types of mappings are performed, as we will point out differences in the way the browsers are used.

To begin, go to the *Enterprise Beans* pane of the EJB Development Environment and select the *TimeSheetGroup*. Open the right-mouse-button menu in the *Enterprise Beans* pane, and select *Add>Schema and Map from EJB Group*, as shown in Figure 19.5.

This simple action accomplishes a lot. A new database schema is created inside VisualAge for Java and maps to the EJBs that were created inside the *TimeSheetGroup* EJB group. Also, a set of table maps are created that map between each individual Entity Bean and its associated database table. In other words, a top-down mapping from your set of EJBs to a database schema has just been performed.

Begin by examining the new database schema that is created from the EJB group. You can view the schema by selecting *Open To>Database*

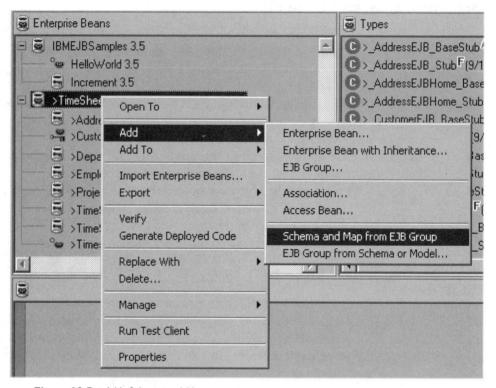

Figure 19.5   *Add>Schema and Map*

Schemas from the *Enterprise Beans* pane of the EJB *Development* tab. This will open the database *Schema Browser,* shown in Figure 19.6.

This useful browser shows the schemas that you currently have loaded into your workspace on the left-hand side and then allows you to select a table within that schema and view the columns and foreign-key relationships that are part of the table. We will return to cover foreign-key relationships in a later chapter, so for the time being, pay attention to the first three panes of this browser.

When you select a table, you can view its columns. Note that the table names match the EJB Remote interface names exactly. Likewise, the column names match the CMP attribute names of our Entity Beans exactly. In this simplest of all possible mappings, each Entity Bean corresponds to a single table, and each attribute in the Entity Bean corresponds to a column in that table. Matching names reduces the possibility of confusion as to which columns map to which attributes. This will work in almost all circumstances, although, as we will see later, in some circumstances, this mapping is too simplistic and must be tailored.

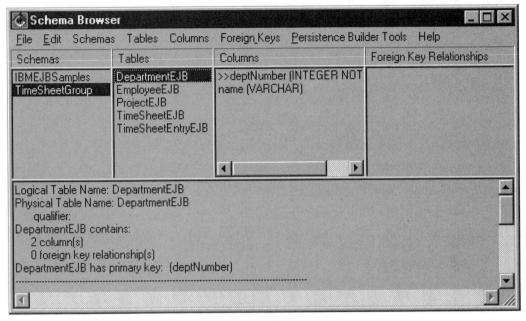

Figure 19.6   The Database *Schema Browser*

Because each attribute maps to a single table column, there must be a way of determining what type of column is created from an attribute. Table 19.2 shows the rules for creating these columns from the Java types that an Entity Bean attribute may use.

To see how this would work, examine the definition of our Entity Bean implementation class, DepartmentBean, and the corresponding CREATE statement in SQL.

```
public class DepartmentEJBBean implements EntityBean {
    public int deptNumber;
    public java.lang.String name;
}
CREATE TABLE DepartmentEJB (
    deptNumber INTEGER NOT NULL,
    name VARCHAR(30))
```

Note that the deptNumber column has been declared as NOT NULL in the CREATE statement in SQL. The reason is that the deptNumber attribute was declared as the key value in the *DepartmentEJB*. This means that the corresponding column will be the key in the database table, and by definition, keys cannot be null in a relational database.

This mapping between columns and attributes can be viewed in another browser, the database *Map Browser* (Figure 19.7). To open this browser,

Table 19.2   Data Type Mappings for WebSphere and VAJ

Java data type	SQL data type
String	VARCHAR
Short/short	SMALLINT
Integer/int	INTEGER
Float/float	FLOAT
Double/double	DOUBLE
Byte/byte	SMALLINT
Long/long	VARCHAR(22)
Character/char	CHAR(1)
Boolean/boolean	SMALLINT
java.math.BigDecimal	NUMERIC
java.sql.Date	DATE
java.sql.Time	TIME
java.sql.Timestamp	TIMESTAMP
Other (serializable)	BLOB

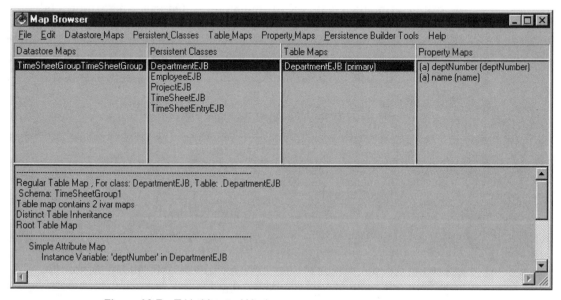

Figure 19.7   Table Mapping Window

return to the *EJB Development Environment* tab and select *Open To>Schema Maps* from the *Enterprise Beans* pane.

The entire mapping between a database schema and a corresponding EJB group is called an EJB *group map:* The list of available maps appears in the *Datastore Maps* pane. When you select a map in this pane, you see in the *Persistent Classes* pane the list of CMP Entity Beans that the group contains. Each Entity EJB corresponds to at least one table map, which contains a set of property maps that map each column in a database table to an attribute in the EJB. The property maps are shown in the far right-hand pane, which lists the map type (*a* stands for attribute), the column name, and the attribute name.

You edit property maps by selecting *Edit>Property Maps...* from the *Table Maps* pane, as shown in Figure 19.8. Selecting this menu item will bring up the *Property Map Editor,* which is shown in Figure 19.9. This pane has two types of maps that you can select. The first is a "simple" map: The attribute on the left-hand side will be mapped to the column on the right-hand side, using the mapping rules set forward in the table earlier.

The second map type is a "complex" map type. Mapping tools can help bridge the gap between the EJB object model and an existing database schema in the area of *dependent objects,* the case in which an Entity Bean has a property whose type is a Java type other than the primitive types that are easily mapped to the common database types. As we have seen, complex EJB properties that are serializable can, by default, be serialized and mapped to an appropriate binary column. Although this does allow for properties of arbitrary Java types, it is not an optimal solution. Because the column is binary, it is impossible to query this column by using standard SQL query tools. Also, the performance of serializing and deserializing an object into a binary large object (BLOB) can be poor.

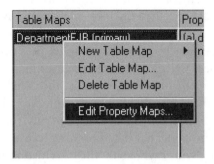

Figure 19.8   Selecting *Edit Property Maps...*

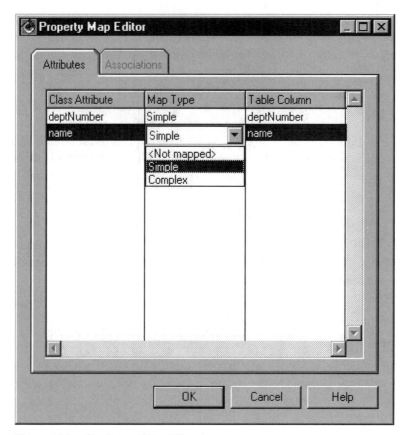

Figure 19.9   The *Property Map Editor*

In order to improve the mapping options for these types, VisualAge for Java introduces the concept of composers and converters. These helper classes provide an open framework for converting between object types and database types. *Converters* are specified on a schema and apply a simple conversion to a column whenever they are used. A *composer* is specified when mapping an EJB field and may decompose the complex Java object into one or more fields of simple types. With a composer, the user maps the individual simple fields to columns in the database. At runtime, the composer class is used to transform between the simple fields and the complex object.

The documentation for both the EJB Development Environment and the Persistence Builder features gives further detail on how to use converters and composers and how to create your own, using the provided framework. For our example, we will use the default simple mapping, which will work in almost all cases.

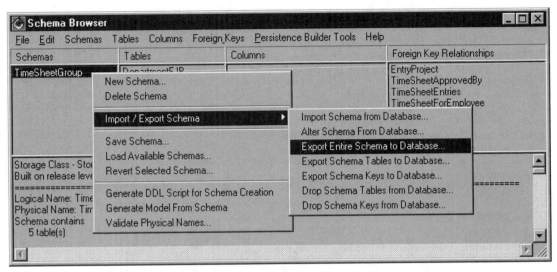

Figure 19.10   Exporting Schemas

Exporting a Schema to a Database

Up to this point, we have been working entirely within VisualAge for Java and that has been effective. But now, to test our EJBs, we need to begin working with an external database as well. WebSphere Advanced Edition includes a copy of DB2 Universal, which we will use as the database for our examples. The examples further include the presupposition that you have created a database named WASBOOK to contain the tables for this example.[1]

The first step in this process is to export the database schema from VisualAge, where it has been held in an internal representation, into the database, in the form of the appropriate CREATE statements. You perform this step by selecting *Import/Export Schema>Export Entire Schema to Database...* from the *Schemas* pane of the *Schema Browser,* as shown in Figure 19.10.

Once you have selected this menu option, you will need to provide some connection information to tell VisualAge where to export the schema. The dialog in Figure 19.11 allows you to provide the information needed to

---

1. You can do this by running the "CreateWASBOOKDB.bat" script file from the CD or by typing "db2 CREATE DATABASE WASBOOK" from a DB2 Command Window.

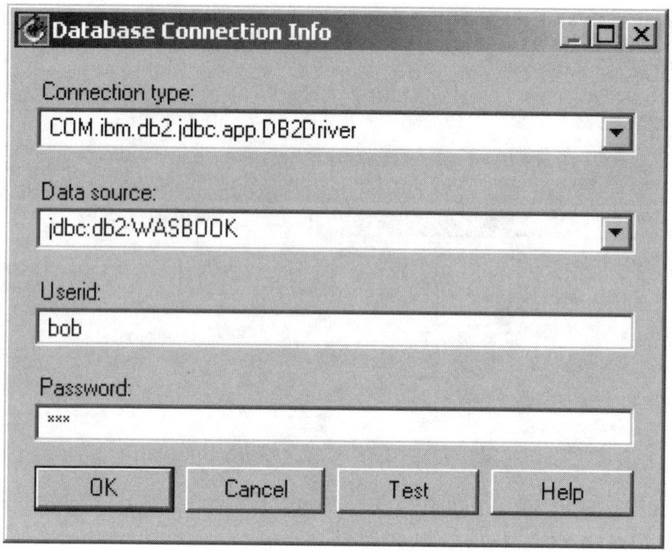

Figure 19.11   *Database Connection* Setup

connect to the database. After entering the information and clicking *OK,* you can watch the progress of the update in the VisualAge console. If any fatal SQL errors occur during this process, a warning dialog will appear. The most common mistake is to provide an incorrect data source URL or to supply an incorrect user ID and password, so be sure to double-check those entries before proceeding.

Now that you've finished exporting the new database schema to the database, the next step is to generate the deployed code for your new Beans. The procedure to generate deployed code is the same for both Entity Beans and Session Beans: Just choose *Generate>Deployed Code* from the *Enterprise Beans* pop-up menu. However, an additional class is generated for Entity Beans. This class, named EJSJDBCPersister<beanname>Bean, handles the persistence of information into the database. If you select one of these generated persister classes for your Beans, you will see that the persister contains the SQL statements that write data to the database and read data from the database. Reading the SQL statements in this class can be instructive in figuring out how the work of mapping to a database is done. Later, we will also see that reading these generated SQL statements can help you understand the deeper issues in mapping EJB relationships to a relational database.

Some Simple Tests

Once you have finished the code generation process, you are ready to test your Bean. However, you need to consider a few things about CMP Entity Bean testing before you begin.

First, most of code in a CMP Entity Bean is generated code. To some people, this would suggest that this code does not need to be tested, and in some respects, that may be true, as you certainly won't have many opportunities to fix it if it is broken. However, there is a deeper reason why testing even generated code is a good idea. When you are writing a test for an Entity Bean, what you are really testing is the interface to the Bean—the methods defined in the Home and the Remote interfaces. This interface to the Bean may remain constant, but over time, the implementation of the interface may change. In the simplest scenario, a new version of VisualAge for Java may come out that implements a later version of the EJB specification. In that case, testing your assumptions about the way each Bean works will be crucial to validating that the rest of your program works as intended. Another possibility may be that you decide to reimplement a CMP Bean as a BMP Bean. In that case, the test will assure you that clients of the Bean will continue to function even with the new implementation.

Second, the way in which you test an Entity Bean may be slightly different from the way in which you test a Session Bean. Earlier, you learned how to test Session Beans by using the generated test client classes that VisualAge for Java provides. However, you may test Entity Beans with not only a test client but also additional test scripts that can be executed from a tool or from the command line. The primary reason for wanting to write supplemental test scripts is that the test client is not able to test the different methods of the interface together in groups *within the context of a transaction*. One of the design decisions that went into the building of the test client was that each method invocation would be its own transaction; this makes testing each method in isolation simpler but does not provide a way to test cases in which multiple methods should be executed within the same transaction.

Let's consider how to write a simple example to demonstrate how you would write tests like this. Begin by creating a new class named Create AndRetrieveDepartment. The class definition from VisualAge for Java follows:

```
import javax.transaction.*;
import java.rmi.*;
import java.util.*;
import javax.naming.*;
import javax.ejb.*;
import com.wsbook.casestudy.ejb.*;
/**
```

```
* This class is a simple test script for testing
* the DepartmentEJB.
* @author: Kyle Brown
*/
public class CreateAndRetrieveDepartment {
    InitialContext initContext;
    DepartmentEJBHome departmentHome;
    boolean failure = false;
}
```

The class has a simple design. It has a set of methods, beginning with test..., that each test one particular aspect of the Home or the Remote interface. If a test fails, it is responsible for setting the failure variable to false. A setup() method initializes the shared initial naming context and DepartmentEJBHome shown in the class definition. The main() method for this class follows:

```
/**
* Starts the application.
* @param args an array of command-line arguments
*/
public static void main(java.lang.String[] args) {
    CreateAndRetrieveDepartment instance = new
    CreateAndRetrieveDepartment();
    instance.setup();
    instance.testCreateDepartment();
    instance.testRetrieveDepartment();
    instance.testRemoveDepartment();
    if (!instance.failure)
        System.out.println("The tests completed with no errors");
    else
        System.out.println("There were errors. Check stdout for details.");
}
```

The setup() method retrieves the initial context and uses it to look up the department EJB Home. The test methods are the more interesting ones. The first method, testCreateDepartment(), is as follows:

```
/**
* This method tests creating a department EJB
* Creation date: (4/22/00 5:55:41 PM)
*/
public void testCreateDepartment() {
    try {
        departmentHome.create(47, "Baboon Sign-language Training");
    } catch (CreateException e) {
        System.out.println("Exception " + e + " caught in testCreateDepartment()");
        failure = true;
    } catch (RemoteException e) {
        System.out.println("Exception " + e + " caught in testCreateDepartment()");
        failure = true;
    }
}
```

There's not a lot going on here. The method simply creates the EJB instance with the create() method defined in DepartmentEJBHome. The only checks necessary are the ones for exceptions; if an exception is thrown, the test obviously fails, so the failure is logged to System.out, and the failure flag is set. The more complicated case, but not much more so, is in the test RetrieveDepartment() method that follows:

```
/**
 * This method is the heart of the test class
 * It verifies that the object created is actually
 * created with the right values.
 *
 * Creation date: (4/22/00 5:56:13 PM)
 */
public void testRetrieveDepartment() {
    UserTransaction tranContext = null;
    try {
        tranContext = (UserTransaction)
initContext.lookup("jta/usertransaction");
        tranContext.begin();
        DepartmentEJB ejb = departmentHome.findByPrimaryKey(new
        DepartmentEJBKey(47));
        String deptName = ejb.getName();
        // The following test would usually be more complex...
        if (!deptName.equals("Baboon Sign-language Training")) {
            failure = true;
            System.out.println("The department name retrieved does not match
            the one set.");
        }
    } catch (Exception e) {
        System.out.println("Exception " + e + " caught in
        testRetrieveDepartment()");
        failure = true;
    } finally {
        try {
            tranContext.commit();
        } catch (Exception e) {
            System.out.println("Fatal failure in testRetrieveDepartment().
            Exception is:" + e);
            failure = true;
        }
    }
}
```

Several things about this method need to be pointed out. First, most of the code in the method executes within a single transaction context because the method obtains the UserTransaction from the initial context and then uses UserTransaction.begin() to start an explicit client-controlled transaction. After the transaction has been started, the test begins; the goal of this method is to retrieve the values from the EJB created in the previous step and compare them to the values that should have been set in that EJB. In our simple case, we are comparing only one value, the department name, but the principle still applies, even though this test would normally be much more complex. Here, however, it is sufficient to compare the string returned from the getName() method to the one used to create the EJB in the previous method.

The final thing to notice is that the transaction is ended in a finally() method to ensure that even if an exception is thrown, the transaction is completed so as not to leave it open. Although the EJB server would end the transaction anyway after a timeout, this would be a needless waste of server resources.

The final test method in this class (testRemoveDepartment()) is simple and similar to the testCreateDepartment() method in that it fails only if an exception is thrown. The source code for this method and the rest of the class are on the accompanying CD-ROM, or you can try to recreate it from the implementation hints we have given.

We are now only a couple of steps away from being able to test our new Entity Bean. First, we need to set the database values in the EJB server that contains the EJBs that you have created. This is so that the EJB server will know what JDBC URL, driver, user ID, and password to use. To set these values, select the EJB server representing your new EJB group in the *EJB Server Configuration* window, and select *Properties* from the right-mouse-button menu of the *Servers* pane. Doing this will bring up the dialog in Figure 19.12.

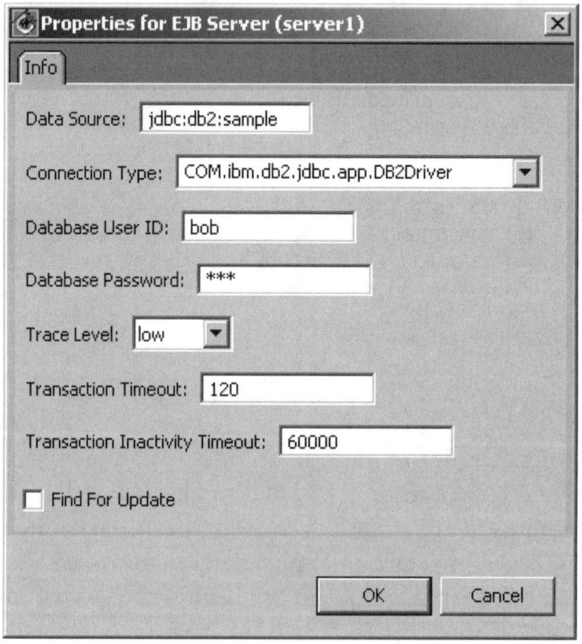

Figure 19.12   EJB Server Properties

Here, you need to type in the same JDBC URL, driver, user ID, and password in the *Data Source:* text field that you used when you exported the relational schema to the database. After making these changes, try starting the EJB processes—the PNS and your EJB server—and observe the console carefully to make sure that your EJB server starts successfully. If the EJB server terminates with an SQL error, go back and examine the values in the *Properties* dialog again to make sure that you have entered the correct JDBC URL, user ID, and password.

Finally, you need to set up the properties for the CreateAndRetrieve Department class so that the main() method will have access to all the classes it needs from other projects to run. Select this class in the *Projects* tab of the workbench, and open the right-mouse-button menu; then select *Properties* to bring up the dialog in Figure 19.13.

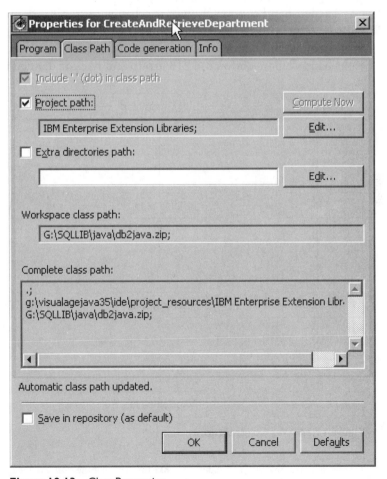

Figure 19.13   Class Properties

Clicking the *Compute Now* button on this dialog instructs VisualAge for Java to find out what other projects are needed by this class's main() method, by traversing the call tree, and add them to the project path. After clicking *Compute Now,* click *OK* to dismiss this dialog. Now you are ready to try running your test. Select *CreateAndRetrieveDepartment* in the *Projects* tab of the workbench, and then start the main() method by clicking the run icon. If you have completed all the tasks so far, this class's main method should run and show the results of your test: ideally, all good![1]

Summary and Preview

You've been introduced to a lot of new concepts and new browsers in this chapter. The UML diagram in Figure 19.14 can help you understand the relationships among all the objects that you've seen.

The left-hand column shows the schema, just as it is defined in the *Schema Map* browser. We did not show how you attach a VapConverter to a table column, but editing the table in the *Schema Browser* can do it. The right-hand column shows the EJB group and EJBs as defined in the EJB

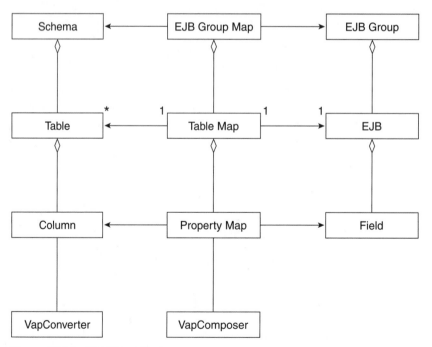

Figure 19.14   VAJ Object Design

1. For a more reusable way of building tests like this, we refer the reader to the open-source JUnit testing framework for Java, available at http://www.junit.org.

Development Environment. The center column shows the mapping objects that are created in the *Table Map* browser and the *Property Map* dialog. If you understand the relationships expressed in this dialog, you've gone a long way toward mastering the various mapping browsers. Finally, you learned about writing test classes that can test Entity EJBs. In the next chapter, we turn to advanced CMP mapping.

CHAPTER 20

Advanced CMP Mapping

In previous chapters, you've learned the basics of the VisualAge for Java EJB Development Environment. You've seen how Entity EJBs are mapped into database tables in a simple one-to-one way. But that hasn't fully met the problem of mapping OO design to EJBs. This chapter addresses some of the more complex object-to-relational mapping issues.

Simple Mapping Rules

The VisualAge for Java EJB Development Environment and WebSphere provide a simple mechanism for mapping Entity Beans to database tables. This simplicity arises from the assumption that each attribute in an EJB maps to a single column in a single table in a database. This mapping is done by type: Strings in Java map to VARCHARs in SQL, ints map to INTEGERs, and so on.

However, one mapping rule sticks out like a sore thumb. All objects that are not convertible to standard SQL types are instead mapped to a BLOB (binary large object) of a maximum size of 1M. This rule applies to any type derived from Object in Java: in other words, every class you might create.

This rule provides a simple solution for storing objects in a relational database, but it's not the best solution for most applications. Of the two approaches to representing object data in a relational database, one is the BLOB approach, with objects serialized into a binary form and then stored into a single column in a table. This approach has the following drawbacks.

- BLOBs are not readable from other applications, such as reporting tools.
- BLOBs cannot be queried from SQL, making data mining and table maintenance difficult.

- BLOBs may not be readable from later versions of the application that created them. This is a tough problem that requires a deep knowledge of how Java serialization works and careful planning to avoid.

These drawbacks have led developers to instead prefer an approach in which objects are mapped to relational databases in such a way that object relationships are preserved in the relational database schema. This approach has been well documented in [Brown 96]. Let's quickly review this approach to see how it applies to EJBs in VisualAge.

Object-Relational Basics

In the most common mapping approach, object relationships are represented by foreign-key relationships in the database. Consider the following relationships, drawn from our case study (Figure 20.1).

Figure 20.1 shows two relationships between TimeSheet and Employee: one representing the approving relationship and another representing the submitting relationship. But another kind of relationship must also be represented. A TimeSheet contains a collection of TimeSheetEntries, as shown in Figure 20.2, which illustrates a multivalued relationship.

In a normal Java class, you would represent the former relationships by having a TimeSheet with two instance variables of the Employee type. Likewise, you might have each TimeSheet hold an array of TimeSheetEntries or a

Figure 20.1   Object Associations

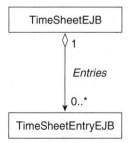

Figure 20.2   One-to-Many Association

vector containing TimeSheetEntry objects. However, this simple solution won't quite work for EJBs. It also doesn't quite map directly to a relational database.

As [Brown 96] discusses, a relationship like TimeSheet to Employee is represented in a relational database by foreign keys that point from the "owning" table (Table 20.1) to the "owned" table (Table 20.2). The columns ApproverFK and SubmitterFK in Table 20.1 contain foreign keys into Table 20.2. Each TimeSheet row will contain pointers to the two Employee rows.

You can also use foreign keys that point the *other* way to also store 1–N (multivalued) relationships. Each "contained" row has a foreign key to the row that "contains" it (Table 20.3). In our example, the two TimeSheetEntry rows both have a foreign key back into the TimeSheet table that provides the link from the two entries (1011 and 1012) back to the TimeSheet with the primary key 1000.

You can now see the basic outlines of our solution. If we want to map from our object model in Java to a relational database, we must have a way of creating and reconstituting these foreign-key relationships. In a nutshell, that is what VisualAge's relational mapping does.

Table 20.1 TimeSheet Table Containing Foreign Keys

PrimaryKey	ApproverFK	SubmitterFK
1000	3015	2013

Table 20-2 Employee Table: The Pointed-to Table

PrimaryKey	Name	Job title
2013	Bob Smith	Programmer
3015	Sue Wong	Manager

Table 20.3 TimeSheetEntry Table: Foreign Key in One-to-Many Relationship

PrimaryKey	TimesheetFK	Hours	Date
1011	1000	8.0	2/13/99
1012	1000	8.0	2/14/99

Concepts in EJB Relationship Mapping

What you want is the best of both worlds. You want to be able to represent object relationships as in standard Java classes, but you also want to take advantage of the automatic persistence, distribution, and transaction features that you get from EJBs. As you might have guessed, you need EJBs for each of the types we have discussed: TimeSheets, Employees, and TimeSheetEntries. The trick comes in how the implementation of these three EJBs ties them together.

Look at the following segment from the Remote interface of our TimeSheet EJB:

```
package com.wsbook.casestudy.ejb;
/**
 * This is the EJB Remote interface for TimeSheetEJB
 */
public interface TimeSheetEJB extends javax.ejb.EJBObject {
EmployeeEJB getApprovingEmployee() throws java.rmi.RemoteException,
javax.ejb.FinderException;
java.util.Enumeration getEntries() throws java.rmi.RemoteException,
javax.ejb.FinderException;
EmployeeEJB getSubmittingEmployee() throws java.rmi.RemoteException,
javax.ejb.FinderException;
}
```

This interface has a method called getApprovingEmployee() that returns an instance of EmployeeEJB and another method called getSubmittingEmployee(). A method named getEntries() returns an Enumeration of TimeSheetEntryEJBs.

Understanding how these methods are implemented is the key to understanding this approach to EJB relationship management. The Remote interface methods declare that you *can* get to the related Employees and the Enumeration of TimeSheetEntries. *How* this is accomplished is the province of our foreign-key trick. Before you see the details of that, though, you need to walk through a hypothetical implementation of one of these methods.

The problem is that EJBs can't directly contain other EJBs: The EJB 1.0 specification explicitly forbade it, and the EJB 1.1 specification doesn't make it clear how this can be accomplished. What is allowed, however, is that an EJB can contain a *key* to another EJB. If we were to implement our TimeSheetEJBBean class to contain two integer variables–the submitting Employee's employeeId and the approving Employee's employeeId, you could implement getApprovingEmployee() as follows:[1]

```
public EmployeeEJB getApprovingEmployee() {
    // assume that employeeHome is already initialized
EmployeeEJB approver = null;
```

---

1. The code in this section doesn't exactly match that generated by VisualAge for Java. However, if you can understand the concepts in this simple example, it will help in understanding the VAJ solution.

```
try {
    EmployeeEJBKey key = new EmployeeEJBKey(approvingEmployeeId);
    approver = employeeHome.findByPrimaryKey(key);
} catch (Exception e) {
    System.out.println("+++Exception caught:" + e);
}
return approver;
}
```

The first section of code before the try block simply declares and initializes a temporary variable of type EmployeeEJB. Before the next section is executed, an implicit assumption is that the instance variable employeeHome, which is of type EmployeeEJBHome, has already been initialized. The only odd thing about the code that follows is that it is *inside* an EJB rather than in an EJB client, as most of the WebSphere examples illustrate. This is key: The *TimeSheet* EJB will be both a client *and* a server, acting as a client for the *Employee* and *TimeSheetEntry EJBs*.

The next section of code, inside the try block, is how the foreign-key reference is turned into an object. The foreign-key reference creates a new instance of EmployeeEJBKey, using the value of the approver foreign key already present in the *TimeSheet EJB*, and then looks up the *EmployeeEJB* at that key with the EmployeeHome, using the findByPrimaryKey() method. Once this is done, the code returns the Employee instance.

The getEntries() method could be done in a similar way. Let's take a look at that code:

```
public java.util.Enumeration getEntries() {
java.util.Enumeration enum = null;
// assume that entryHome is already initialized
try {
    enum = entryHome.findEntriesByTimesheet(primaryKey);
} catch (Exception e) {
    System.out.println("+++Exception caught:" + e);
}
return enum;
}
```

The first section of code simply declares a variable of type java.util.Enumeration. The code inside the try block is the more intriguing portion. The Enumeration returned by this method is obtained by sending the message findEntriesBy Timesheet() to the TimesheetEntryEJBHome instance held in entryHome. The argument to this method is the primaryKey of the *TimeSheet*. This method is defined in the TimeSheetEntryEJBHome:

```
package com.wsbook.casestudy.ejb;

/**
```

```
 * This is the Home interface for the TimeSheetEntry Entity Bean
 */
public interface TimeSheetEntryEJBHome extends javax.ejb.EJBHome {

com.wsbook.casestudy.ejb.TimeSheetEntryEJB create(int arg1, double arg2,
java.lang.String arg3, int arg4, int arg5) throws javax.ejb.CreateException,
java.rmi.RemoteException;

com.wsbook.casestudy.ejb.TimeSheetEntryEJB findByPrimaryKey(com.wsbook.
casestudy.ejb.TimeSheetEntryEJBKey key) throws java.rmi.RemoteException,
javax.ejb.FinderException;

java.util.Enumeration findEntriesByTimesheet(com.wsbook.casestudy.ejb.
TimeSheetEJBKey inKey) throws java.rmi.RemoteException, javax.ejb.
FinderException;

}
```

Remember that 1–N relationships are represented by rows pointing back to the row that represents the object that contains them. The TimeSheetEntry EJBHome would implement this method by executing SQL code that returns a set of rows representing those TimeSheetEntries that have a foreign key corresponding to the TimeSheet primary key passed in as a parameter. This is the set of objects that you want to be associated with our *TimeSheet,* so the trip has now come full circle.

Now you've seen how the getter part of the problem would be solved. The corresponding setter part works in the reverse order: by taking the primary key out of the EJB reference passed in and then placing it back in the instance variable that holds the foreign-key value.

You have now seen two kinds of object relationships that can be represented in EJBs. Table 20.4 summarizes those relationships and how they were implemented in the relational database tables and in our EJBs.

VisualAge uses the same strategies that we used to implement these relationships in the previous section in its generated code for associations. By showing you the generated code for our example in VisualAge for Java 3.5, you will learn exactly how the strategies we examined are implemented.

Table 20.4   EJB Relationship Implementation Strategies

Relationship type	Database implementation	EJB implementation
0, 1–1	Foreign key in owning table	The get() method uses findByPrimaryKey() in the owned class Home to return a single EJB reference.
0, 1–N	Foreign key in owned table	The get() method uses a special finder method in the owned class Home to return an Enumeration.

Associations in UML

Before we embark on our investigation of the association support in VAJ 3.5, however, let's briefly discuss some of the elements of support for associations in UML. This may seem like a sidetrack, but it really does help in understanding some of the decisions behind the association support in VAJ 3.5.

In UML, a solid line between two classes represents an association between them. An association in UML simply represents a link between objects, but it does not imply anything about the implementation of that link. In fact, UML is intentionally vague to allow for multiple implementation strategies. An association can carry along with it information about the relationship between the objects that are linked. In our case, we are concerned only with links between two classes, so we can limit our discussion to the types of information that relate to those relationships.

Each end of an association can have certain information associated with it. In general, UML relationships are always bidirectional, thereby keeping the options for implementation open. The first kind of information associated with an end of an association is *navigability*. Navigability is represented in UML by an open-ended arrow on an association end. Navigability simply means that you can traverse the link in the direction of an arrow. An association with no arrows is reachable from either end. An association with an arrow is reachable only in the direction of the arrow.

Each association end has associated with it a *role name,* or "view" of the object from the other end. The role name is the name by which each object is known to the other object in the relationship. Finally, each association end has a *multiplicity* associated with it. A multiplicity specifies how many values an association end may have. This can be a number (1, 2,...) or a range (0..1), or it may be the unbound expression (*), which means "any number" or any combination of the preceding. These decorations are shown in Figure 20.3.

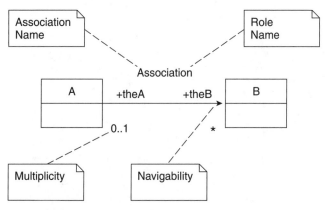

Figure 20.3 UML Notation for Associations

Associations in VisualAge for Java 3.5

The reason for our sidetrack into UML becomes clear when we begin to examine the new dialogs for generating associations in VisualAge for Java 3.5. Selecting an Entity EJB in the *Enterprise Beans* pane of the *EJB* tab of the workbench and then selecting *Add>Association* from the pop-up menu allows you to reach the *Association Editor* dialog (Figure 20.4).

This dialog has controls that correspond to most of the association qualifiers we examined earlier. To begin with, the *Association name:* has the same meaning as in UML: the name by which this association will be referred to. This name can be seen in the schema browsers and in other places. Next, each association end has a corresponding set of controls:

- A drop-down list that allows the user to select the class on that end of the association.
- A role name for the association end.
- A check box indicating whether this association end is navigable, that is, whether you can reach the class on this end from the other side.
- A check box indicating which side should be represented by a foreign key in the database.

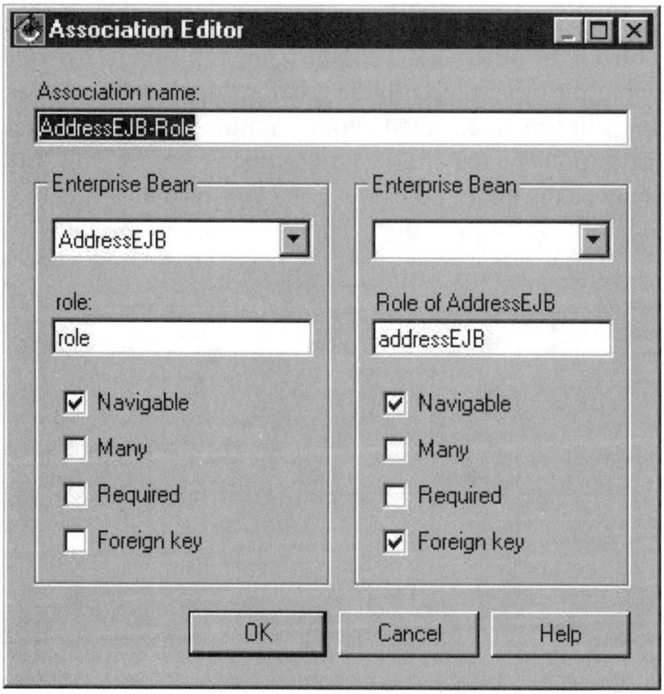

Figure 20.4   *Association Editor* Dialog in VisualAge for Java

• Two check boxes indicating the multiplicity of the association. They correspond to the UML multiplicities according to Table 20.5, which can also be found in the *help* file for this dialog.

You will begin to see the meaning of these check boxes by seeing them in use, as the following examples will illustrate.

Implementing a Simple Association

The problem with introducing to you the process for adding simple one-to-one relationships is that, at this point, there are no such relationships in the EJB model we have been developing. We will add one now. Consider the following scenario: During the time-sheet reporting process, we may find that we have to mail weekly or monthly summary reports of time worked to the managers who approve time sheets. We don't have in the system any information that would give us the address of an employee to whom we could mail a report like this.

We need to add a simple relationship to attach this information. We will add to our system an *AddressEJB* that is related in a one-to-one manner to each *EmployeeEJB*. Although this could have been implemented just as easily as additional attributes of the *EmployeeEJB,* this implementation will allow you to learn a little bit about how to generate one-to-one EJB associations in VisualAge for Java.

Just as you previously built the *ProjectEJB, DepartmentEJB*, and so on, you now need to add an *AddressEJB* with the container-managed attributes listed in Table 20.6.

To implement the one-to-one association between *EmployeeEJB* and *AddressEJB*, we begin by selecting *EmployeeEJB* in the *Enterprise Beans* pane and then selecting *Add>Association....* menu selection. This brings up the *Association* dialog we introduced earlier. Now, what we really want is for each *EmployeeEJB* to be able to obtain its corresponding *AddressEJB*, of which there will be one and only one. This means that the association should be 1..1 from the point of view of the *EmployeeEJB*.

Table 20.5   Mapping Many and Require to Multiplicity Values

Many?	Required?	Multiplicity
Yes	Yes	1..*
Yes	No	0..*
No	Yes	1..1
No	No	0..1

Table 20.6   Attributes for *AddressEJB*

Attribute	Type
AddressKey (key value)	int
StreetAddress	String
City	String
State	String
ZipCode	String

We need to set up an association with one end being an *EmployeeEJB* and the other end being an *AddressEJB*. We do this by selecting these two classes from the drop-down lists. In our example, we will name the role of *AddressEJB* address and the role of *EmployeeEJB* employeeEJB. The association as a whole we can name EmployeeEJBToHomeAddress.

After making these simple decisions, you need to address the questions of navigability and multiplicity. Obviously, because each *EmployeeEJB* has a single address, we can leave out the *Many* selections. So we need to check *Required* only for the address role to enforce the 1..1 cardinality. This setting on a role specifies whether the lower limit of the multiplicity should be 0 or 1. This setting has two effects on the generated EJB. First, it will control whether the role may be part of the object identity (OID). Only a required role may be an OID component. Second, a required role will be mapped to a real database constraint if a default schema is generated. An optional role would not be compatible with a referential integrity constraint in the database, so a corresponding "logical" foreign key will be created in a default schema. In our case, not every employee must have an address, so we can leave *Required* clear on the *EmployeeEJB* side. Likewise, we may easily find a use for an address from other EJBs, so we will leave the selection clear on the *AddressEJB* side as well.

Next, we need to consider navigability. VisualAge for Java takes a simple approach to navigability with EJB associations. VisualAge will generate accessor methods, such as getAddressEJB() or getEmployeeEJB(), only for the association ends for which the navigable property has been set. This especially makes sense in the 1–*N* case, as we will see, as we obviously must have accessors on the "Many" side to gain access to the foreign-key attribute. In our case, we won't need to be able to retrieve an Employee from its Address, so we will check *Navigable* on the *EmployeeEJB* side only.

Finally, we need to decide which end of the relationship should contain the foreign key. In our case, we want to take the simplest, most standard approach, representing a connection from an *EmployeeEJB* to an *AddressEJB* by placing a foreign key in the database table representing an *EmployeeEJB*,

Figure 20.5 Setting for Association Between Employee and Address

pointing to the primary key of the *AddressEJB* table. So, you will need to select *Foreign key* on the *EmployeeEJB* side but leave the selection blank on the *AddressEJB* side. Once you have made all these selections, the associations dialog for this example, with all the selections that correspond to the decisions we have made, will look like Figure 20.5.

Single-Valued Association Implementation Details

The next step in completing this example is to click the *OK* button on the associations dialog and see what code VisualAge for Java will generate to represent the associations. VisualAge for Java makes the following changes to the EmployeeEJB class. First, it adds the following user-accessible methods to the *EmployeeEJB* Remote interface and the EmployeeEJBBean class:

public AddressEJB getHomeAddress()

public void setHomeAddress(AddressEJB aHomeAddress)

These two methods correspond to the same kind of single-valued association methods that we looked at in our hypothetical implementation of

TimeSheetEJB's getApprovingEmployee(). The former method will return the associated instance of AddressEJB for this *EmployeeEJB,* and the second will set the association. You should not use several other "internal" methods specific to VisualAge's implementation of associations:

public void secondarySetHomeAddress(AddressEJB aHomeAddress)

public void privateSetHomeAddressKey(com.wsbook.casestudy.ejb.Address EJBKey inKey)

public AddressEJBKey getHomeAddressKey()
protected com.ibm.ivj.ejb.associations.interfaces.SingleLink getHomeAddressLink()

To understand what these methods do and how they are used by the code generated by VisualAge for Java, you'll need to understand the concept of a link. VisualAge for Java's generated code manages associations through the use of link classes. A link is an object that physically manages the connection between the two objects. A link contains a reference to the EJB whose association "owns" the link, as well as a reference to the EJB Home of the "target" EJB.

VisualAge has three types of links. Single links, which implement single-valued relationships, come in two subtypes: single-to-single links and many-to-single links. Single-to-many links implement multivalued relationships. In any case, VisualAge will generate a subclass of the appropriate link subclass that is unique to each particular role: EmployeeEJBToHomeAddressLink, in this example.

VisualAge generates the getHomeAddressLink() method on the *EmployeeEJB* to allow the code in the getHomeAddress() and the setHomeAddress() methods to find the link instance that manages that relationship. Once you look inside a link, you will find that the code is very similar to the hypothetical code we examined earlier. For instance, the fetchTarget() method of the EmployeeEJB ToHomeAddressLink looks like the following:

```
protected javax.ejb.EJBObject fetchTarget() throws java.rmi.RemoteException,
javax.ejb.FinderException {
    EJBObject target = null;
    com.wsbook.casestudy.ejb.AddressEJBKey key = ((com.wsbook.
    casestudy.ejb.EmployeeEJBBean) source).getHomeAddressKey();
    try {
        target = ((com.wsbook.casestudy.ejb.AddressEJBHome)this.
        getTargetHome()).findByPrimaryKey(key);
    }
    catch (NamingException e) {
        throw new FinderException(e.toString());
    }
    return target;
}
```

This method does exactly what we would expect it to. It uses the get

HomeAddressKey() method that we saw generated earlier to obtain an instance of AddressEJBKey from the container-managed homeAddress_addressKey attribute and then uses findByPrimaryKey() on the AddressEJBHome to obtain a reference to the appropriate AddressEJB stub for this particular EmployeeEJB.

In general, the following methods will be generated for single-valued associations. The end holding the foreign key will get the following methods, if the *Navigable* flag is set:

<Remote Interface of associated EJB> get<RoleName>()

void set<Rolename> (<Remote Interface of associated EJB>)

The following internal methods will be generated:

public void secondarySet<Rolename>(<Related EJB Remote Interface>)

public void privateSetHome<Role of Related EJB>Key(<Related EJB primary key class>)

public.<Related EJB Remote Interface> get<Role of Related EJB>Key()

The end that does not have the foreign key will have the following methods generated, regardless of whether the *Navigable* flag is set:

void set<Rolename> (<Remote Interface of associated EJB>)

public void secondarySet<Rolename>(<Related EJB Remote Interface>)

If the *Navigable* flag is set, the associated get<Rolename> method will also be generated on the end not having the foreign key, so you can navigate from either end.

Just as VisualAge for Java generates the link class on the "owning" end of a relationship to manage changes to the relationship, such as changing the value of the relationship, it also adds a corresponding link class on the other end of the relationship to manage that end. In this way, bidirectional relationships can be kept in sync with each other.

So far, we have seen only links that are single-valued on both ends. VisualAge also handles the situation in which a link is multivalued on the other end: for instance, the relationships between Employee and TimeSheet. In this case, the new link class will extend ManyToSingleLink, but the general approach to managing the relationships will remain the same.

Implementing Many-Valued Relationships

To see how multivalued associations are implemented, we'll implement the relationship between *TimeSheetEJB* and *TimeSheetEntryEJB*. As in the previous example, we'll start by going to the associations dialog by selecting the *TimeSheetEJB* in the *Enterprise Beans* pane and choosing *Add>Association*. In this case, we have the following choices to make:

- Because each *TimeSheetEJB* can have many *TimeSheetEntryEJBs*, this is a *Many*-valued relationship on the *TimeSheetEJB* side.
- A *TimesheetEntryEJB* can exist only as part of a *TimeSheetEJB*. Therefore, the *Required* attribute must be set on the *TimeSheetEJB* side.
- The relationship should be navigable from both ends, as it may become necessary in the future to set up things by TimeSheet that each Entry will use, such as special project codes.

So, if we set the check boxes in the dialog according to these decisions, the associations dialog will look like Figure 20.6.

This dialog is different from the previous dialogs in that the *Foreign key* check box is automatically disabled when you set a *Many*-valued relationship. The reason is that the only place to put the foreign key is in the "owned" object and table, as we saw in the beginning of the chapter.

As in the previous example, the next thing to do is to click the *OK* button and examine what code is generated to represent this relationship. In this case, we will have to look at code in three different places: the TimeSheet EntryEJB, the TimeSheetEJB, and the TimeSheetEntryEJBHome. The code here will

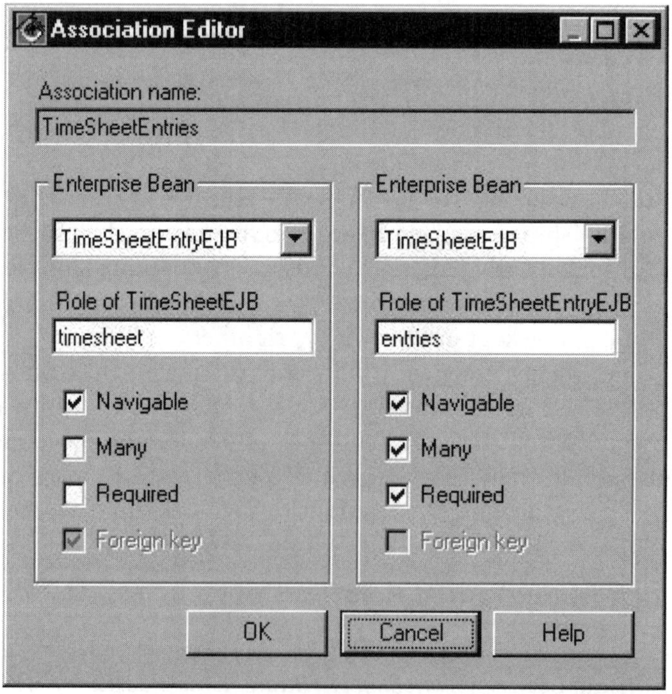

Figure 20.6   One-to-Many Association: TimeSheet to TimeSheetEntry

seem familiar to you, as it's an extension of the ideas and implementations that you've already seen in the earlier examples.

First, you need to examine TimeSheetEJB. The most interesting methods are found in this class. You will find the following publicly accessible methods have been added to the class:

```
public java.util.Enumeration getEntries()

public void addEntries(TimeSheetEntryEJB anEntries)

public void removeEntries(TimeSheetEntryEJB anEntries)
```

The first method (getEntries()) is similar in concept to the hypothetical example that we examined earlier. To understand the implementation, you need to recall that we defined a method named findEntriesByTimesheet() as a custom finder method. In the same way, VisualAge has also defined a method of the same name in the TimeSheetEntryEJBHome. This method is used by the method fetchTargetEnumeration() in the class TimeSheetEJBToEntriesLink, as follows:

```
protected java.util.Enumeration fetchTargetEnumeration() throws
java.rmi.RemoteException, javax.ejb.FinderException {
    Enumeration enum = null;
    try {
        enum = ((com.wsbook.casestudy.ejb.TimeSheetEntryEJBHome) this.
        getTargetHome()).findEntriesByTimesheet((com.wsbook.casestudy.ejb.
        TimeSheetEJBKey)((com.wsbook.casestudy.ejb.TimeSheetEJBBean)
        source).getEntityContext().getPrimaryKey());
    }
    catch (NamingException e) {
        throw new FinderException(e.toString());
    }
    return enum;
}
```

As in our previous example, this method simply calls the findEntries ByTimesheet() finder method in the EJB Home, sending the TimeSheetEJB's primary key as the argument, and then returns the enumeration of TimeSheetEJBs that are returned by the finder.

The next two methods (addEntries() and removeEntries()) are also worth investigating. They point out some of the advantages of the implementation of Links, particularly SingleToManyLinks, in VisualAge. The method addEntries()

- Sets the back-pointer (parent foreign key) of the TimeSheetEntryEJB to be the primary key of the TimeSheetEJB that receives the message. This ensures that the relationship is preserved in the database when the EJBs are persisted.
- Sets the reference to the TimeSheetEJB held in the TimeSheetEntryEJB to be this instance of TimeSheetEJB.

- Adds the TimeSheetEntryEJB to a cache (a vector) of TimeSheetEntryEJBs. This vector is used by VisualAge's generated code to allow enumerations over the set of TimeSheetEntryEJBs, even though changes may not yet have been committed to the database. This allows the EJBs and the database to both remain consistent at all times.

As you can imagine, the message removeEntries() performs the inverse of these operations.

In addition to the publicly accessible methods, some methods that are not user-accessible will also be added to the TimeSheetEntryEJB:

protected com.ibm.ivj.ejb.associations.interfaces.ManyLink getEntriesLink()

public void secondaryAddEntries(com.wsbook.casestudy.ejb.TimeSheetEntryEJB anEntries)

public void secondaryRemoveEntries(com.wsbook.casestudy.ejb.TimeSheet EntryEJB anEntries)

These methods are used by the implementation of getEntries(), addEntries(), and removeEntries() and by the new link subclass, TimeSheetEJBToEntriesLink, to handle adding and removing elements. The total set of user-accessible methods that you will see on a *Many* end of a many-valued association is:

java.util.Enumeration get<RoleName>()

void add<RoleName>(<Related EJB Remote Interface>)

void remove<RoleName>(<Related EJB Remote Interface>)

The following internal methods will be generated:

public void secondaryAdd<Rolename>(<Related EJB Remote Interface>)

public void secondaryRemove<Role of Related EJB>Key(<Related EJB primary key class>)

protected com.ibm.ivj.ejb.associations.interfaces.ManyLink get<Rolename> Link ()

The set of methods generated on the other end of the association, the *Single* end, are the same as they are in the single-valued association case, so you won't see anything different on that end.

Wrapping Up Relationships

To complete the association used in the case study, add the two associations between the *TimeSheetEJB* and *EmployeeEJB*. You can use Figures 20.7 and 20.8

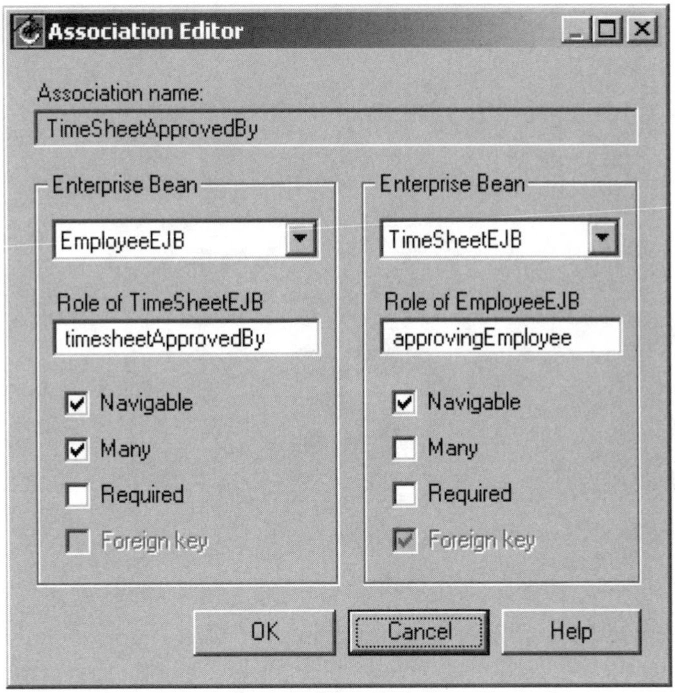

Figure 20.7 *TimeSheetApprovedBy* Relationships

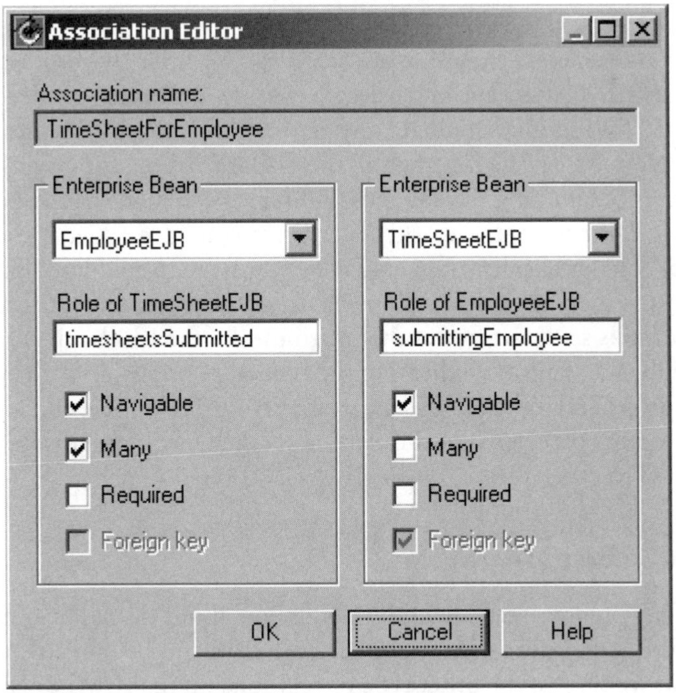

Figure 20.8 *TimeSheetForEmployee* Relationships

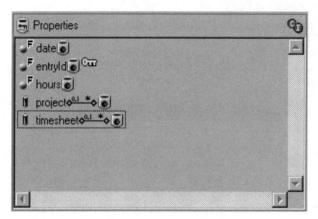

Figure 20.9   Associations as Properties

to see how to configure the settings in the *Create Association* dialog. After generating the associations between the EJBs by using the association dialog, you will need to regenerate the deployed code for the EJBs in the *TimeSheetGroup* EJB group. Adding the associations changes not only the Bean implementations but also the Home and Remote interfaces. Because the definitions of these interfaces have changed, you must regenerate the RMI over IIOP stubs and skeletons that implement those interfaces.

To regenerate these classes, select the *TimeSheetGroup* EJB group in the *Enterprise Beans* pane and select *Generate Deployed Code* from the pop-up menu. This should eliminate any errors (red X marks) by these classes.

Now we can tie together all the disparate threads of relationship management by examining the changes that have been made to the *Properties* pane of the EJB page of the workbench. Once you have added the EJB relationships for TimeSheetEntryEJB, its *Properties* pane should look like Figure 20.9.

Note how the relationships have been represented in this pane. Each relationship is set apart from other attributes of the EJB by the presence of a small UML diagram indicating the type of relationship defined. For example, the project relationship has a cardinality of 0..1 on one end and a cardinality of * on the other end. In this way, a quick glance can indicate how this EJB is related to other EJBs.

EJB Inheritance in VisualAge

So far, you have seen a lengthy discussion about the association relationship in UML and how associations between EJBs can be implemented in VAJ. Now, we turn to the other type of relationship that UML specifies: generalization. Generalizations are of two types. The *inheritance* relationship corresponds to the notion of implementation inheritance ("extends" in Java), and the *realization* relationship corresponds to the notion of interface inheritance ("implements" in Java).

When they start to talk about inheritance in EJBs, people tend to be a little vague, probably because the EJB specification itself is a little vague on the issue. The EJB specification has only two clear indications about what inheritance means in the context of EJBs:

The EJB 1.0 specification [EJB] states: "The remote interface is allowed to have superinterfaces. Use of interface inheritance is subject to the RMI-IIOP rules for the definition of remote interfaces."[2] Further, "the home interface is allowed to have superinterfaces. Use of interface inheritance is subject to the RMI-IIOP rules for the definition of remote interfaces."[3]

The 1.0 specification refers to inheritance in only two other places. In both the Session Bean and the Entity Bean scenarios, all three of Home and Remote interfaces and Bean implementations are shown in a generalization relationship to other respective interfaces and implementations. However, the specification is vague on how this can be accomplished. For instance, in the Entity Bean scenario, it states that "tools can use inheritance, delegation, and code generation to achieve mix-in of the two classes [participating in the generalization relationship]."[4]

The EJB 1.1 specification clarifies this situation in its FAQ, specifically stating that component inheritance—how an entire EJB descends from another EJB—is beyond the scope of the specification. However, it goes on to discuss how developers can take advantage of the Java language support for inheritance, as follows:

> Interface inheritance. It is possible to use the Java language interface inheritance mechanism for inheritance of the home and remote interfaces. A component may derive its home and remote interfaces from some "parent" home and remote interfaces; the component then can be used anywhere where a component with the parent interfaces is expected. This is a Java language feature, and its use is transparent to the EJB Container.
>
> Implementation class inheritance. It is possible to take advantage of the Java class implementation inheritance mechanism for the enterprise Bean class. For example, the class CheckingAccountBean class can extend the AccountBean class to inherit the implementation of the business methods.

So the specification seems to give quite a bit of latitude to tools and container implementers when it comes to how to implement "component inheritance" between EJBs. It is good to keep this in mind when we look at the implementation of EJB inheritance in WebSphere Application Server, Advanced Edition, Version 3.5 and VisualAge for Java, Enterprise Edition, Version 3.5. The developers of these products have sought to create a sensible,

---

2. [EJB], p.132.
3. Ibid, p. 133.
4. Ibid., p. 158.

consistent implementation of both "interface inheritance" and "implementation class inheritance" while still staying within the context of the specification. They have even taken a stab at defining some aspects of "component inheritance." This has proved to be challenging, but, as we will see, it has been possible.

Remote Interface Inheritance for Sessions and Entities

Perhaps the easiest inheritance feature to understand is the direct support for inheritance of methods defined in Remote interfaces. For instance, what if, in our example system, we need to add some subclasses of our EmployeeEJB, as shown in the UML diagram in Figure 20.10?

Our goal here is to have two subclasses of EmployeeEJB: SalariedEmployee and HourlyEmployee, with the two types of employees being paid differently. The first task is to define how the Remote interfaces, which specify the externally available methods of the EJB, are related. This turns out to be just as simple as you might think, as the following two code snippets show. (From now on, we'll deal with only one of the subclasses, for the sake of space.)

```
public interface Employee extends javax.ejb.EJBObject {
...
}

public interface SalariedEmployee extends Employee {
...
}
```

In VAJ and WebSphere, any Remote interface can inherit from any other Remote interface, so long as the entire tree is rooted in javax.ejb.EJBObject. The part that is more interesting than inheriting Remote interfaces—which, as we

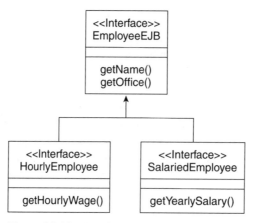

Figure 20.10   Interface Inheritance between EJB Remote Interfaces

saw, were clearly defined in the specification—is in the inheritance of Bean implementations that realize those interfaces.

Figure 20.11 shows how inheritance is used in WebSphere and VAJ. Although the example is that of an Entity EJB, the principles discussed apply just as well to Session EJBs.

As you can see, a parallel hierarchy of EJB implementation classes matches that of the Remote interfaces. The following two code snippets show how this is done:

```
public class EmployeeBean implements EntityBean {
...
}

public class SalariedEmployeeBean extends EmployeeBean {
...
}
```

A few rules govern EJB inheritance in both VisualAge and WebSphere. First, Entity Bean implementations cannot inherit from Session Bean implementations and vice versa. Second, with Session Bean implementations, you

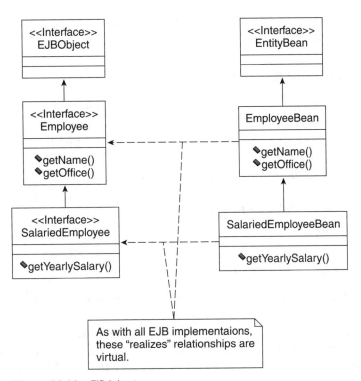

Figure 20.11   EJB Inheritance

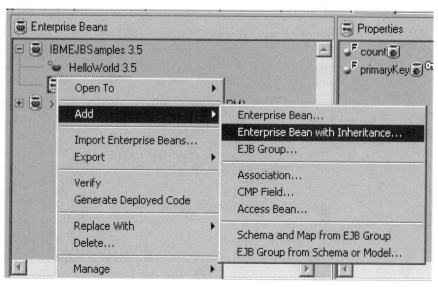

Figure 20.12   *Add>Enterprise Bean...with Inheritance*

cannot mix and match stateless and stateful Session Beans; the type of the parent must match the type of all its descendants.

Building Inherited Beans in VisualAge

Now that we've seen what inheritance of Remote interfaces and Bean implementations look like in EJBs, we can understand the support that VAJ gives developers in building EJBs with these relationships. To create an EJB that inherits from another EJB, you select a new menu selection from the *Add* menu in the *Enterprise Beans* pane of the EJB page called *Enterprise Bean with Inheritance...*, as seen in Figure 20.12. When this menu item is selected, you see the dialog in Figure 20.13, which allows you to create an EJB that uses inheritance.

Inheritance of Home Interfaces

At this point, inheritance of Home interfaces cannot be supported while maintaining compliance with the EJB specification, mostly, as the EJB 1.1 FAQ suggests, because of the required method signatures for "find-by-primary-key" methods. Each Home interface must include a method findByPrimaryKey (Key inKey), which returns an instance of its EJB class. If a parent class and

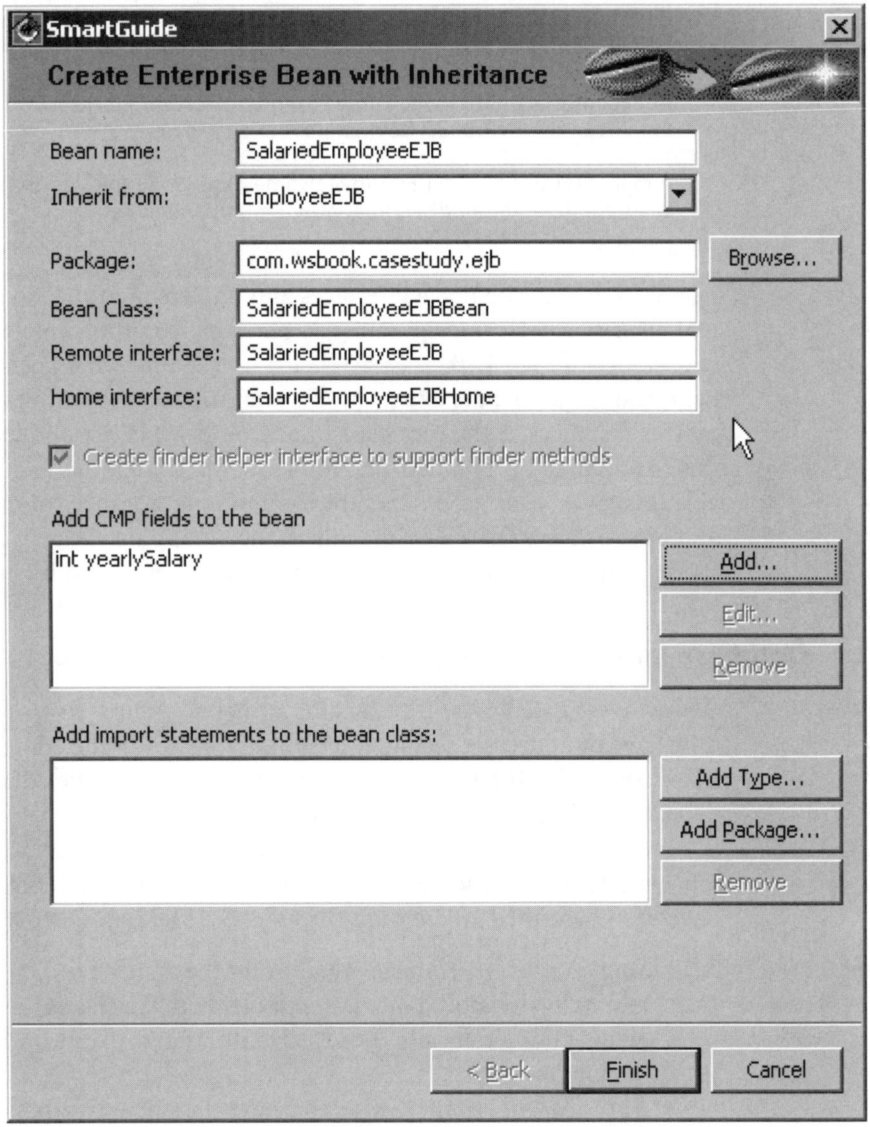

Figure 20.13 Inheritance *SmartGuide*

subclass tried to define these methods, a signature conflict would be created in the subclass. For example:

```
public interface EmployeeHome extends javax.ejb.EJBHome {
Employee findByPrimaryKey(EmployeeKey key)...;
}
public interface SalariedEmployeeHome extends EmployeeHome {
SalariedEmployee findByPrimaryKey(EmployeeKey key);
}
```

Even though the Home interfaces and implementations do not have a formal inheritance relationship, they do participate in the implementation of the inheritance of their EJB classes. When a user defines an association to an inheritance hierarchy, the expectation is that the members of that association may be instances of the root class or any of its subclasses. In order to satisfy this requirement, the finders on Homes in inheritance hierarchies need to be able to answer a mixed enumeration containing instances of the root EJB class and its subclasses. Based on the inheritance-mapping strategy chosen, the root Home will implement its finders with queries over the tables of its subclasses.

Database Inheritance Strategies

We've investigated what it means for an EJB to inherit from another EJB. We now have to address a second question that arises in the context of an Entity EJB: How is this inheritance relationship preserved in the database that makes up the Bean's persistent store?

Inheritance can be represented in a relational database in two different schemes. These schemes and their relative advantages and disadvantages have been described at length in [Brown 96]. The two schemes are

- *Single-table inheritance,* whereby all the attributes of all the classes in a hierarchy are stored in a single table, with special SQL select statements taking out only those attributes that are appropriate for any particular class.
- *Root-leaf inheritance,* whereby each class in a hierarchy corresponds to a table that contains only those attributes defined in that class and the key columns that are shared by all members of the hierarchy. An *n*-way SQL join is required to assemble any particular instance of a class from its corresponding table and all the tables above it in the inheritance hierarchy.

Briefly, the major advantage of the first scheme is speed, and its major disadvantage is the size of the table: for example, the number of null columns. The major advantage of the second scheme is its close correspondence to the object model; its major disadvantage is the time it takes to do the necessary joins.

CMP Entity Support for Inheritance

Both of these schemes are supported to one degree or another in VAJ for container-managed (CMP) EJBs. Which scheme a programmer chooses depends on his or her own interpretation of the benefits and liabilities of each in a particular situation.[6]

The choice of which to use is also limited by the method by which the Entity EJBs are constructed. In a top-down EJB approach, in which database tables are generated from the attributes present in EJBs, a single-table model is used for simplicity. In a bottom-up approach, in which Entity EJBs are generated from the columns and tables available in a database schema, inheritance cannot be reliably inferred from a database schema, so no inheritance mapping is applied, by default. However, in the meet-in-the-middle approach, in which schema and EJB design are developed independently and then mapped into each other, all schemes are supported.

We don't have a good reason to use EJB inheritance in the time-sheet-management application. Most cases for EJB inheritance stem from having the inheritance in the object model and wanting this directly reflected in the EJB implementation, particularly when there is benefit to the root Home interface finder methods returning heterogeneous collection of EJBs. The other big benefit of object inheritance in general, decoupling between client type dependence and runtime type implementation, is supplied with all EJBs through the two Remote interfaces.

Summary and Preview

In this chapter, you've learned how VisualAge for Java supports single-valued and multivalued associations between CMP Entity EJBs. This feature allows you to represent relationships in the database and in the EJB model in the same way. This support is crucial for implementing the EJBs in our sample application and will be necessary for most real-world client applications using CMP Entity EJBs as well. We also introduced the notion of inheritance in EJBs and the support VAJ provides to implement this relationship. In the next chapter, we look at Bean-managed persistence.

---

6. You may wish to reference the following two articles by Kyle Brown and Scott Rich when building EJB inheritance hierarchies, particularly CMP Entity Bean hierarchies, in VAJ: "Basic Schema Mapping and EJB Inheritance," http://www7.software. ibm.com/vad.nsf/Data/Document2330?OpenDocument&p=1&BCT=3&Footer=1, Advanced Schema Mapping and EJB Inheritance", http://www7. software.ibm.com/vad.nsf/Data/Document2341?OpenDocument&p=1&BCT=3&Footer=1.

CHAPTER 21

Bean-Managed Persistence

In earlier chapters, you have seen how the EJB specification provides for persistence management in EJB implementations. Although data can be stored and retrieved from a database by both Session and Entity EJBs, the primary component type defined in the specification for persistent data storage and retrieval is the Entity EJB. The specification describes two options for Entity Beans: container-managed persistence (CMP) and Bean-managed persistence (BMP). CMP implicitly applies persistence to Enterprise Beans, relieving the Bean developer of having to code for it. A detailed discussion of the implementation of CMP EJBs in WebSphere and VisualAge for Java can be found in Chapters 17, 19, and 20. BMP, on the other hand, requires the Bean developer to implement persistent operations within Bean class methods. This chapter helps you understand the basics of writing BMP Beans that work in WebSphere.

Applying BMP

By definition, the life span of a Session Bean is the same as the lifetime of the user or "session" referencing the Bean instance. Therefore, persistence is not usually applied to Session Beans. On the other hand, Entity Beans can exist between server recycles, so persistence is a requirement. Entity Beans represent an underlying data source or application and as such require access to them (Figure 21.1). The data access calls necessary to store the state of a BMP Entity Bean in a persistent store are defined in methods implemented to satisfy the Entity Bean component contract (Table 21.1).

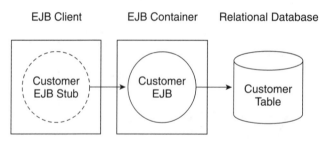

Figure 21.1   Entity Bean Data Source Relationship

Table 21.1   Entity Bean Persistence Methods

Method	Purpose
ejbCreate()	Insert Entity Bean state into a data source.
ejbRemove().	Remove Entity Bean from an underlying data source.
ejbFind<method>()	Retrieve Entity Bean instances based on the finder method signature.
ejbLoad()	Refresh Entity Bean state from the data source.
ejbStore()	Update data source attributes with the Entity Bean state.

Bean developers can use the Java Database Connectivity (JDBC) API or any other vendor-supplied framework, such as an object relational (OR) mapping product, to access data sources. We begin by examining this approach and then investigate some of its ramifications.

At first, simply nesting JDBC calls in Entity Bean methods might seem like a reasonable approach to implementing persistence. However, a more flexible and reusable design can be produced if requests are forwarded to a mapping class, similar to the mapping design described in Chapter 3 and Appendix A. We will cover that approach at the end of this chapter.

A Simple BMP Bean

We will go ever so slightly outside the bounds of our example so far in order to investigate how BMP Beans are written and what advantages they offer. So far, we have dealt with only one aspect of our business domain: the time-sheet aspect of a human resources system. However, any large company also has other systems. Suppose that we are building our system for an airline or a travel agency and are dealing with a frequent-traveler program. In this sort of program, one of the primary objects involved will be a Customer. Viewing

Customer information and making modifications to it constitutes the bulk of the activity in this system. Thus, we can imagine that we have an object, CustomerEJB, having the following interface:

```
import javax.ejb.*;
import java.rmi.*;
package com.wsbook.casestudy.ejb;

/**
 * CustomerEJB Remote Interface
 */
public interface CustomerEJB extends EJBObject {
int getAccountBalance() throws RemoteException;
String getCustomerName() throws RemoteException;
int getCustomerNumber() throws RemoteException;
void setAccountBalance(int acctBal) throws RemoteException;
void setCustomerName(String custNm) throws RemoteException;
}
```

That interface definition shows a simple Remote interface that defines a Customer consisting of a unique number—the primary key of our BMP Bean—a name, and an account balance. The Home interface for the EJB too is simple and straightforward:

```
import java.rmi.*;
import javax.ejb.*;
package com.wsbook.casestudy.ejb;

/**
 * The Home interface for the CustomerEJB Entity Bean
 */
public interface CustomerEJBHome extends EJBHome {

CustomerEJB create(int cNum, String cName) throws CreateException,
RemoteException;

CustomerEJB findByPrimaryKey(CustomerEJBKey key) throws RemoteException,
FinderException;
}
```

In this case, we are taking a very simple approach, having defined the simplest Home interface possible: a create() method taking as its arguments a new Customer number and name and a findByPrimaryKey() method.

Rather than walk through the entire EJB class, we'll look at selected parts of the EJB and see how it was written using VisualAge for Java and how it can be tested there and used in WebSphere. First, let's examine the class definition of our CustomerEJBBean:

```
import javax.naming.*;
import java.sql.*;
import java.rmi.RemoteException;
```

```
import java.security.Identity;
import java.util.Properties;
import javax.ejb.*;
import com.ibm.db2.jdbc.app.stdext.javax.sql.*;

/**
 * CustomerEJBBean is an Entity Bean class with BMP fields
 */
public class CustomerEJBBean implements EntityBean {
    private javax.ejb.EntityContext entityContext = null;
    final static long serialVersionUID = 3206093459760846163L;

    private int customerNumber;
    private java.lang.String customerName;
    private int accountBalance;

    public static final String LOAD_STRING = "SELECT cNum, cName, acctBal
from Cust WHERE cNum = ?";
    public static final String FIND_BY_PRIMARYKEY_STRING = "SELECT cNum from
Cust WHERE cNum = ?";
    public static final String UPDATE_STRING = "UPDATE Cust SET cName = ?,
acctBal = ? WHERE cNum = ?";
    public static final String INSERT_STRING = "INSERT INTO Cust(cNum, cName,
acctBal) VALUES (?, ?, ?)";
    public static final String REMOVE_STRING = "DELETE from Cust where cNum =
?";
    /* Create SQL is CREATE TABLE Cust (cNum INTEGER NOT NULL, cName
VARCHAR(60), acctBal INTEGER) */

    private DataSource ds;
    public static final String DATASOURCE_NAME = "jdbc/MyDataSource";
}
```

The first few lines declare the class as being an implementer of the EntityBean interface and declare the entityContext and serialVersionUID instance variables. The *Create EJB SmartGuide* in VisualAge for Java generated that much for us. The only difference in the initial generation of this EJB was that we chose the EJB to be an *Entity EJB with Bean-Managed Fields,* a choice we have not previously made. We also added three instance variables—customer Number, customerName, and accountBalance with the *Add Field SmartGuide* and then promoted the getters and setters for each of these variables to the Remote Interface. One exception is that we did not promote the setter for customerNumber to the Remote interface; as this variable will hold our primary-key value, we don't want clients to be able to change the primary key of a CustomerEJB object.

The next few lines begin to get interesting. Here, we declare several final static String variables to hold SQL statements: the SQL that our persistence methods will execute to store or to retrieve our Bean data from the database. We will look at some of these in more depth later.

Finally, we declare an instance variable of type DataSource and declare a final static String value that names a DataSource. To understand what this means and why we need it, we need to investigate how JDBC connection pooling works in WebSphere.

WebSphere JDBC Connection Pooling

One of the most expensive JDBC operations in both time and memory is obtaining a database connection. Connections are the primary objects in the JDBC API; everything else in JDBC depends on having a valid connection. Connections are expensive to obtain, and any particular database can handle only a limited number of concurrent client connections. Therefore, it behooves a Java developer to create connections only when absolutely necessary. A common mechanism by which this is done is to "pool" connections: to have a set of open connections from which a connection may be drawn, used, and returned to the pool so that it is created only once but may be used many times. This sort of connection pooling is a standard feature of the JDBC 2.0 API as implemented in WebSphere.

In WebSphere, the basis for connection pooling is that you obtain a DataSource object from the JNDI context: the same JNDI context used to obtain EJB Home references. A DataSource object is created in the administration console and is specific to a particular database driver and database name. Your code can obtain database connections from the DataSource by sending it the getConnection() method. This can be seen in the getConnection() method of our CustomerEJB BMP Bean, as follows:

```
/**
 * This method returns a JDBC Connection from a DataSource
 * Creation date: (7/15/2000 3:53:52 PM)
 * @return java.sql.Connection
 */
public Connection getConnection() throws SQLException, RemoteException {
    if (ds == null) {
        try {
            Properties props = new Properties();
            props.put(Context.INITIAL_CONTEXT_FACTORY,
"com.ibm.ejs.ns.jndi.CNInitialContextFactory");
            props.put(Context.PROVIDER_URL, "iiop:///");
            // fill in the properties
            InitialContext initContext = new InitialContext(props);
            ds = (DataSource) initContext.lookup(DATASOURCE_NAME);
            if (ds == null)
                throw new RemoteException("Could not initialize
DataSource in getConnection()");
        } catch (NamingException e) {
```

```
              throw new RemoteException("Could not initialize DataSource
        in getConnection() —" + e);
            }
        }
        return ds.getConnection();
    }
```

We will use this getConnection() method in each of the persistence methods in our EJB. One more attribute of using JDBC connection pooling needs to be pointed out to emphasize why it is so crucial that you use the Web-Sphere JDBC connection pooling mechanism in your BMP Beans that use JDBC. One of the key points of the BMP portion of the EJB 1.0 specification is that the EJB container—or at least that part of it known as the transaction service in the EJB specification—is responsible for coordinating the EJB transaction and the database transaction. In other words, the EJB container, not the Bean implementation class, is responsible for committing the changes to the database. If it were the other way, each Bean would function within its own transaction, and it would be possible to have some changes within an EJB transaction committed to the database and others not.

WebSphere handles this coordination in BMP Beans through the JDBC connection pooling mechanism. In a container, all EJB Beans that request a JDBC database connection from a particular DataSource within a single EJB transaction are given references to the *same* JDBC database connection. The EJB container will handle committing this JDBC connection at EJB transaction commit time or roll the transaction back if the EJB transaction aborts. This is possible only if a JDBC connection is obtained through the connection pool. If a connection is obtained from outside the pool, by the standard JDBC mechanism of using a driver manager, the EJB container will not be aware of this connection and will not be able to control transactions for the connection.

If you want to use a DataSource in VisualAge for Java, you first have to set it up in the WTE. This can be easily done in the *WTE Control Center*. First, though, you have to start the persistent naming service (PNS), if it is not already started. Once the PNS has started, you can select the *DataSource Configuration* link in the *WTE Control Center*. Selecting this link displays the page in Figure 21.2.

When you click on the *Add* button, the dialog in Figure 21.3 appears, which allows you to specify the properties of a new DataSource. In this dialog, you can select the driver and enter the database URL of the database this DataSource will use. After filling out this dialog, click *OK* to add the DataSource to the previous list (Figure 21.4).

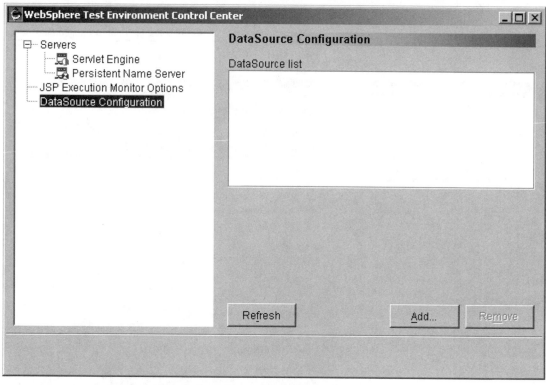

Figure 21.2 Selecting *DataSource Configuration*

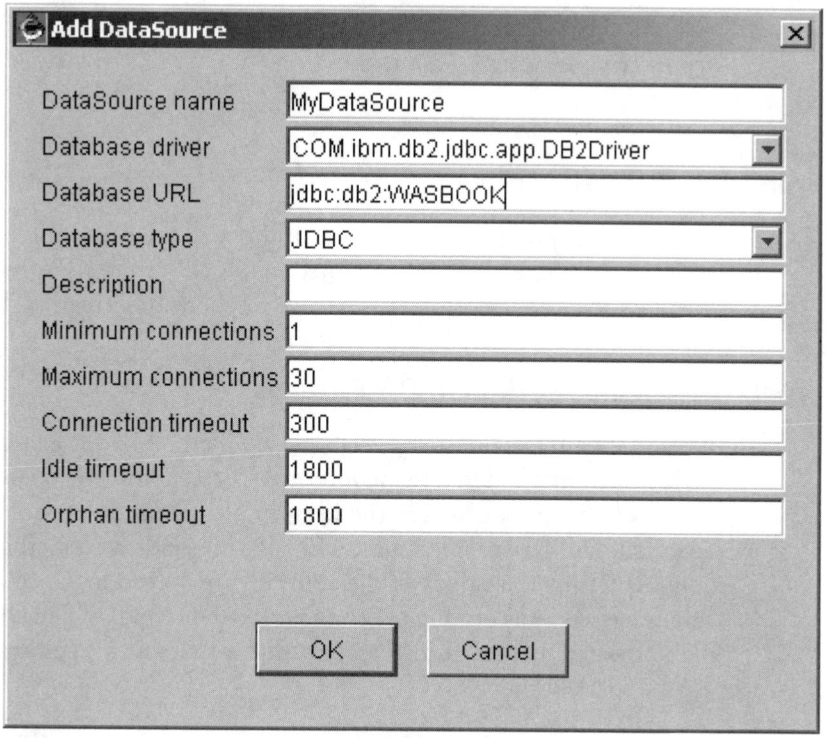

Figure 21.3 The *Add DataSource* Dialog

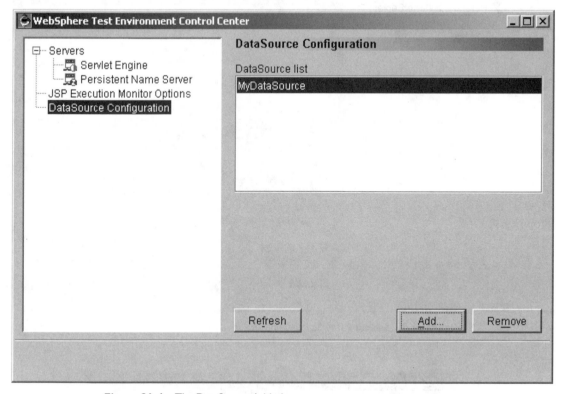

Figure 21.4   The DataSource Added

Examining BMP Persistence

Now that the preliminaries are out of the way, we can begin investigating how the persistence methods defined in a BMP Entity EJB are implemented. We will look at each of the persistence methods described earlier.

Writing ejbCreate() Method in BMP Beans

We will start by examining the ejbCreate() method in our example. Recall that each create() method in a Home interface corresponds to an ejbCreate() method with the same parameters in the Bean implementation class. However, this is where the similarity ends. In a CMP EJB, the ejbCreate() method is responsible only for setting the values of the container-managed instance variables to the values passed in as arguments to the create() method, whereas in a BMP EJB, the ejbCreate() method is also responsible for creating a persistent representation of the object in the data source. In our simple case, this means that it must *insert* a row into the SQL database. The code for the sample ejbCreate() method is as follows:

```
/**
 * ejbCreate method for a BMP entity bean
 * @return com.wsbook.casestudy.system.CustomerEJBKey
 * @param key com.wsbook.casestudy.system.CustomerEJBKey
 * @exception javax.ejb.CreateException The exception description.
 * @exception java.rmi.RemoteException The exception description.
 */
public com.wsbook.casestudy.ejb.CustomerEJBKey ejbCreate(int cNumber,
String cName) throws javax.ejb.CreateException, java.rmi.RemoteException {

        this.setCustomerNumber(cNumber);
        this.setCustomerName(cName);
        this.setAccountBalance(0);

        Connection jdbcConn = null;
        PreparedStatement sqlStatement = null;
        try {
            jdbcConn = getConnection();
            sqlStatement = jdbcConn.prepareStatement(INSERT_STRING);
            sqlStatement.setInt(1, customerNumber);
            sqlStatement.setString(2, customerName);
            sqlStatement.setInt(3, accountBalance);
            if (sqlStatement.executeUpdate() != 1) {
                throw new CreateException("Failure in ejbCreate() — row already
                exists");
            }
            return new CustomerEJBKey(cNumber);
        } catch (SQLException e) {
            throw new CreateException("Failure in ejbCreate() — " +
            e.getMessage());
        } finally {
            try {
                if (sqlStatement != null) sqlStatement.close();
                if (jdbcConn != null) jdbcConn.close();
            } catch (SQLException e1) {
                System.out.println("Exception caught in ejbCreate() — failure to
                close connection");
            }
        }
}
```

This method begins much as the corresponding method in a CMP implementation would; it sets the values of the instance variables customerNumber and customerName to the values passed in to the method. However, the lines following that section of code are unique to a BMP. The method next creates a PreparedStatement from the database connection it obtains

from the getConnection() method we discussed earlier. The Prepared
Statement will execute the following SQL, defined in the INSERT_STRING
constant:

    INSERT INTO Cust(cNum, cName, acctBal) VALUES (?, ?, ?)

Here, we substitute the customerNumber, customerName, and account
Balance values for the substitution parameters (?s) in the SQL statement. Finally, the method executes the SQL statement and checks to see that only one
row was added to the database. The final statement in the main branch of the
method is to then return a new instance of CustomerEJBKey created from the
newly assigned customer number.

Around this standard method flow is a set of try...catch blocks that handle
the various exceptions that may occur. You should pay particular attention to
the finally clause in this method; it ensures that the PreparedStatement is always
closed and that the JDBC connection is closed. In the case of a JDBC connection obtained from the WebSphere connection pooling classes, this means
that the connection is returned back to the pool rather than being deallocated
and destroyed.

Writing BMP Finder Methods

Now, we can move on to the process of finding a BMP EJB or a set of BMP
EJBs and then loading their state from the database. This process starts with
the execution of a finder method on the EJB Home, which in BMP EJBs corresponds exactly to an ejbFind...() method in the EJB Bean implementation
class. This is different from CMP EJBs, in which the finder implementation
was handled entirely in the generated EJB Home, with only some SQL provided by the programmer in a FinderHelper interface.

In our case, we have only one finder method in our EJB Home interface:
findByPrimaryKey(CustomerEJBKey). This corresponds to the ejbFindByPrimaryKey
(CustomerEJBKey) method whose code follows:

```
/**
 * ejbFindByPrimaryKey method. This method corresponds to findBy
 PrimaryKey() in the Home Interface.
 * @return com.wsbook.casestudy.system.CustomerEJBKey
 * @param primaryKey com.wsbook.casestudy.system.CustomerEJBKey
 * @exception java.rmi.RemoteException The exception description.
 * @exception javax.ejb.FinderException The exception description.
 */
public com.wsbook.casestudy.ejb.CustomerEJBKey
ejbFindByPrimaryKey(com.wsbook.casestudy.ejb.CustomerEJBKey key) throws
java.rmi.RemoteException, javax.ejb.FinderException {
```

```
            boolean wasFound = false;
            boolean foundMultiples = false;
            //CustomerEJBKey key = (CustomerEJBKey)
    getEntityContext().getPrimaryKey();
            Connection jdbcConn = null;
            PreparedStatement sqlStatement = null;
            try {
                // SELECT from database
                jdbcConn = getConnection();
                sqlStatement =
    jdbcConn.prepareStatement(FIND_BY_PRIMARYKEY_STRING);
                sqlStatement.setInt(1, key.primaryKey);
                // Execute query
                ResultSet sqlResults = sqlStatement.executeQuery();
                // Advance cursor (there should be only one item)
                // wasFound will be true if there is one
                wasFound = sqlResults.next();
                // foundMultiples will be true if more than one is found.
                foundMultiples = sqlResults.next();
            } catch (SQLException e) { // DB error
                throw new RemoteException("Database Exception " + e + "caught in
    ejbFindByPrimaryKey()");
            } finally {
                try {
                    if (sqlStatement != null) sqlStatement.close();
                    if (jdbcConn != null) jdbcConn.close();
                } catch (SQLException e1) {
                    System.out.println("Exception caught in
    ejbFindByPrimaryKey() — failure to close connection");
                }
            }
            if (wasFound && !foundMultiples) {
                return new CustomerEJBKey(key.primaryKey);
            } else {
                // Report finding no key or multiple keys
                throw new FinderException("Multiple rows or no rows found for
    unique key in ejbFindByPrimaryKey().");
            }
        }
```

The flow of this method is simple but surprising. This method simply creates a PreparedStatement executing the following SQL:

```
SELECT cNum from Cust WHERE cNum = ?
```

Why are we selecting only one column? The reason lies in the way in which BMP EJBs are instantiated from the database. When a finder method is called on an EJB Home, the container selects, more or less at random, an instance of the Bean implementation class to run the ejbFind... method on. When the ejbFind... method executes, it must return either a single primary-key object or, for finders that should return multiple objects, an enumeration

of primary keys. The container will then either retrieve from the instance
pool or create as many Entity Bean instances as necessary and set these primary key(s) in the EntityContext of those Beans. Finally, the finder method will
invoke ejbLoad() on these EJBs so that the latest values of the data can be
loaded from the database. In this way, the ejbFind... methods are more or less
"disconnected" from the rest of the EJB implementation and do not operate
on any of the instance variables of the Bean class but instead use only the arguments of the method as arguments to the SQL. Because all the SQL needs
to do is run a SELECT to find the primary-key columns of the table, based on
the parameters, we select only a single column in our example.

Because this is a single-valued EJB finder method, we need to return only
a single primary-key object. For this reason, we also want to make sure that
only *one* row exists in the table for this particular primary-key value, which
is why we check for additional rows being returned. We could do this by executing a COUNT function in the SQL, but this approach is probably just as
easy and as efficient.

Writing BMP ejbLoad() Methods

Now that we've seen how the finder methods will create the primary-key objects and set them into the Entity contexts, we are ready to move on to writing our ejbLoad() method. The source code for this method is as follows:

```
/**
 * ejbLoad method for CustomerEJB.
 * @exception java.rmi.RemoteException The exception description.
 */
public void ejbLoad() throws java.rmi.RemoteException {
    boolean wasFound = false;
    boolean foundMultiples = false;
    CustomerEJBKey key = (CustomerEJBKey) getEntityContext().getPrimaryKey();
    Connection jdbcConn = null;
    PreparedStatement sqlStatement = null;
    try {
        jdbcConn = getConnection();
        // SELECT from database
        sqlStatement = jdbcConn.prepareStatement(LOAD_STRING);
        sqlStatement.setInt(1, key.primaryKey);
        // Execute query
        ResultSet sqlResults = sqlStatement.executeQuery();
        // Advance cursor (there should be only one item)
        // wasFound will be true if there is one
        wasFound = sqlResults.next();
        if (wasFound) {
            // set the internal variables
            this.setCustomerNumber(sqlResults.getInt(1));
```

```
                this.setCustomerName(sqlResults.getString(2));
                this.setAccountBalance(sqlResults.getInt(3));
            }
            // foundMultiples will be true if more than one is found.
            foundMultiples = sqlResults.next();
        } catch (SQLException e) { // DB error
            throw new RemoteException("Database Exception " + e + "caught in
            ejbLoad()");
        } finally {
            try {
                if (sqlStatement != null) sqlStatement.close();
                if ( jdbcConn != null) jdbcConn.close();
            } catch (SQLException e1) {
                System.out.println("Exception caught in ejbLoad() — failure to close
                connection");
            }
        }
        if (wasFound && !foundMultiples) {
            return;
        } else {
            // Report finding no key or multiple keys
            throw new RemoteException("Multiple rows found for unique key in
            ejbLoad().");
        }
    }
```

The logic of this method is similar to that in ejbFindByPrimaryKey() but with a few key differences. First, the primary-key information used in the WHERE clause of the SELECT statement is obtained from the EntityContext, as we discussed earlier. Second, the SELECT statement itself retrieves values for all the columns in the table:

```
SELECT cNum, cName, acctBal from Cust WHERE cNum = ?
```

After retrieving the row from the ResultSet, the method sets the values of the instance variables in this EJB to be the values obtained from the corresponding rows in the result set. Note that this may involve some data type conversions or other translations. Although VisualAge and Web-Sphere provide helpful converter classes for converting data types, such as changing VARCHARS with yes or no to Booleans or converting Dates to Strings with a nonstandard format, these are available only in CMP Beans; if any data conversion is to be done in a BMP Bean, you must code it yourself.

Writing ejbStore() Methods

The next method to investigate is the ejbStore(), which the container calls at the end of a transaction or a business method to record the state of the EJB to the database. The implementation of this method is much like the implementation of the other methods you've seen:

```
/**
 * ejbStore method for CustomerEJB
 * @exception java.rmi.RemoteException RemoteException for errors.
 */
public void ejbStore() throws java.rmi.RemoteException {
    Connection jdbcConn = null;
    PreparedStatement sqlStatement = null;
    try {
        jdbcConn = getConnection();
        sqlStatement = jdbcConn.prepareStatement(UPDATE_STRING);
        sqlStatement.setString(1, customerName);
        sqlStatement.setInt(2, accountBalance);
        sqlStatement.setInt(3, customerNumber);
        if (sqlStatement.executeUpdate() != 1) {
            throw new RemoteException("No rows added — failure in ejbStore()");
        }
    } catch (SQLException e) {
        throw new RemoteException(e.getMessage());
    } finally {
        try {
            if (sqlStatement != null) sqlStatement.close();
            if (jdbcConn != null) jdbcConn.close();
        } catch (SQLException e) {
            System.out.println("Error in ejbStore() — failure to close");
        }
    }
}
```

In many ways, this method is the inverse of the ejbLoad() method. The SQL executed for this method follows:

```
UPDATE Cust SET cName = ?, acctBal = ? WHERE cNum = ?
```

As you can see, we set the SQL substitution parameters to contain the values of the customerName, accountBalance, and customerNumber variables. Just as in the case of ejbLoad(), if any data type conversion is to be done, you must do it in this method. That's as far as we will pursue this example. If you are interested in the implementation of ejbRemove(), consult the source code on the CD-ROM accompanying this book.

Why Use PreparedStatements?

When using JDBC, you have three options for your statements: A Statement is a class that can execute an arbitrary SQL String passed in to it. A Prepared-Statement refines a Statement by adding substitution parameters and by separating the SQL compilation process from the execution of the Statement. Finally, a CallableStatement takes away the SQL compilation process entirely by executing a SQL stored procedure. Normally, a PreparedStatement is used when you may reuse it and execute it multiple times. So, why have we used a PreparedStatement rather than a Statement in each of our examples, where this is not the case? The reason is that WebSphere implements a Prepared Statement cache on its JDBC connection pooling mechanism. WebSphere entirely skips the compilation process for any statement that matches one that it has stored in its cache. This can provide a significant performance boost at runtime, even though it might not appear from reading the code that any performance gain would be evident.

BMP versus CMP

What is the best approach to persistence? BMP builds data access within the Bean source. CMP keeps persistence requirements independent of the Bean itself. However, CMP may be limited to data sources supported by a vendor container mapping tool. The decision lies in data access requirements and whether an EJB server container supports these requirements. In this section, we examine some questions you can ask yourself about your particular project to help you determine whether BMP, CMP, or neither is right for a particular requirement.

Is there a set of objects—perhaps constituting a logical subsystem—that are both read and updated relatively frequently, with complex relationships between them changing rapidly? In a nutshell, this is the case for CMP Entity EJBs. When a set of complex relationships exists between different EJBs, the complexity of the programming of the relationship management becomes a key driver in choosing a solution. CMP Entity EJBs, especially as the code generators in VisualAge for Java, Enterprise Edition, implement them and are a compelling solution to this problem. The code generators in VisualAge for Java can handle complex single and multivalued relationships between different EJBs and handle EJB inheritance issues. VAJ also handles complex mapping between the EJB design and underlying relational database stores. When a tool can generate this code rather than its being laboriously hand coded, a system can be more easily adapted to changes in the requirements or the underlying data model.

Another attractive feature of CMP is its ability to manage optimization of the set of SQL calls that must be made in order to read or to write the persistent state of an EJB. For instance, the CMP model in WebSphere allows a set

of Entity EJBs to be read from a relational database in a find() method with
only a single SQL SELECT call, which is much more efficient than the default
BMP case, which requires N + 1 SQL calls to do the same thing.

*Do you have an object structure in your design that corresponds to a rela-
tional join, or do you see the need for a relational join to improve overall system performance?* For instance, suppose that the Customer has an Address
that indicates where the Customer lives. If we take the approach of making
both the Customer and the Address CMP Entity EJBs, as in the previous solution, we find that to obtain a Customer and an Address, we need to do two
SQL SELECT statements: one to select the Customer from the Customer table,
inside the findByPrimaryKey() of the *Customer* Bean, and another to select the
Address from the Address table, inside the findByPrimaryKey() of the *Address*
Bean.

However, this isn't necessary. In SQL, we can retrieve the data in both the
Customer and the Address objects with a single SELECT statement, using a
join if the two tables are linked by a foreign-key relationship.

The problem is that although you can do this in SQL, you can't do this in
the current implementation of CMP in WebSphere. In fact, no EJB server
handles relational joins well. VisualAge for Java does generated code for
WebSphere to handle simple relational joins with Entity EJBs but only where
two tables share the same primary key; it will not handle general foreign-key
relationships like the one described previously.

So, we are stuck with using a BMP solution. However, this is a good
thing. We can create what is called a *dependent object,* which simply means a
JavaBean, not an EJB, that the *Customer* EJB will create and return when
asked for an Address. We will create our *Address* JavaBean in the ejbLoad() of
our *Customer* BMP EJB.

We show how this would work in the following code fragment, which illustrates part of the implementation of the *Customer* BMP Entity Bean. (The
new part is in boldface.)

```
public class CustomerEJBBean implements EntityBean {
    ...
    private int customerNumber;
    private String customerName;
    private int accountBalance;
    private Address address;
    ...
}
```

Here, we see that in addition to such fields as customerName and account
Balance, we have a dependent object of type Address. The Address is defined as
follows. (Note that it would also have methods, which are not shown, for
setting and retrieving these values.)

```
public class Address implements java.io.Serializable {
    public String streetAddress;
    public String city;
    public String state;
    public String zip;
}
```

Now we can see how the ejbLoad() method would work and fill in the appropriate pieces of the EJB from each table:

```
/**
 * ejbLoad method comment
 * @exception java.rmi.RemoteException The exception description.
 */
public void ejbLoad() throws java.rmi.RemoteException {
    boolean wasFound = false;
    boolean foundMultiples = false;
    CustomerEJBKey key = (CustomerEJBKey) getEntityContext().getPrimaryKey();
    Connection jdbcConn = null;
    PreparedStatement sqlStatement = null;
    try {
        jdbcConn = getConnection();
        // SELECT from database
        sqlStatement = jdbcConn.prepareStatement(LOAD_STRING);
        sqlStatement.setInt(1, key.primaryKey);

        // Execute query
        ResultSet sqlResults = sqlStatement.executeQuery();
        // Advance cursor (there should be only one item)
        // wasFound will be true if there is one
        wasFound = sqlResults.next();
        if (wasFound) {
            // set the internal variables
            this.setCustomerNumber(sqlResults.getInt(1));
            this.setCustomerName(sqlResults.getString(2));
            this.setAccountBalance(sqlResults.getInt(3));
            this.setAddressFK(sqlResults.getInt(4));
            // Now create the dependent object
            // And set its variables, then add it to this bean
            Address addr = new Address();
            addr.setStreetAddress(sqlResults.getString(5));
            addr.setCity(sqlResults.getString(6));
            addr.setState(sqlResults.getString(7));
            addr.setZip(sqlResults.getString(8));
            this.setAddress(addr);
        }
        // foundMultiples will be true if more than one is found.
        foundMultiples = sqlResults.next();
    } catch (SQLException e) { // DB error
        throw new RemoteException("Database Exception " + e + "caught in
        ejbLoad()");
    } finally {
        try {
```

```
            if (sqlStatement != null) sqlStatement.close();
            if (jdbcConn != null) jdbcConn.close();
        } catch (SQLException e1) {
            System.out.println("Exception caught in ejbLoad() — failure to close
            connection");
        }
    }
    if (wasFound && !foundMultiples) {
        return;
    } else {
        // Report finding no key or multiple keys
        throw new RemoteException("Multiple rows found for unique key in
        ejbLoad().");
    }
}
```

Note that this method is very much like the previous implementation of the method, with the exception of loading the Address instance with the appropriate values. The SQL that is executed will also be different and will look like the following:

```
SELECT a.cNum, a.cName, a.acctBal, a.addressFK, b.streetaddress, b.city,
b.state, b.zipcode from Cust a, AddressEJB b WHERE cNum = ? AND a.addressFK
= b.addressKey
```

As you can see, this SQL performs a join on the Cust and AddressEJB tables, returning a result that contains columns from both tables. Now, this approach is probably best for those objects whose parts can be divided into read/write and read-only objects. When you try to update a dependent object, you encounter some additional problems. For instance, when the dependent object changes, you would need to be able to set it back into the EJB. Likewise, because updating a JOIN is problematic in SQL, you would need to execute multiple SQL UPDATE statements, one for each table, in the ejbStore() method.

Do you have an object structure that represents an $M \times N$ relationship in your underlying database? Here, we have an extreme version of the problem we just addressed. So far, we have examined 1–N and one-to-one relationships in EJBs: both CMP and, now, in BMP. However, $M \times N$ relationships are more problematic. In SQL, representing an $M \times N$ relationship is accomplished with the aid of a third table, often called a *relationship,* or *association, table.* This table maps the primary keys of the table on one end of the $M \times N$ relationship to the primary keys of the table on the other end of the relationship. However, this represents a problem when we try to map this to EJBs.

One of the assumptions that we have been implicitly making all along is that each EJB maps to one database table and one table only. In the dependent-objects case we have just seen, a situation in which an EJB may map to two tables, this can create problems in updating. However, this may

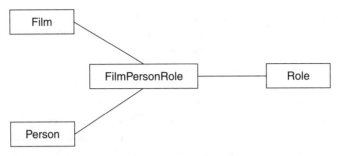

Figure 21.5   A Three-Way $M \times N$ Relationship

be the *only* solution that is acceptable. For instance, let's say that we have the three-way $M \times N$ relationship shown in Figure 21.5. This would occur if you were part of a project team that's building a Web site for purchasing newly pressed DVDs of classic American cinema. You will need to know how to search your database for different information about the films, the members of the cast and crew, and the roles that people played in the film. Figure 21.5 illustrates the relationship. For instance, Ron Howard was an actor before becoming a successful director. Similarly, Rob Reiner has sometimes appeared in his own films in both roles and still makes guest appearances as an actor in films directed by others.

   Although it is easy to state this problem, it is difficult to solve efficiently by using CMP EJBs. To solve this problem, we would create a CMP EJB for each table. The primary key of the middle EJB (FilmPersonRole) would be the entire set of columns in that table. We can show that the preceding procedure will work, but we haven't yet thought about how *efficient* the process is. What we are comparing against is the standard SQL solution; if you want to retrieve the People and Roles for a particular film, you can do this in the database in a single SQL statement: a relational join. However, it's not possible to do things quite as efficiently in the CMP EJB solution we've just outlined.

   For instance, here's the procedure for fetching back N Person-Role pairs for any particular film.

1. The custom finder method that locates FilmPersonRoles by film will require the execution of one SQL statement. (Select * from FilmPersonRole, where film = ?.) This statement will retrieve all the information for a FilmPersonRole.

2. N SQL calls to retrieve each Person corresponding to each individual FilmPersonRole. (Select * from Person, where personId = ?.) The reason is that each call to getPerson() will invoke findByPrimaryKey() on the PersonHome class uniquely.

3. *N* SQL calls to retrieve each Role that corresponds to each individual FilmPersonRole. (Select * from Role, where roleId = ?.) The reason is that each call to getRole() will invoke findByPrimaryKey() on the RoleHome class uniquely.

So, we conclude that for *N* rows in the FilmCrewRole table, $2N + 1$ SQL calls must be made to retrieve all the EJBs that correspond to those relationships. Obviously, this is not a very efficient solution. We need a way to retrieve this information in fewer SQL calls. That will be the driving force behind the BMP solution that we will evaluate next.

The basic idea of this solution is the same as in the previous case: that we can reduce the total number of SQL calls required if we do *not* make some of the objects EJBs in our small system. If we create only a single EJB named *FilmPersonRole* that has three methods—getFilm(), getPerson(), and getRole()—that are dependent objects, we can reduce the total overhead of SQL calls.

How much improvement does this new solution have over our previous solution? Let's look at the number of SQL calls executed to retrieve *N* FilmPersonRoles:

- A single SQL call will retrieve the keys of the FilmPersonRole table that is called from the custom finder (the ejbFindByFilm()) method.
- *N* SQL calls will be invoked from the ejbLoad() methods to load the data for each FilmCrewRole (the join between the Film, Person, and Role tables).

So, the BMP solution ends up with a total of $N + 1$ SQL calls, significantly fewer than the previous all-CMP solution.[1]

Is there a set of objects that are updated very infrequently but whose state is frequently read? Almost every program has at least some object of this sort. For instance, insurance applications have a number of codes for various medical procedures that change vary rarely, perhaps only once a year. Another, more common type of object like this is a political entity, such as a county or a state. These change exceedingly rarely, but the list of them may be expanded if an application must be made to work internationally.

Here, we have a problem that sounds as though it could be solved in the same way as the previous case but instead is best done by a stateless Session Bean that returns JavaBeans—dependent objects—whose states are read once, usually on program startup, and stored in a static variable of a nonEJB

---

1. For more information on this solution, including source code for the BMP solution, see *http://www7.software.ibm.com/vad.nsf/data/document2354?OpenDocument&p=1&BCT=1& Footer=1.*

class. So why not use the previous solution and let a BMP Entity manage these? The reason is that these objects are not transactional at all but rather read-only. Although it depends on the caching option used by the EJB container, usually a BMP's state is read once per transaction. In this case, the state will always be the same, regardless of the transaction. If we read the state once and hold it in memory for the lifetime of the JVM Bean, we will save a large number of needless calls to the back-end storage mechanism.

Do you need to display and scroll through a large (>50-element) list in your application? Many applications need to be able to display large lists of data from which users select. In general, this should be avoided because scrolling through a large list is a poor user-interface design choice, but sometimes, it is the only option.

When you are retrieving data to display in a list, you generally need only a small subset of data. Often, lists contain only a unique identifier and some sort of user-readable representation of the list element. In this case, using a custom finder method to retrieve a large set of Entity EJBs, only to then use a few data elements in each EJB, is a huge waste of resources. Instead of retrieving an enumeration of EJBs and then walking over the enumeration, create a simple stateful Session EJB that can retrieve only those pieces of data that are necessary through a very minimal SQL query. You can then return the information in a very simple form, such as a hash table of key values to the Strings that will be displayed in the list.

Once the user has made a selection from the list, you can use an EJB to retrieve and to operate only that selected object by finding the EJB with a findByPrimaryKey() method, using the key value that corresponds to the selected element. In practice, we have found this solution to be more than twice as fast as iterating through an enumeration of Entity EJBs in most circumstances and to generate less garbage as well.

Summary and Preview

We've only scratched the surface of BMP in this chapter. We have examined what the EJB API provides for BMP Entity Beans, but we haven't had a chance to fully examine the issues of object-relational mapping or even to investigate obtaining BMP EJBs from data sources other than a relational database. However, this discussion should ground you in the principles necessary for moving on to these more advanced options when you are ready. Next, we turn to building layered architectures for EJB Systems.

CHAPTER 22

Building Layered Architectures for EJB Systems

You may be wondering how we will connect the code that we developed on servlets and JSPs, which operate in terms of JavaBeans, with the EJBs. But first, let's review a few of the basic points about EJB programming.

- Clients can obtain information from an EJB only by sending messages defined in the Remote interface to the EJB.
- Remote method invocations on an EJB use RMI over IIOP as the communication mechanism between JVMs.
- All reads, changes, and updates of an EJB should occur within the context of an EJB transaction.

Together these three points can lead to great inefficiencies in a system design that does not take them into account. The basic problem is that the overhead of the number of network calls required to manipulate complex data entirely by EJB Remote methods, such as using the Proxy pattern, is restrictive [Gamma]. Proxy is a powerful mechanism, but it's not the right solution in all situations. Proxy has the unfortunate side effect that *every* call to a proxy crosses the network. In many situations, this is not only too expensive, but also unnecessary.

Problems with an All-EJB Solution

Consider what would happen if we simply made a one-for-one replacement of the JavaBeans we used in the earlier chapters with EJBs. In many cases, this would work fine: The EJBs that you have seen are in many ways identical to the JavaBeans that you saw in the earlier chapters. However, the fact remains that each call to the EJBs has the potential of being a network call, which means that if you want to write a servlet to display a TimeSheet and all its component TimeSheet entries, a huge number of network calls could be made. For instance, consider the following scenario.

Our hypothetical "TimeSheetDisplay" servlet obtains a reference to a TimeSheet and sends it messages to obtain the state, week-end date, and approving Employee. However, the Employee is an EJB also, so obtaining the approver's name requires another network call. Finally, the servlet obtains the enumeration of TimeSheetEntries. The servlet dereferences each TimeSheetEntry and sends the Entry messages to obtain the date, hours, and Project. *Project* is another EJB, so obtaining the project name is yet another network call. So, what we've seen is that displaying even this small amount of data has resulted in $(N * 4) + 4$ calls that can cross the network, where N is the number of entries attached to the TimeSheet. If each RMI-over-IIOP call had even a small overhead of, say, 50 msec from marshaling and unmarshaling parameters and if a time sheet has ten entries, we have added 2000 msec = 2 *seconds* of extra execution time just in crossing the network.

Using Entity Beans as application-specific domain objects also has other significant problems. Let's say that our time-sheet tracking program is a hit, and teams start investigating the other areas of bookkeeping related to time-sheet reporting. Another team wants to use your *Employee* EJB but, alas, needs a slightly different set of domain behavior, such as different validation or a different Bean representation. Because you don't want the Entity Bean to turn into a single object that knows everything and does everything, the second team instead subclasses its EJB from the first EJB.

This works just fine until the team comes across the following hierarchy created by the first team: an *Employee* EJB with two subclasses, Hourly Employee and SalariedEmployee. Now, to add its behavior, the second team must now make two new subclasses. As you can see, if the inheritance hierarchy increases in width, this problem becomes bigger and bigger.

Then the team decides to take the easy way out and practice copy-cut-and-paste reuse of the code. Unfortunately, this doubles the amount of work that the application deployer has to do: assigning security and transaction capabilities to two sets of Beans. Also, you now have an interesting problem inside the EJB server: two Beans in competition to the same database rows. Unless the isolation level is set to TRANSACTION_SERIALIZABLE, you have the possibility of phantom reads and other transaction problems. However, setting the isolation level to TRANSACTION_SERIALIABLE can have significant performance penalties.

So, the only real answer to this situation is not to do that. It becomes apparent to people thinking about reuse that you should not put application-specific business logic in Entity EJBs at all. Simply treat an Entity EJB as an OO view of a database. Having association navigation methods on your Entity EJBs is OK and is not domain behavior per se. The key here is that if your Entity Beans are data gateways—pure data sources—they have a better chance of being shared among multiple applications. Just as in the previous pattern, business logic should be placed in its own set of application-specific JavaBeans that operate on the information in the Entity Beans.

So, how do we arrive at a solution that does this? How do we keep our Entity Beans generic and globally useful while still allowing for application-specific business logic? Is there a way to reduce that $(N * 4) + 4$ network-crossing calls we saw earlier? Finally, what if we could also gain the advantage of having the "TimeSheet" servlet be unaware of the fact that it was using EJBs—for example, not having to handle RemoteExceptions, know about JNDI lookups, and so on. What if we could also make it transparent to the controller (servlet) code if we were using EJBs or another persistence mechanism, such as JDBC? The solution that we are going to suggest can in fact gain all these advantages. At its heart, it is just another application of application layering.

The Session Facade and Data Bean Solution

The first linchpin to solving the problem is a simple observation about how WebSphere's implementation of RMI over IIOP works. The observation is that WebSphere's ORB is smart enough to implement EJB Remote methods differently, based on whether the client—the class making the Remote method call—and the server—the EJB or EJB Home—are within the same JVM. If both client and server are within the same JVM, WebSphere does not make a call using RMI over IIOP but instead makes a local method call from client to server. Only if client and server are in different processes is a call over the network necessary. So, obviously, part of the strategy to make our EJBs perform well is to reduce the overhead of the network calls by keeping as many calls as possible within the same JVM.

Next, because RMI over IIOP is an extension of RMI, any serializable object can be passed as a method argument to an EJB Remote method call or returned as a method result from an EJB Remote method call. This one fact allows us to develop an architecture that can help reduce drastically the number of network-crossing calls needed by our servlets.

Simply put, our solution is to use a pass-by-value approach to obtain information from our EJBs rather than a pass-by-reference (proxy) approach.

We will ask a special EJB, which we will call a *session facade,* for a serializable Java object, which we will call a *data Bean,* that contains all the information necessary to display an entire business result or to perform a business operation. The data Bean will be the repository for business logic, such as validation and calculations that do not need to be persistent and whose results are unique to each instance. Likewise, when we need to update information in an EJB, we will send that information as a data Bean to the session facade, which will determine which EJBs to update, so that all updates can happen within the context of a single EJB transaction. Figure 22.1 illustrates this process.

As you can see, a servlet asks a Session EJB for a data Bean. The Session EJB is responsible for obtaining the information that will make up the data Bean from one or more Entity EJBs. The Session EJB is then responsible for creating a serializable object, a data Bean, and copying the information into the data Bean. Finally, the data Bean is returned as the result of the message sent to the Session EJB. On the client side, the servlet will then obtain the individual data items from the data Bean and display them to the user by either embedding the Bean directly in a JSP or by another mechanism. The point is that all the calls made from the servlet to the data Bean are local calls; only the call made from the servlet to the Session EJB is a network call. This avoids the additional overhead of the all-EJB solution and usually results in a faster overall system, even though the total number of Java methods invoked is greater.

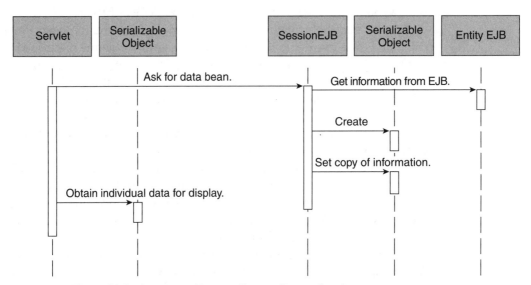

Figure 22.1   Interaction Diagram Showing Session Facade

As important as the performance increase is in using a Facade and Data Bean solution, however, there is an even more important architectural reason to employ this pattern. If an Entity Bean is accessed directly from a client program, then each individual method sent to the Entity Bean will be its own transaction, unless the client-demarcated transactions are used. As we mentioned earlier in Chapter 18, using client-demarcated transactions is never a good practice because of the complexity that managing them adds to the client. This also violates the principles of layering that we have been discussing all along—exposing an Entity Bean (essentially a persistence layer object) to the client code will unnecessarily tie the client to a particular persistence implementation.

In fact, when you consider that each Entity Bean method invoked from a client will be its own transaction, you see that the performance overhead of such a solution quickly becomes unacceptable. Remember that when using Option C caching, each new transaction involving an Entity Bean will result in the Entity Bean having to reload its data from the database. If read-only methods are not marked as such, then the data will be replaced in the database at the end of the transaction as well. This will result in two completely unnecessary SQL calls (a SELECT and an UPDATE) for each remote method invocation. Obviously if you multiply the overhead for each call by hundreds or thousands of remote calls you can see that the performance degradation to the system will be huge. For these reasons, we cannot recommend ever accessing an Entity Bean directly from a client program, and always will instead recommend using a Facade and Data Bean solution.

Examples of the Session Facade/Data Bean Solution

A Simple Example from the Case Study

Now that you have seen the basic outline of the session facade/data Bean solution, you are ready to start stepping through the code of one of the simplest examples of how this solution is put to use in our case study. We will see how to obtain a set of data Beans corresponding to the list of projects available for selection. This list will be used a few times in our case study code; for example, the TimeSheetMediator asks for a list of projects to display in a drop-down list so that someone entering a new TimeSheetEntry can assign it to a project.

Figure 22.2 shows a high-level object interaction diagram of how this is accomplished. After glancing through the diagram, look at the in-depth treatment of the example code that follows to see why each of the classes in the interaction diagram is necessary.

A few basic points underlying the OID are worth pointing out, as they have a bearing on understanding the code that is presented later.

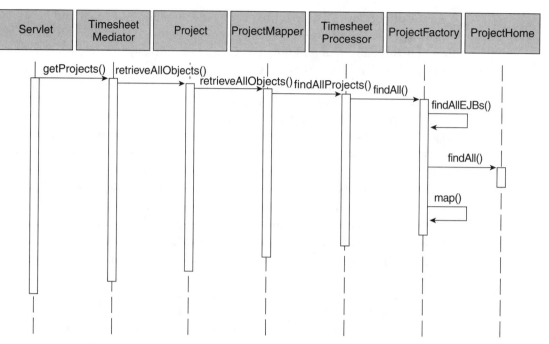

Figure 22.2   Interaction Diagram to Get List of Projects

- Each Domain object class has a Mapper class that is responsible for retrieving instances of the class from the persistent store.
- The Mapper classes all interact with a single session facade, a stateless Session EJB of the type TimesheetProcessor.
- Methods in the TimesheetProcessor pass responsibility for creating and mapping domain objects into Entity Beans (and vice versa) to Factory objects that are subclasses of the class DomainFactory.

The last point may cause some confusion. Why add another layer of objects beyond the session facades and data Beans? The problem is that data Beans are not full-fledged components like EJBs and so don't have built-in support for object creation and management. We could put the necessary code to build and maintain these objects directly into the session facade EJBs themselves, but the result would be lots of unnecessarily duplicated code. Instead, you should put the responsibility for building them into a separate set of Factory objects, whose facilities can be used from multiple session facades or other parts of your program.

Before we move on, we need to evaluate an alternative to building Factory classes. VisualAge for Java's EJB Development Environment also contains a set of code generators to generate CopyHelper JavaBeans that contain copies of the information in Entity Beans. These CopyHelper Beans are also capable of synchronizing this information back to the database by generating, on the Entity EJB, two methods, called copyToEJB() and copyFromEJB(), that update and read, respectively, the information from the Entity Bean. In this case, the Entity Bean itself acts as the data Bean Factory and creates a JavaBean that contains a copy of the information it contains.

However, this solution assumes that "one size fits all," that all clients of an Entity Bean will want the same (complete) set of attributes from the Entity Bean copied to a JavaBean. When you begin to consider Entity Beans that have relationships to other Entity Beans, it becomes clear that this may cause problems, as the question arises as to how "deep" the copy should be. Having external Factories is a more flexible solution in that it allows for the construction of different data Bean JavaBeans containing different subsets of the data in the Entity Bean(s).

So, having covered that, you're now ready to start at the beginning, at the retrieveAllObjects() method in the TsObject superclass:

```
/**
 * Return Vector of objects for Type.
 * Creation date: (2/2/00 10:38:18 PM)
 */
public Vector retrieveAllObjects() throws MappingRuntimeException {

    Mapper aMapper = null;
    try {
     aMapper = computeMapper(); }
    catch (Throwable e) {AppService.trace(e.toString()); }
    return aMapper.retrieveAllObjects();
}
```

In our case, the type of object that this message will be sent to is a Department; the computerMapper() method will return an instance of Project Mapper. The outline of this class is shown in Figure 22.3.

ProjectMapper implements all the abstract methods defined by the interface Mapper. ProjectMapper is a subclass EJBMapper, which gives it some utility methods for creating an initial context and obtaining an instance of TimesheetProcessor. For instance, createProcessor() is the method that obtains an instance of the TimesheetProcessor, as the following code demonstrates:

```
/**
 * Return a reference to a TimesheetProcessor.
 * Creation date: (3/20/00 12:38:33 PM)
 */
public void createProcessor() {
   try {
```

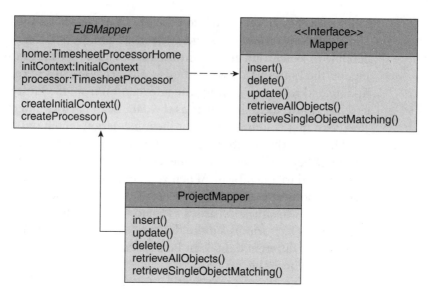

Figure 22.3   Object Model Showing Mapper Design

```
        java.lang.Object homeObject = initContext.lookup("TimesheetProcessor");
        home = (TimesheetProcessorHome)javax.rmi.PortableRemoteObject.
        narrow(
                (org.omg.CORBA.Object) homeObject,
        TimesheetProcessorHome.class);
        processor = home.create();
    } catch (Exception e) {
        System.out.println("Exception " + e + " in createTimesheetProcessor()");
    }
}
```

Now that you've seen where the TimesheetProcessor instance—held in the processor variable—comes from, you can understand the implementation of the retrieveAllObjects() message in the ProjectMapper class:

```
public java.util.Vector retrieveAllObjects() {
    Vector allObjects = null;
    try {
        allObjects = processor.findAllProjects();
    } catch (FactoryException e) {
        System.out.println("Exception caught: " + e);
    } catch (RemoteException e) {
        System.out.println("Remote Exception caught: " + e);
    }
    return allObjects;
}
```

As you can see, there's not much to this method. All the work is done on the

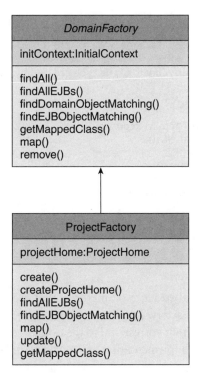

Figure 22.4 Factory Hierarchy

server side. To see this, take a look inside the implementation of findAll Projects() in the TimesheetProcessorBean class:

```
public java.util.Vector findAllProjects() throws FactoryException {
    return projFactory.findAll();
}
```

Again, this method is simply "passing the buck" to the Factory. The ProjectFactory that is held in the projFactory instance is held in a private variable that is initialized during the ejbCreate() method. The methods of this class are thread safe, so it is not a problem for the EJB implementation to hold on to an instance of that type, even though the TimesheetProcessor is a stateless Session Bean. Remember that the TimesheetProcessor is a facade and therefore shouldn't do much on its own but instead should hide the complexity of an underlying subsystem. In this case, the Entity Beans and the Factories make up the subsystem hidden by this facade.

To finally see some "real work" done, you need to look into the Project Factory class. Figure 22.4 illustrates the inheritance hierarchy of the Project Factory class.

ProjectFactory inherits a number of template methods from its superclass, DomainFactory. One of these methods is the findAll() method:

```
/**
 * Return a Vector of all Domain objects of the type created by this factory.
 * Creation date: (3/19/00 7:59:51 PM)
 * @return java.util.Vector
 */
public Vector findAll() throws FactoryException {
    Enumeration allEJBs = findAllEJBs();
    Vector vector = new Vector();
    while (allEJBs.hasMoreElements()) {
        Object next = allEJBs.nextElement();
        Object foo = javax.rmi.PortableRemoteObject.narrow(next,
        getMappedClass());
        Object mapped = map((EJBObject) foo);
        vector.addElement(mapped);
    }
    return vector;
}
```

This method relies on three abstract hook methods that are redefined in each of the subclasses of DomainFactory. The first, findAllEJBs(), returns an Enumeration of all the Entity EJBs that correspond to the domain object type. To see what is meant, take a look at the implementation of findAllEJBs() in ProjectFactory:

```
protected Enumeration findAllEJBs() throws FactoryException {
    try {
        return projectHome.findAll();
    } catch (Exception e) {
        throw new FactoryException("Wrapped exception : " + e);
    }
}
```

At this point, we've almost unwound all the way to the bottom. Project Home's findAll() method is a custom finder method. As with all custom finders in WebSphere and VisualAge, the only user-provided code necessary to implement this finder is in the ProjectEJBBeanFinderHelper interface, which simply defines a findAllWhereClause string as being 1 = 1 so that all rows will be included in the result Enumeration.

The findAll() uses two more hook methods. The first, getMappedClass(), simply returns the class object that EJBObjects should be narrowed to. In the ProjectFactory case, the object returned here is ProjectEJB.class. The final hook method map(EJBObject obj), the more interesting one, returns a domain object that contains the information in the EJBObject passed into it as an argument. The following implementation of map() in ProjectFactory shows a simple example of this:

```
/**
 * Return an instance of Project created from the ProjectEJB passed in as an
 * argument
```

```
 * Creation date: (2/20/00 9:41:44 PM)
 */
public Object map(EJBObject input) throws FactoryException {
    ProjectEJB ejb;
    try {
        ejb = (ProjectEJB) input;
    } catch (ClassCastException e) {
        throw new FactoryException("Attempt to map a non ProjectEJB in
        ProjectFactory:" + e);
    }
    Project proj = null;
    try {
        proj = new Project();
        proj.setNumber(Integer.toString(((ProjectEJBKey) ejb.getPrimaryKey()).
        projNumber));
        proj.setName(ejb.getName());
    } catch (Exception e) {
        System.out.println("Exception " + e + " caught in ProjectFactory.map()");
        throw new FactoryException("Wrapped Exception " + e+ " caught in
        ProjectFactory.map()");
    }
    return proj;
}
```

This method is a bit more interesting than some of the earlier ones. The first try...catch block in the method is meant to catch runtime problems that would result from trying to map something that is not a ProjectEJB. The second try...catch block does the bulk of the work of this method. As you can see, the method first creates a new instance of Project and sets its number and name variables to the values obtained from the ProjectEJB passed in as an argument. Presuming that this all works correctly, the result returned from this method is an instance of Project and works its way back to the previous method and is finally added to the vector that is returned by the TimesheetProcessor.

A More Complex Example

Now that you understand the basic way in which facades, Factories, data Beans, and Entity Beans interact, you are ready to move on to understanding a more complex interaction: the way in which Timesheets, including all their component objects, are fetched for display. We start by showing the entire hierarchy of Factories that we have used in our solution (Figure 22.5).

As you can see, most of the complexity in this solution is in the Timesheet Factory and TimeSheetEntryFactory classes. A TimesheetFactory contains references to both an EmployeeFactory and a TimeSheetEntryFactory. In fact, TimeSheetEntryFactories exist only in the context of a TimesheetFactory; you never map TimeSheetEntries to their corresponding EJBs outside the context of

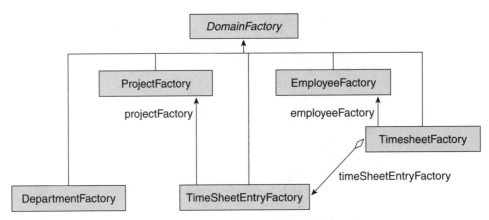

Figure 22.5   Factory Relationships for Underlying Object Relationships

a Timesheet. Likewise, a TimeSheetEntryFactory contains a reference to a ProjectFactory. These relationships exactly parallel those of the JavaBeans these Factories create and the Entity EJBs from which they store and retrieve their data.

The Timesheet creation process matches that of the Project creation process because they share most of the same classes and methods. Because everything upstream of the TimesheetProcessor is very nearly the same, you can start learning about the differences there. You can start examining the creation of Timesheets at TimesheetProcessor's getAllTimesheets() method:

```
public java.util.Vector findAllTimesheets() throws FactoryException {
    return timesheetFactory.findAll();
}
```

Remember that just as in the previous example, the implementation of findAll() in DomainFactory relies on the findAllEJBs() and map() hook methods. In fact, the implementation of findAllEJBs() looks almost exactly like that in the previous example:

```
protected Enumeration findAllEJBs() throws FactoryException {
    try {
        return timesheetHome.findAll();
    } catch (Exception e) {
        throw new FactoryException("Wrapped exception : " + e);
    }
}
```

The real difference occurs in the implementation of map(). Examine the following code and then take a look at the explanation that follows:

```
/**
 * Insert the method's description here.
 * Creation date: (2/26/00 3:53:49 PM)
```

```
        * @return com.wsbook.casestudy.domain.TimeSheet
        * @param ejb com.wsbook.casestudy.ejb.TimeSheetEJB
        */
       public Object map(EJBObject input) throws FactoryException{
          TimeSheetEJB ejb;
          TimeSheet timeSheet;
          try {
             ejb = (TimeSheetEJB) input;
          } catch (ClassCastException e) {
             throw new FactoryException("Attempt to map a non TimeSheetEJB in
             TimeSheetFactory:" + e);
          }
          try {
             timeSheet = new TimeSheet();
             timeSheet.setTimesheetID(Integer.toString(((TimeSheetEJBKey)
             ejb.getPrimaryKey()).timeSheetId));
          // handle Employee mappings
             Employee approver = (Employee)getEmployeeFactory().map
             (ejb.getApprovingEmployee());
             timeSheet.setApprovedBy(approver);
             Employee submitter = (Employee)getEmployeeFactory().map
             (ejb.getSubmittingEmployee());
             timeSheet.setEmployee(submitter);
             Enumeration entries = ejb.getEntries();
          // handle Entry mappings
             Vector newEntries = new Vector();
             while (entries.hasMoreElements()) {
                Object next = entries.nextElement();
                Object foo = javax.rmi.PortableRemoteObject.narrow(next,
                TimeSheetEntryEJB.class);
                Object entry = getEntryFactory().map((TimeSheetEntryEJB) foo);
                newEntries.addElement(entry);
             }
             timeSheet.setEntries(newEntries);
          // Now handle date mapping
             DateFormat df = new SimpleDateFormat ("MM/dd/yyyy");
             Date date = df.parse(ejb.getWeekend());
             Calendar aCalendar = Calendar.getInstance();
             aCalendar.setTime(date);
             timeSheet.setWeekend(aCalendar);
          // Finally handle State creation and mapping
             String stateName = ejb.getState();
             TimeSheetState state = null;
             if (stateName.equals("APPROVED"))
                state = new ApprovedState(timeSheet);
             else
                state = new PendingState(timeSheet);
             timeSheet.setState(state);
          } catch (Exception e) {
             System.out.println("Exception " + e + " caught in
             TimeSheetFactory.map()");
             throw new FactoryException("Wrapped Exception " + e+ " caught in
             TimeSheetFactory.map()");
```

```
    }
    return timeSheet;
}
```

If you dissect this method, you can learn how the various pieces work and understand it as a whole. First, note, that the initial try...catch block that checks the type of the argument is exactly the same as in the map() method for ProjectFactory.

The first real difference occurs when the method begins to handle the relationships between the Timesheet and the Employees that submit and approve the Timesheet. Take a look at the following code snippet taken from the middle of the method:

```
Employee approver = (Employee)getEmployeeFactory().map
(ejb.getApprovingEmployee());
timeSheet.setApprovedBy(approver);
```

The first line of code turns over the problem of creating a new instance of Employee from an *Employee* EJB to the EmployeeFactory class. The code uses the EJB relationship getter method getApprovingEmployee() to obtain an EJB object (an *Employee* EJB) and then asks the EmployeeFactory to return an Employee that is created from that information. Finally, the code sets the Timesheet's approving employee to be that Employee. The same solution is repeated for the submitting employee a few lines later.

The next problem the method addresses is creating the TimeSheetEntry instances that a Timesheet holds. The following code snippet illustrates how this is done:

```
Enumeration entries = ejb.getEntries();
Vector newEntries = new Vector();
while (entries.hasMoreElements()) {
    Object next = entries.nextElement();
    Object foo = javax.rmi.PortableRemoteObject.narrow(next,
    TimeSheetEntryEJB.class);
    Object entry = getEntryFactory().map((TimeSheetEntryEJB) foo);
    newEntries.addElement(entry);
}
timeSheet.setEntries(newEntries);
```

First, the method obtains the list of entries—*TimeSheetEntry* EJBs—from the *Timesheet* EJB and then enumerates over this list of entries. However, the interesting thing is that after obtaining each entry from the Enumeration, with nextElement(), the method uses PortableRemoteObject.narrow() on the object that is returned from the Enumeration. This is a key point in using EJB relationships in WebSphere and VisualAge. You always need to narrow() objects returned from 1–N relationships before you begin sending methods to them. The object returned from the Enumeration is not a stub for the actual EJB stub but rather is only a generic EJB stub.

Once it has narrowed the EJB stub returned from the Enumeration, the method then calls the map() method in TimeSheetEntryFactory to map this EJB to a *TimeSheetEntry* JavaBean. Having done this, the method adds the new TimeSheetEntry to the vector and loops around again. Finally, the method sets the list of entries in the Timesheet to the vector of TimeSheetEntries that it has just created.

Next, the method performs some Date manipulation to take the String that is returned from the EJB and convert it into a Calendar so that it can be set into the Timesheet. Only the last part of this method, which creates the State, deserves more inspection. Take another look at the following code snippet:

```
String stateName = ejb.getState();
TimeSheetState state = null;
if (stateName.equals("APPROVED"))
    state = new ApprovedState(timeSheet);
else
    state = new PendingState(timeSheet);
timeSheet.setState(state);
```

The method creates a brand new state object whose type is based on the information stored in the state attribute of the EJB. This kind of object creation based on static information is common in cases in which the object created has no internal state or whose internal state can be entirely recreated, as it can here. When storing objects like this—which are often Flyweights, as in [Gamma]—you are frequently better off storing a simple String that can be interpreted at runtime rather than storing a more complex representation of the object.

An Updating Example

The inverse operation of creating a Timesheet from the corresponding EJB is updating the state of a *Timesheet* EJB from information held in a Timesheet object. Again, start at the TimesheetProcessor class, this time in the update(Timesheet) method:

```
/**
 * Update a Timesheet's EJBs from information in a Timesheet
 * Creation date: (3/19/00 5:42:35 PM)
 * @param param com.wsbook.casestudy.domain.Department
 */
public void update(TimeSheet timesheet) throws FactoryException {
    timesheetFactory.update(timesheet);
}
```

Moving into the TimesheetFactory class, you see the following code in the update(Timesheet) method:

```
/**
 * This method updates the EJBs that are related to the TimeSheet passed in.
 * Creation date: (2/27/00 2:44:43 PM)
```

```
/**
 * This method updates the EJB's that are related to the TimeSheet passed in.
 * @param timesheet com.wsbook.casestudy.domain.TimeSheet
 */
public void update(TimeSheet timesheet) throws FactoryException {

    try {
        int timeSheetId = Integer.parseInt(timesheet.getTimesheetID());
        TimeSheetEJBKey newKey = new TimeSheetEJBKey(timeSheetId);
        TimeSheetEJB ejb = timesheetHome.findByPrimaryKey(newKey);

        String stateName = timesheet.getState().getStatename();
        ejb.setState(stateName);

        // This date code updates the ejb's weekend field with a String
        Calendar calendar = timesheet.getWeekend();
        DateFormat df = new SimpleDateFormat ("MM/dd/yyyy");
        String dateString = df.format(calendar.getTime());
        ejb.setWeekend(dateString);

        // Next handle the submitter and approver

        EmployeeEJB submitter = (EmployeeEJB) employeeFactory.findEJBObject
Matching(timesheet.getEmployee());
        ejb.setSubmittingEmployee(submitter);

        EmployeeEJB approver = (EmployeeEJB) employeeFactory.findEJBObject
Matching(timesheet.getApprovedBy());
        ejb.setApprovingEmployee(approver);

        // When changing a dependent object in a 1-N relationship there are two
ways of handling the
        // update problem.  Since objects can be removed or added to the
relationship, you can either
        // track each remove/add individually, or instead remove everything and
then re-add them.
        // We are taking the second tack.  It is slower, but easier to implement.

        Enumeration ejbEntries = ejb.getEntries();
        while (ejbEntries.hasMoreElements()) {
            EJBObject ejbObject = (EJBObject) ejbEntries.nextElement();
            ejbObject.remove();
    }

        // Now cycle through the TimeSheetEntries and add the new EJB's
        Enumeration enum = timesheet.getEntries().elements();
        while (enum.hasMoreElements()) {
            TimeSheetEntry entry = (TimeSheetEntry) enum.nextElement();
            entryFactory.create(entry, newKey);
        }

    } catch (Exception e) {
        System.out.println("Exception " + e + " caught in create()");
```

```
    throw new FactoryException("Wrapped Exception " + e + " caught in
create()");
    }
```

Again, take a look at the method as a whole and then dissect it into its component parts. The first few lines are quite simple: The method creates a new EJB key instance from the Timesheet's ID value and then uses that key to obtain a reference to the proper *TimeSheet* EJB by using findByPrimaryKey(). The next couple of lines are also simple. The method sets the state name and week-end attributes to the appropriate values by asking the Timesheet for its values and doing the appropriate conversions.

Employee relationships are set in the reverse of what happened on the map() case. Take a look at the following code fragment:

```
EmployeeEJB submitter = (EmployeeEJB)
employeeFactory.findEJBObjectMatching(timesheet.getEmployee());
ejb.setSubmittingEmployee(submitter);
```

Here, you see that the method uses the EmployeeFactory method findEJBObject Matching() to obtain a reference to the *Employee* EJB that corresponds to the Employee object held by the Timesheet. The method then sets the submitting employee attribute in the *TimeSheet* EJB by using the setSubmittingEmployee() method. The code for setting the approving employee works in the same way.

The final, and most interesting, section of this method handles setting the relationship between the *TimeSheet* EJB and its *TimeSheetEntry* EJBs. Look closely at the following segment of code:

```
Enumeration ejbEntries = ejb.getEntries();
while (ejbEntries.hasMoreElements()) {
    EJBObject ejbObject = (EJBObject) ejbEntries.nextElement();
    ejbObject.remove();
}

// Now cycle through the TimeSheetEntries and add the new EJBs
Enumeration enum = timesheet.getEntries().elements();
while (enum.hasMoreElements()) {
    TimeSheetEntry entry = (TimeSheetEntry) enum.nextElement();
    entryFactory.create(entry, newKey);
}
```

As the comment in the method text explains, you can handle changing the elements of a 1–N relationship in two ways. The client code could have added new TimeSheetEntries, deleted old TimeSheetEntries, or changed existing ones, so we could either track each change individually by, say, using the Command pattern, or we could instead delete all the old entries and recreate new ones. The second solution is definitely easier to implement, but it works only in cases in which the total number of objects participating on the N side of the 1–N relationship is very small. In our case, this is true, so the inefficiency of deleting the old objects and recreating new ones won't significantly slow the application down.

So, that's exactly what this code does. The first while loop cycles through all the existing EJB relationships and deletes the *TimeSheetEntry* EJB objects connected to this particular *TimeSheet* EJB. The second while loop then creates new *TimeSheetEntry* EJBs, using the create() method of the TimeSheet EntryFactory class. That method follows:

```
/**
 * This method creates a TimeSheetEntryEJB associated with the TimeSheetEJB
   having parentKey
 * Creation date: (2/27/00 3:09:30 PM)
 * @param entry com.wsbook.casestudy.domain.TimeSheetEntry
 */
public void create(TimeSheetEntry entry, TimeSheetEJBKey parentKey) throws
FactoryException {
try {
    int timeSheetEntryID = Integer.parseInt(entry.getTimeSheetEntryID());
    double hours = entry.getHours();

    // This date logic obtains a date string for the create() method below
    Calendar calendar = entry.getDate();
    DateFormat df = new SimpleDateFormat ("MM/dd/yyyy");
    String dateString = df.format(calendar.getTime());

    int project = Integer.parseInt(entry.getProject().getNumber());
    TimeSheetEntryEJB entryEJB = timesheetEntryHome.create(timeSheetEntryID,
    hours, dateString, project, parentKey.timeSheetId);

} catch (Exception e) {
    System.out.println("Exception " + e + " caught in create()");
    throw new FactoryException("Wrapped Exception " + e+ " caught in create()");
    }
}
```

You've now made it all the way to the end. The create() method called by this method is implemented in the *TimeSheetEntry* EJB, which you saw in an earlier chapter. There's nothing much else to note in this method, other than the ever-present conversion of Date to String format.

Summary and Preview

In this chapter, you've learned how to build an architecture that reduces the total number of network-crossing EJB Remote method calls while still allowing for the display and manipulation of complex data. You've also seen how to make Entity EJBs generic data sources for multiple projects, enterprise-wide, while still maintaining the ability to have application-specific business logic. The key to achieving this is to have the following types of objects in your architecture:

- Data Beans are serializable Java objects that contain a subset of the information held in an Entity EJB. They should contain some of the system business logic, such as validation, dynamic calculations, and so on. They can manage their own relationships to other data Beans; for instance, an Employee can contain an Address. These JavaBeans are suitable for display by a JSP.
- Session facades are Session EJBs that provide distributed access to common ways of creating, updating, and managing data Beans for client programs, such as servlets. Making the facades Session EJBs allows for flexibility in distributing the database lookup logic to other machines beyond the second-tier application servers running presentation logic. Session facades also serve as the initial point of contact for control of transactions; that is, they start the transactions that other EJBs participate in. The facades themselves should be somewhat small, probably no more than 40 methods. The methods in the facades should be *very* small—five lines of code or less—because they pass all the "work" on to the Factories.
- Factories are standard Java classes responsible for building data Beans and updating data sources from the information passed to them as data Beans that have changed. Factories know about the different data sources, manage connections to the data sources, create instances of the data Beans, fill in the instances of the data Beans, and so on. Each Factory can retrieve and update data to/from multiple data sources. Every "root" object in your object model should have a Factory. (Root objects are those that "contain" other objects.)
- Entity EJBs are standard data sources that can be globally useful across the enterprise. Entity Beans should not contain application-specific domain logic; nor should they be constrained to work within a single application.

You've learned about building these objects and how they interact to form a layered architecture that incorporates the best advantage of EJBs. In the next chapter, we'll deploy EJBs into WebSphere.

CHAPTER 23

Deploying EJBs into WebSphere

The VisualAge for Java IDE is excellent for creating and testing EJBs. Previous chapters have shown the convenience and time-saving features of the EJB *SmartGuides,* which provide a wizard-driven approach to generating Session and Entity Beans and their supporting classes. Complete applications can be tested in the environment, using its full debugging and inspection capabilities.

Eventually, however, the code you develop must be exported out of the VisualAge for Java environment into a production environment. Typical Java applications can be deployed on any workstation that has a JVM and the required Java class files. The most efficient way to deploy these types of applications is in the form of a JAR file, which allows any number of application class files to be packaged and compressed into a single file. As you know, EJBs are housed and accessed from an EJB container that resides on an Enterprise JavaBean server (EJS), separate from the application or the client. The client requires only a subset of the files required by the EJS. Therefore, applications using EJBs must be deployed and packaged for a client and also deployed for a vendor-supplied EJB container, such as WebSphere.

The EJB specification does not indicate how an EJB container carries out Bean persistence, transaction support, and management. Because the specification provides APIs only from a client's point of view, only application server vendors provide containers. Likewise, deployment conditioning of constructed Beans is a function of the vendor-supplied container. If in the future, a container specification is adopted, a market of container providers and tools could possibly thrive.

In the meantime, EJBs' deployment semantics are neutralized across various vendors through the EJB.*jar* file specification. This chapter describes the production of this file and provides instructions on how EJBs can be deployed to the EJB container supplied with the WebSphere application server.

Because the VisualAge for Java development environment has built-in EJB construction and deployment capabilities, we focus on the deployment capabilities of the IDE. Later in this chapter, we discuss how to use the WebSphere application server, independent of VisualAge for Java, to deploy any valid EJB.*jar* file.

Exporting EJBs from VisualAge for Java

VisualAge for Java supplies three ways to export EJBs from the development environment.

- If exporting for a nonWebSphere EJS, the EJB *.jar* file option can be used to export EJB information to a standard *deployable JAR file*. The resulting JAR file will be processed into deployed code by the EJS.
- If the EJBs are being deployed to WebSphere, a *deployed JAR file* can be exported that includes EJS (WebSphere) required classes. Required classes consist of stubs, skeletons, and supporting "helper" and "holder" classes for WebSphere's RMI over IIOP implementation.
- EJB classes required only by the client can be exported in a *client JAR file,* ready for deployment to a client runtime environment.

The following sections describe how each of these options is used in the VisualAge for Java IDE. After that, we discuss some best practices in deploying applications and outline the steps for deploying our case study application.

EJB JAR File

The EJB specification explains how unassembled EJBs are packaged, along with information about how they are deployed in a standardized EJB JAR file. *Unassembled* is the operative word in the previous sentence. Because containers implement EJB management in a nonstandardized fashion, they are obliged to read the information stored in the EJB JAR file and to produce classes to manage the persistent and transactional state of the EJB. Likewise, the container will also produce appropriate client access mechanisms, such as stubs and skeletons, so that the EJBs can be remotely accessed by client applications. This provides EJB vendor neutrality, as any compliant EJB container can turn any standard EJB JAR file into a set of vendor-specific deployed JAR files. Each EJB container will produce its own set of support classes to implement the distribution, persistence, and management functions. These support classes, which are specific to each EJS vendor, should be transparent to Bean providers and application assemblers (Bean users).

According to the EJB 1.0 specification, an EJB JAR file must also contain a deployment description in the form of a serialized set of objects; the EJB

1.1 standard uses an XML document instead. WebSphere 3.0.2 and 3.5, which follow the EJB 1.0 standard, use a serialized deployment descriptor instance. Future releases of WebSphere will follow the EJB 1.1 standard and use an XML document. (For a discussion of our recommendation for various transaction-related deployment descriptor and attribute settings, see Chapter 18.) One deployment descriptor per file is allowed and must be stored in the file with the following name:

META-INF/ejb-jar.ser

Along with the deployment descriptor, each EJB must include the following class files:

- The Bean class
- The Home and Remote interfaces
- If an Entity Bean, the primary key class

Classes and interfaces that the Home and remote interfaces are dependent on can also be included in the JAR file and can include inherited classes and interfaces.

Creating an EJB JAR File from VisualAge for Java

Generating an EJB JAR file is similar to exporting a typical nonEJB *.jar* file from VisualAge. Begin by opening the EJB panel of the workbench. When you select an EJB group or a specific Bean, you can then select *Export* from the right-mouse-button menu. The available menu options are shown in Figure 23.1.

As you can see, the three *.jar* file types are available from this menu. A fourth menu option, *EJB JAR for CB,* is useful only if you are programming to WebSphere Enterprise Edition (Component Broker). But because we are concerned only with WebSphere Advanced Edition, we can safely ignore that option.

When you select the *Export>EJB JAR...* option, a dialog similar to the standard export file will appear (Figure 23.2).

Whether selecting a single EJB or an EJB group, you will, in most cases, want to keep the default selections on this dialog. However, you may sometimes want to include other classes and resources in the exported JAR file. For instance, if your EJB uses a utility class that is part of your application, you may want to include that class in your EJB *.jar* file. Clicking the *Select referenced types and resources* button will ensure that these classes are included. Later in this chapter, we discuss how the exported EJB is made deployable by the WebSphere application server. We also discuss some best practices for segregating your application in order to help you understand what classes to include in your *.jar* files.

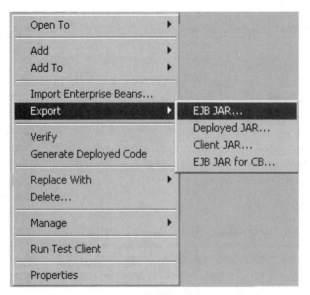

Open To	▶
Add	▶
Add To	▶
Import Enterprise Beans...	
Export	▶
Verify	
Generate Deployed Code	
Replace With	▶
Delete...	
Manage	▶
Run Test Client	
Properties	

Export submenu:
- EJB JAR...
- Deployed JAR...
- Client JAR...
- EJB JAR for CB...

Figure 23.1   VisualAge EJB Exporting Options

SmartGuide   ☒

Export to an EJB JAR File

JAR file: `d:\IBMVJava\ide\export\export.jar`   Browse...

What do you want to include in the JAR file?

☑ beans   Details...   1 selected

☑ .class   Details...   3 selected

☐ .java   Details...   3 selected

☑ resource   Details...   0 selected

Select referenced types and resources

Options

☑ Include debug attributes in .class files.

☑ Compress the contents of the JAR file.

☐ Overwrite existing files without warning.

< Back   Finish   Cancel

Figure 23.2   EJB *.jar* Export Option

VisualAge Deployed JAR File

As mentioned previously, an EJB *.jar* file contains only the bare minimum of information required for deployment by an EJB-compliant application server. However, when you are developing in VisualAge for WebSphere, you will instead usually want to export the full set of classes required by WebSphere. Exporting a *deployed JAR file* means that the support classes required for WebSphere will be included in the resulting JAR file. The JAR file will then simply be added to the WebSphere container, discussed later.

Exporting a deployed *.jar* file is very similar to the process for exporting EJB JAR files. The only difference is that once you have selected an EJB or an EJB group, select the *Export>Deployed JAR* option. A dialog similar to the EJB JAR export will appear (Figure 23.3).

Deployed JAR files can also include any referenced types and resources required by EJBs defined in the group. Remember that only the WebSphere

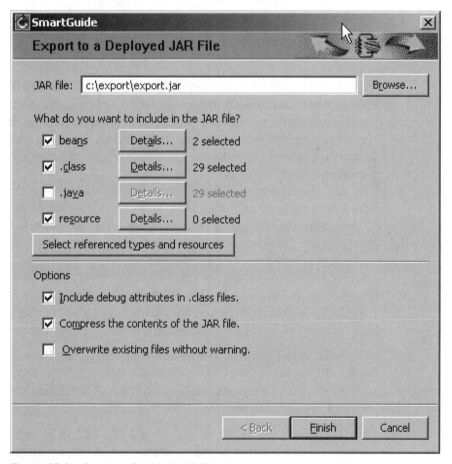

Figure 23.3 Export to Deployed JAR File

application server can use deployed JAR files; other application servers cannot use them.

Client JAR File

Another convenient feature of VisualAge for Java is the option to export a special JAR file that contains only the classes required by an application client. This will include the Home and Remote interfaces and the client stubs for the EJB Home and EJB but not any of the server-side implementation classes. A client JAR file can be generated from VisualAge for Java, just as an EJB JAR file was exported.

Best Practices for EJB Deployment

In Chapter 6, we discussed some issues in deploying servlets and JSPs into Web applications within an application server. The issue becomes even more complex when we add EJBs into the mix of objects to be deployed into WebSphere.

A full consideration of deployment into WebSphere involves issues well beyond the scope of this book; for instance, a deployment plan for WebSphere has to take into account failover planning, capacity planning, and consideration of time and effort spent in administering the WebSphere system. However, we can address some of the simpler yet crucial issues. Perhaps the simplest but most key question is, "How do I structure my applications and files?"

In Chapter 6, we explained that a Web application specifies a class path for servlets and other classes used by your servlets. This class path, sometimes called the *reloadable servlet class path,* is unique to that particular Web application. However, we also need to consider two other class paths, as they have a bearing on the deployment of EJBs into a WebSphere Application Server. Web applications can share classes through these other class paths, called the *dependent class path* and the *application class path.* Table 23.1 outlines the class paths, where they are set, and how they are used.

When you deploy an EJB, WebSphere will need to find three sets of things:

- The EJB base files: Remote and Home interfaces, Bean implementation, and so on
- The EJB deployment files: stubs, skeletons, and ties
- Dependent classes

The first two will be contained in a deployed EJB file generated by VisualAge or by WebSphere. However, we recommend that the dependent

Table 23.1 Class Paths

Class path	Set in	Used for
Reloadable servlet class path	Administration console at the Web application level.	Servlet and related class files specific to a Web application are placed on this class path.
Application class path	Administration console at the application server level. This is set by using the —classpath option of the JVM command line.	Files specific to a single application server used by either servlets or EJB deployed to that application server.
Dependent class path	Administration console at the node level.	Files shared by all application servers and the administration server on a node. Files that are required for EJB deployment, such as stub generation, must be placed on this class path.

classes instead be placed on the dependent class path of the node rather than in the EJB JAR file. The first reason for this is the high likelihood that these classes will be used by more than one EJB. Placing them in a separate, shared *.jar* file allows you to set up the dependent class path only once and then to deploy as many EJBs that use these dependent classes as you need. The alternative—deploying dependent classes into each EJB *.jar* file—is more problematic: You have to remember to include them in every *.jar* file, but it's very easy to forget one or more, which, depending on your code, may not become apparent until runtime.

You also need to be sure to place a client *.jar* file for your EJBs in the reloadable servlet class path of any Web applications that have servlet clients of your EJBs. This will allow your servlet clients to find and to use the stubs necessary to connect to the EJB Homes and EJBs. If your servlet client also needs any of the same dependent classes used by your EJB, the JVM will look for them on the application server class path and the dependent class path, after looking on the Web application class path. One thing to keep in mind is that you should minimize the scope of any class as much as possible; if a class is not needed by anything other than a servlet or a group of servlets in a Web application, place it only on the Web application class path. If the class is needed by an EJB but is not needed for deployment, place it on the application server class path. Only if a class is needed for EJB deployment or when multiple application servers will share it should it be placed on a node-level dependent class path. This will reduce the coupling between applications by reducing the "overlap" of the set of classes they will share.

Now that we've examined some of the issues of WebSphere class paths and how *.jar* files should be placed on those class paths, we are ready to turn our attention to some best practices for deploying *.jar* files and other components of WebSphere applications. First, we should investigate some of the basic ways in which the default directories are structured in WebSphere. When you install WebSphere application server, it will create two directories:

- A directory named *[WebSphere_Root]\WebSphere\AppServer\ deployableEJBs,* which can be used to hold EJB JAR files that need deployment code generated
- A directory named *[WebSphere_Root]\WebSphere\AppServer\ deployedEJBs,* which can contain EJB JAR files already in a deployed state, or containing all necessary generated code

Finally, WebSphere will also contain another directory structure descending down from *[WebSphere_Root]\WebSphere\AppServer\ hosts\ default_host,* which will contain a subdirectory for each Web application that is created. This directory can contain servlets and other classes specific to a Web application.

However, although WebSphere does provide this complete directory structure, you should not rely on this structure in a production WebSphere environment. The reason is quite simple: although these directories are provided for your convenience, WebSphere does not require you to use them; in fact, you can configure WebSphere to look in any directory you choose for any of the kinds of files we have described. The best practice that we have seen in many production environments is instead to create a separate directory structure, apart from the WebSphere directories, with separate subdirectories for each project's specific JAR files and another directory for shared JAR files. This gives you two benefits. First, because the directory is separate from WebSphere's files, it is easy to package and compress this directory, using PKZIP or TAR, for purposes of backup and of replicating the directory structure on multiple machines. This second reason is key to taking advantage of the "cloning" features of WebSphere Advanced Edition. Remember that a "clone" of an application server is a copy, or model, of a server that can be started any number of times on any number of machines. WebSphere automatically performs workload management of requests for servlets, JSPs, and EJBs among clones of a model. However, when you install a clone on a machine from the administrative console, one of the requirements is that the directory structure containing the application server's files be the same as the structure on the original "model" machine. Thus, being able to easily reproduce this structure through a process like FTP and TAR or PKZIP becomes crucial to making cloning manageable.

The final reason to avoid placing your application files within WebSphere's directory structure is to make it easier to upgrade WebSphere or to reinstall WebSphere on your system. Although the WebSphere install script does make a copy of all user directories when you upgrade WebSphere, if you forget to click on the button during the install, instructing it to perform the copy, all your application files will be lost. Not only that, but occasionally, a WebSphere installation will fail, leaving the WebSphere directory structure in an inconsistent state. Therefore, it is probably safer for you to rely on copying your own application files rather than depending on the install script.

Deploying EJBs into WebSphere

Exported JAR files, whether they are in a deployed format or not, can be deployed into a WebSphere application server. The process by which this happens is somewhat indirect: EJBs are added to a WebSphere Application Server *EJB container,* using the WebSphere administration console. Containers can house multiple EJBs; in general, each container contains several EJBs.

Next, we walk through the process of using WebSphere to deploy our case study into an application server. Along the way, you will see how some of the best practices we have already discussed are put into practice and will learn the mechanics of taking code out of VisualAge for Java and putting it into WebSphere.

Deploying .jar Files

In Chapter 6, we provided an example of how to deploy servlets and JSPs into WebSphere. We will develop that example to show how to deploy EJBs in the same way. We will have to make some changes to the deployment decisions that we made in Chapter 6; these changes should be minimal, and we will explain why we have made these changes as we go.

First, we need to create a new directory structure to contain the *.jar* files that make up the example we developed earlier. Then we will discuss how to take classes out of VisualAge for Java and deploy them into WebSphere. As recommended earlier, we need to create a new directory structure specific to this particular application. (You can copy this entire structure, including the files contained in it, from the CD-ROM.) We would recommend that you create the following directory structure, which will be rooted at a drive letter (in NT) or root directory (in UNIX) and will look like the following:

[root]\WebSphereBookExports\domain
[root]\WebSphereBookExports\ejbs
[root]\WebSphereBookExports\servlet
[root]\WebSphereBookExports\tests
[root]\WebSphereBookExports\utils
[root]\WebSphereBookExports\web

Next, we will show you how to deploy our example to these directories. The basic principle we will follow is that each package in our case study example roughly equates to a layer in a layered architecture and also equates to a single *.jar* file for deployment. This allows us to both easily build new applications by reusing existing code and deployment structures and minimize the impact of single-class changes on deployed applications.

We will begin by exporting the *.jar* files that represent the UI, mediator, domain, and mapping layers, as well as the utility classes used by these and other layers. Table 23.2 details the *.jar* files that are created, the directories in which they are placed, and the packages from which they were created.

These *.jar* files are the ones used by our EJBs and servlets and also the servlet classes; we haven't yet exported our EJBs. That is the next step in the process. To do this, go into VisualAge for Java and select the *EJB* tab; then select the *TimeSheetGroup* EJB group. Finally, choose *Export>Deployed Jar...* from the middle-mouse-button menu. Name the EJB JAR file *timesheetejbs.jar* and place it in the *[root]\WebSphereBookExports\ejbs* directory. After this process has completed, select the *TimeSheetGroup* EJB

Table 23.2   JAR Files

Jar file name	Deployment directory	Package(s)
domain.jar	*/domain*	com.wsbook.casestudy.domain
domainmapping.jar	*/domain*	com.wsbook.casestudy.mapping
ejbmapping.jar	*/domain*	com.wsbook.casestudy.mapping.ejb
mediators.jar	*/servlet*	com.wsbook.casestudy.mediator
tsservlets.jar	*/servlet*	com.wsbook.casestudy.servlets
tsjunit.jar	*/tests*	com.wsbook.casestudy.tests.junit
tsutils.jar	*/utils*	com.wsbook.casestudy.system
		com.wsbook.casestudy.util

group again, and this time choose *Export>Client Jar...* from the menu. Name the new *.jar* file *timesheetejbsclient.jar* and place it in the *[root]\ WebSphereBookExports\ejbs* directory also.

Deploying Files from Studio

Next, you will need to publish the nonJava assets to this directory structure from WebSphere Studio. First, you will define a publishing stage for your production environment. This stage will have at least three publishing targets defined: *html, servlet,* and *jspPages*. The first two of these targets are defined by Studio; the third is one that you will add. The *html* target should point to your Web server's document root for your site. The servlet target should point to our *[root]\WebSphereBookExports\servlet* folder. Finally, the *jspPages* publishing target should point to *[root]\WebSphereBookExports\ web\pages*. This corresponds to a folder under the Web application's document root.

Next, establish the URL hierarchy of the application as folders under the publishing stage. For our case study, we have a top-level folder, */TimeApp*, which corresponds to our Web application's root URI. Under that we have established a */pages* folder, which holds the JSPs for the project. This folder will be marked as publishable to the *jspPages* target (Figure 23.4). By

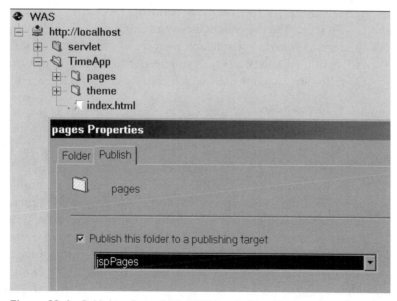

Figure 23.4   Publishing Pages Folder (JSPs) to *jspPages* Target

isolating the JSPs in a separate folder, the rest of the assets (HTML pages, images, and so on) will be published to the default *html* target; the Web server's document root. Finally, publish the production stage to publish the HTML pages, images, and JSPs to the appropriate directories.

Defining EJBs

Having completed filling in the directory structure for our application with the correct files, we are ready to move on to the next step: defining the EJBs in our application in WebSphere. First, however, we need to address some other issues in the administration console. We will begin that process by starting the WebSphere administration console.

Our first task is to prepare our node for EJB deployment by setting up the dependent class path. As described earlier, the dependent class path is used during EJB deployment: The admin server will look for classes that are referenced in the Home or Remote interfaces of an EJB in this class path. However, the dependent class path is also part of the total class path for an application server; for this reason, it makes a good place to put *.jar* files that are referenced by your EJBs. The only thing to be careful about here is that if you have multiple application servers running on a single node, they will share the same dependent class path. This would create difficulties, for instance, if you wanted to host two application servers, one for test and one for production, on the same physical node, as they would have to always use the same version of the *.jar* files on the dependent class path.

To set up the dependent class path for a node, simply select the node in the administrator's console and then change the *Dependent Classpath* property to add whatever *.jar* files you need into the list. In our case, we will add the following two *.jar* files, which contain classes referenced by our EJBs:

- *Domain.jar*
- *Ejbmapping.jar*

The last thing to address before beginning to deploy our EJBs is to set up a DataSource for the EJB container. This DataSource will be used in two ways. Recall that each CMP Entity EJB corresponds to a table in the database. The DataSource specifies in *which* database these tables are found. The admin server will use this information to create the table, if necessary, and the application server will use the DataSource to obtain connections to the database for these EJBs at runtime. You set up a Datasource for an EJB container by selecting the EJB container and turning to the *DataSource* tab (Figure 23.5).

Note that to set up a DataSource, you have to specify it by selecting from a list, using the *Change* button. You also specify a user ID and password for

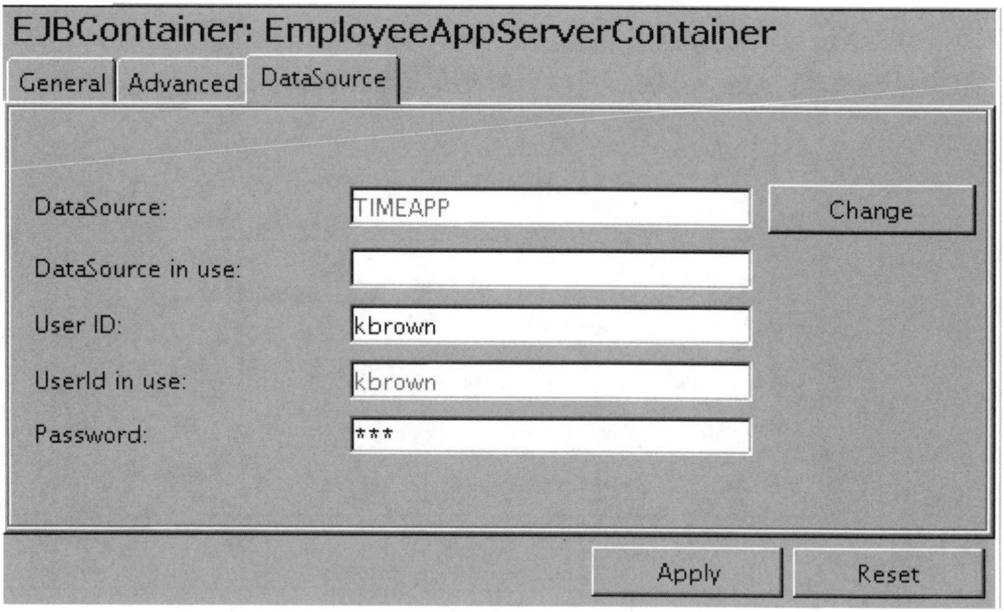

Figure 23.5 DataSource Setup

the database on that DataSource. Because it is used for two purposes, this user ID must have both read/write and create rights on the database for which the DataSource is set up. If you need more help on creating a Data-Source, consult the WebSphere documentation.

Now we can move on to deploying our EJBs. Once a container has been selected, the EJBs defined in a deployed JAR file can be added to the container, using the *Create Enterprise Bean* menu option, which will open a dialog prompting for an EJB to add to the container. The dialog for defining an Enterprise Bean is shown in the Figure 23.6. This view also has a *Browse* option that opens a dialog that displays available Beans defined in a specified *.jar* file (Figure 23.7).

When you select the *timesheetejbs.jar* file, you will see the dialog (Figure 23.8) that will lead you to deploying the EJBs in the *.jar* file. In our case, you will want to respond to this dialog by choosing *Yes*. If instead you choose *No*, you will see the dialog in Figure 23.9, which allows you to choose to deploy EJBs in the *.jar* file individually.

What happens next depends on whether you are deploying from an EJB *.jar* file or a deployed *.jar* file. If the specified JAR does not have all the appropriate EJS code generated, a dialog will appear prompting for generation of deployment code (Figure 23.10).

If *Deploy and Enable WLM* is selected, the appropriate deployed code, including the special "smart stubs" for EJB workload management, will be

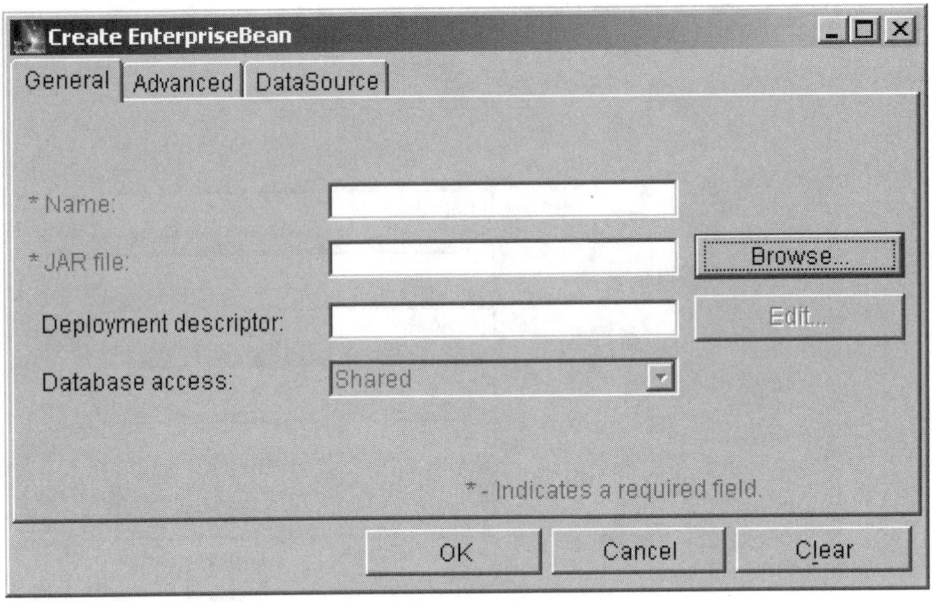

Figure 23.6 *Create Enterprise Bean* Dialog

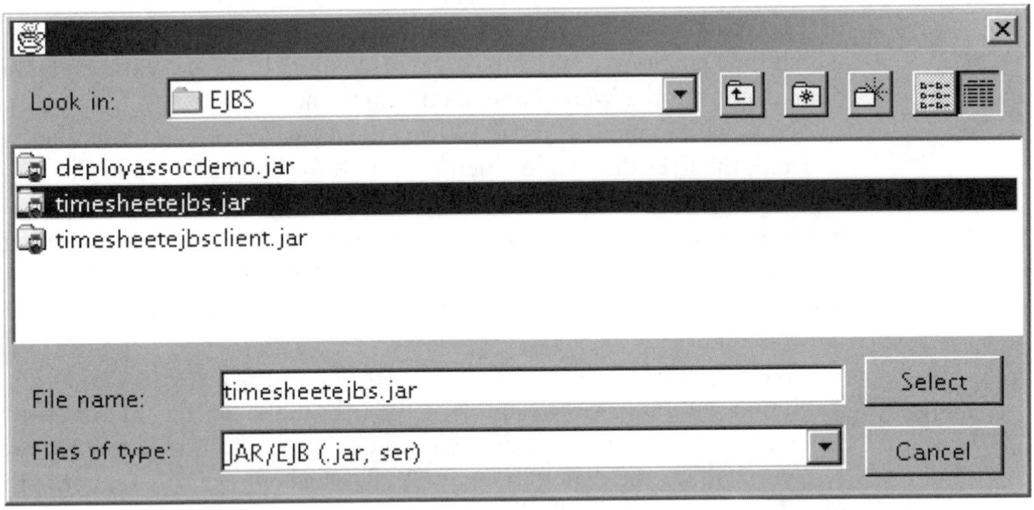

Figure 23.7 *Browse* JAR *Files*

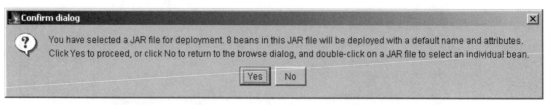

Figure 23.8 *Confirm* Dialog

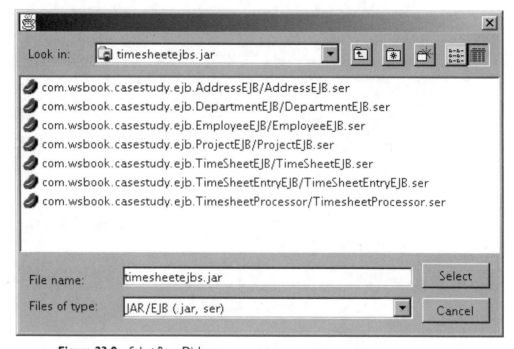

Figure 23.9 *Select Bean* Dialog

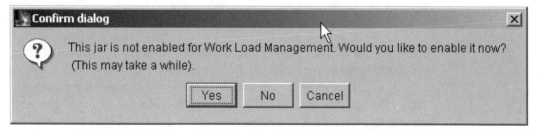

Figure 23.10 Deployment Confirmation Dialog

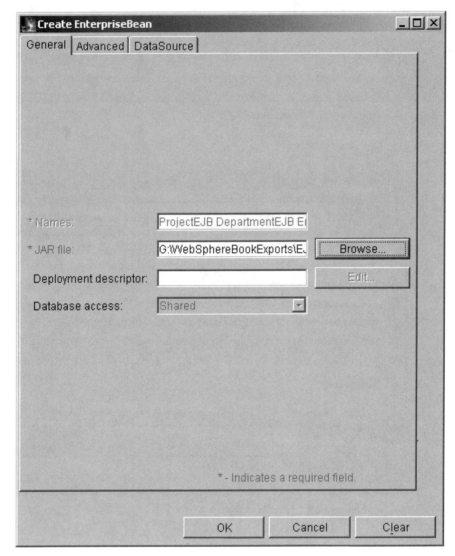

Figure 23.11   Completed *Create EnterpriseBean* Dialog

generated and a new deployed JAR produced from the EJB JAR file. This
new *.jar* file will be placed in the *Deployed .jar file directory* that is specified
in the application server configuration. On the other hand, if you choose
"*NO,*" the smart stubs will not be generated. After this dialog is dismissed,
you will again see the *Create EnterpriseBean* dialog, but this time with the
EJBs filled in (Figure 23.11).

  To complete the deployment of your EJBs, just click the *OK* button on this
dialog. Each EJB will be added to the EJB container, as seen in Figure 23.12.

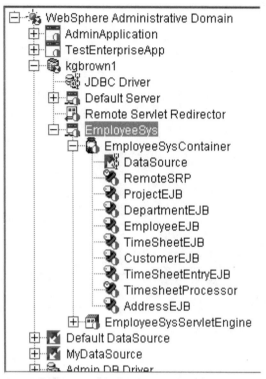

Figure 23.12   Deployed EJB Tree

Final Changes

Finally, we need to change the application server class path to include other files needed by the EJBs and also change the Web app class path to include the EJB clients. We will begin by setting up the application server class path. We do this by selecting the *EmployeeSys Application Server* and turning to the *General* tab. You can then enter the class path by typing the class path argument into the *Command line arguments:* entry field and clicking *Apply*. (*Note:* You will replace *G:* with the root directory in which you placed the *WebSphereBookExports* directory.)

```
-classpath G:\WebSphereBookExports\domain\domainmapping.jar;
G:\WebSphereBookExports\utils\tsutils.jar
```

The *General* tab with the *Command line arguments:* filled in is shown in Figure 23.13.

Next, you will need to set up the Web application class path. To do that, select the Web application in the administration console and then turn to the *Advanced* tab, as shown in Figure 23.14. In the *Classpath* part of the form,

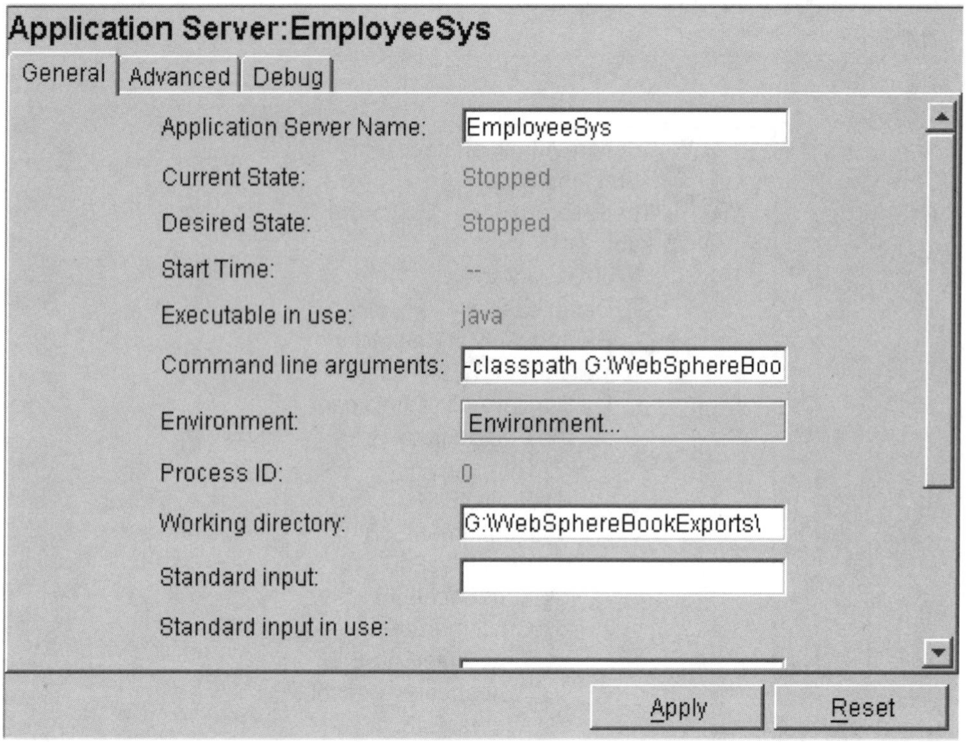

Figure 23.13 Command Line Arguments

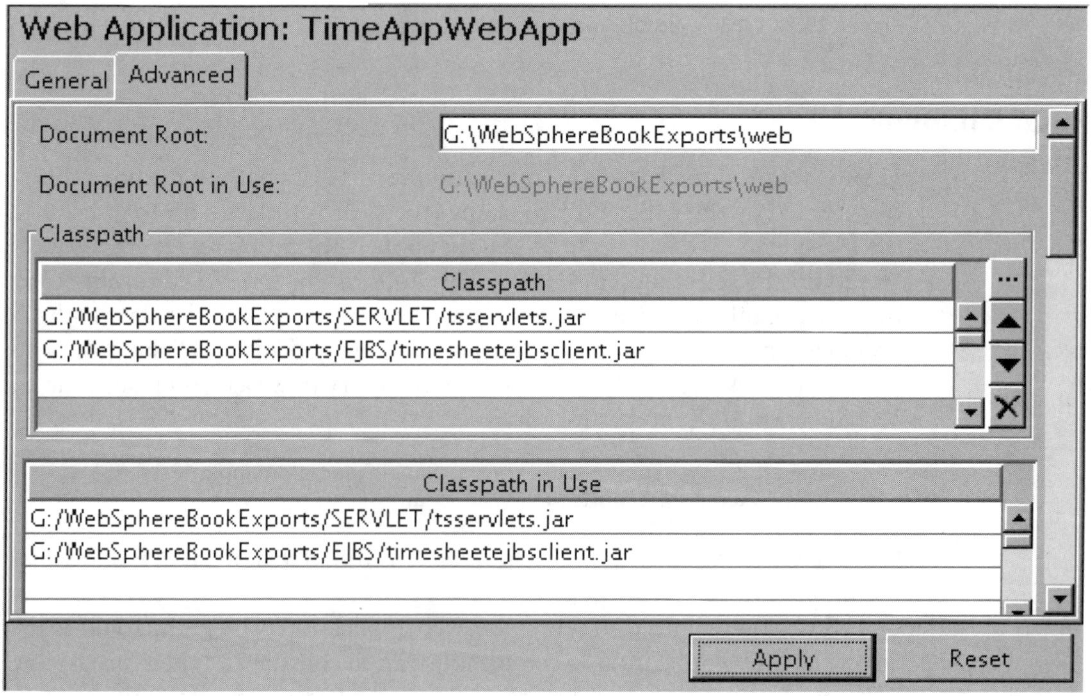

Figure 23.14 Web App Class Path

add the EJB client *.jar* file that you created earlier into the Web app class path. You also need to add the *tsservlets. jar* file that contains the servlets and the *mediators.jar* file containing the mediator classes. After adding the new path, click *Apply*. You can then start the application server. Now comes the moment of truth. If everything has worked, you should now be able to test out the application![1]

Summary and Preview

In this chapter, we have surveyed the process of deploying EJBs from VisualAge for Java into WebSphere, Advanced Edition. We've examined some best practices for deployment and seen how the deployment process is accomplished. In the next chapter, the final one, we will wrap up our discussion of WebSphere by reviewing what you've learned.

---

1. Note that to make the application work, you must first populate the database with some sample data. You can insert this by hand using DB2's tools or modify the EntityBean test case to insert the data.

CHAPTER 24

A Final Look

Throughout this book, we have explored the building of business-to-business (B2B) and business-to-customer (B2C) enterprise applications. We have assumed that these applications will be deployed in an *n*-tiered architecture that exploits J2EE application server(s) in the middle tier. In covering this spectrum, we have addressed the core technologies that are used to build active components in this environment, namely, servlets, JSPs, and EJBs. We have also looked at many of the supporting enterprise APIs, such as JNDI, JDBC, and JTA, that round out the J2EE architecture.

J2EE Application Servers

The application server framework provides a rich platform on which to deploy distributed enterprise applications. A rich runtime associated with each JVM provides the vast array of middle-tier (middleware) services, such as naming, distribution, transaction, persistence, and security. By building an application on top of such a platform, application developers can concentrate on application-specific functionality and use standard APIs for the platform's enterprise services.

For the most part, the deployment architecture for an application is orthogonal to the development activity. Deploying to high-end application server products, such as IBM WebSphere Application Server, Advance Edition, permits strong application scaling through server group clustering, workload management services, and support for application failover.

Layering: MVC Revisited

To facilitate the opportunities for reuse, extensibility, and scalability inherent in the J2EE architecture, it is important to apply a well-defined *application architecture* to organize and to structure your development assets. The application architecture presented over the expanse of the book is based on the principle of application layering. We focused primarily on MVC as a structuring principle, in part because the Web components—servlets and JSPs—are mostly about supporting a communication channel between the Web (application) client and the application. Separating the user interface components (View) from the application components (Model) is a long-proven design principle. Here, it is particularly important to stress this separation, as it is too easy to intermix business logic with UI support even within a single method, such as doPost() or doGet().

Layering is also essential within the Model to promote reuse and easy-to-maintain code. We saw this most clearly through

- The role for Entity EJBs
- Use of Session EJB facades
- Use of domain objects and/or XML to exchange data in and out of the model
- Use of mapper (Factory) objects to facilitate moving between the *pass-by-value* domain objects and the *pass-by-reference* persistent objects

Best practices in the use of this application architecture establish some very distinct and perhaps narrowly defined roles for several key J2EE application elements. In particular, Entity EJBs are strongly encouraged to be OO views on your persistent data store and should be applicable across your enterprise. In other words, they should be application neutral. Application-specific business rules and processes need to be defined in other layers.

JSPs are recommended to be presentation engines only. They are given JavaBeans that contain dynamic data, which can be used to populate the resulting dynamic Web page.

Servlets are viewed as the HTTP request conduits within the application server. With the help of mediators, servlets translate requests and request data—in the form of HTML form parameters, query strings, and headers—and delegate to the Model layer to perform the necessary work with parameters supplied as server-side domain objects. The servlet-assisted Controller must also be responsible for any application state management, which is also tied to HTTP, namely, the use of HttpSessions.

Tools

The tools used to develop, test, and deploy your application received a lot of attention throughout this book. Enterprise applications comprise many diverse components, ranging from HTML-based assets to stored procedures on your database and everything in between. Large development efforts will more than likely have a number of developers with specialized roles, such as developing Web-based user interfaces or developing domain objects and their mappers. In each situation, it is vital to use the correct set of tools for the development task. These tools should also directly support team development—source and version control—or should be operated within an infrastructure that provides this support.

We concentrated on two tool sets:

- IBM VisualAge for Java, Enterprise Edition
- IBM WebSphere Studio

VisualAge provides one of the most productive Java development environments available today. However, two additional features of the Enterprise Edition provide the high productivity for building Web applications: WebSphere Test Environment (WTE) and EJB Development Environment.

- The WTE provides a nearly complete test bed for Web container (servlet engine)–based application testing. This permits extensive iterative testing without the delays associated with deployment.
- The EJB Development Environment provides the developer with the ability to think about EJBs as individual components rather than as a collection of interfaces and classes. The tool manages all the interdependencies between these Java types. In addition, this environment provides some of the best CMP mapping tools available today.

VisualAge also is demonstrated to be the deployment tool of choice for WebSphere Application Server. The EJB Development Environment feature also facilitates this.

IBM WebSphere Studio provides a framework for managing assets that, taken together, make up an application that is to be deployed to two or more servers, such as Web server and application server. Studio assists in managing these assets in a team development–friendly fashion. It offers a publishing metaphor to provide deployment support for application assets.

WebSphere Page Designer, a component of Studio, is one of the premier JSP development environments. Its support of using JavaBean properties to deliver dynamic content to pages greatly assists the developer who is trying to minimize writing scriptlet in JSPs.

The final tool piece that is addressed in this book is the IBM WebSphere Application Server itself. This is a representative application server with very good support for high-end security, scalability, reliability, and performance. The development tools are well integrated to support development of applications to be deployed on the WebSphere server.

Parting Comments

We recognize the complexity of the task of building enterprise applications. Today, for many organizations, a growing percentage of new development will migrate to these application server–based architectures. Good design principles are vitally important to a development team operating in this environment. We hope that you have gained key insights from these pages so that you will be able to successfully compete in this ever accelerating marketplace. Good luck in all your development efforts.

APPENDIX A

Mapping Domain Objects to Data Stores

Many organizations have a heavy investment in legacy data sources and require the ability to access them collectively in support of a single application domain model (Figure A.1). The way to support this kind of heterogenous architecture is through the use of object mappers.

Implementing the domain as JavaBeans offers several benefits to the iterative software development process and also promotes reusability. Application domain objects ultimately must be rendered from persistent data sources. In some cases, new data sources are created; more often than not, existing legacy sources must be accessed. In any case, this is a mapping function and, ideally, should be carried out in parallel with the evolution of domain/presentation objects or whenever the domain has solidified. Additionally, data sources and connectivity to them might not be possible during early iterations, so it should not hinder domain evolution. This approach does not compromise the J2EE model, as Enterprise JavaBeans exist as distributed data sources and therefore can be mapped to the JavaBean domain like a traditional data source.

The challenge of this design is to decouple and to isolate the JavaBean domain from any type of data source while allowing individual domain class definitions to be mapped to a data source at will. This accounts for the isolation challenge; decoupling dictates that specific data source access objects, such as JDBC connection or column/table data, should not appear anywhere in the domain. In essence, the domain represents a purely logical view of a problem space, and it does not contain any specific data source access logic. However, an agreed on message flow that engages data source objects and carries out persistent retrieve and modification requests from underlying "mapped" data sources is needed.

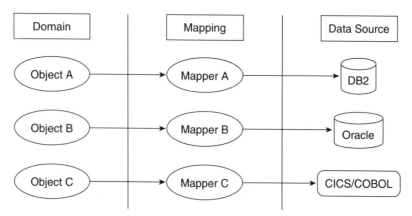

Figure A.1   Object Mapping Relationship

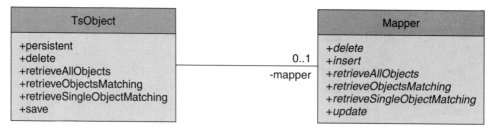

Figure A.2   Base Class TsObject

Inheritance, message forwarding, and interfaces are the design elements used to decouple the JavaBean domain from specified data sources. A generalized set of persistent methods is made available to domain JavaBeans through a base class that domain Beans will extend from. Persistent operations are forwarded to a Mapper instance defined for the receiving domain Bean class. Mapper instances are defined to access a specific data source, such as JDBC, RMI, and EJB. Persistent messages received by the base class TsObject (Figure A.2) are forwarded to a mapping object that implements the Mapping interface. Mapping instances are found and created for a domain Bean by applying a naming convention whereby the class name for the domain object's class name is suffixed with Mapper. For example, a class named Foo would have a mapper class name of FooMapper.

This indirect access to data source–specific mapping objects allows the mapping, at a class-level granularity, of a single logical JavaBean domain to multiple data sources. In other words, every class in a domain model can be mapped to a different data source.

Another advantage of this design is the support it provides the iterative development process, whereas presentation and domain efforts can proceed independently of physical data source requirements. Of course, this presumes that a facsimile test mapper is in place that emulates a real data source. The case study implements such a mapper.

Object Mappers

Allowing developers to iterate domain implementations independently of data source connectivity infrastructure goes a long way toward enhancing productivity and supporting the iterative development process. During a development process, data sources often may not exist or cannot be accessed, causing other development elements, such as presentation construction, to become bottlenecked. The case study implements such a mapper, which emulates a persistent data source, allowing the creation and presentation of a domain model independently of a physical data source.

The case study uses a mapper that emulates a data store by defining a crude object caching mechanism. Therefore, simple persistent requests, such as save() and retrieveAllObject(), issued from the domain model affect the mapper's cache instead of interacting with a real data source.

Caching is accomplished by using a collection defined in the Object Mapper class, implemented as a vector. Each class defined in the domain model, subclass of TsObject, will reference a single instance of an Object Mapper for a domain type, effectively preserving the cache-emulating collection for each mapper type. Of course, when the application's JVM Machine is terminated, objects occupying the cache are gone. However, for testing purposes, the approach is sufficient.

Because the ObjectMapper is emulating a data store, an initial population of objects might be required for each ObjectMapper defined. This behavior is optional; by default, issuing a retrieveAllObjects() results in an empty Vector. An initial population of objects can be defined by overriding the initialLoad() method that will create and return a Vector of domain objects. An example of this can be seen in the case study's ProjectMapper implementation, which returns an initial population of Project instances.

```
/**
 * Create and return a Vector of Project Objects.
 */
Vector initialLoad() {
    Vector v = new Vector();
    Project p = new Project();
    p.setNumber("P1");
    p.setName("Development at ABC Corp.");
```

```
                v.addElement(p);
                p = new Project();
                p.setNumber("P2");
                p.setName("Project work at XYZ Corp.");
                v.addElement(p);
                return v;
        }
```

The ObjectMapper implements the following persistent operations.

```
retrieveAllObjects()
save()
delete()
```

The ability to request objects based on a query predicate relies on a query mechanism defined by a data source. An example of this would be a where clause used to access a table in a relational database. Therefore, the ObjectMapper does not implement operations requiring a query value.

Once a domain object has a defined ObjectMapper, persistent operations can be exercised, as the following line of code shows:

```
// retrieve objects.

Project aProject = new Project().retrieveAllObjects();
```

APPENDIX B

Application Service Layers

Application Services

There are application responsibilities that developers must apply to all application development efforts. Implementing these activities consistently by using a design that is extensible will facilitate reuse and minimize side effects when requirements change. Moreover, standardizing these services across all applications can yield efficiencies in determining and communicating new development and maintenance activities.

Obvious application responsibilities include error handling, status tracing, application startup and shutdown, accessing externalized properties, and applying interface preferences. A design must be put in place that allows developers to consistently apply error handling across all applications but support the ability to install and change these behaviors on an application basis. For example, application status is sometimes reported to a console, but what happens if the application is server based and a console does not exist? The design should allow tracing to be routed to a flat file or maybe to the console. The following sections describe a solution to meet these design challenges.

The AppService Class

Central to the application service design is the implementation of the AppService class, which borrows its presence from the java.lang.System class. This class implements static attributes that reference service-capable objects, which are defined to supply basic application services, such as exception handling and logging.

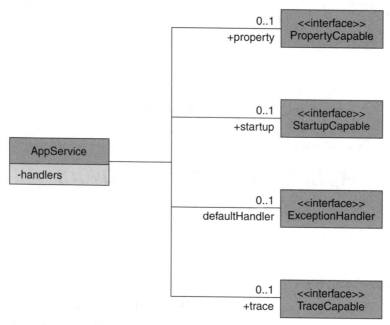

Figure B.1   AppService Interfaces

Attributes in the AppService class are typed as Java interfaces (Figure B.1). In this way, service objects can be defined independently of a hierarchy and can exist autonomously. The significance of this design is the ability of the developer to express application service behavior independently of specific application requirements.

Startup Sequence

Every application, whether it is a traditional client/server GUI application or a more state-of-the-art distributed application running on servers across the enterprise, performs some kind of initialization or resource allocation at startup time. Moreover, housekeeping behavior is also required when an application is closed or, in the case of a distributed application, shut down.

Application startup mechanisms can be formalized by defining a Java class that implements the StartupCapable interface (Figure B.2). The start() method is responsible for creating and seeding other AppService objects and for performing any application-specific initialization, such as cache loading or performing required resource connectivity. The following example shows the StartupCapable class implemented for the time-sheet case study.

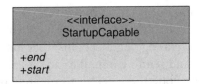

Figure B.2 StartupCapable Interface

```
/*** Time Sheet Startup Class.*/
public class TimeSheetStartup implements StartupCapable {

public void end() {}
/*** perform startup sequence.*/
public void start() {
    // Initiliaze StrataSystem class
    AppService.startup = this;
    // Initialize Properties Object
    AppService.property = new TimeSheetProperties();}
}
```

Initialization requirements can differ, depending on the environment the application is deployed in. Servlet-based applications, which reside on the server, might require cache loading and will also have the ability to access resources directly on the server. However, applet-based applications will not be able to access resources without using the document base; therefore, they will require a different property-access mechanism to be initialized at startup. Defining two different classes that implement the StartupCapable interface can capture these differences.

As simplistic as it might seem, the benefits of standardizing application startup should not be dismissed. Many developers can be involved in performing new development and ongoing maintenance; therefore, communication among developers becomes more efficient.

Exception Handling

Exception-handling requirements change from application to application. If a reusable domain is desired, exception-handling behavior needs to be configured without having to affect a domain source. This allows a common domain source to apply exception-handling behavior without committing to a specific handling mechanism, such as outputting exception information to the console. Exception-handling requirements can change, depending on the application deployment environment. A standalone GUI application might require the reporting of exception information only to the end user's console, but a server-based application probably does not have a console and will require information to be written to a logging mechanism, or maybe logging exception information to a file and sending e-mail to an on-call developer. In any case, the design needs to facilitate these decisions on an application basis without burdening the development process.

A well-known design pattern can be applied to facilitate multiple exception handlers in response to a raised exception. The Observer design pattern has been applied to the Java component event-handling mechanism and can be used as an ideal solution.

Observer Pattern

The intent of the Observer design as it appears in [Gamma] states: "Define a one-to-many dependency between objects so that when one object changes state, all its dependents are notified and updated automatically." The most ubiquitous application of this pattern is in the event-notification implementation of the Java AWT/Swing user interface packages. In this implementation, individual GUI components can have any number of "observable" objects added. When an event produced by a component, also known as the *subject,* is encountered, it enumerates over installed observers, forwarding the event in the form of an object.

Observers do not require knowledge of components, only of event types forwarded to them, effectively decoupling the component implementation. A contract is established to help enforce the type of notification observers must listen for and what types of objects can be listeners. This contractual arrangement is implemented using interfaces that enforce a type and method signature constraint. Interfaces help enforce the Observer/Listener contract at compile time, alleviating a possible class hierarchy explosion if an inheritance approach is used.

Exception handlers are created by implementing the ExceptionHandler interface (Figure B.3). The interface requires the definition of a handle() method that accepts an ExceptionEvent as an argument. Events are created by the AppSystem class and forwarded to install handlers when the AppService handle() method is expressed in a catch block. The ExceptionEvent instance sent to "observing" handlers will reference date, time, and the exception instance. Handlers can then use this information to perform their prescribed behavior (Figure B.4).

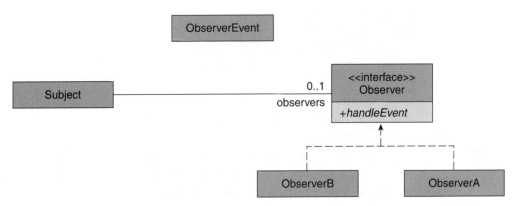

Figure B.3 ExceptionHandler Interface

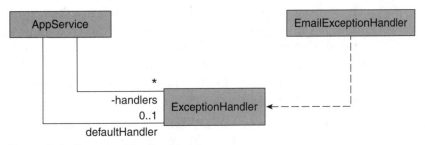

Figure B.4 Exception-Handling Model

ExceptionHandler instances are installed during application startup by creating ExceptionHandler instances and exercising the install(ExceptionHandler) method defined in the Service class. Any number of handlers can be installed.

```
// startup code , install exception handlers
AppService.install( new PagerHandler() );
AppSer vice.install( new FileHandler() );
```

Developers can apply exception handling generically across application boundaries by exercising the handle(Throwable e) defined in the AppService class, which creates an ExceptionEvent and forwards to installed handlers (Observers).

```
try {
    float f = 1.0/0; // raised Divide by zero exception
  }
catch (ArithmeticException e )
{AppService.handle(e); } // handle exception
```

Creating an exception handler requires the implementation of the Exception Handler interface, which requires a method with the handle(ExceptionEvent)

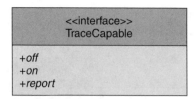

Figure B.5   Trace Interface

signature to be implemented. Handlers will be notified of the occurrence of an exception through this method and can then use the ExceptionEvent information to apply prescribed handling behavior. (For more details, see the accompanying code on the CD-ROM for an implementation example of a handler that will e-mail an exception stack trace to an on-call developer.)

Developers routinely output application state trace information to the Java console at strategic locations in an application's execution path. Moving the application into production typically requires that these statements be removed. However, when problems or defects are encountered, the developer must sometimes reintroduce these trace statements. Moreover, it cannot be assumed that a console exists. Application servers typically output console data to a circular-type log.

```
// Log information, appears only if trace is turned on...
 AppService.trace.report("Hello World");
```

The AppService class can be assigned an instance of a class that implements the TraceCapable interface (Figure B.5), which requires the implementation of methods that support turning logging behavior on and off and reporting trace messages. The ability to toggle tracing on/off during runtime allows strategically placed trace statements to exist in production code. Additionally, encapsulating this toggle logic inside the trace object prevents it from appearing in production source.

```
<application logic...>
// Record date time
AppService.trace( "Date time = "+new Date() );
<more logic...>
```

Application Property and Resource Access

Almost every application requires access to external resource information, such as an image file path name or a database name. Because these values can change frequently, they are typically externalized to a property file and are accessed from an application by using an assigned key. The JDK supplies a mechanism to load properties from an external property file and then gain

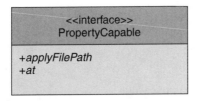

Figure B.6   PropertyCapable Interface

access to them by using a property ID or key. However, this serves as a mechanism to access only values defined in the property file. Supplying defaults or converting a resource value to a platform-specific format and location, as is the case with file paths, requires more than just returning keyed values.

A more robust property access mechanism is achieved by defining a class that encapsulates property access requests. Additionally, file path requests can be normalized in this class, alleviating hard-coded path information from appearing in the application source. In the spirit of the application service design, property access expressions implemented by developers should be performed consistently and be configured independently of an application and the server it is currently located at. Therefore, the AppService class, akin to other services such as exception handling, implements a property reference typed to a Java interface of PropertyCapable (Figure B.6). The PropertyCapable interface defines methods that will be expressed by developers to access application property values and file paths:

```
// Access a database name
AppService.getProperty().at("database");
// Apply file path
AppService.getProperty().applyFilePath( "myfile.txt");
//Apply qualified file path
AppService.getProperty().applyFilePath("image","myimage.gif");
```

Another advantage to this design is in supplying default values. During development, default values can be hard coded inside the PropertyCapable instance, eliminating the presence of an externalized file on the developer workstation. This might not seem like a big benefit, but having to track down an up-to-date property file can be time consuming. Also, for security reasons putting values in a text file might not be a good idea. Therefore, hard coding them in a class can provide a limited form of encryption.

Objects implementing this interface are assigned to the AppService class and can then be used by application source to gain access to properties and to apply file paths. An example implementation of the at(String) method follows:

```
/**
 * Return value for key, if default value
 * not in properties file, return default.
```

```
        */
        public Object at(String aKey) {

            // Heading RGB color string
            if (aKey.equalsIgnoreCase("heading"))

                // Check to see if property has value
                {
                if (System.getProperty("heading") != null) {
                    return System.getProperty("heading");
                }
                // Servlet URL defaults to Local host
                else {return "#6699FF";
                }
            }
            // Detail RGB color String
            if (aKey.equalsIgnoreCase("detail"))
                // Check to see if property has value
                {
                if (System.getProperty("detail") != null) {
                    return System.getProperty("detail");
                }
                // Servlet URL defaults to Local host
                else {
                    return "#AABBCC";
                }
            }
            if (aKey.equalsIgnoreCase("footing"))
                // Check to see if property has value
                {
                if (System.getProperty("footing") != null) {
                    return System.getProperty("footing");
                }
                // Servlet URL defaults to Local host
                else {
                    return "#BBBBBB";
                }
            }
            return null;
        }
```

Java in and of itself is portable; however, developers can apply behavior that is platform specific, thereby hampering application portability. The most obvious example is operating system–specific file paths. Windows and UNIX file paths are formatted differently. Java provides the ability to sense the runtime operating system. So, using the PropertyCapable applyFilePath() method allows application code to reference only external resource names, without regard to the actual path and its format. Instead, information and logic are centralized in this interface method.

APPENDIX C

Setting Up a Database Driver and DataSource

In previous chapters we discussed how to configure an EJB Server in the WebSphere Test Environment (WTE), in VisualAge for Java, to connect to a database. We also showed how to configure DataSources in the VisualAge for Java WTE. Here we show how to set up a database driver and Data-Source in the WebSphere Application Server Administrator's Console for Servlets and EJBs to use.

To begin, we will need to add a new database driver to the WebSphere domain and then configure it. We will demonstrate how to do this for DB2, but the process is similar for all other supported databases. The only difference is in the class name of the database driver and the name of the associated .zip or .jar file. Start by opening the WebSphere Administrator's console. Select the root of the topology tree (labeled "WebSphere Administrative Domain"). Then pop up the right-mouse-button menu and select "Create>JDBC Driver". This will open the "Create a JDBC Driver Wizard" (Figure C.1).

To set up a database driver for DB2, pull down the "class name" drop-down and select "com.ibm.db2.jdbc.app.DB2Driver". If you were going to use a different database (like Oracle) you would select a different driver. (Note that it is possible to create database drivers for databases that WebSphere does not support; you can type any class name into the Class Name drop-down. However, it is not guaranteed that these drivers will function correctly.) Finally, type a name into the Name field (e.g. "WASDriver") and press OK to add the database driver to the domain.

Next we have to install the database driver on the node you are currently using to run WebSphere and the Administrator's console. Select that node in

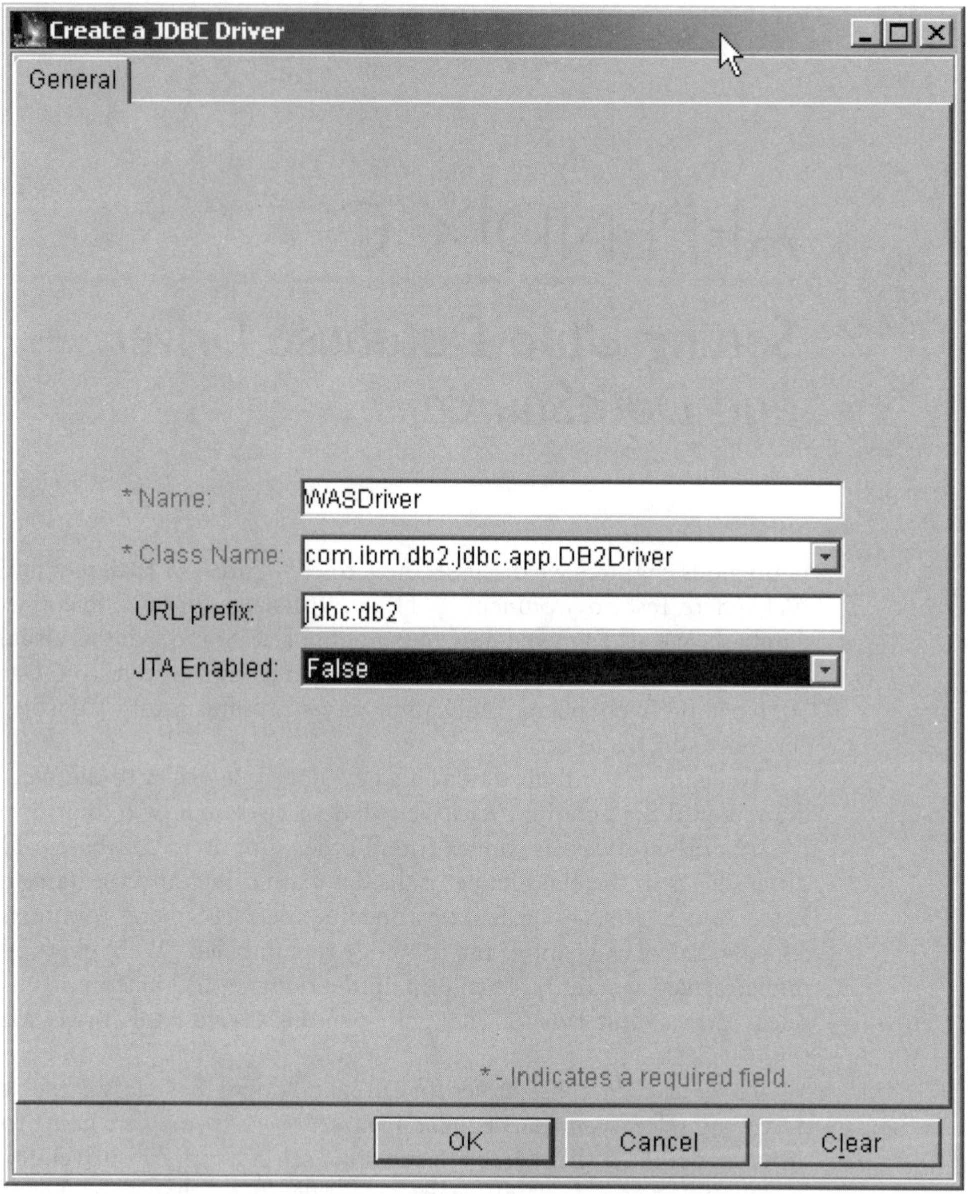

Figure C.1   Create a JDBC Driver Wizard

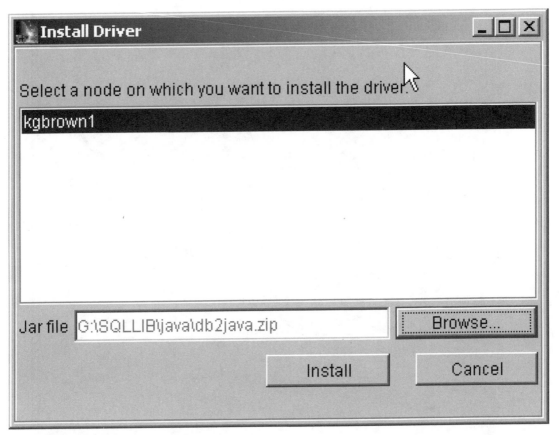

Figure C.2   Install Driver Wizard

the topology view and open the right-mouse-button menu. Select "Install" and the "Install Driver" dialog will appear (Figure C.2).

Use the "Browse" button to locate the zip or jar file that contains the driver class we referenced in the previous dialog. For DB2 this is <drive:> \SQLLIB\java\db2java.zip, where <drive:>is the drive on which DB2 was installed. Finally, select the node on which this is to be installed (e.g., this node) and press the "Install" button.

Finally, we will need to create a DataSource for our Entity EJBs to use. Again, select the top of the topology tree and open the menu. This time, select "Create>DataSource". The "Create a DataSource" wizard will appear (Figure C.3).

In this dialog, enter the name of the Database we created earlier (WAS-BOOK) and select the WASDriver JDBC driver we created earlier. Name this Data Source TIMEAPP and press OK. This will create the DataSource and enable it for use by Servlets and EJBs.

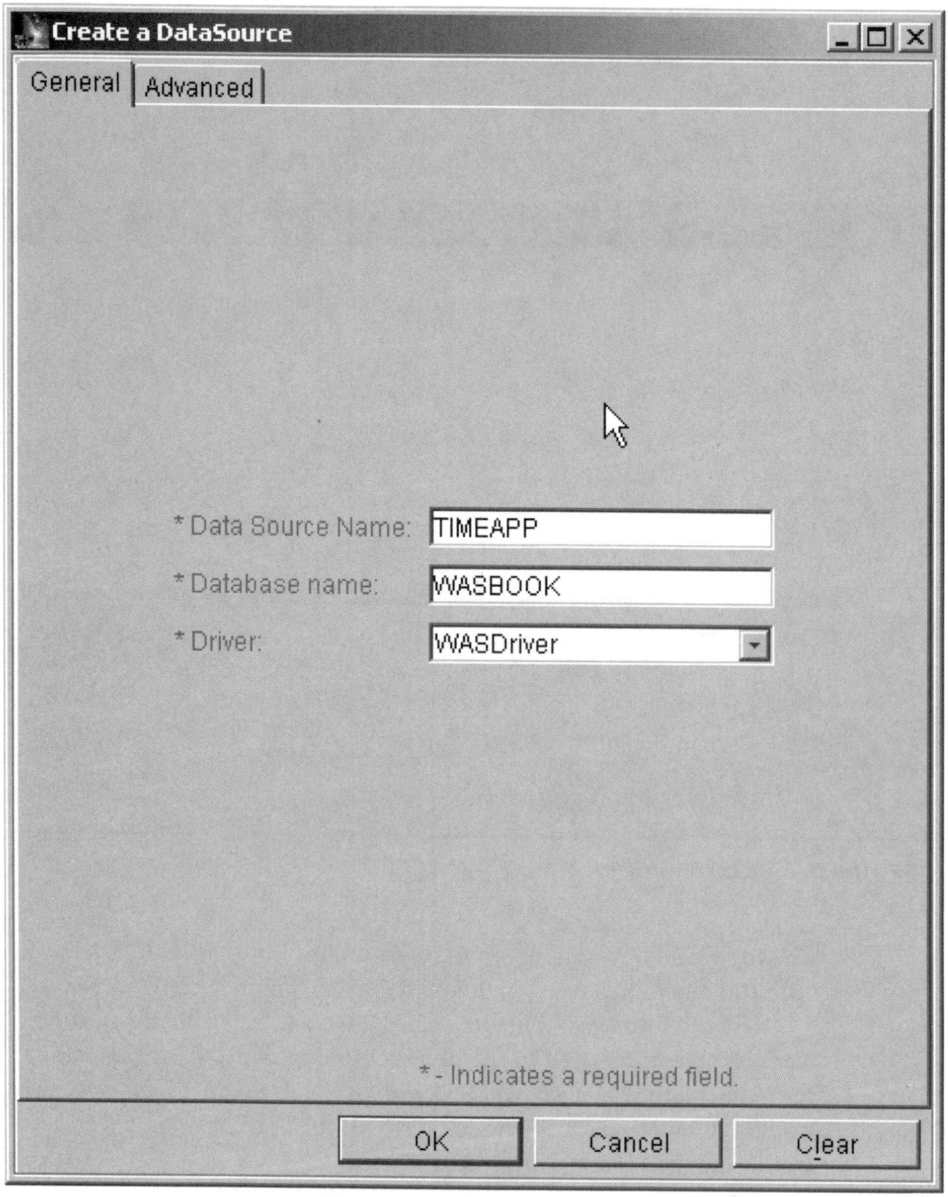

Figure C.3   Create a DataSource Wizard

# BIBLIOGRAPHY

[Beck] Kent Beck, *Extreme Programming Explained: Embrace Change* (Reading MA: Addison-Wesley, 2000).

[Booch] Grady Booch, "Object Oriented Analysis and Design With Applications," Second Edition, Reading, MA: Addison-Wesley, 1994.

[Brown 96] Kyle Brown and Bruce Whitenack, "Crossing the Chasm from Objects to Relational Databases," in *Pattern Languages of Program Design 2* (Reading, MA: Addison-Wesley, 1996).

[Brown 99] Kyle Brown, Philip Eskelin, and Nat Pryce, "A Component Distribution Mini-Language," Submission to the Pattern Languages of Programs 1999 Conference, Monticello, Illinois. Available at *http://members.aol.com/kgb1001001/*.

[Buschmann] Frank Buschmann, Regine Meunier, Hans Rohnert, Peter Sommerlad, and Michael Stal, *Pattern Oriented Software Engineering: A System of Patterns*, (West Sussex, England: Wiley, 1996).

[Elmasri] Ramez Elmasri and Shamkent Navathe, *Fundamentals of Database Systems*, 3rd ed. (Menlo Park, CA: Benjamin Cummings, 1999).

[EJB] Sun Microsystems, Enterprise JavaBeans Specification, version 1.0. Available at *http://java.sun.com*.

[EJB 99] Sun Microsystems, Enterprise JavaBeans Specification, version 1.1. Available at *http://java.sun.com*.

[Fowler] Martin Fowler with Kendall Scott, *UML Distilled*, 2d ed. (Reading MA: Addison-Wesley, 2000).

[Gamma] Erich Gamma, Richard Helm, Ralph Johnson, and John Vlissides, *Design Patterns: Elements of Reusable Object-Oriented Design*, (Reading, MA: Addison-Wesley, 1995).

[Horstmann] Cay Horstman and Gary Cornell, *Core Java 2: Volume I, Fundamentals* (New York: Prentice-Hall, 1999).

[Ivanov] Vesselin Ivanov, "EJB's and Transaction Management in WebSphere Advanced Edition," VisualAge Developer's Domain. Available at *http://www.soft ware.ibm.com/vadd*.

[Jakab] Peter Jakab, Dale Nilsson, Bill Sarantakos, and Russell Stinehour, *Enterprise Development with VisualAge for Java Version 3* (New York: Wiley, 2000).

[Jacobson 92] Ivar Jacobson, Magnus Christerson, Patrik Jonsson, and Gunnar Overgaard, *Object Oriented Software Engineering: A Use Case Driven Approach* (Workingham, UK: Addison-Wesley, 1992).

[Jacobson 99] Ivar Jacobson, Grady Booch, and James Rumbaugh, *The Unified Software Development Process* (Reading, MA: Addison-Wesley, 1999).

[JTS] Sun Microsystems, Java Transaction Service Specification, version 1.0. Available at *http://java.sun.com*.

[Krasner] Glenn Krasner and Stephen Pope, "A Cookbook for Using the Model-View-Controller User Interface Paradigm," *Journal of Object Oriented Programming,* 1:3, pp. 26–49 (August-September 1988).

[Monson-Haefel] Richard Monson-Haefel, *Enterprise JavaBeans,* 2d ed. (O'Reilly, 2000).

[Orfali] Robert Orfali and Dan Harkey, *Client Server Programming with Java and CORBA,* 2d ed. (New York: Wiley, 1998).

[RFC 1945] W3C Informational RFC 1945, "HTTP/1.0." Available at *http://www.w3.org/Protocols/Specs.html*.

[RFC 2616] W3C RFC 2616, "HyperText Transfer Protocol HTTP/1.1." Available at *http://www.w3.org/Protocols/Specs.html*.

[RFC 2396] W3C RFC 2396, "Uniform Resource Identifiers Generic Syntax." Available at *http://www.ietf.org/rfc/rfc2396.txt*.

[Ueno] Kenichuro Ueno et al., *WebSphere V3 Performance Tuning Guide, SG24-5657-00.* Available at *http://www.redbooks.ibm.com*.

INDEX

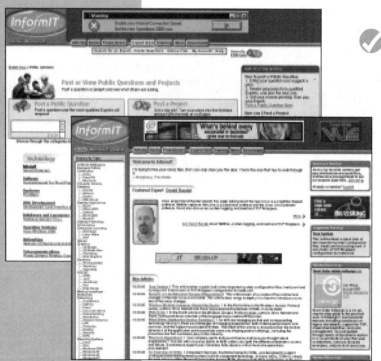